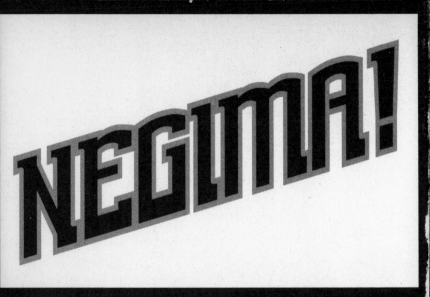

NEGIMA!

Ken Akamatsu

TRANSLATED BY
Hajime Honda

ADAPTED BY
Peter David and Kathleen O'Shea David

LETTERED BY
Studio Cutie

BALLANTINE BOOKS • NEW YORK

A Word from the Author

Hi, this is Ken Akamatsu. It's been a while.

After taking over a year off after *Love Hina*, I have returned to work with my new serial, *Magister Negi Magi*! I hope you enjoy it.

The protagonist of *Negima!*, Negi, is cute, smart and talented—the kind of protagonist you'd never find in my previous manga! Ironically enough, though, top student personalities like him don't usually stand out (ha ha)!

So, are you gonna take the plunge!?

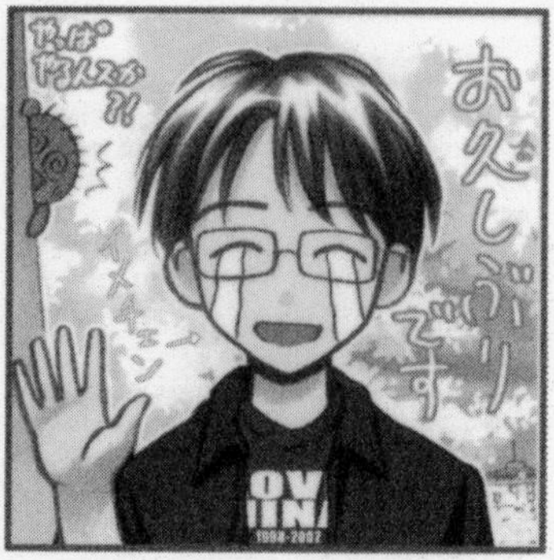
お久しぶりです

It's been so long.

The 31 beautiful girls in his class all have unique personalities, each with her share of trials and tribulations. (Actually, some of them aren't even human. . . .) Maybe they're the real protagonists of *Negima!*?

So let's take our time and watch over Negi as he grows up.

Ken Akamatsu

http://www.ailove.net

Translator—Hajime Honda
Adaptors—Peter David and Kathleen O'Shea David
Lettering—Studio Cutie
Cover Design—David Stevenson

This is a work of fiction. Any resemblance to actual persons, living or dead, is unintentional and purely coincidental.

A Del Rey® Book
Published by The Random House Publishing Group

Published in the United States by Del Rey Books, an imprint of The Random House Publishing Group, a division of Random House, Inc., New York, and simultaneously in Canada by Random House of Canada Limited, Toronto. First published in serial form by Shonen Magazine Comics and subsequently published in book form by Kodansha, Ltd., Tokyo in 2003. Copyright © 2003 by Ken Akamatsu.

www.delreymanga.com

Library of Congress Control Number: 2004090830

ISBN 0-345-47046-X

Manufactured in the United States of America

First Edition: May 2004

19 18 17 16 15 14 13

Honorifics

Throughout the Del Rey Manga books, you will find Japanese honorifics left intact in the translations. For those not familiar with how the Japanese use honorifics, and more important, how they differ from American honorifics, we present this brief overview.

Politeness has always been a critical facet of Japanese culture. Ever since the feudal era, when Japan was a highly stratified society, use of honorifics—which can be defined as polite speech that indicates relationship or status—has played an essential role in the Japanese language. When addressing someone in Japanese, an honorific usually takes the form of a suffix attached to one's name (example: "Asuna-san"), or as a title at the end of one's name or in place of the name itself (example: "Negi-sensei," or simply "Sensei!").

Honorifics can be expressions of respect or endearment. In the context of manga and anime, honorifics give insight into the nature of the relationship between characters. Many translations into English leave out these important honorifics, and therefore distort the "feel" of the original Japanese. Because Japanese honorifics contain nuances that English honorifics lack, it is our policy at Del Rey not to translate them. Here, instead, is a guide to some of the honorifics you may encounter in Del Rey Manga.

-*san*: This is the most common honorific, and is equivalent to Mr., Miss, Ms., Mrs., etc. It is the all-purpose honorific and can be used in any situation where politeness is required.

-*sama*: This is one level higher than *san*. It is used to confer great respect.

-*dono*: This comes from the word *tono*, which means *lord*. It is an even higher level than *sama*, and confers utmost respect.

-*kun*: This suffix is used at the end of boys' names to express familiarity or endearment. It is also sometimes used by men among friends, or when addressing someone younger or of a lower station.

-chan: This is used to express endearment, mostly toward girls. It is also used for little boys, pets, and even among lovers. It gives a sense of childish cuteness.

Sempai: This title suggests that the addressee is one's "senior" in a group or organization. It is most often used in a school setting, where underclassmen refer to their upperclassmen as "sempai." It can also be used in the workplace, such as when a newer employee addresses an employee who has seniority in the company.

Kohai: This is the opposite of *sempai*, and is used toward underclassmen in school or newcomers in the workplace. It connotes that the addressee is of lower station.

Sensei: Literally meaning "one who has come before," this title is used for teachers, doctors, or masters of any profession or art.

-[blank]: Usually forgotten in these lists, but perhaps the most significant difference between Japanese and English. The lack of honorific means that the speaker has permission to address the person in a very intimate way. Usually, only family, spouses, or very close friends have this kind of permission. Known as *yobisute*, it can be gratifying when someone who has earned the intimacy starts to call one by one's name without an honorific. But when that intimacy hasn't been earned, it can also be very insulting.

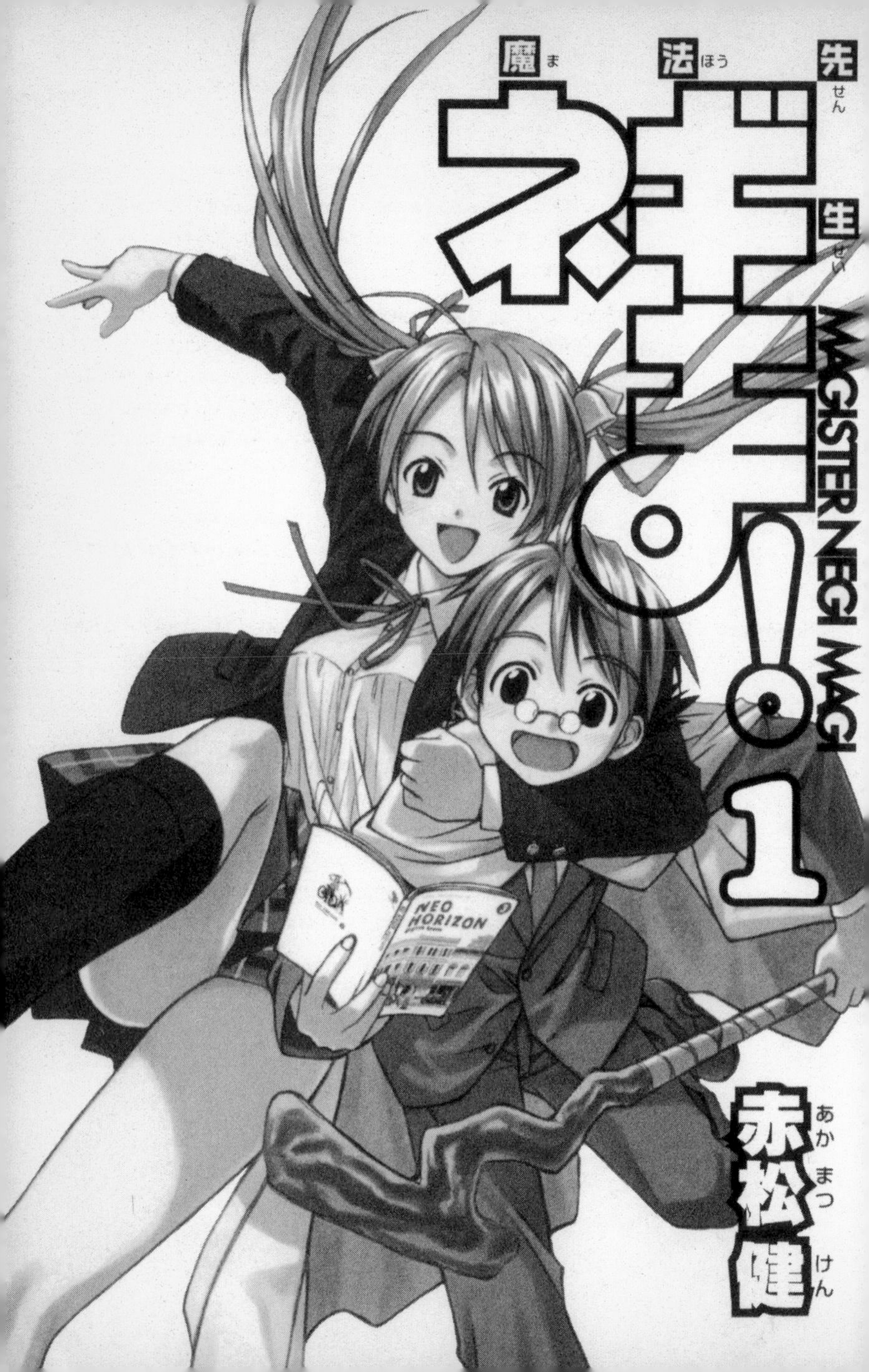
魔法先生ネギま!
まほうせんせい
MAGISTER NEGI MAGI
1
NEO HORIZON
赤松健
あかまつけん

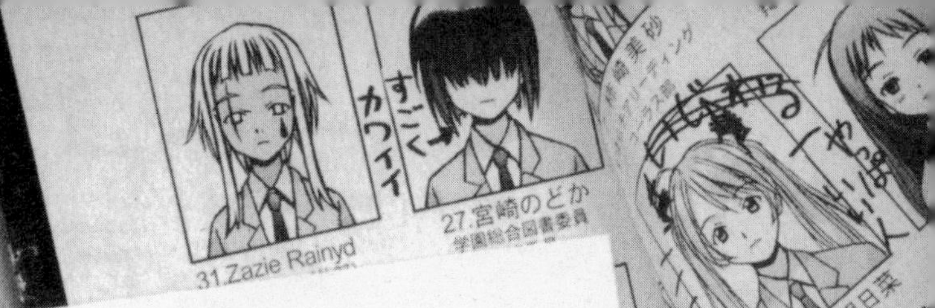

31.Zazie Rainyd
すごくカワイイ
27.宮崎のどか
学園総合図書委員
8. 神楽坂明日菜
美術部

Contents

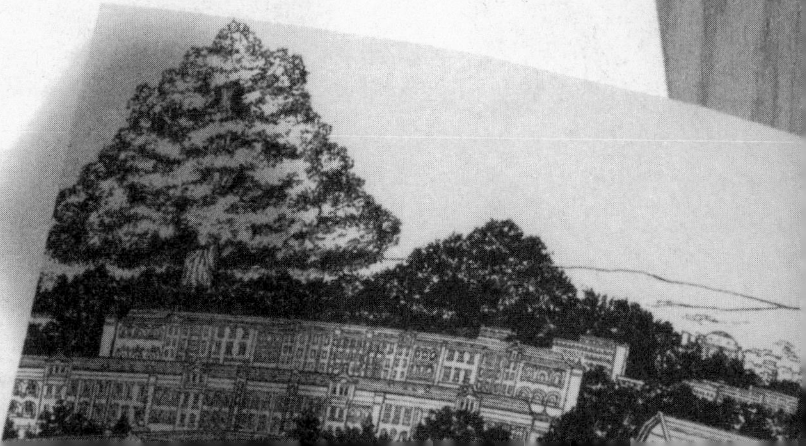

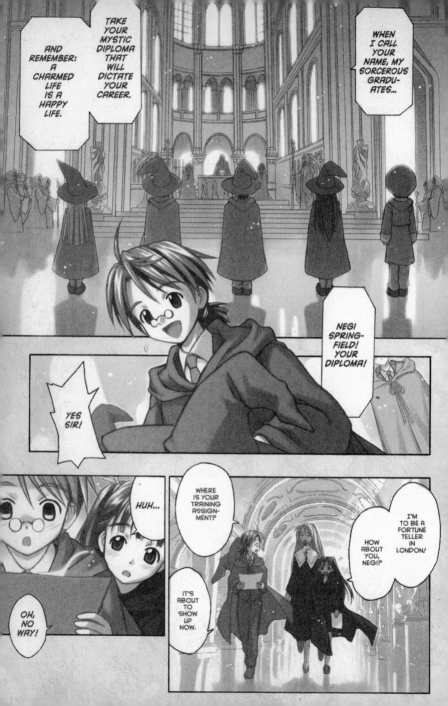

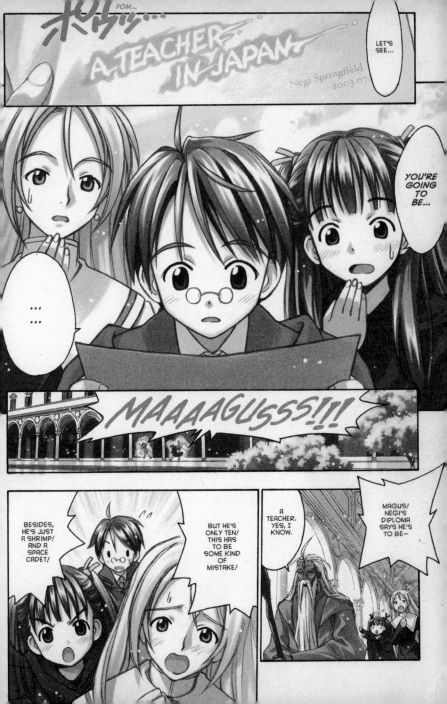

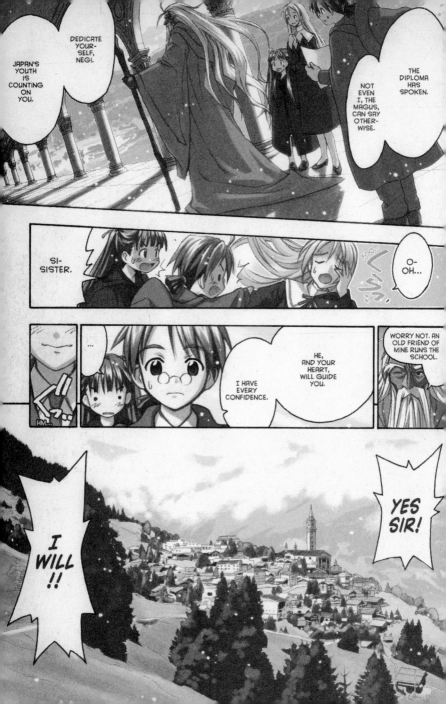

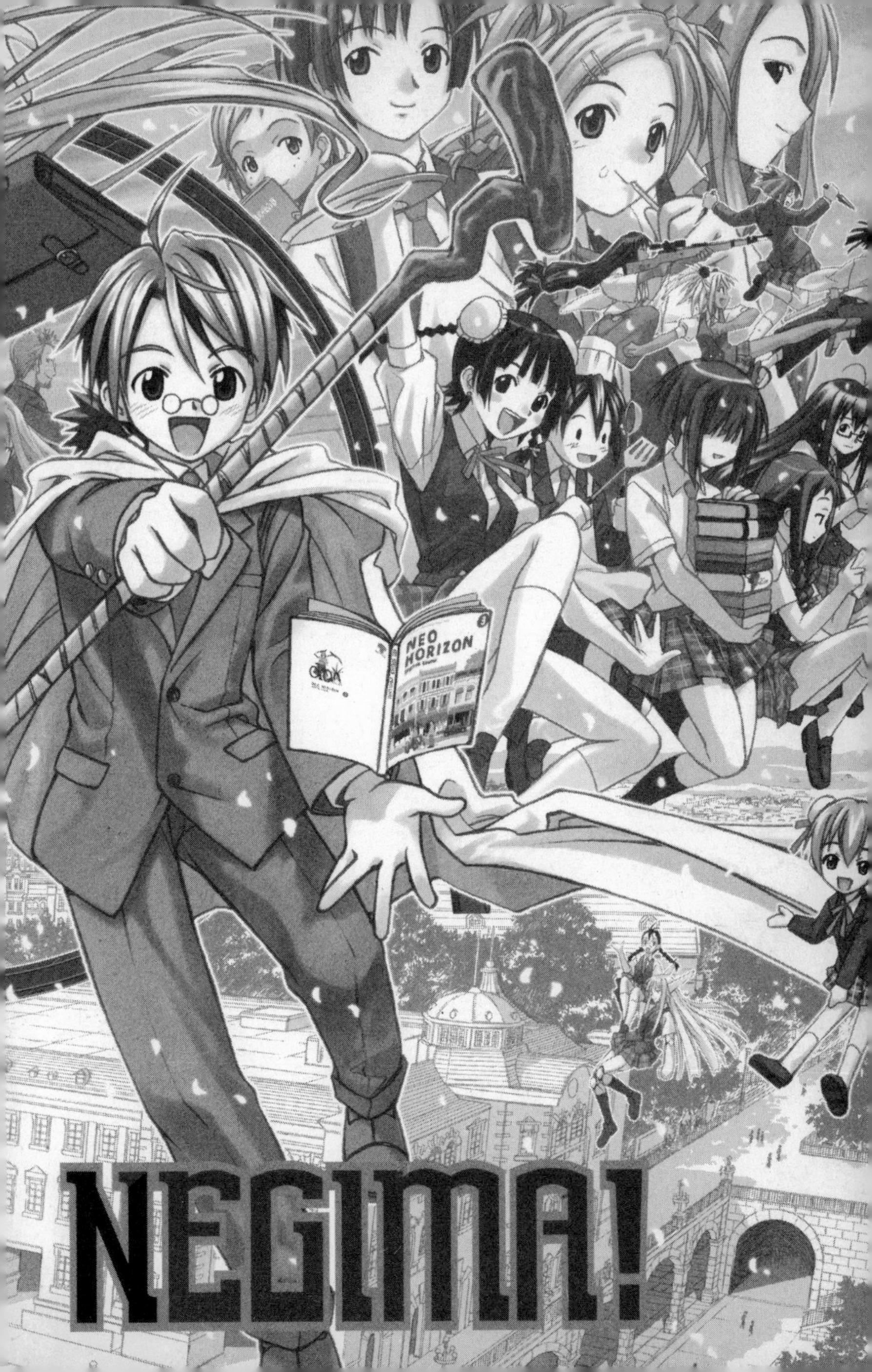
NEO HORIZON
NEGIMA!

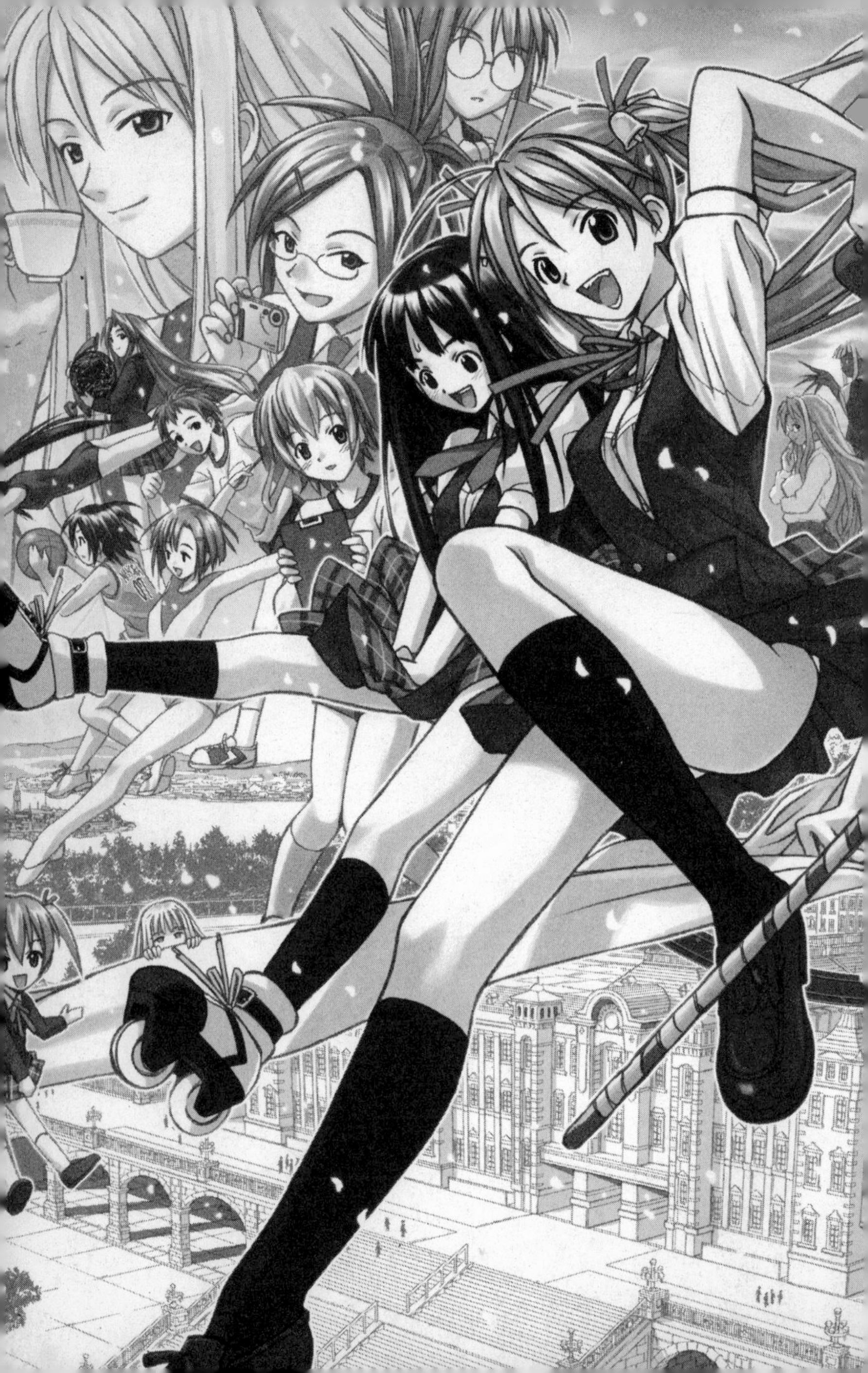

MAHORA
NEGIMA!

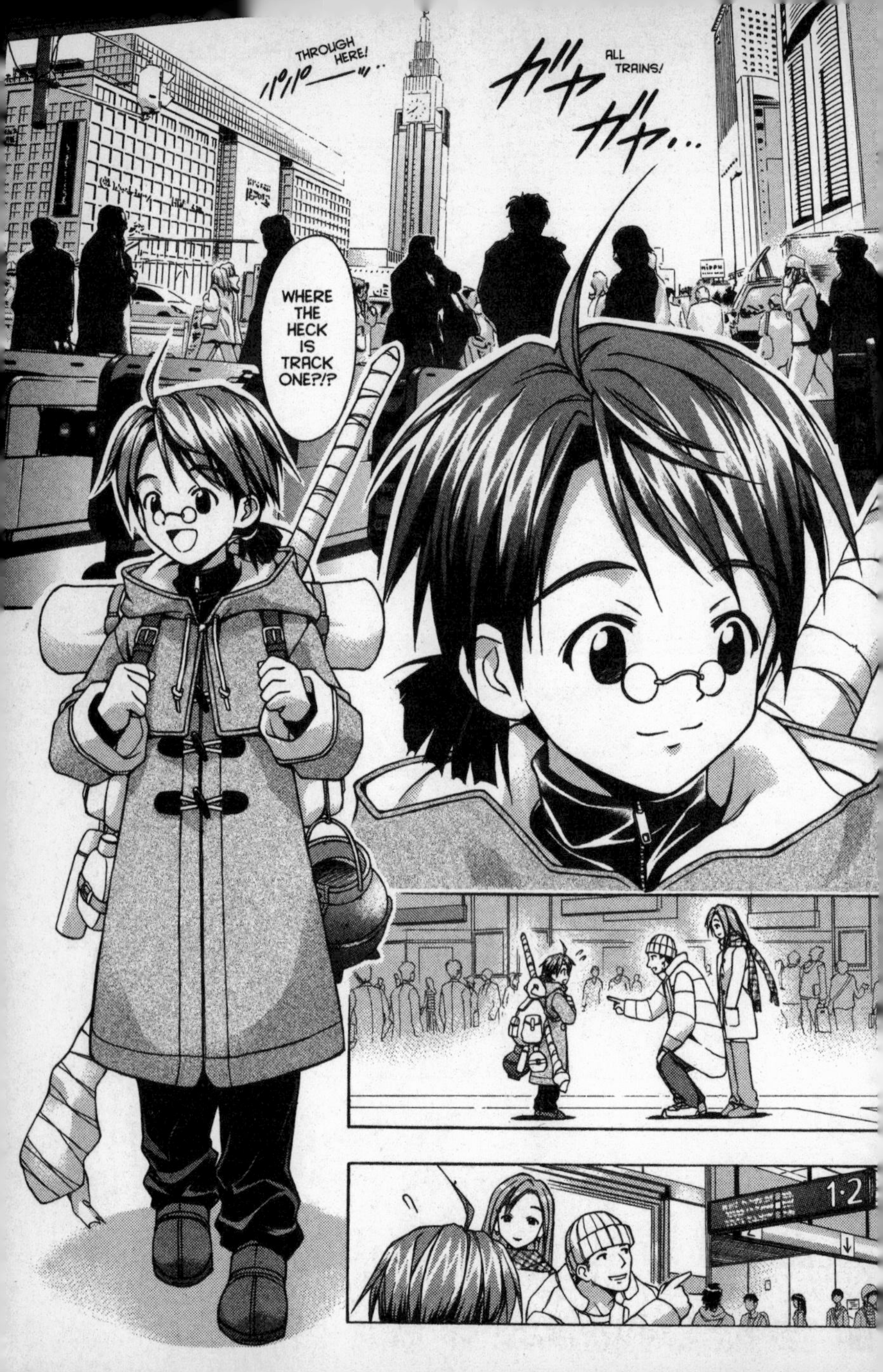
ガヤ ガヤ…
ALL TRAINS!
THROUGH HERE!
パパー…
WHERE THE HECK IS TRACK ONE?!?

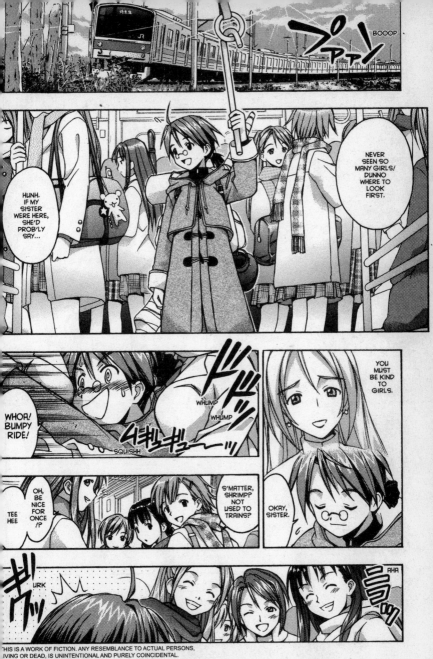

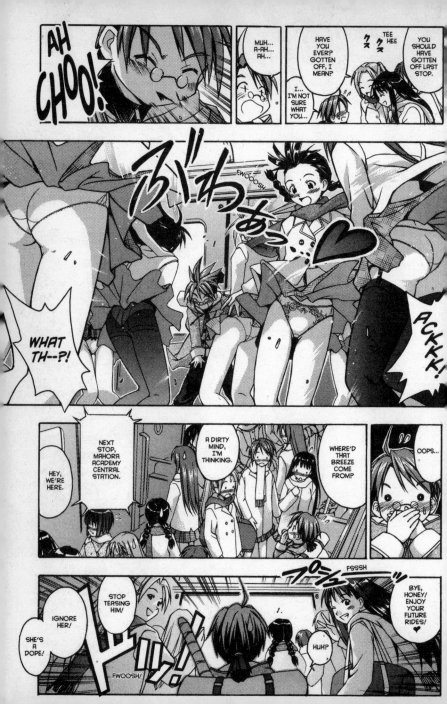

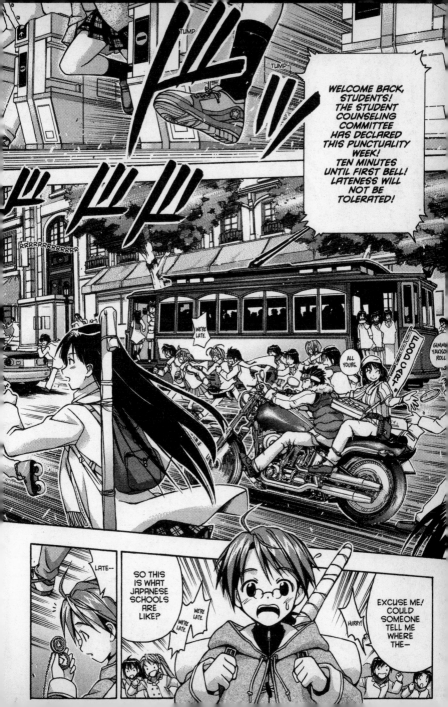

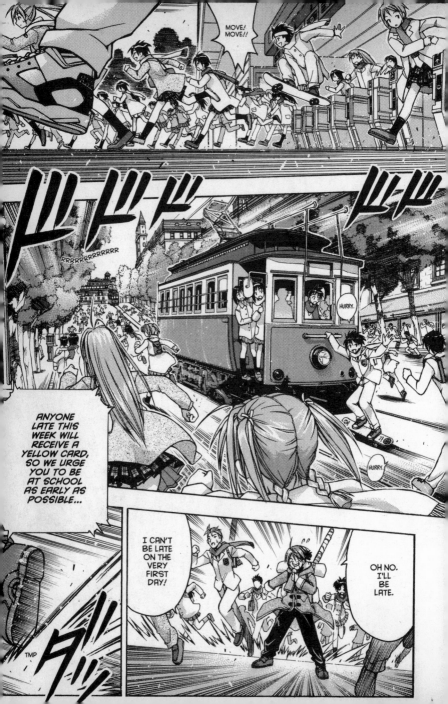

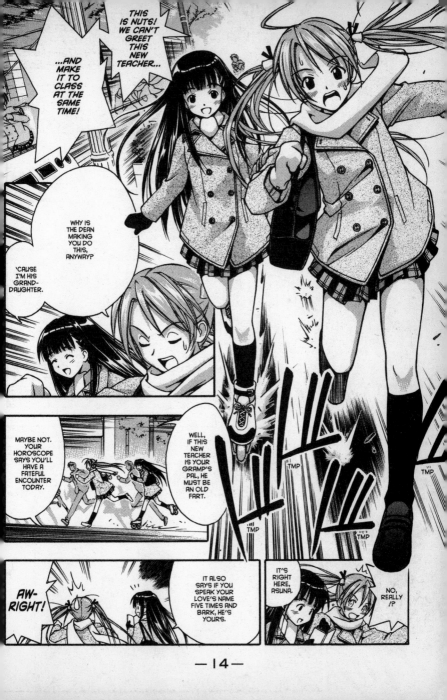

THIS IS NUTS! WE CAN'T GREET THIS NEW TEACHER...

...AND MAKE IT TO CLASS AT THE SAME TIME!

WHY IS THE DEAN MAKING YOU DO THIS, ANYWAY?

'CAUSE I'M HIS GRAND-DAUGHTER.

MAYBE NOT. YOUR HOROSCOPE SAYS YOU'LL HAVE A FATEFUL ENCOUNTER TODAY.

WELL, IF THIS NEW TEACHER IS YOUR GRAMP'S PAL, HE MUST BE AN OLD FART.

TMP

TMP

TMP

TMP

AW-RIGHT!

IT ALSO SAYS IF YOU SPEAK YOUR LOVE'S NAME FIVE TIMES AND BARK, HE'S YOURS.

IT'S RIGHT HERE, ASUNA.

NO, REALLY!?

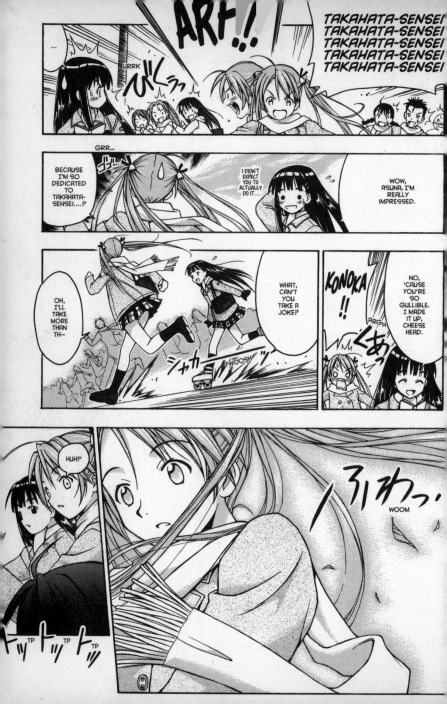

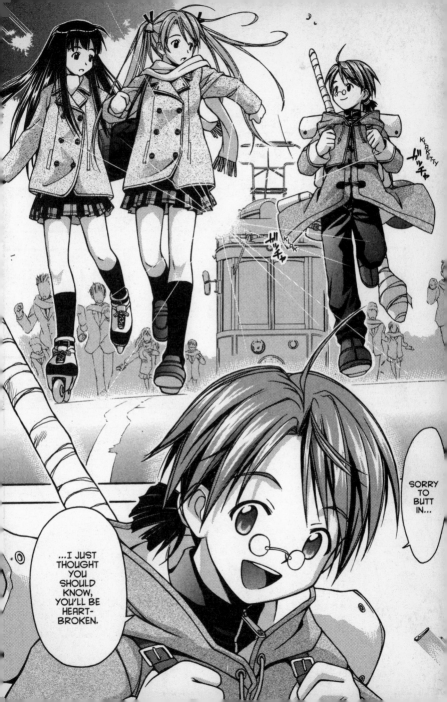

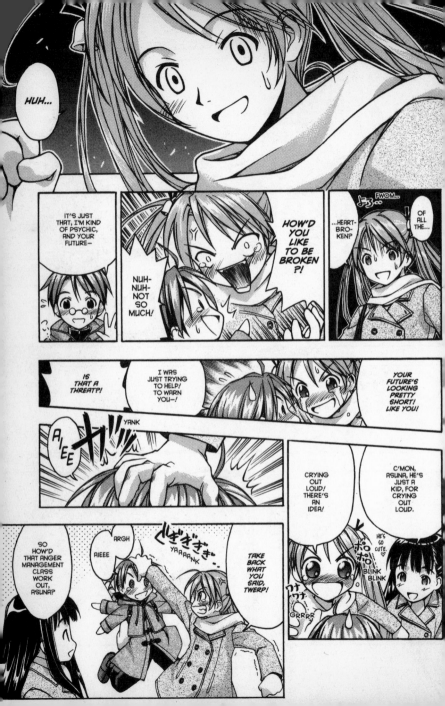

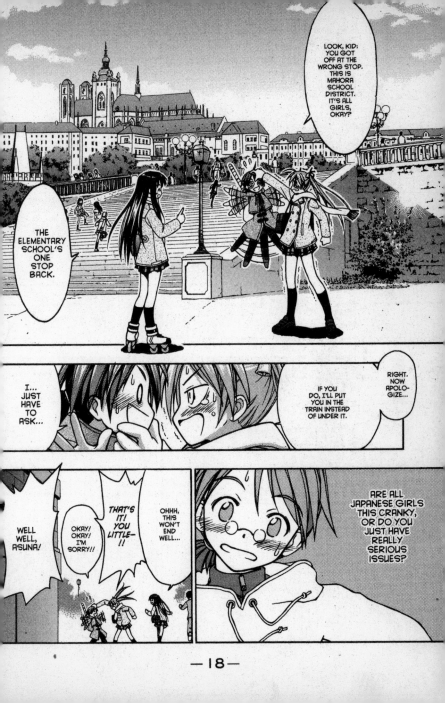

LOOK, KID: YOU GOT OFF AT THE WRONG STOP. THIS IS MAHORA SCHOOL DISTRICT. IT'S ALL GIRLS, OKAY?

THE ELEMENTARY SCHOOL'S ONE STOP BACK.

I... JUST HAVE TO ASK...

IF YOU DO, I'LL PUT YOU IN THE TRAIN INSTEAD OF UNDER IT.

RIGHT. NOW APOLO- GIZE...

WELL WELL, ASUNA!

OKAY! OKAY! I'M SORRY!!

THAT'S IT! YOU LITTLE—!!

OHHH, THIS WON'T END WELL...

ARE ALL JAPANESE GIRLS THIS CRANKY, OR DO YOU JUST HAVE REALLY SERIOUS ISSUES?

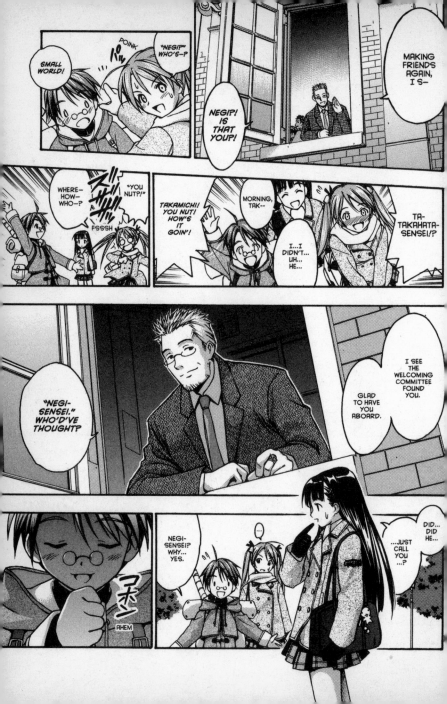

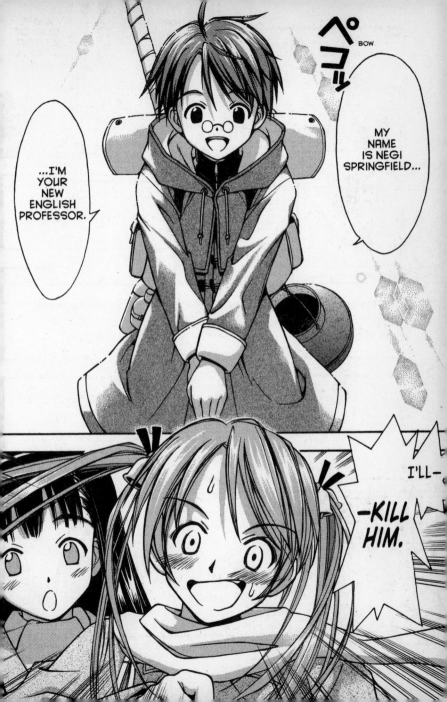

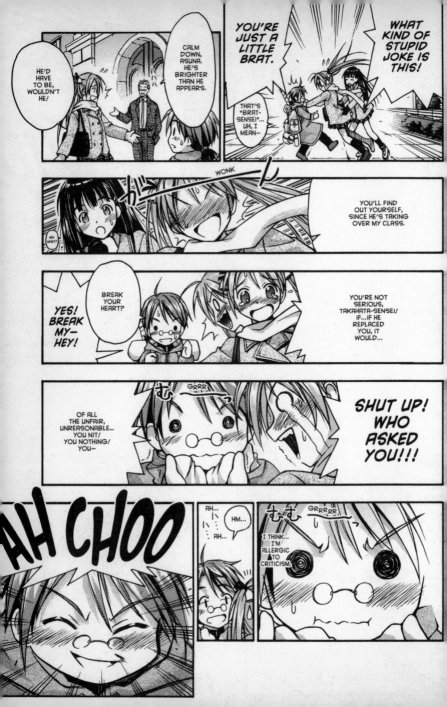

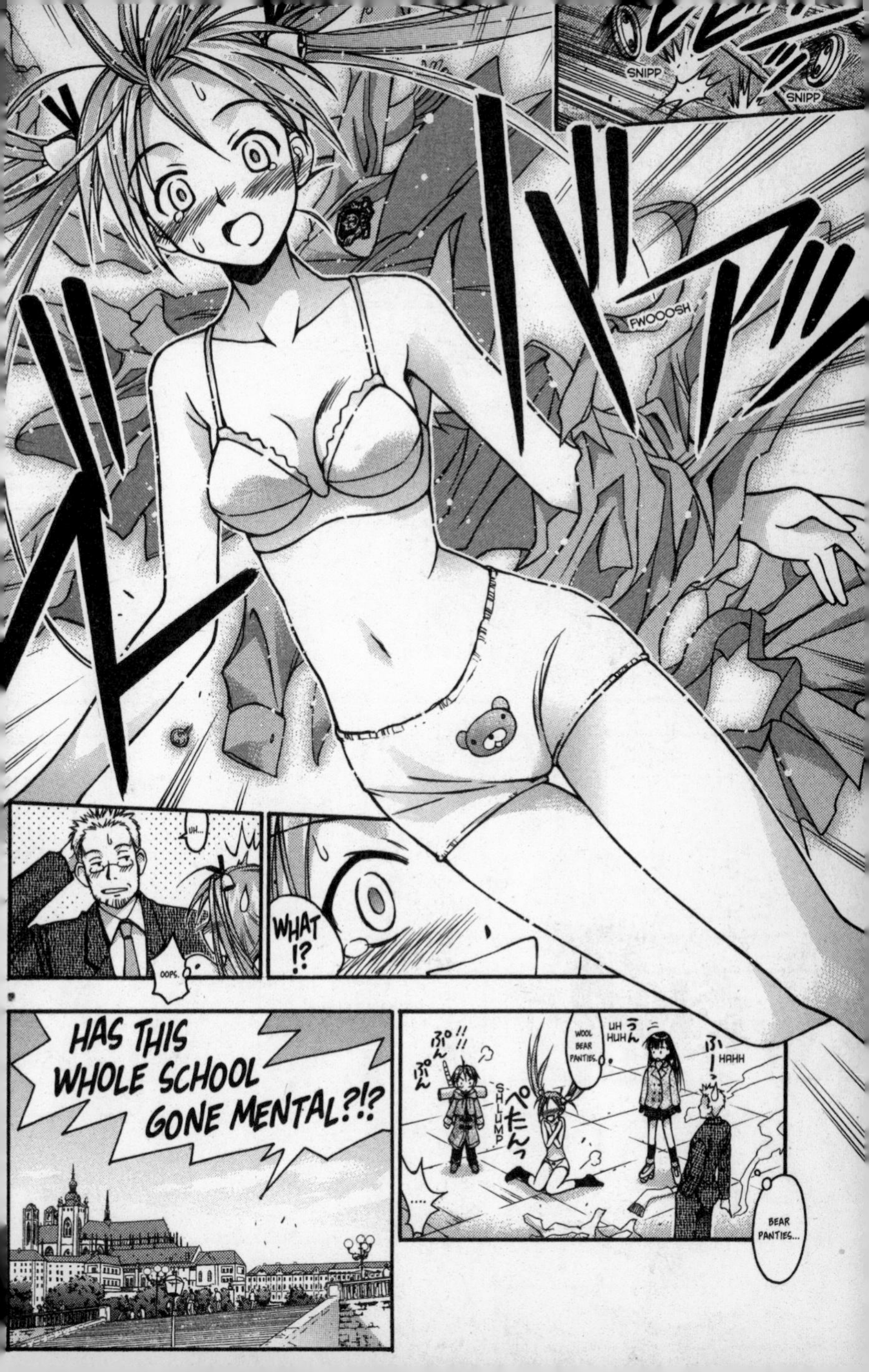
SNIPP
SNIPP
FWOOOSH
WHAT !?
UH...
OOPS.
UH HUH うん
WOOL BEAR PANTIES...
ふー! HAHH
BEAR PANTIES...
ぺたんっ SHLUMP
ぷん!! ぷん!!
....
HAS THIS WHOLE SCHOOL GONE MENTAL?!?

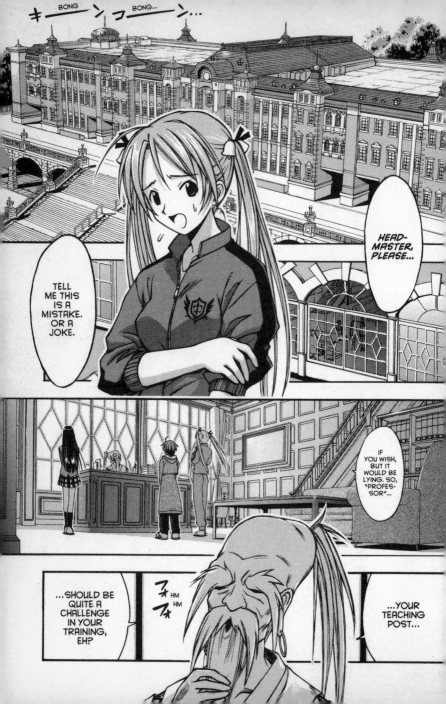

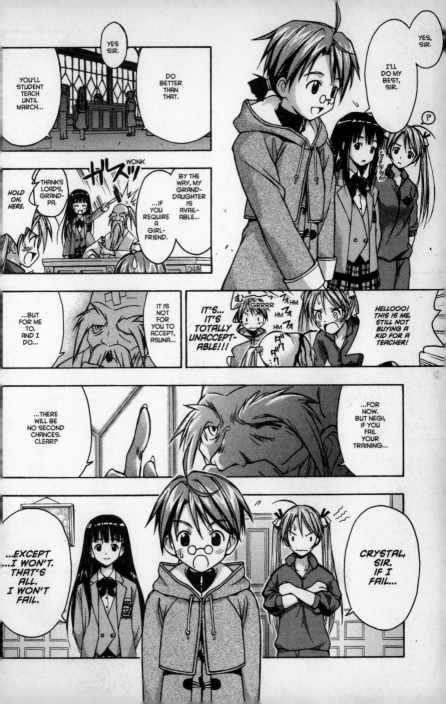

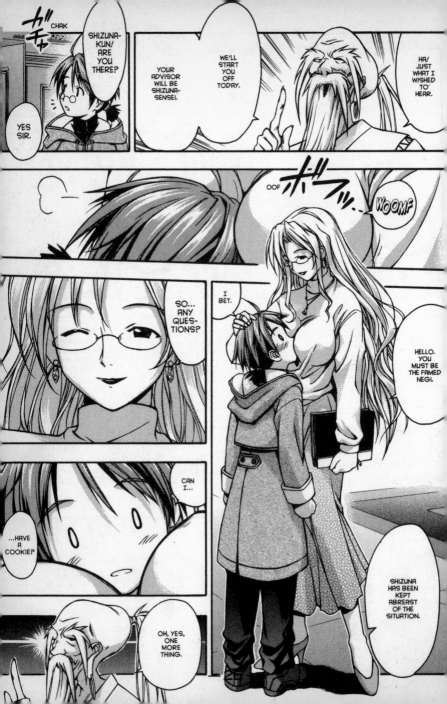

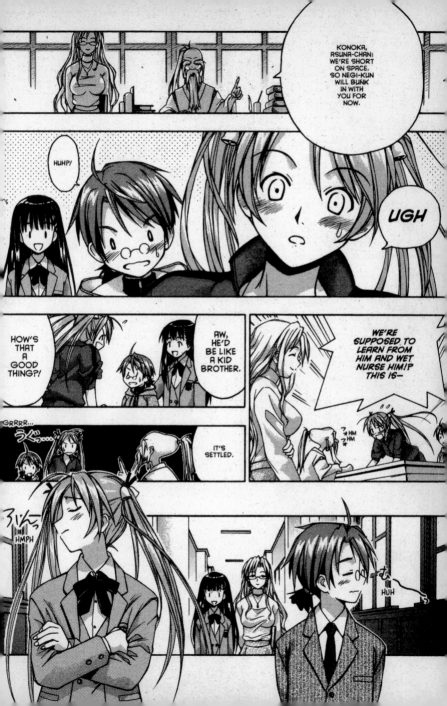

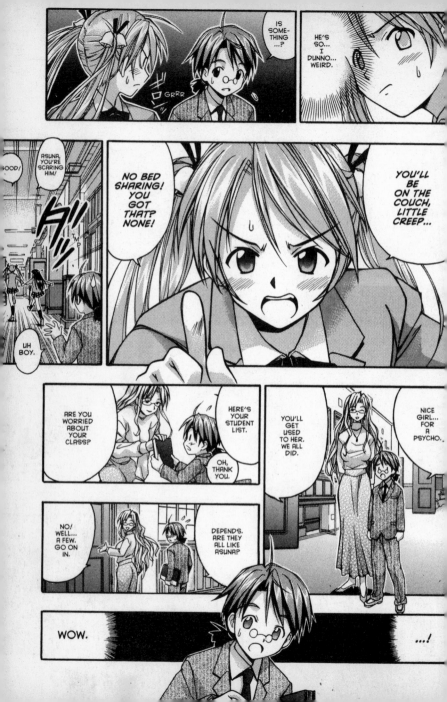

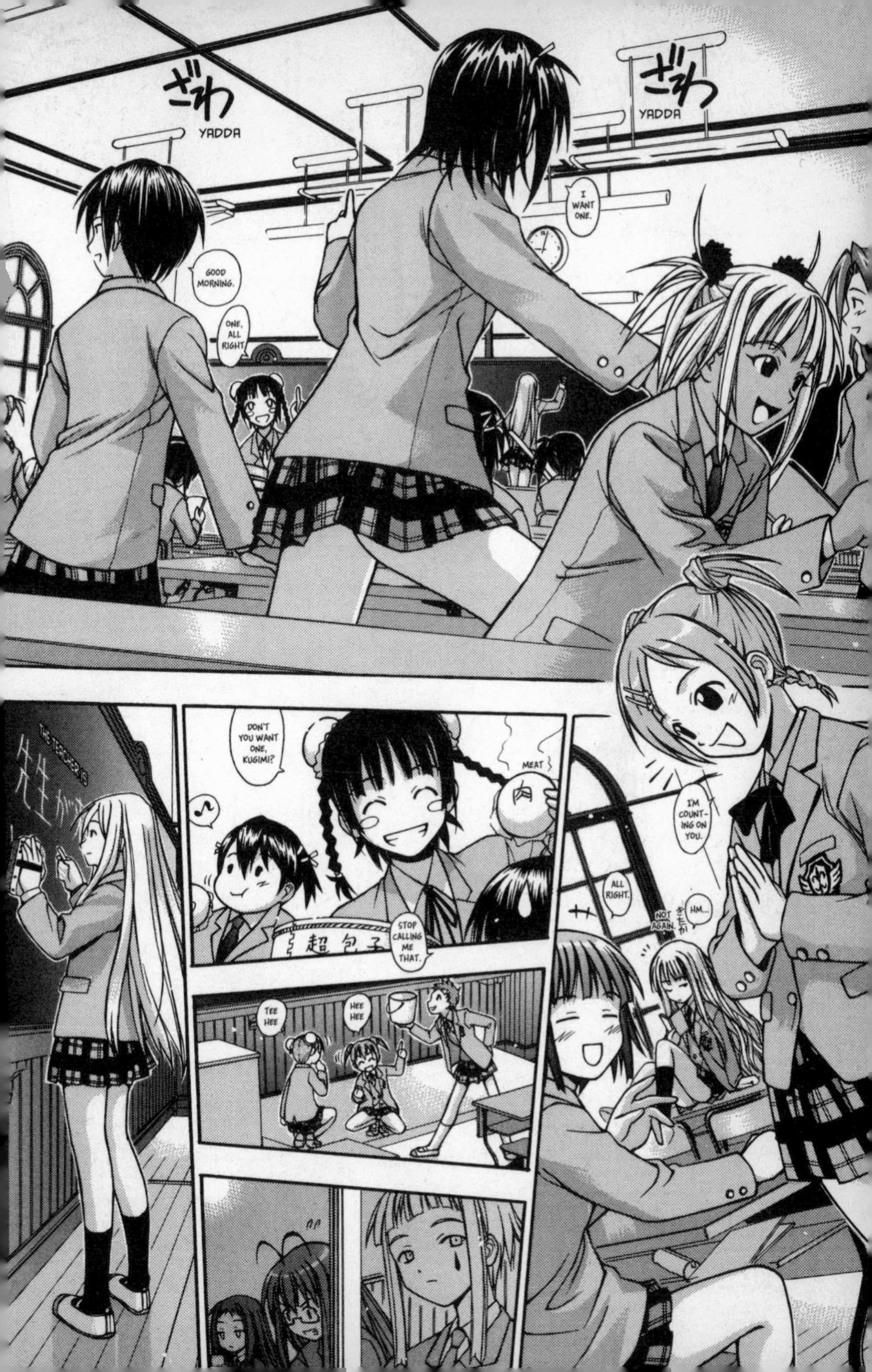
ざわ
YADDA
I WANT ONE.
ざわ
YADDA
GOOD MORNING.
ONE, ALL RIGHT
I'M COUNTING ON YOU.
HM...
NOT AGAIN.
ALL RIGHT.
MEAT
肉
DON'T YOU WANT ONE, KUGIMI?
超包子
STOP CALLING ME THAT.
HEE HEE
TEE HEE
THE TEACHER IS

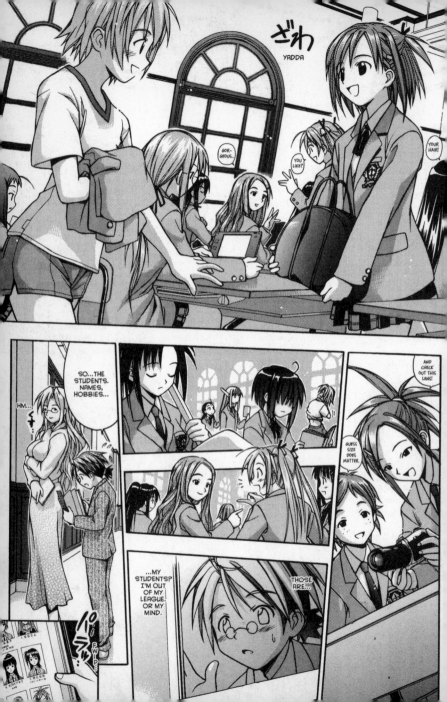

YADDA

GORGEOUS...

YOU LIKE?

YOUR HAIR!

SO... THE STUDENTS. NAMES, HOBBIES...

HM...

AND CHECK OUT THIS LENS!

GUESS SIZE DOES MATTER.

...MY STUDENTS? I'M OUT OF MY LEAGUE! OR MY MIND.

THOSE ARE...

FWIP?

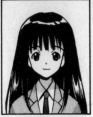

13. KONOKA KONOE
SECRETARY
FORTUNE-TELLING CLUB
LIBRARY CLUB

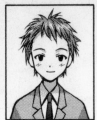

9. KASUGA MISORA

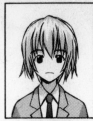

5. AKO IZUMI
NURSE'S OFFICE
SOCCER TEAM
(NON-SCHOOL ACTIVITY)

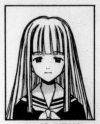

1. SAYO AIZAKA
1940~
DON'T CHANGE HER SEATING

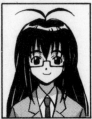

14. HARUNA SAOTOME
MANGA CLUB
LIBRARY CLUB

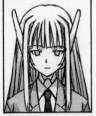

10. CHACHAMARU RAKUSO
TEA CEREMONY CLUB
GO CLUB
CALL ENGINEERING (ext. A08-7796)
IN CASE OF EMERGENCY

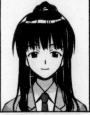

6. AKIRA OKOCHI
SWIM TEAM

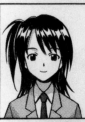

2. YUNA AKASHI
BASKETBALL TEAM
PROFESSOR AKASHI'S DAUGHTER

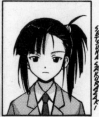

SETSUNA SAKURAZAKI
JAPANESE FENCING
KYOTO SHINMEI STYLE

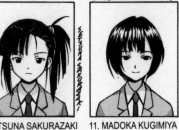

11. MADOKA KUGIMIYA
CHEERLEADER

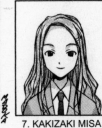

7. KAKIZAKI MISA
CHEERLEADER
CHORUS

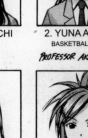

3. KAZUMI ASAKU
SCHOOL NEWSPAPER
MAHORA NEWS (ext.B09

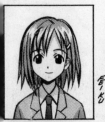

16. MAKIE SASAKI
GYMNASTICS

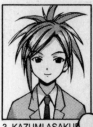

12. FEI KU
CHINESE MARTIAL ARTS
GROUP

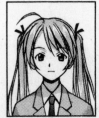

8. ASUNA KAGURAZAKA
ART CLUB

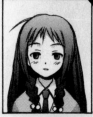

4. YUE AYASE
KID'S LIT CLUB
PHILOSOPHY CLUB
LIBRARY CLUB

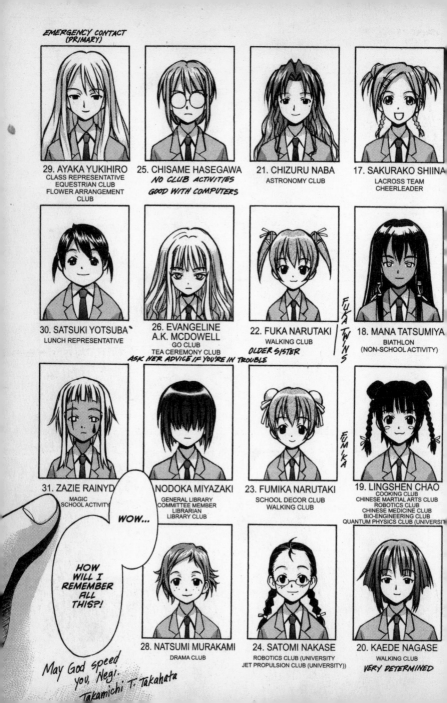

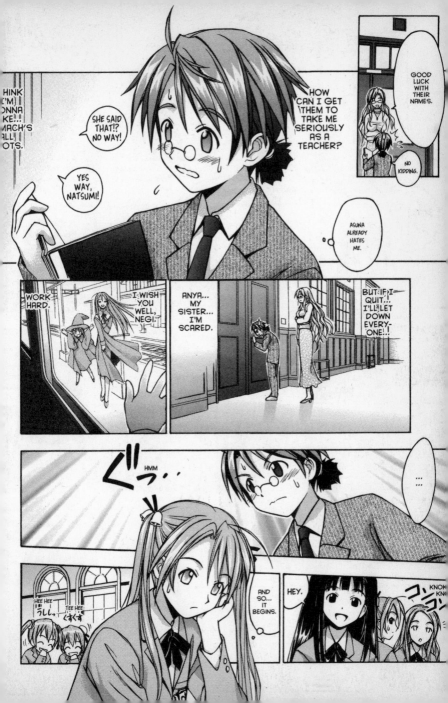

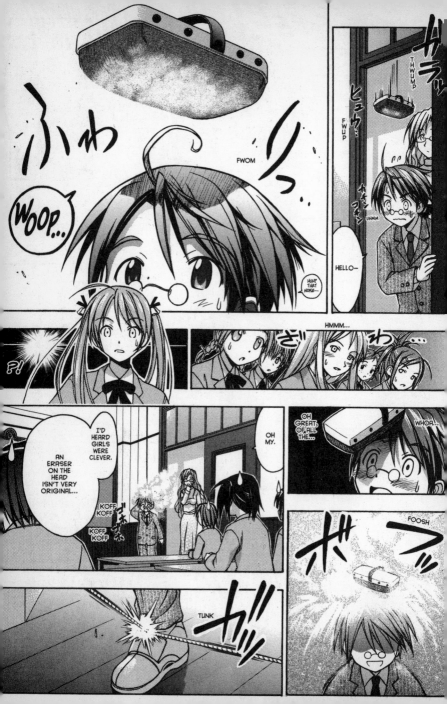

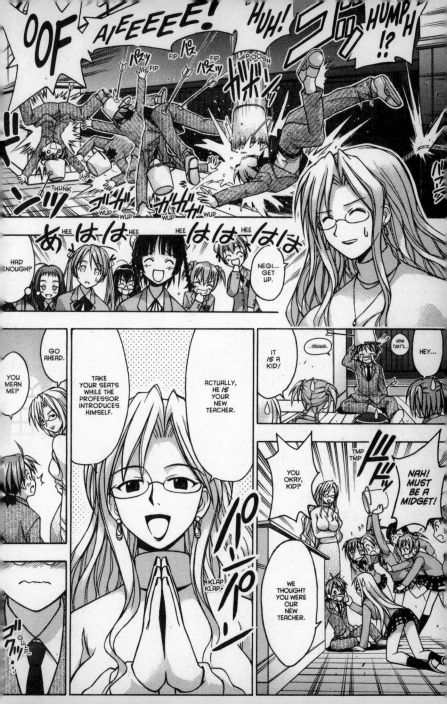

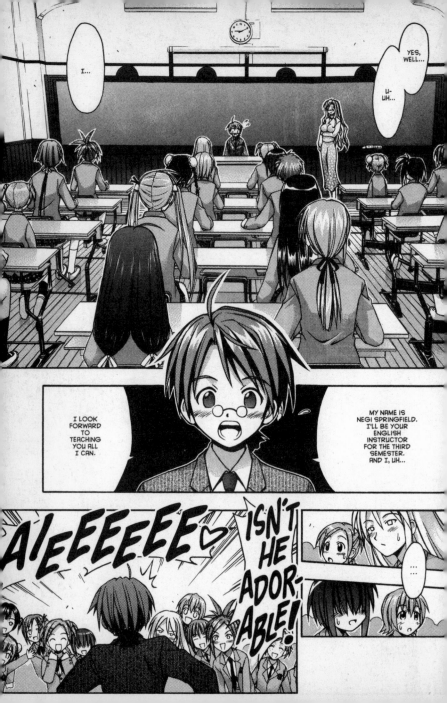

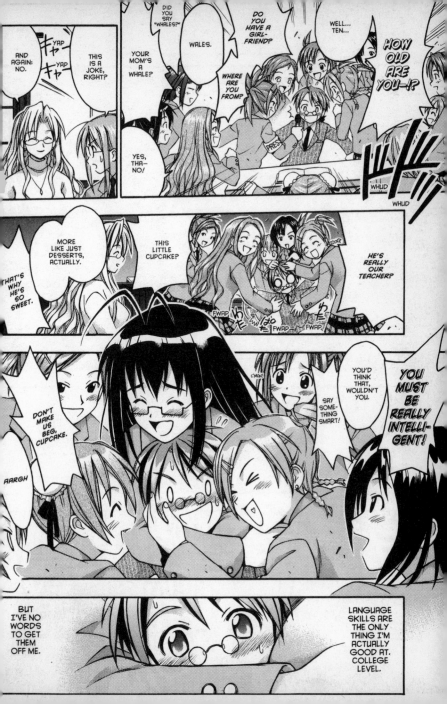

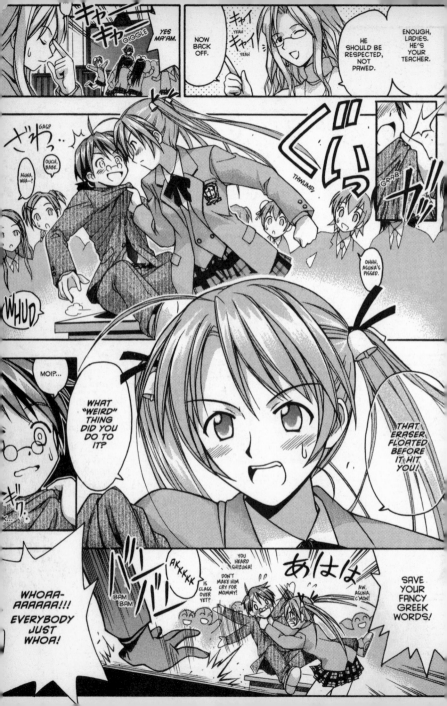

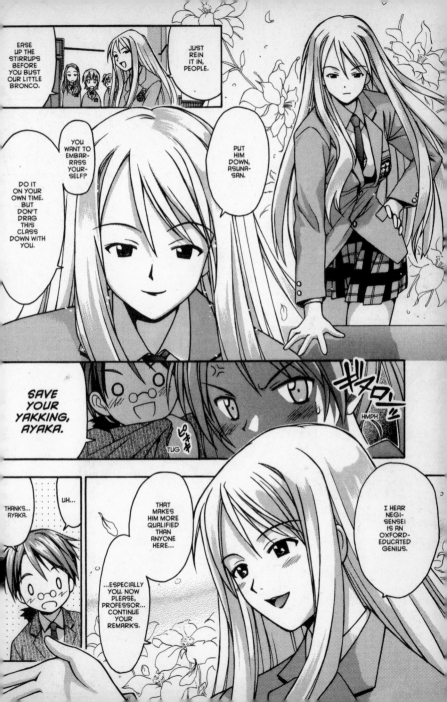

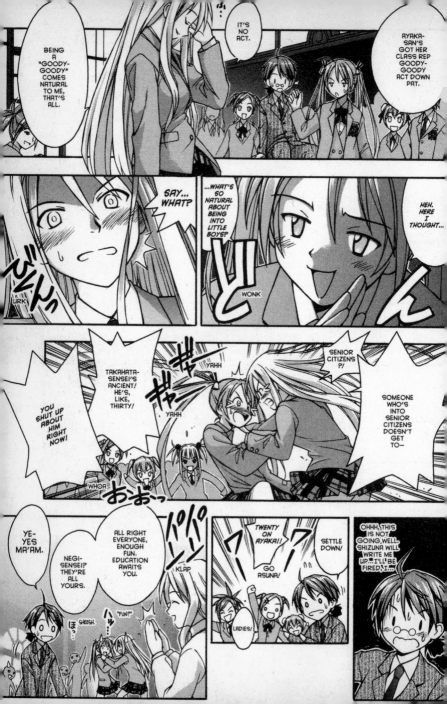

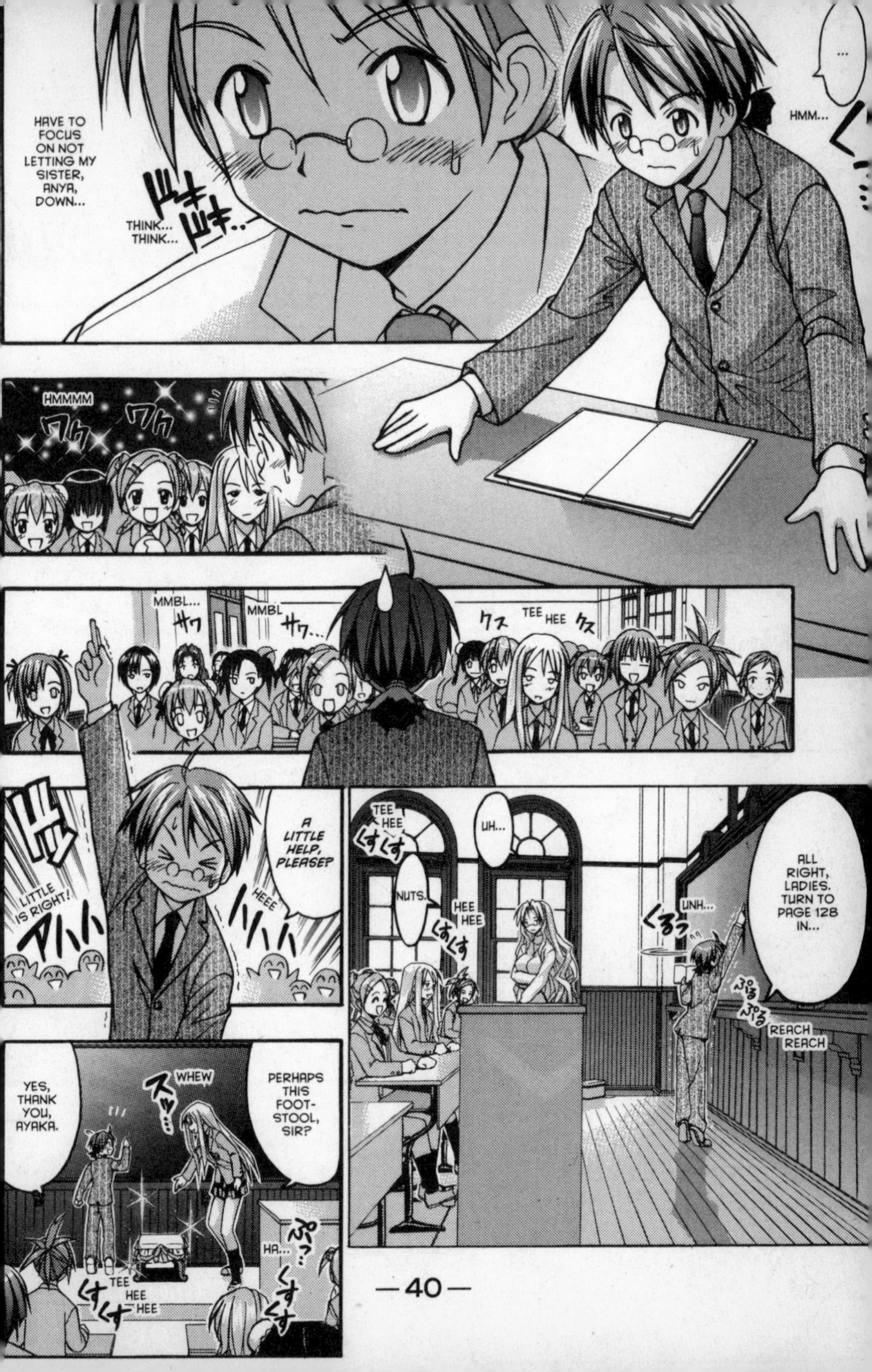
...
HMM...
HAVE TO FOCUS ON NOT LETTING MY SISTER, ANYA, DOWN...
THINK... THINK...
HMMMM
ワク ワク
MMBL... サワ
MMBL サワ...
クス TEE HEE クス
ALL RIGHT, LADIES. TURN TO PAGE 128 IN...
UNH... くるっ
UH...
TEE HEE くすくす
NUTS.
HEE HEE くすくす
ぷるぷる REACH REACH
ピッ
A LITTLE HELP, PLEASE?
HEEE ハハハ
LITTLE IS RIGHT! アハハ
PERHAPS THIS FOOT-STOOL, SIR?
WHEW スッ...
YES, THANK YOU, AYAKA.
HA... ぷっ くすくす
TEE HEE HEE くすくす

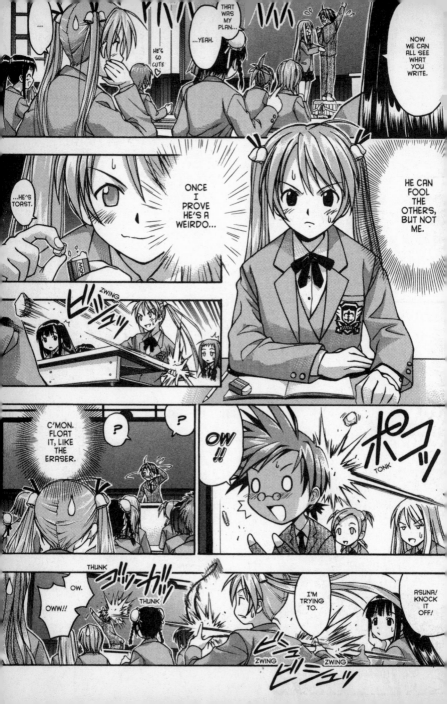

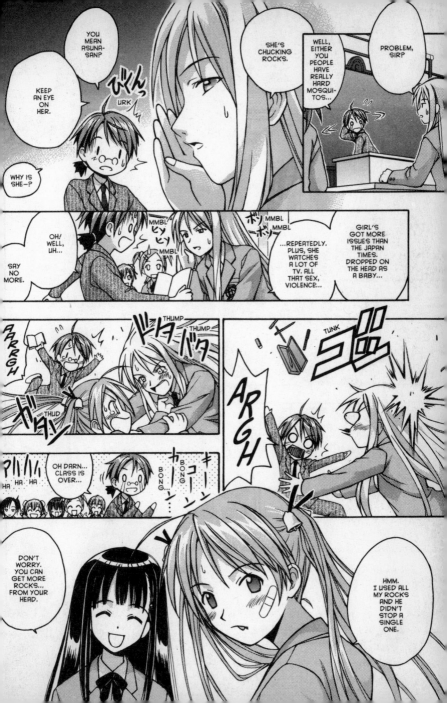

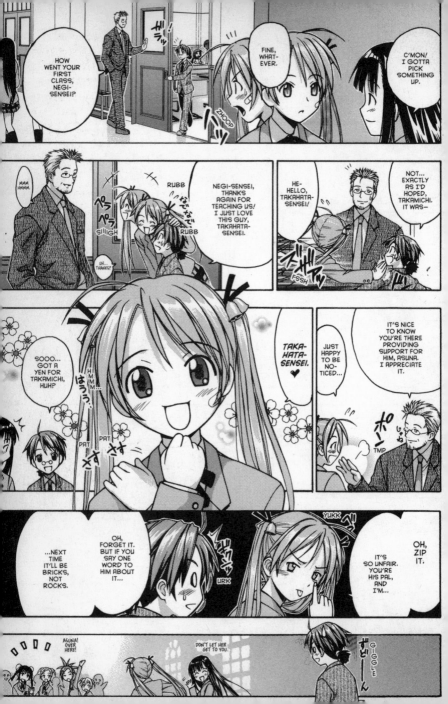

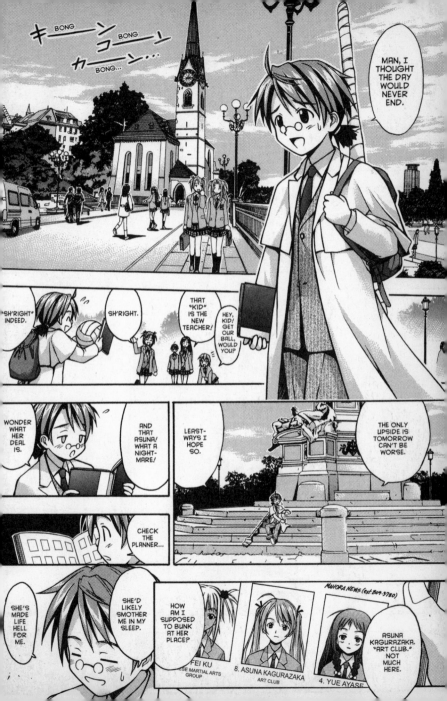

キーーン コーーン カーーン...

BONG BONG BONG...

MAN, I THOUGHT THE DAY WOULD NEVER END.

"SH'RIGHT" INDEED.

SH'RIGHT.

THAT "KID" IS THE NEW TEACHER!

HEY, KID! GET OUR BALL, WOULD YOU?

WONDER WHAT HER DEAL IS.

AND THAT ASUNA! WHAT A NIGHTMARE!

LEAST-WAYS I HOPE SO.

THE ONLY UPSIDE IS TOMORROW CAN'T BE WORSE.

CHECK THE PLANNER...

SHE'S MADE LIFE HELL FOR ME.

SHE'D LIKELY SMOTHER ME IN MY SLEEP.

HOW AM I SUPPOSED TO BUNK AT HER PLACE?

ASUNA KAGURAZAKA. "ART CLUB." NOT MUCH HERE.

MAHORA NEWS (ext. 809-3780)

FEI KU
CHINESE MARTIAL ARTS GROUP

8. ASUNA KAGURAZAKA
ART CLUB

4. YUE AYASE

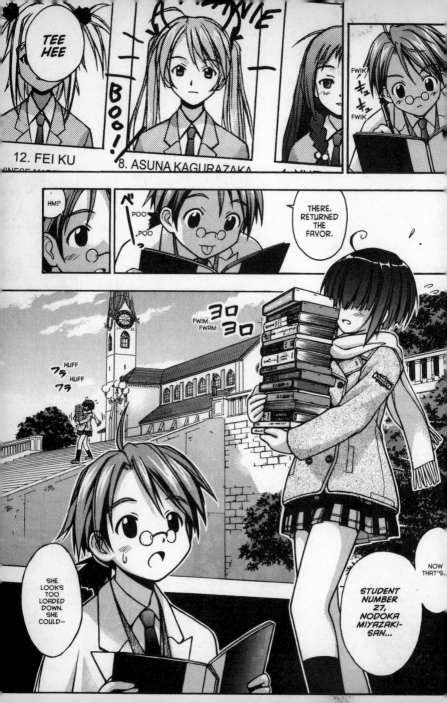

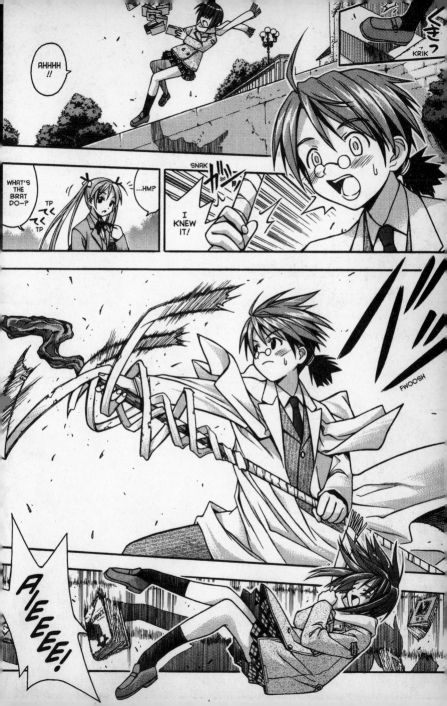

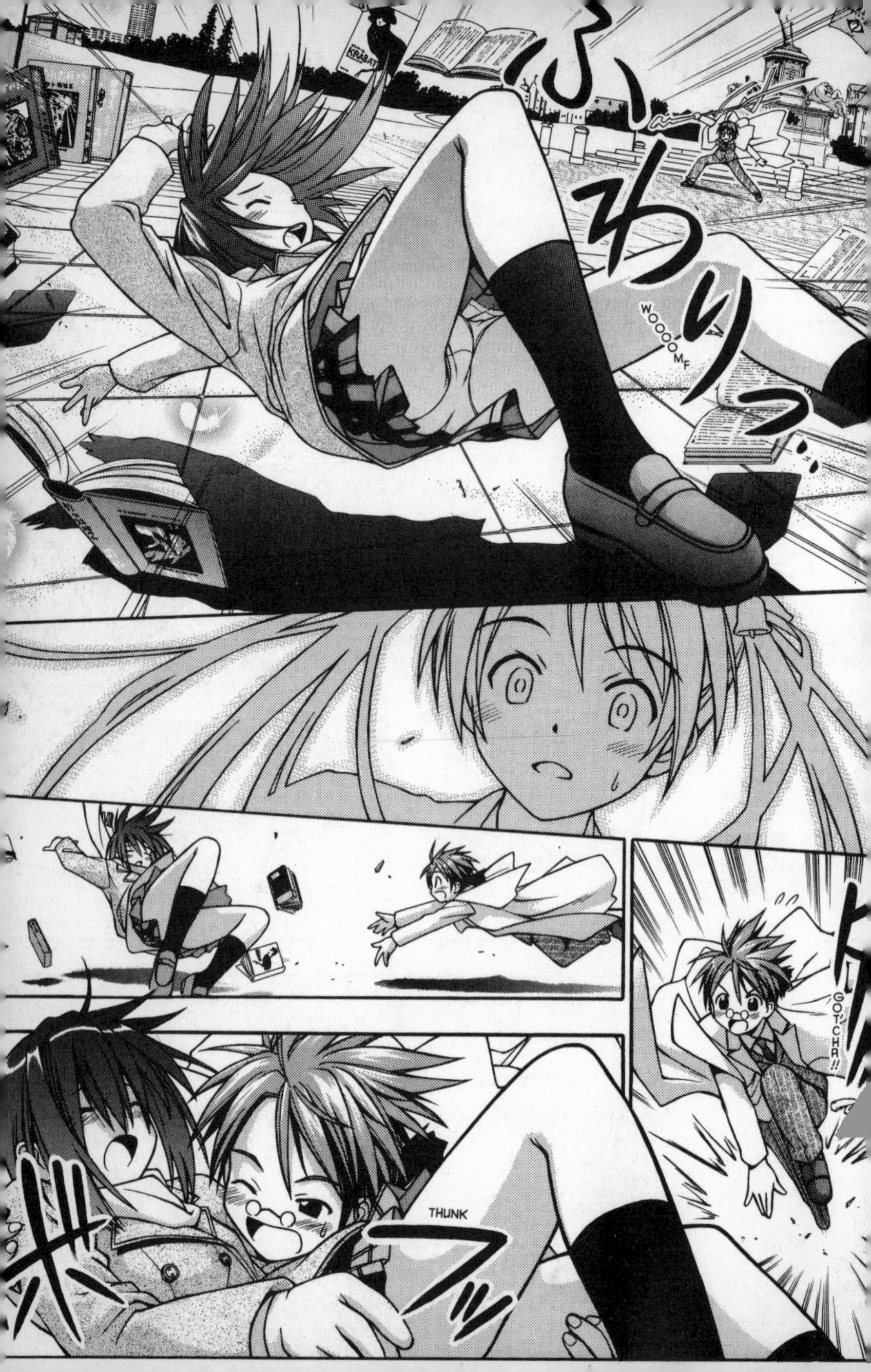
ふわりっ
WOOOOOMF
GOTCHA!!
THUNK

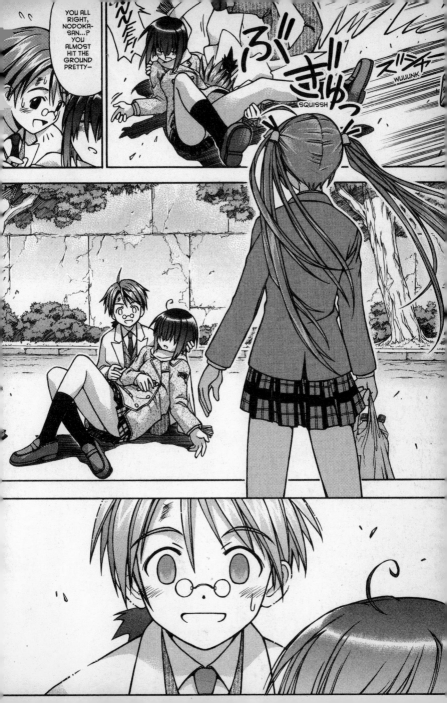

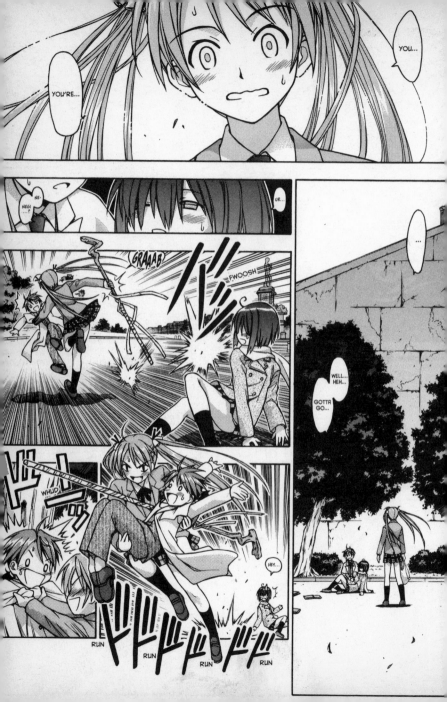

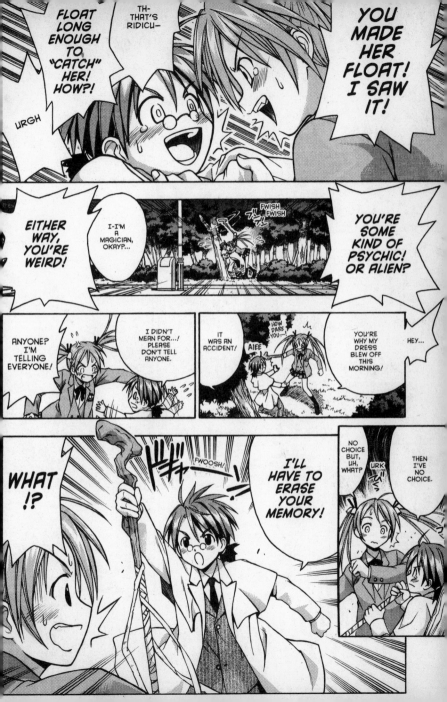

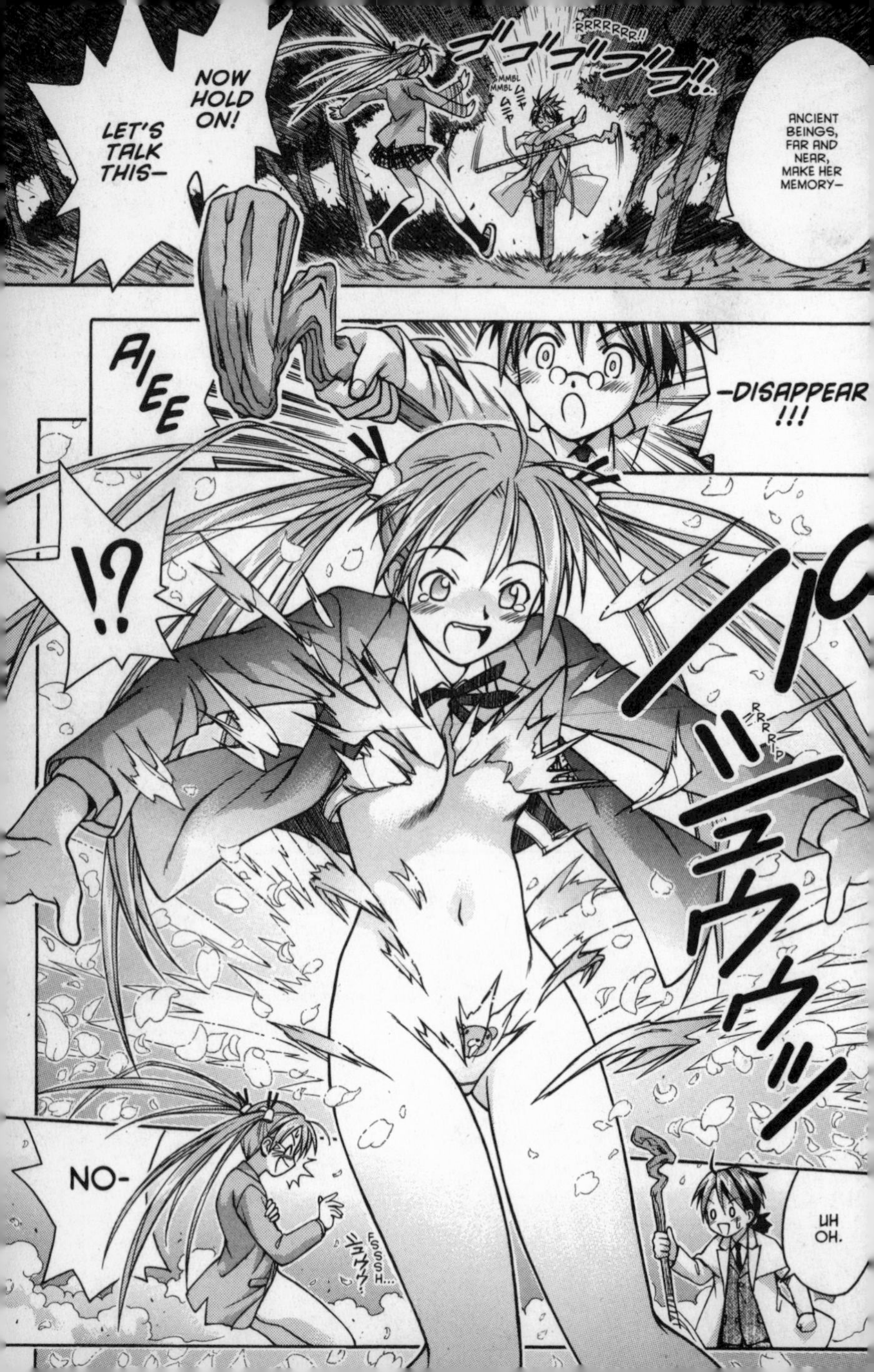
ANCIENT BEINGS, FAR AND NEAR, MAKE HER MEMORY—
RRRRRRR!!
MMBL MMBL
NOW HOLD ON!
LET'S TALK THIS—
—DISAPPEAR!!!
AIEE
!?
RRRRRIP
UH OH.
FSSSH...
NO-

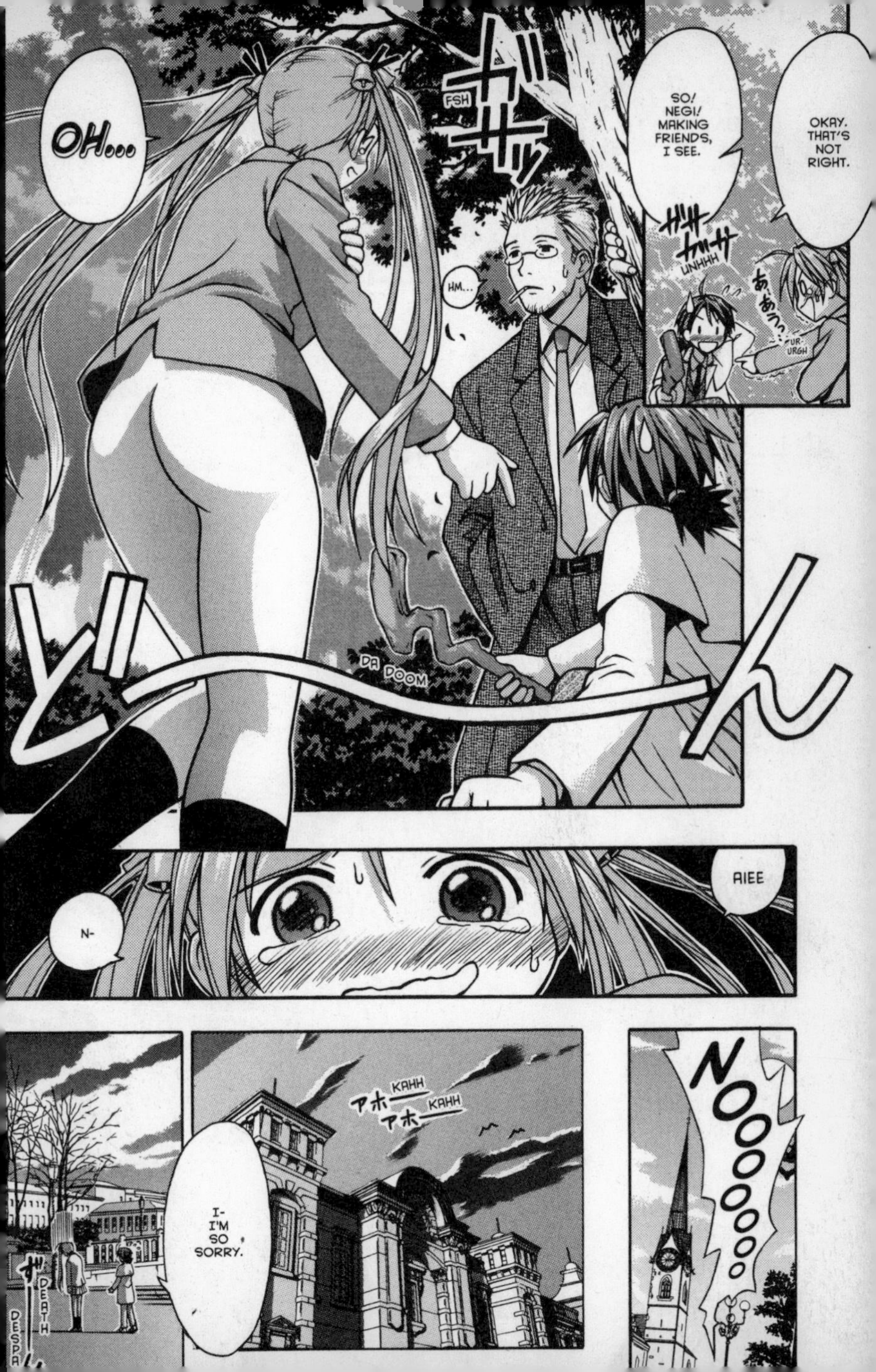
OKAY. THAT'S NOT RIGHT.
SO! NEGI! MAKING FRIENDS, I SEE.
UNHHH
UR-URGH
FSH
OH...
HM...
DA DOOM
AIEE
N-
NOOOOOOO
KAHH
KAHH
I- I'M SO SORRY.
DEATH
DESPA

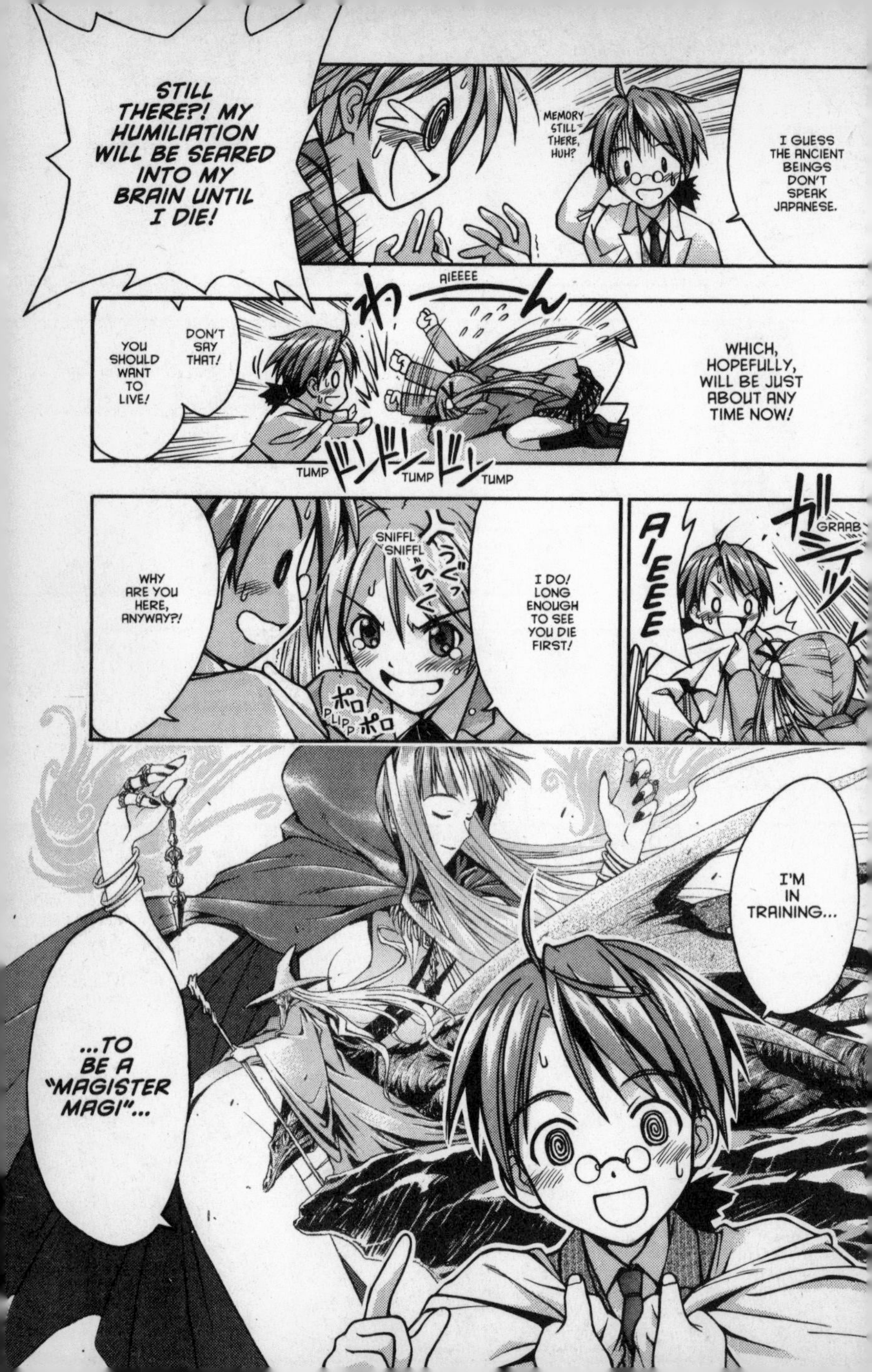
I GUESS THE ANCIENT BEINGS DON'T SPEAK JAPANESE.
MEMORY STILL THERE, HUH?
STILL THERE?! MY HUMILIATION WILL BE SEARED INTO MY BRAIN UNTIL I DIE!
WHICH, HOPEFULLY, WILL BE JUST ABOUT ANY TIME NOW!
わーん
AIEEEE
DON'T SAY THAT!
YOU SHOULD WANT TO LIVE!
ドンドンドン
TUMP TUMP TUMP
ガシィッ
GRAAB
AIEEE
I DO! LONG ENOUGH TO SEE YOU DIE FIRST!
SNIFFL SNIFFL
WHY ARE YOU HERE, ANYWAY?!
ポロポロ
PLIPP
I'M IN TRAINING...
...TO BE A "MAGISTER MAGI"...

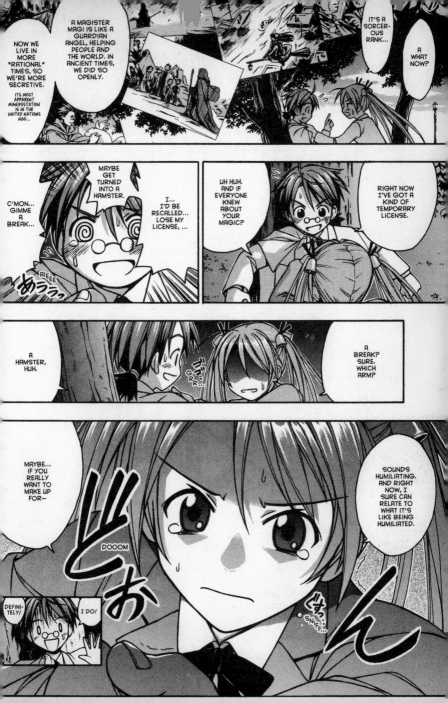

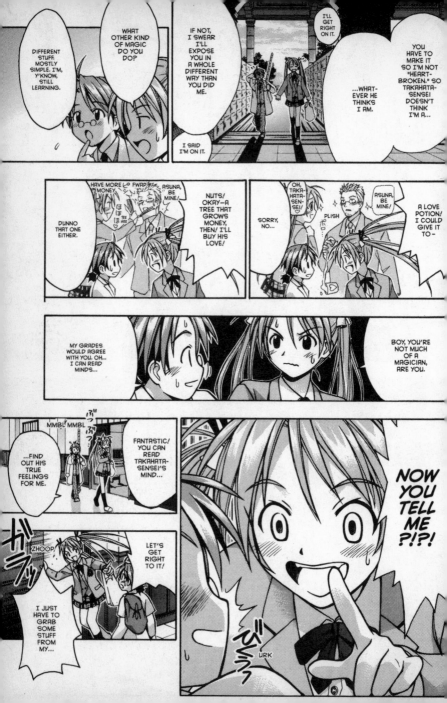

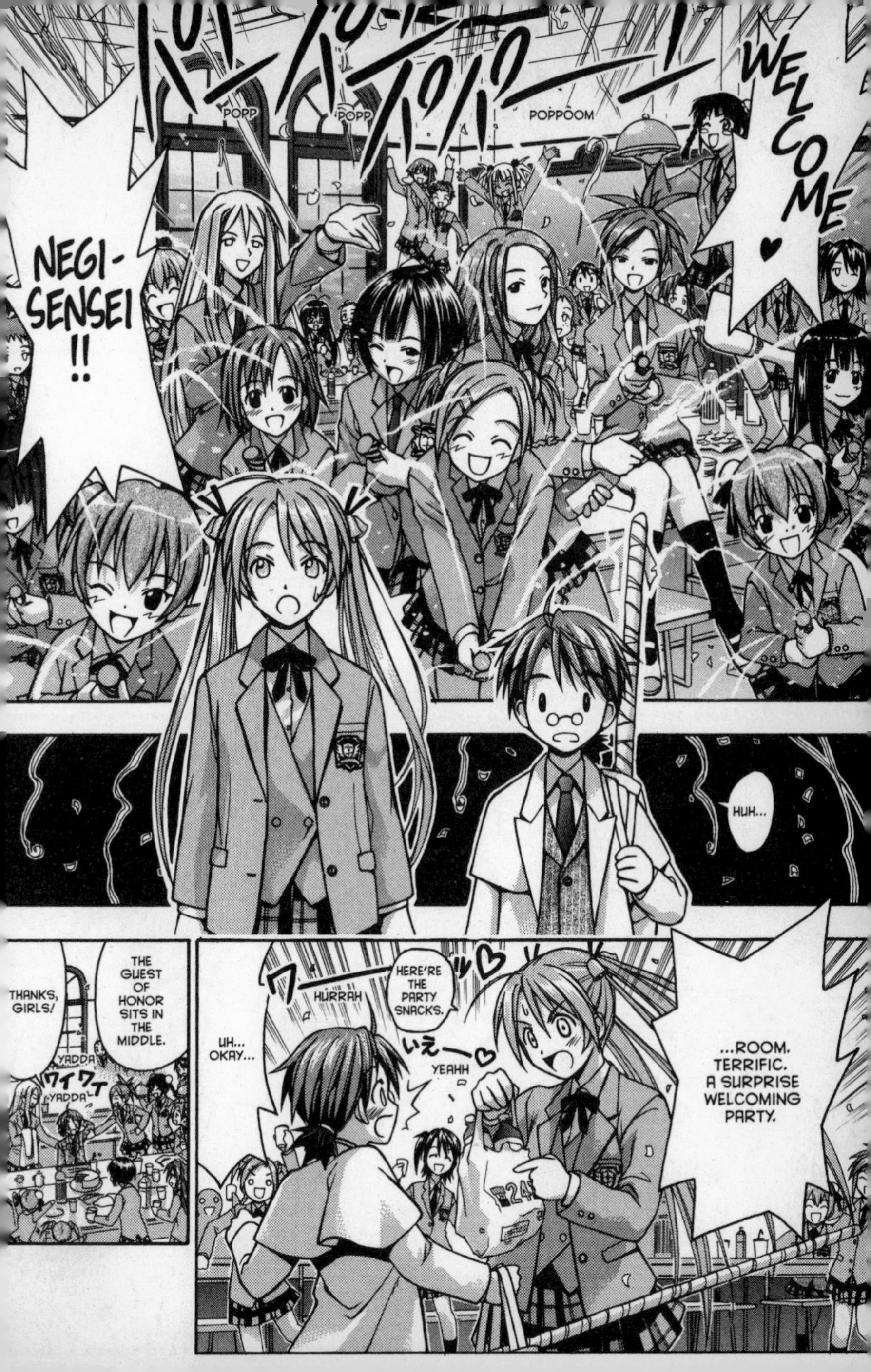
WELCOME ♥
POPPOOM
POPP
POPP
NEGI-SENSEI !!
HUH...
...ROOM. TERRIFIC. A SURPRISE WELCOMING PARTY.
HERE'RE THE PARTY SNACKS.
ワー
HURRAH
いえー♥
YEAHH
UH... OKAY...
THE GUEST OF HONOR SITS IN THE MIDDLE.
THANKS, GIRLS!
ワイワイ
YADDA
YADDA

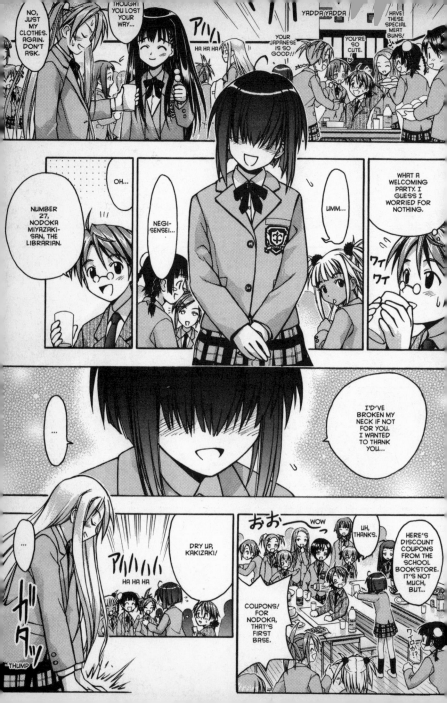

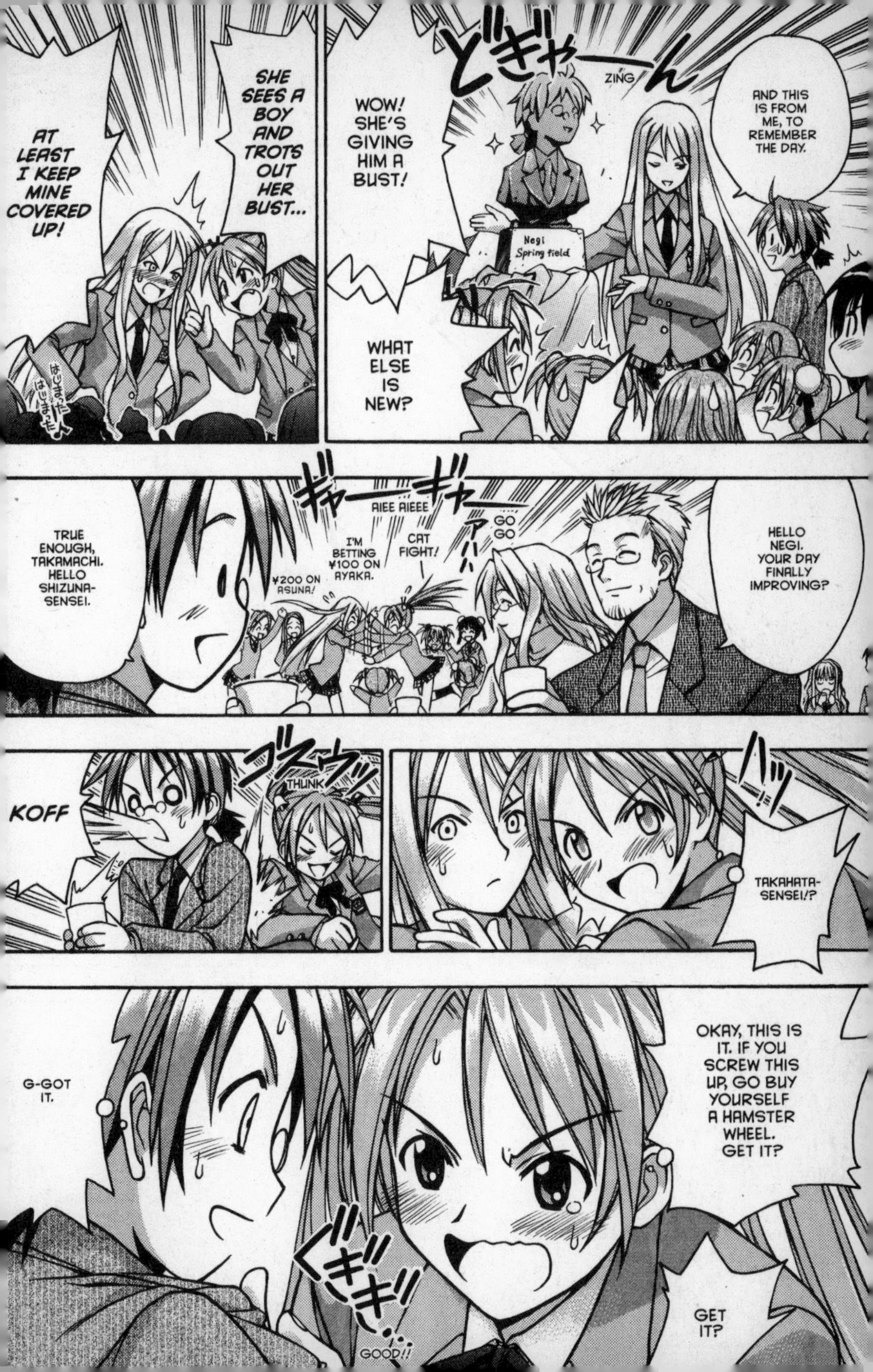
どぎゃーーん
ZING
AND THIS IS FROM ME, TO REMEMBER THE DAY.
WOW! SHE'S GIVING HIM A BUST!
Negi Springfield
WHAT ELSE IS NEW?
SHE SEES A BOY AND TROTS OUT HER BUST...
AT LEAST I KEEP MINE COVERED UP!
HELLO NEGI. YOUR DAY FINALLY IMPROVING?
ギャーギャー
AIEE AIEEE
GO GO
CAT FIGHT!
I'M BETTING ¥100 ON AYAKA.
¥200 ON ASUNA!
TRUE ENOUGH, TAKAMACHI. HELLO SHIZUNA-SENSEI.
TAKAHATA-SENSEI!?
THUNK
KOFF
OKAY, THIS IS IT. IF YOU SCREW THIS UP, GO BUY YOURSELF A HAMSTER WHEEL. GET IT?
GET IT?
G-GOT IT.
GOOD!!

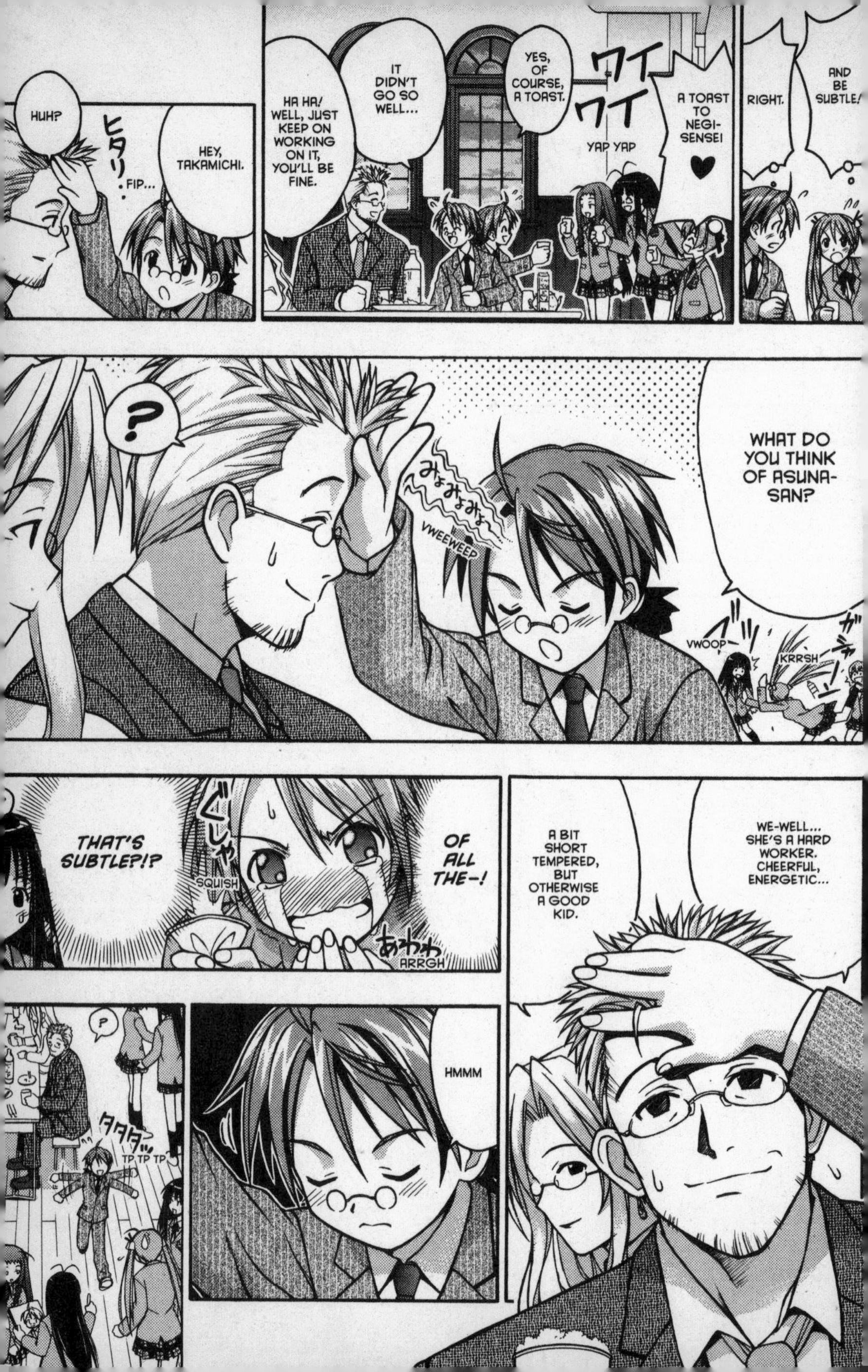
AND BE SUBTLE!
RIGHT.
A TOAST TO NEGI-SENSEI ♥
ワイワイ
YAP YAP
YES, OF COURSE, A TOAST.
IT DIDN'T GO SO WELL...
HA HA! WELL, JUST KEEP ON WORKING ON IT, YOU'LL BE FINE.
HEY, TAKAMICHI.
ヒタリ
FIP...
HUH?
WHAT DO YOU THINK OF ASUNA-SAN?
KRRSH
VWOOP
みょみょみょ
VWEEWEEP
?
WE-WELL... SHE'S A HARD WORKER. CHEERFUL, ENERGETIC...
A BIT SHORT TEMPERED, BUT OTHERWISE A GOOD KID.
OF ALL THE-!
ぐしゃ
SQUISH
あわわ
ARRGH
THAT'S SUBTLE?!?
HMMM
P
タタタッ
TP TP TP

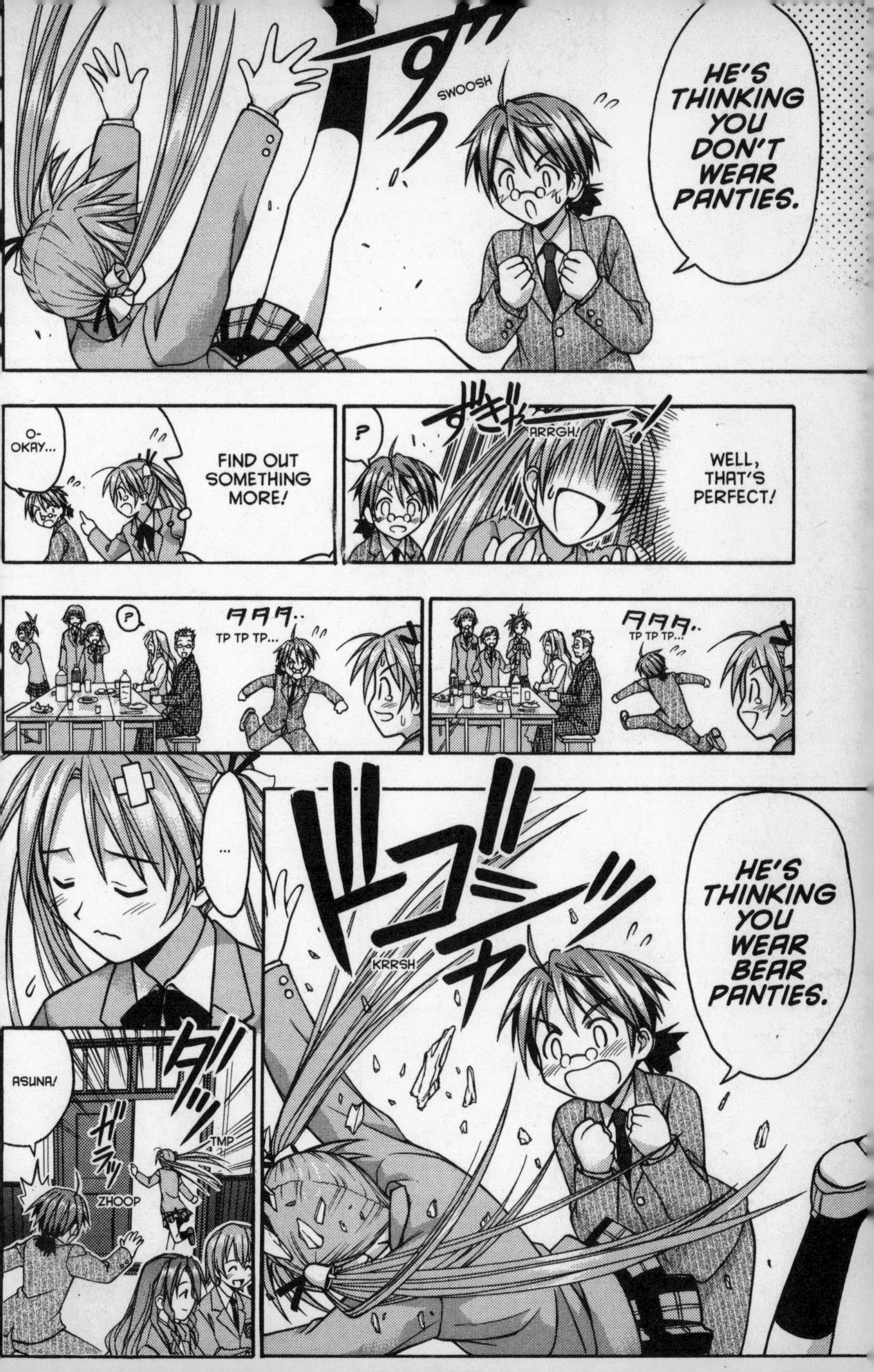
HE'S THINKING YOU DON'T WEAR PANTIES.
SWOOSH
WELL, THAT'S PERFECT!
ARRGH!
?
FIND OUT SOMETHING MORE!
O-OKAY...
TP TP TP...
TP TP TP...
?
HE'S THINKING YOU WEAR BEAR PANTIES.
KRRSH
...
TMP
ZHOOP
ASUNA!

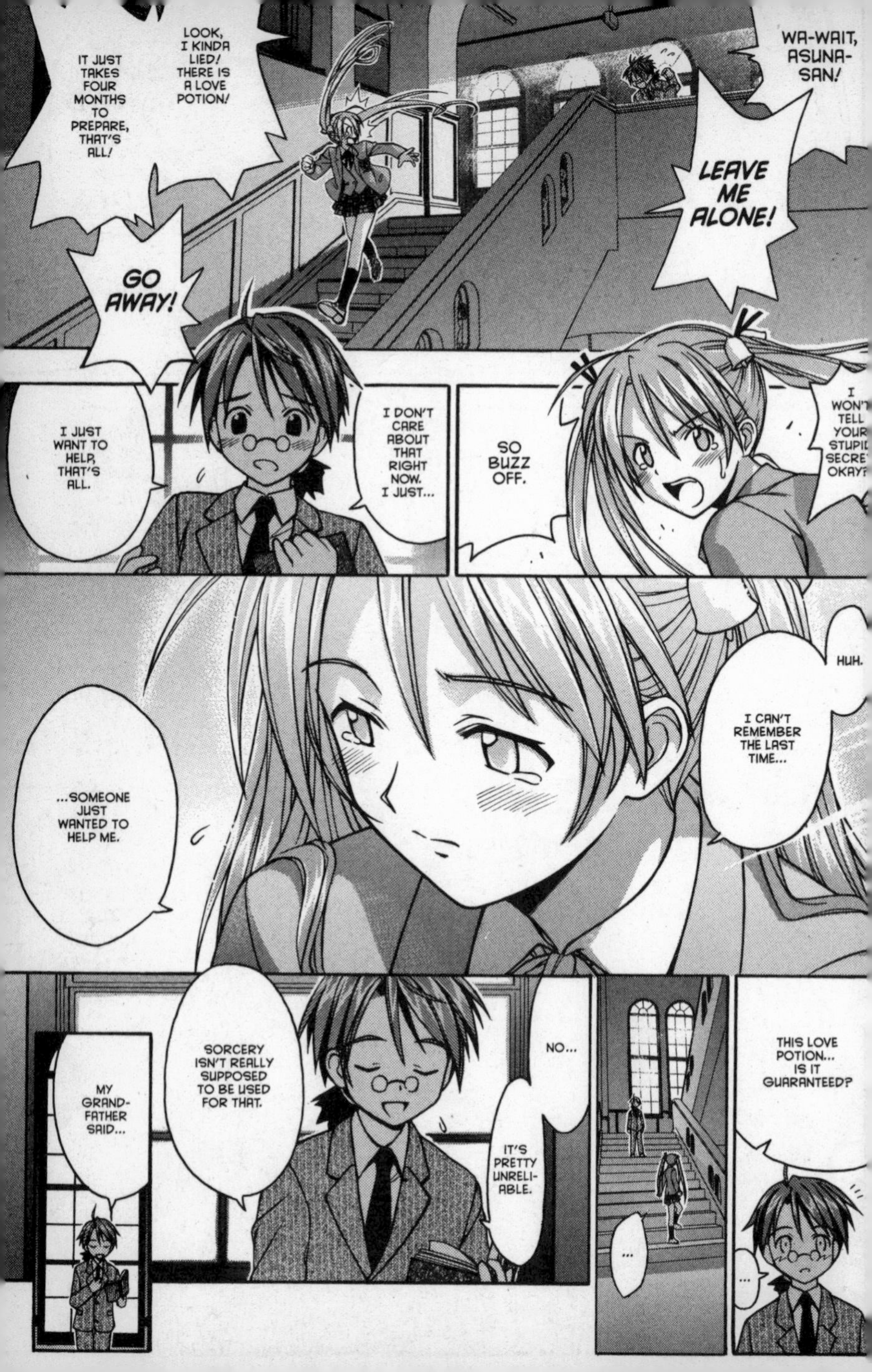
WA-WAIT, ASUNA-SAN!
LEAVE ME ALONE!
LOOK, I KINDA LIED! THERE IS A LOVE POTION!
IT JUST TAKES FOUR MONTHS TO PREPARE, THAT'S ALL!
GO AWAY!
I WON'T TELL YOUR STUPID SECRET OKAY?
SO BUZZ OFF.
I DON'T CARE ABOUT THAT RIGHT NOW. I JUST...
I JUST WANT TO HELP, THAT'S ALL.
HUH.
I CAN'T REMEMBER THE LAST TIME...
...SOMEONE JUST WANTED TO HELP ME.
THIS LOVE POTION... IS IT GUARANTEED?
...
...
NO...
IT'S PRETTY UNRELI-ABLE.
MY GRAND-FATHER SAID...
SORCERY ISN'T REALLY SUPPOSED TO BE USED FOR THAT.

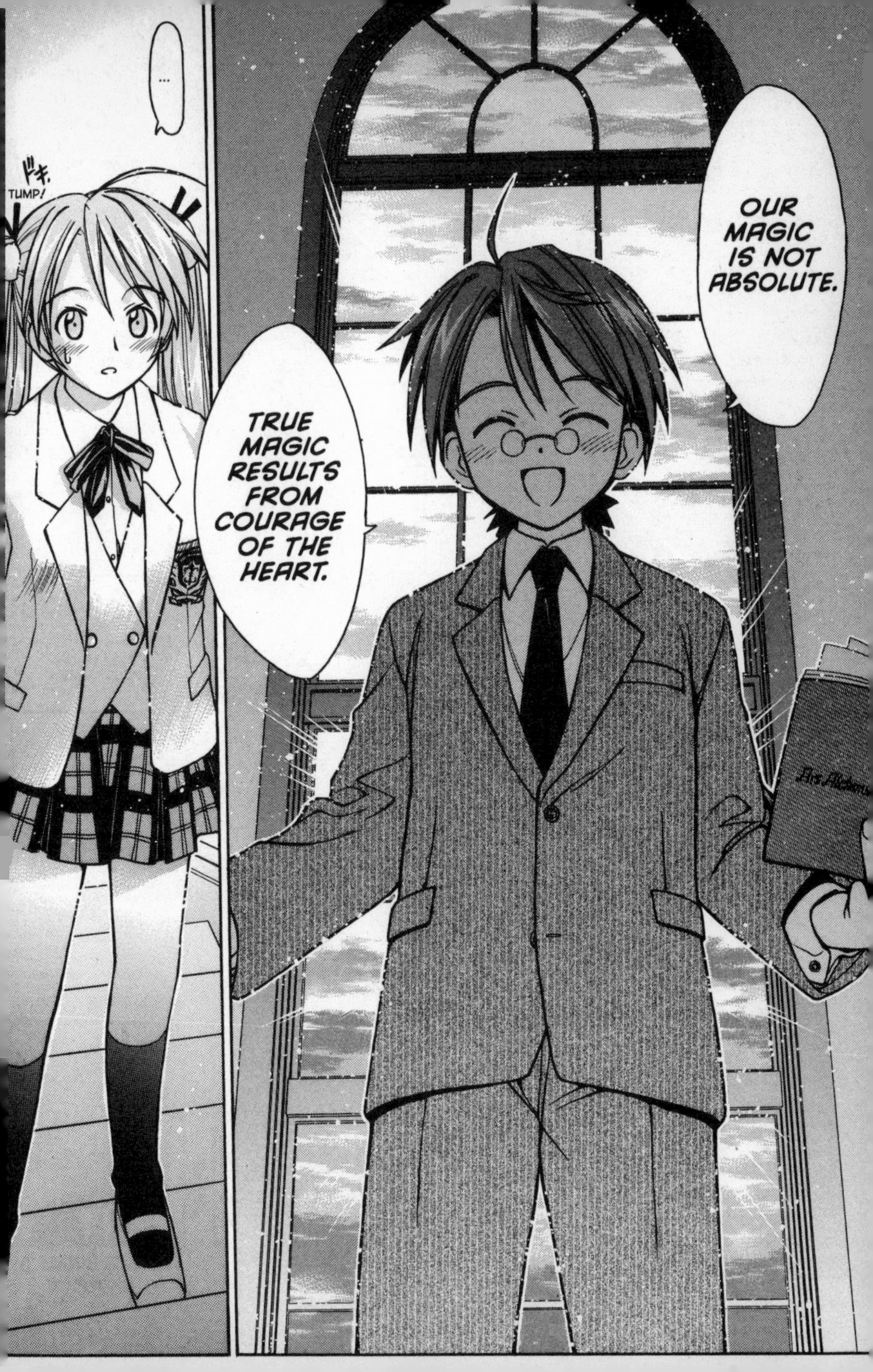
OUR MAGIC IS NOT ABSOLUTE.
TRUE MAGIC RESULTS FROM COURAGE OF THE HEART.
...
ドキ
TUMP!

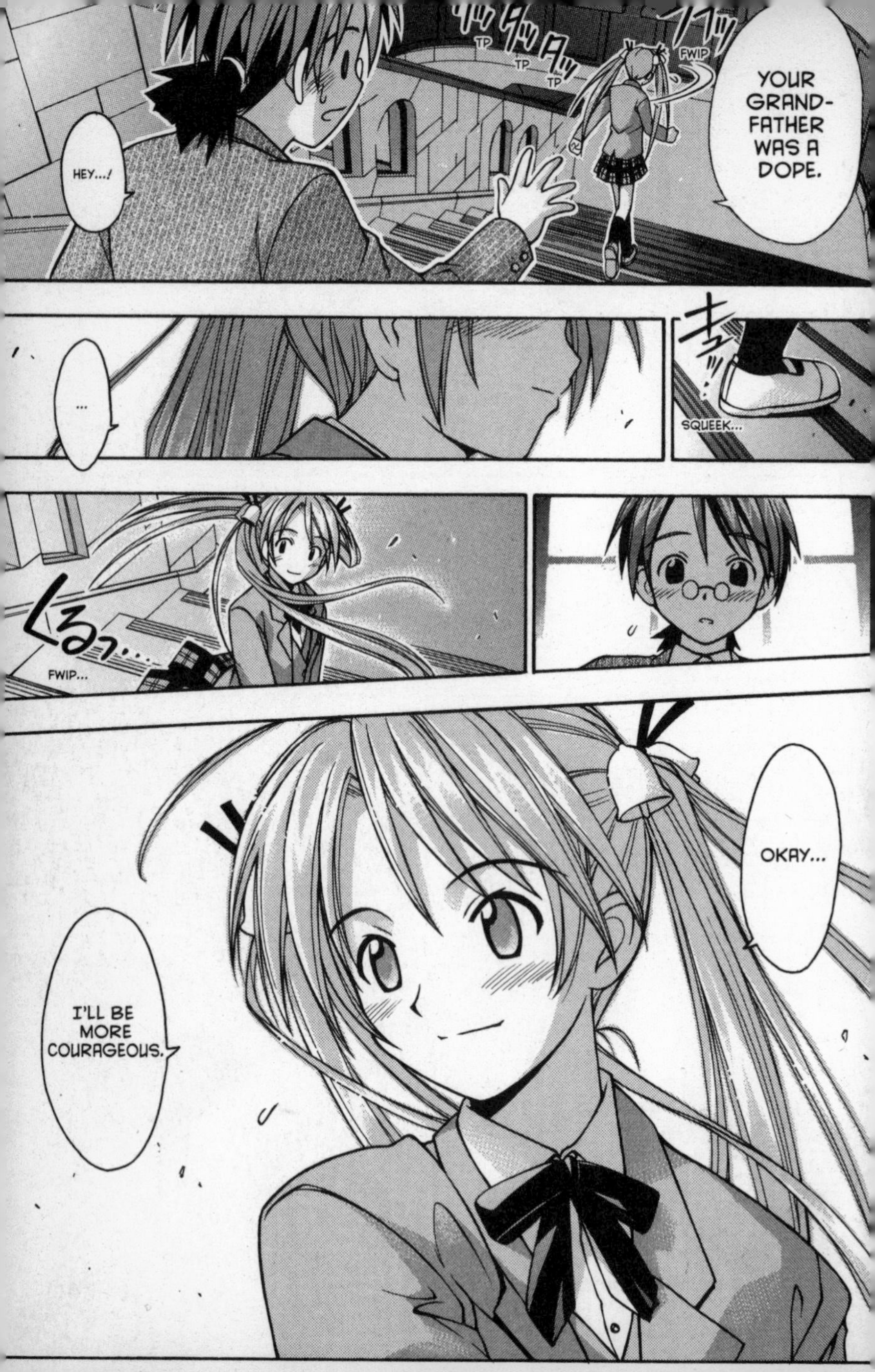
FWIP
YOUR GRANDFATHER WAS A DOPE.
TP
TP
TP
HEY...!
SQUEEK...
...
FWIP...
OKAY...
I'LL BE MORE COURAGEOUS.

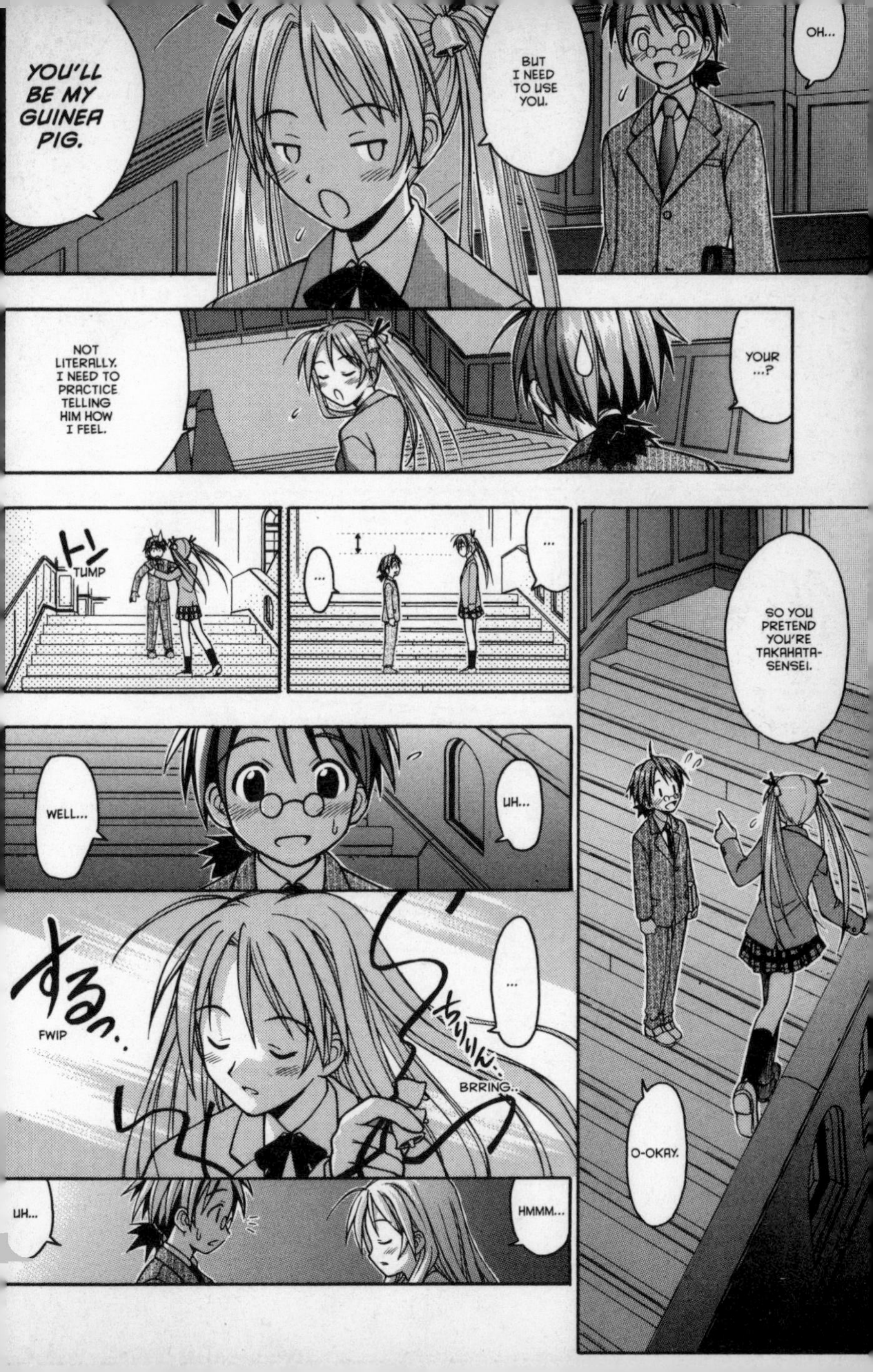
OH...
BUT I NEED TO USE YOU.
YOU'LL BE MY GUINEA PIG.
YOUR ...?
NOT LITERALLY. I NEED TO PRACTICE TELLING HIM HOW I FEEL.
SO YOU PRETEND YOU'RE TAKAHATA-SENSEI.
O-OKAY.
...
...
トン
TUMP
UH...
WELL...
...
BRRING..
FWIP
HMMM...
UH...

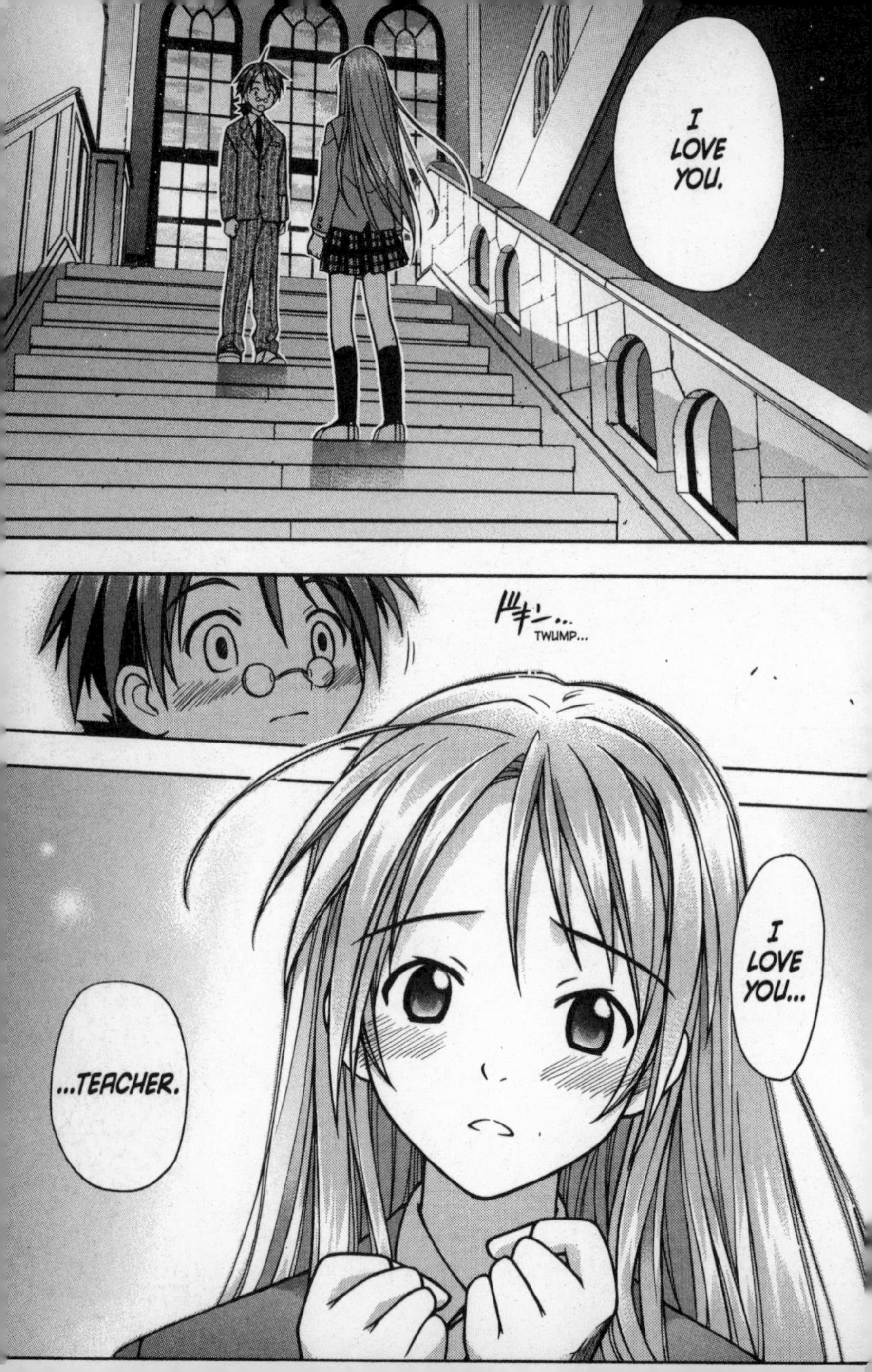
I LOVE YOU.
ドキン…
TWUMP...
I LOVE YOU...
...TEACHER.

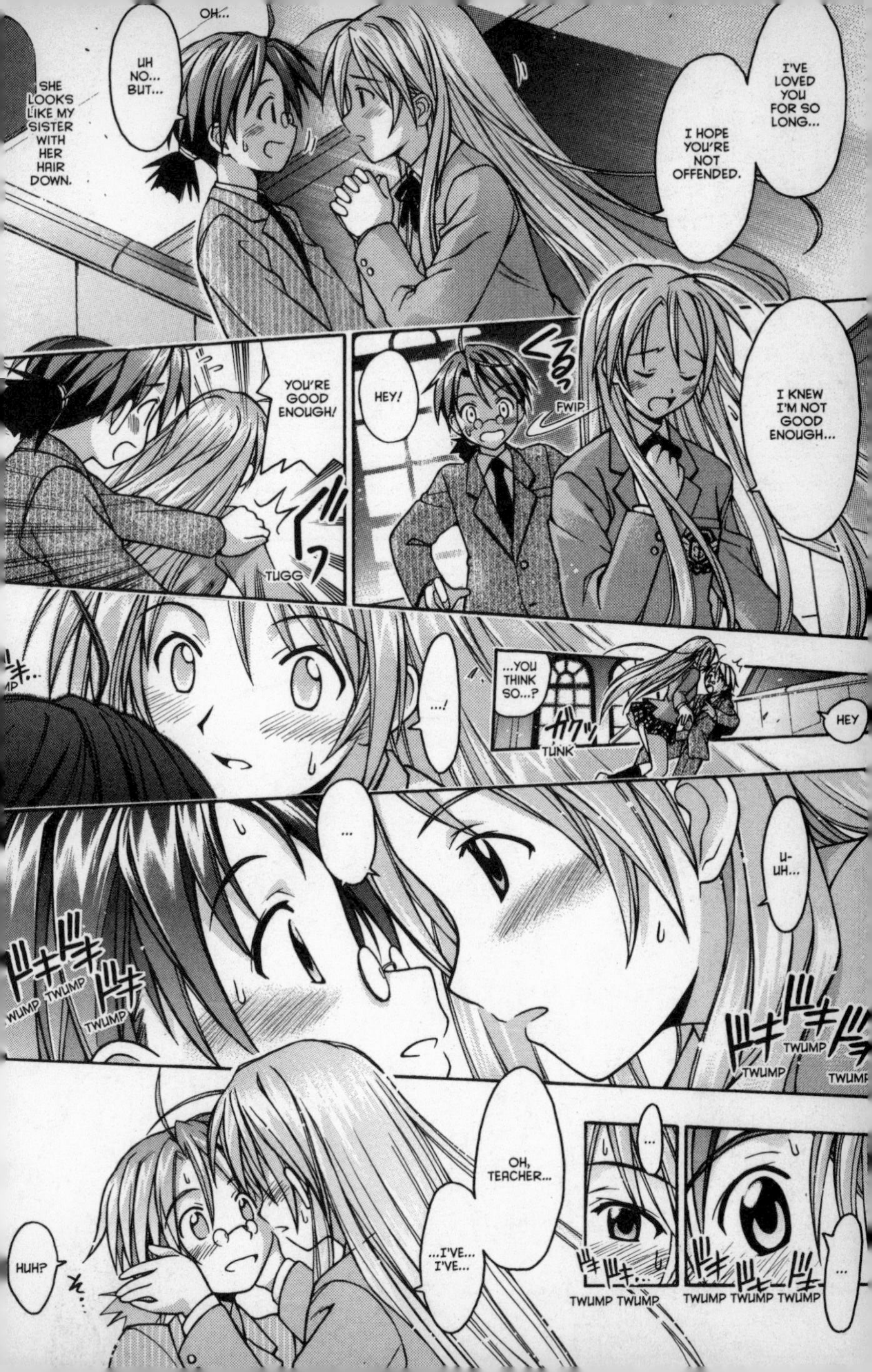
I'VE LOVED YOU FOR SO LONG...
I HOPE YOU'RE NOT OFFENDED.
OH...
UH NO... BUT...
SHE LOOKS LIKE MY SISTER WITH HER HAIR DOWN.
I KNEW I'M NOT GOOD ENOUGH...
FWIP
HEY!
YOU'RE GOOD ENOUGH!
TUGG
HEY
...YOU THINK SO...?
TUNK
...!
U-UH...
TWUMP
TWUMP
TWUMP
...
TWUMP
TWUMP
TWUMP
...
TWUMP TWUMP TWUMP
...
TWUMP TWUMP
OH, TEACHER...
...I'VE... I'VE...
HUH?

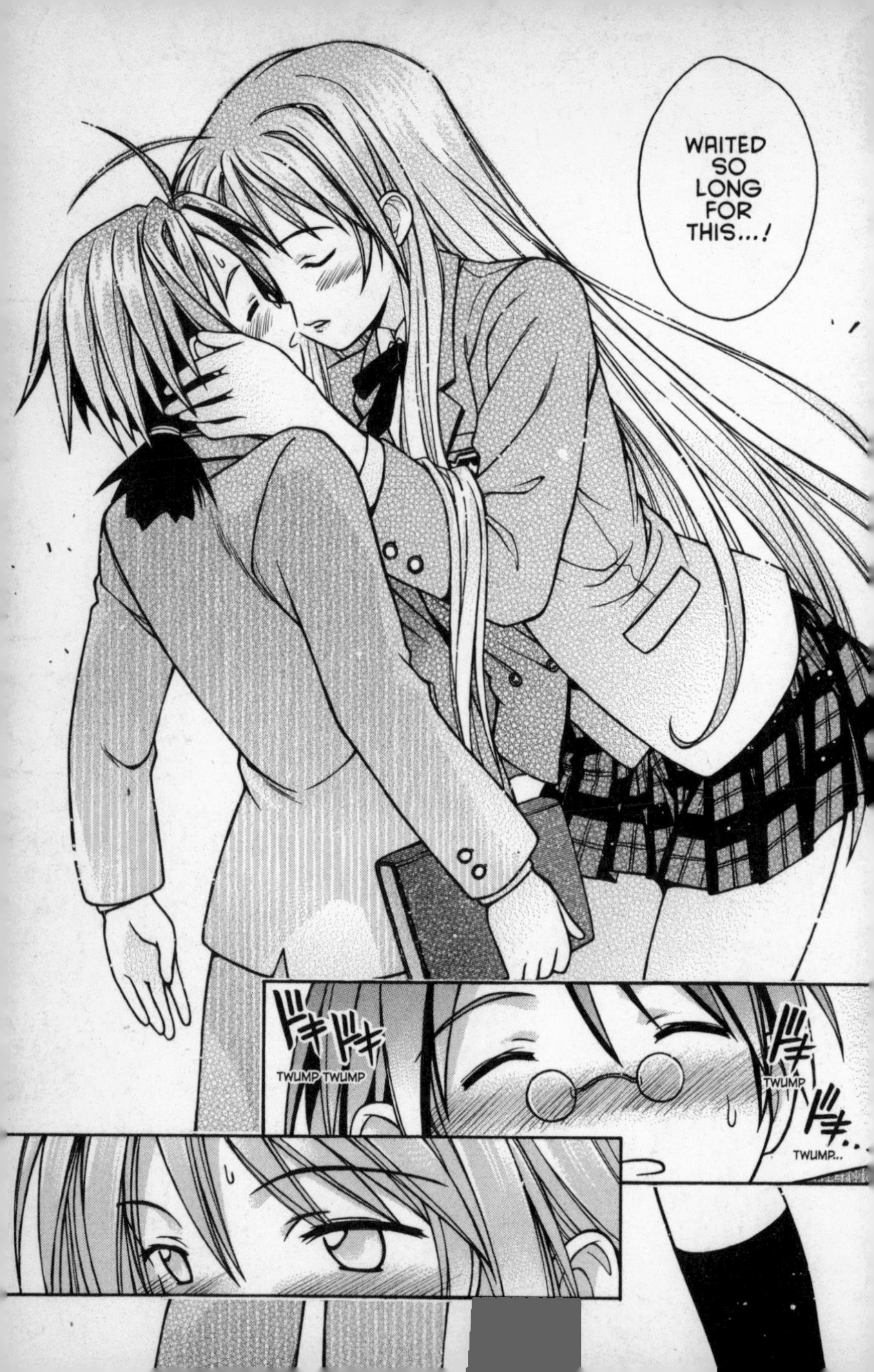
WAITED SO LONG FOR THIS...!
ドキ
TWUMP
ドキ...
TWUMP...
ドキドキ
TWUMP TWUMP

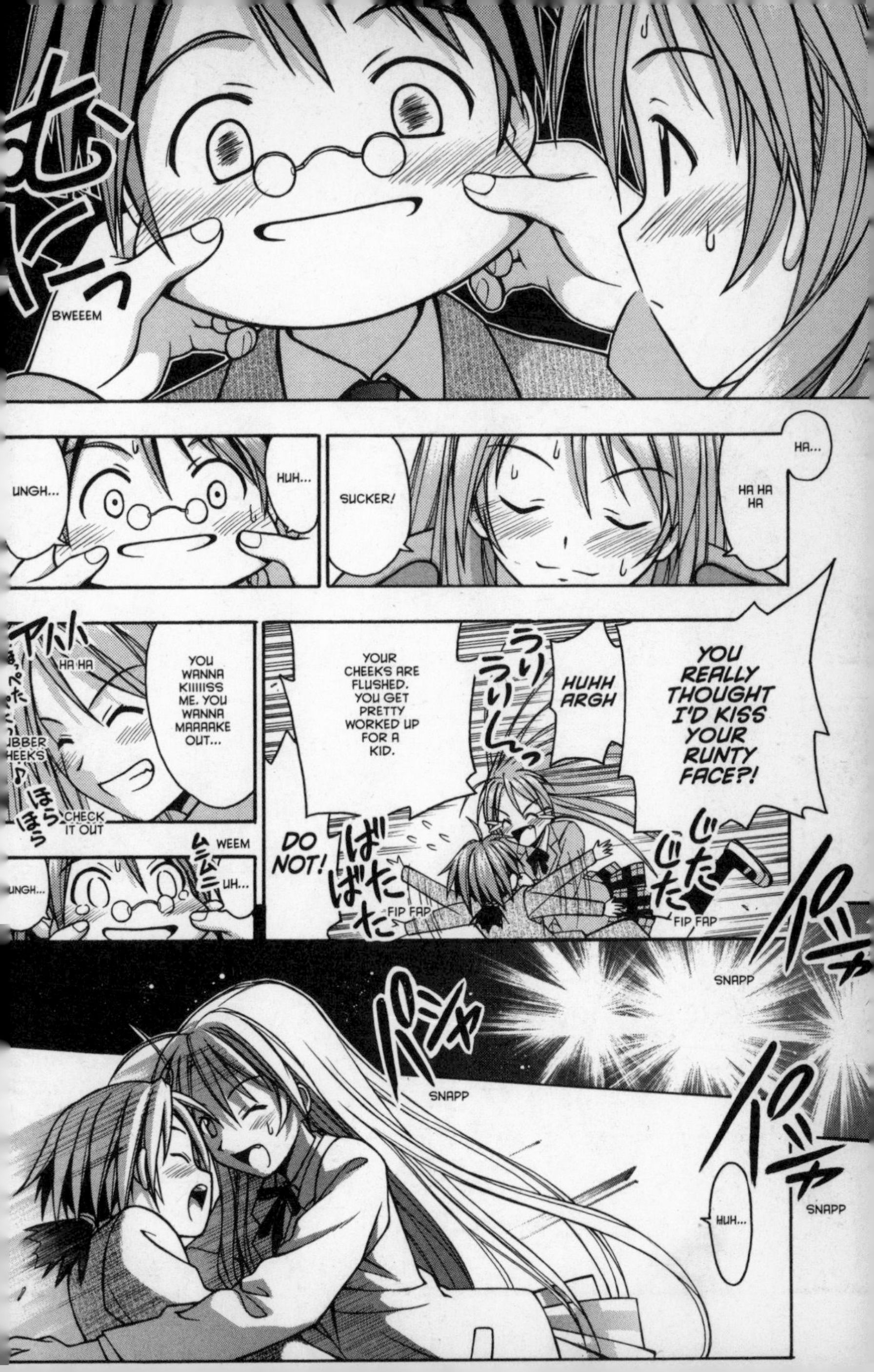

BWEEEM
HA...
HA HA HA
SUCKER!
HUH...
UNGH...
YOU REALLY THOUGHT I'D KISS YOUR RUNTY FACE?!
HUHH ARGH
YOUR CHEEKS ARE FLUSHED. YOU GET PRETTY WORKED UP FOR A KID.
DO NOT!
FIP FAP
FIP FAP
YOU WANNA KIIIIISS ME. YOU WANNA MAAAAKE OUT...
HA HA
CHECK IT OUT
WEEM
UH...
UNGH...
SNAPP
SNAPP
SNAPP
HUH...

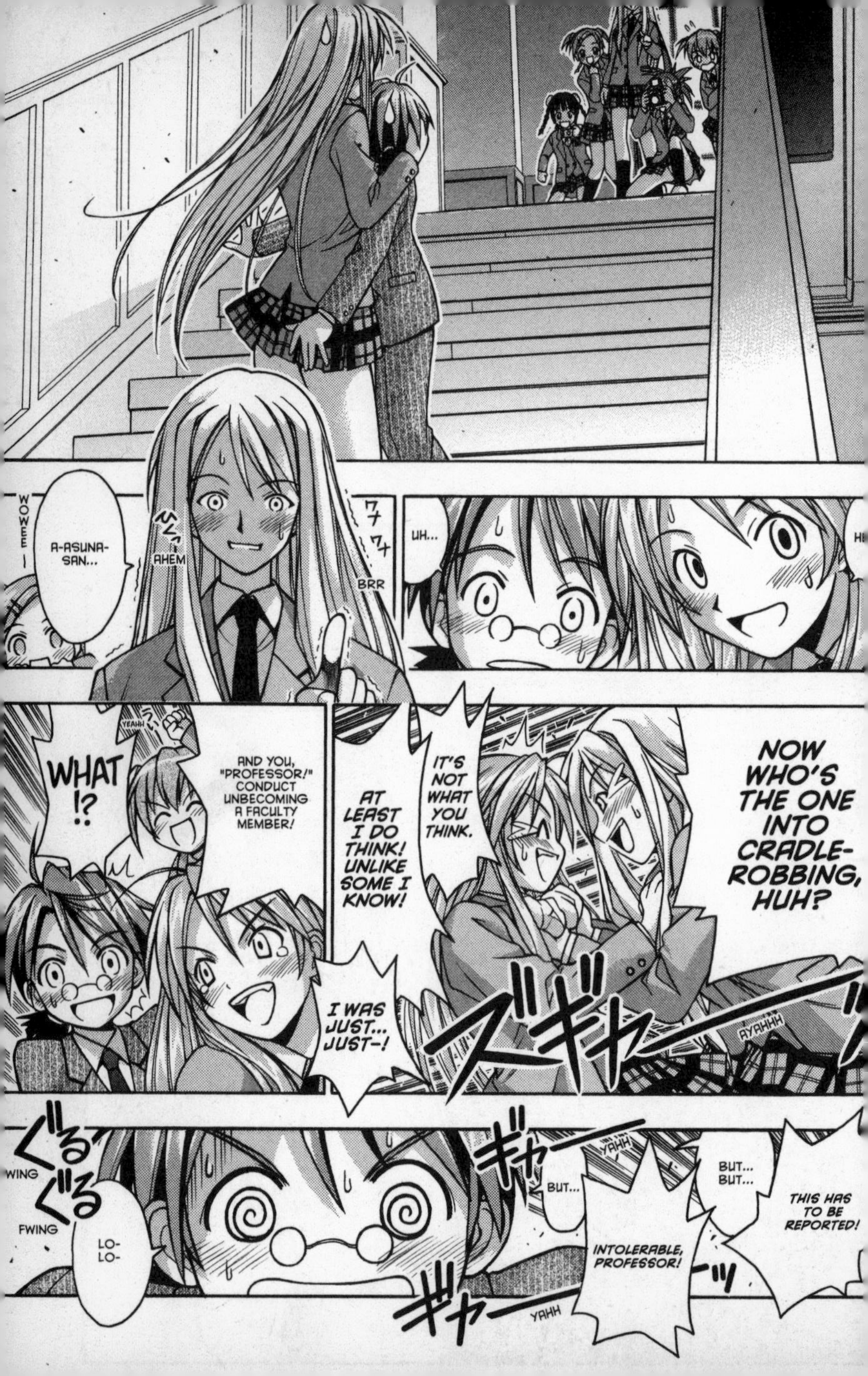
UH...
WOWEE
A-ASUNA-SAN...
AHEM
BRR
NOW WHO'S THE ONE INTO CRADLE-ROBBING, HUH?
IT'S NOT WHAT YOU THINK.
AT LEAST I DO THINK! UNLIKE SOME I KNOW!
AYAHHH
I WAS JUST... JUST-!
AND YOU, "PROFESSOR!" CONDUCT UNBECOMING A FACULTY MEMBER!
YEAHH
WHAT!?
THIS HAS TO BE REPORTED!
BUT... BUT...
INTOLERABLE, PROFESSOR!
YAHH
BUT...
YAHH
WING
FWING
LO-LO-

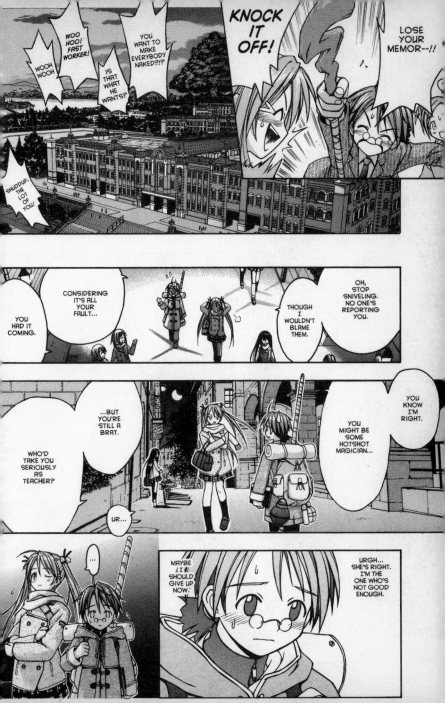

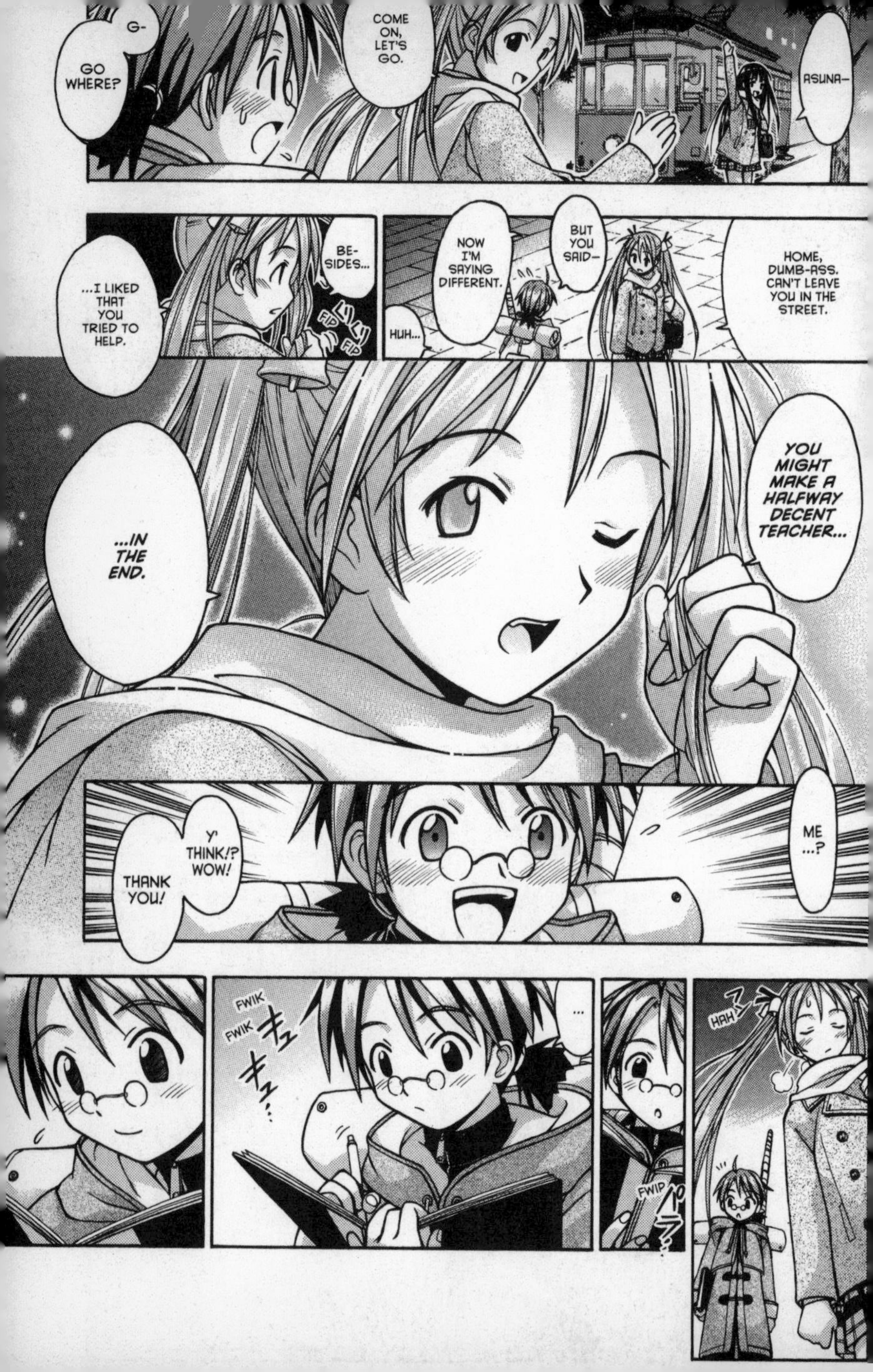

ASUNA—
COME ON, LET'S GO.
G-
GO WHERE?
HOME, DUMB-ASS. CAN'T LEAVE YOU IN THE STREET.
BUT YOU SAID—
NOW I'M SAYING DIFFERENT.
HUH...
BE-SIDES...
FIP FIP
...I LIKED THAT YOU TRIED TO HELP.
YOU MIGHT MAKE A HALFWAY DECENT TEACHER...
...IN THE END.
ME ...?
Y' THINK!? WOW!
THANK YOU!
HAH
...
FWIP
FWIK FWIK

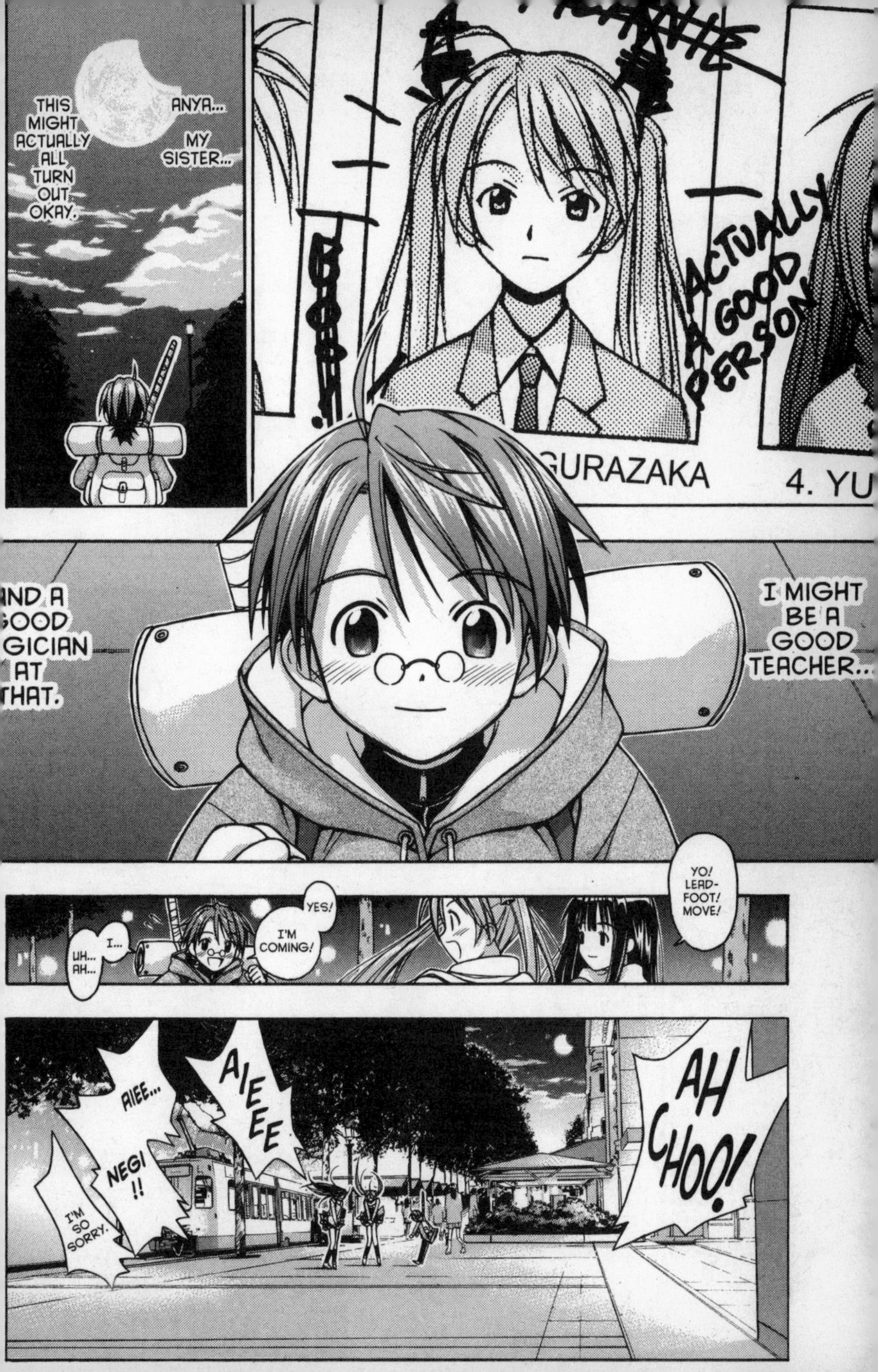
ACTUALLY A GOOD PERSON
GURAZAKA
4. YU
ANYA...
MY SISTER...
THIS MIGHT ACTUALLY ALL TURN OUT OKAY.
I MIGHT BE A GOOD TEACHER...
ND A GOOD GICIAN AT THAT.
YO! LEAD-FOOT! MOVE!
YES!
I'M COMING!
I...
UH... AH...
AH CHOO!
AIEEE
AIEE...
NEGI !!
I'M SO SORRY.

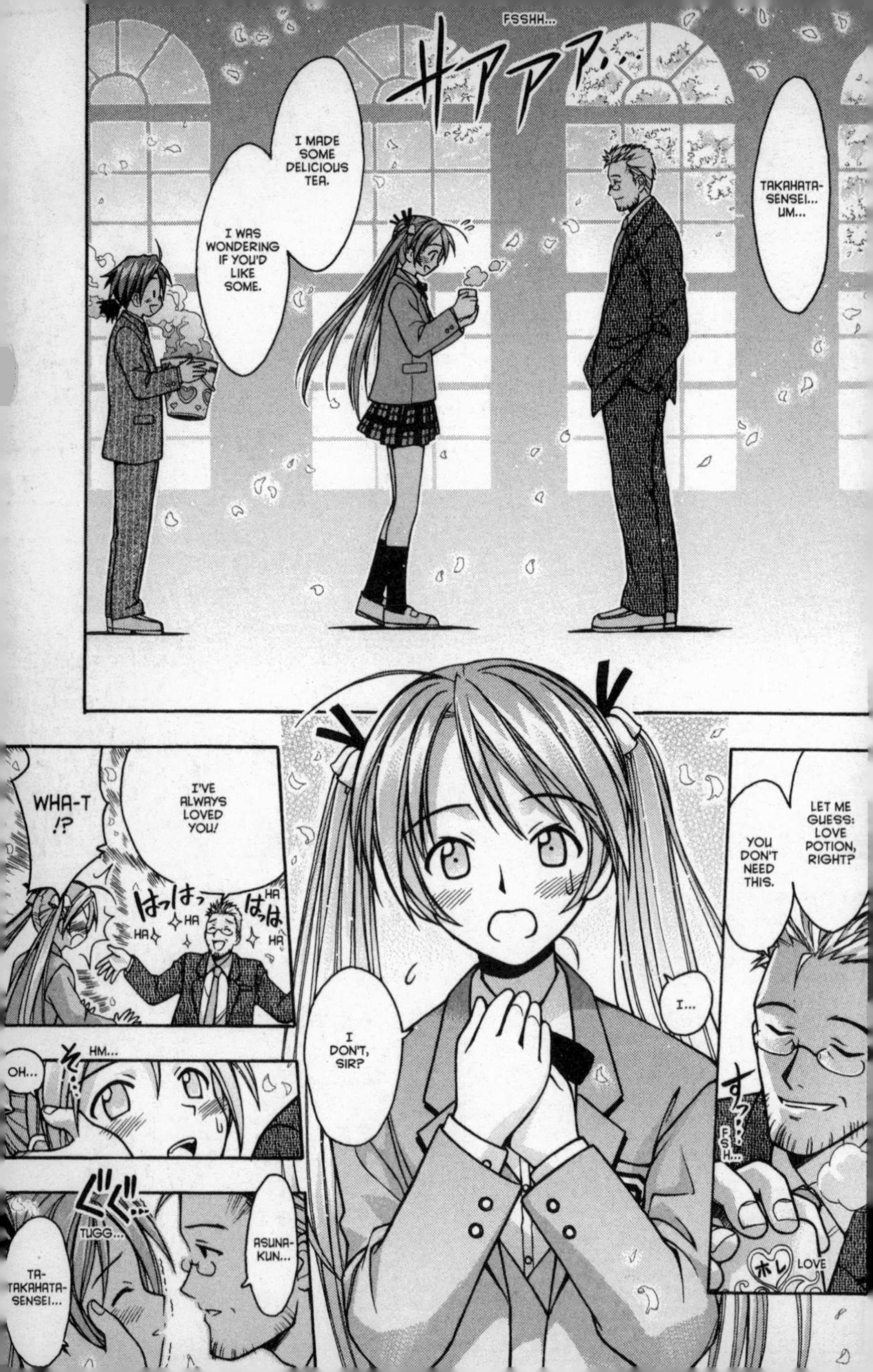
FSSHH...
TAKAHATA-SENSEI... UM...
I MADE SOME DELICIOUS TEA.
I WAS WONDERING IF YOU'D LIKE SOME.
LET ME GUESS: LOVE POTION, RIGHT?
YOU DON'T NEED THIS.
FSH...
LOVE
I...
I DON'T, SIR?
I'VE ALWAYS LOVED YOU!
WHA-T !?
HA HA HA HA HA
HM...
OH...
ASUNA-KUN...
TUGG...
TA-TAKAHATA-SENSEI...

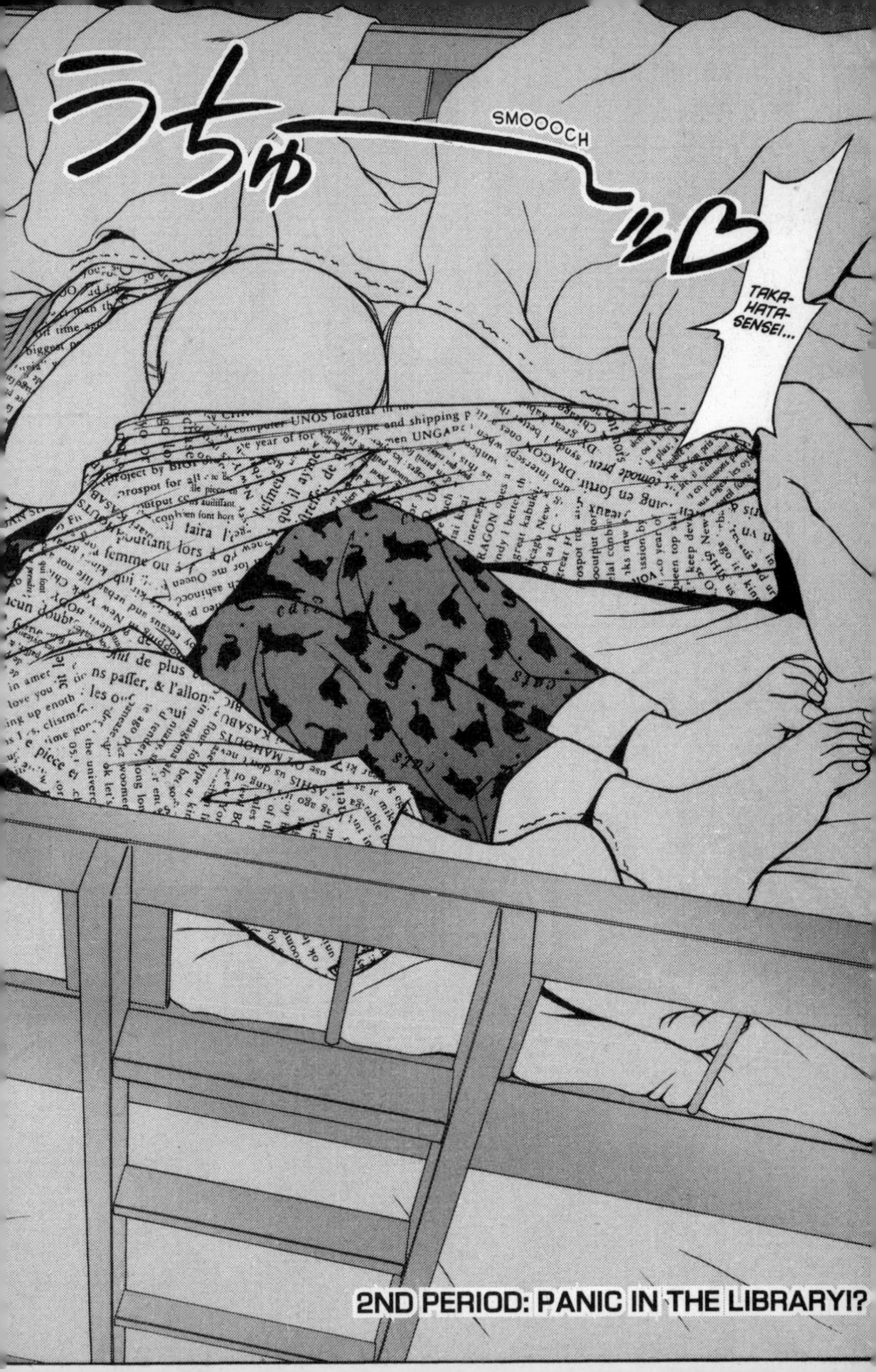
うちゅ〜〜っ♡
SMOOOCH
TAKA-HATA-SENSEI...
2ND PERIOD: PANIC IN THE LIBRARY!?

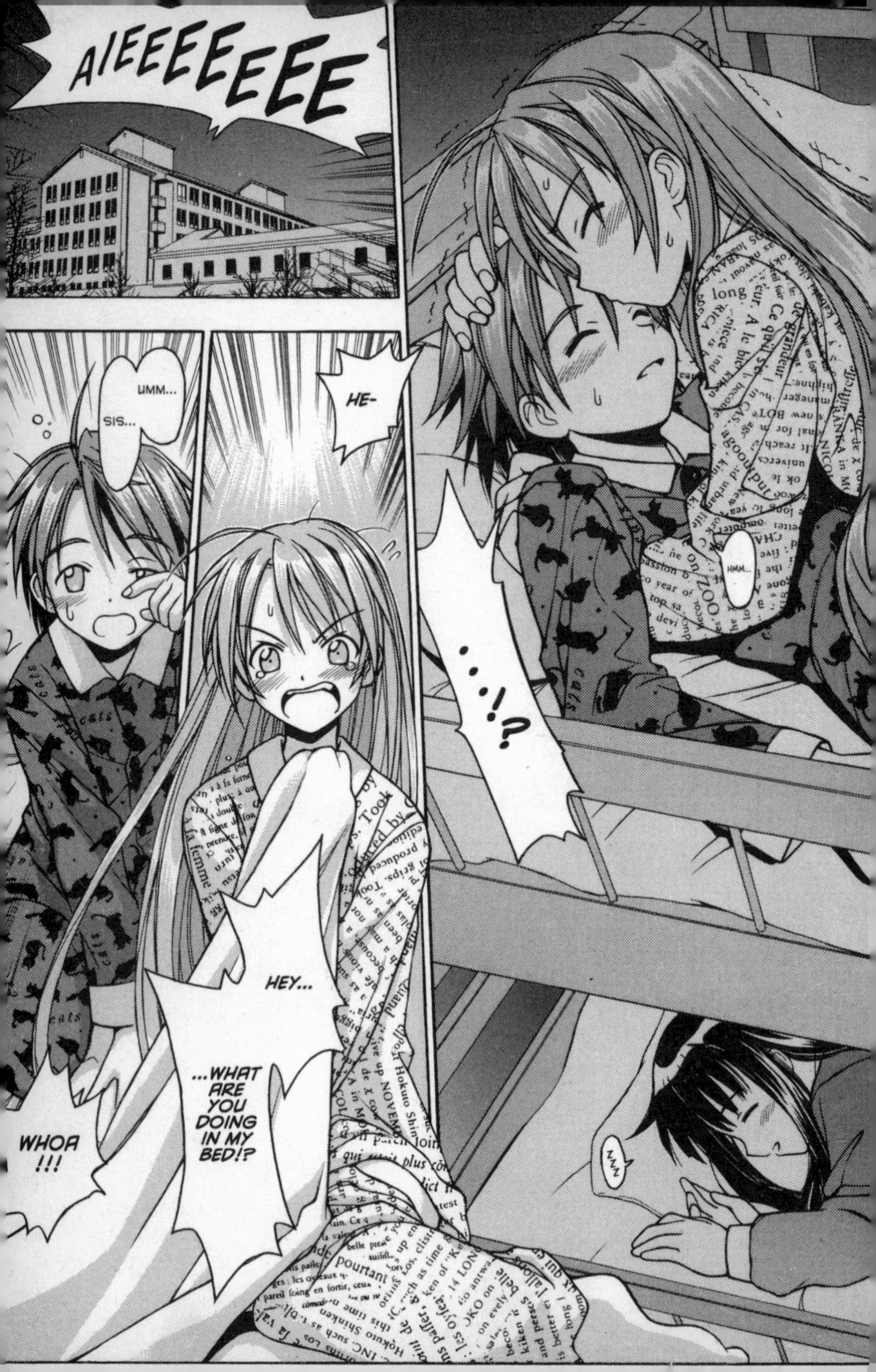
HMM...
...!?
NNN
AIEEEEEEEE
HE-
HEY...
...WHAT ARE YOU DOING IN MY BED!?
UMM... SIS...
WHOA !!!

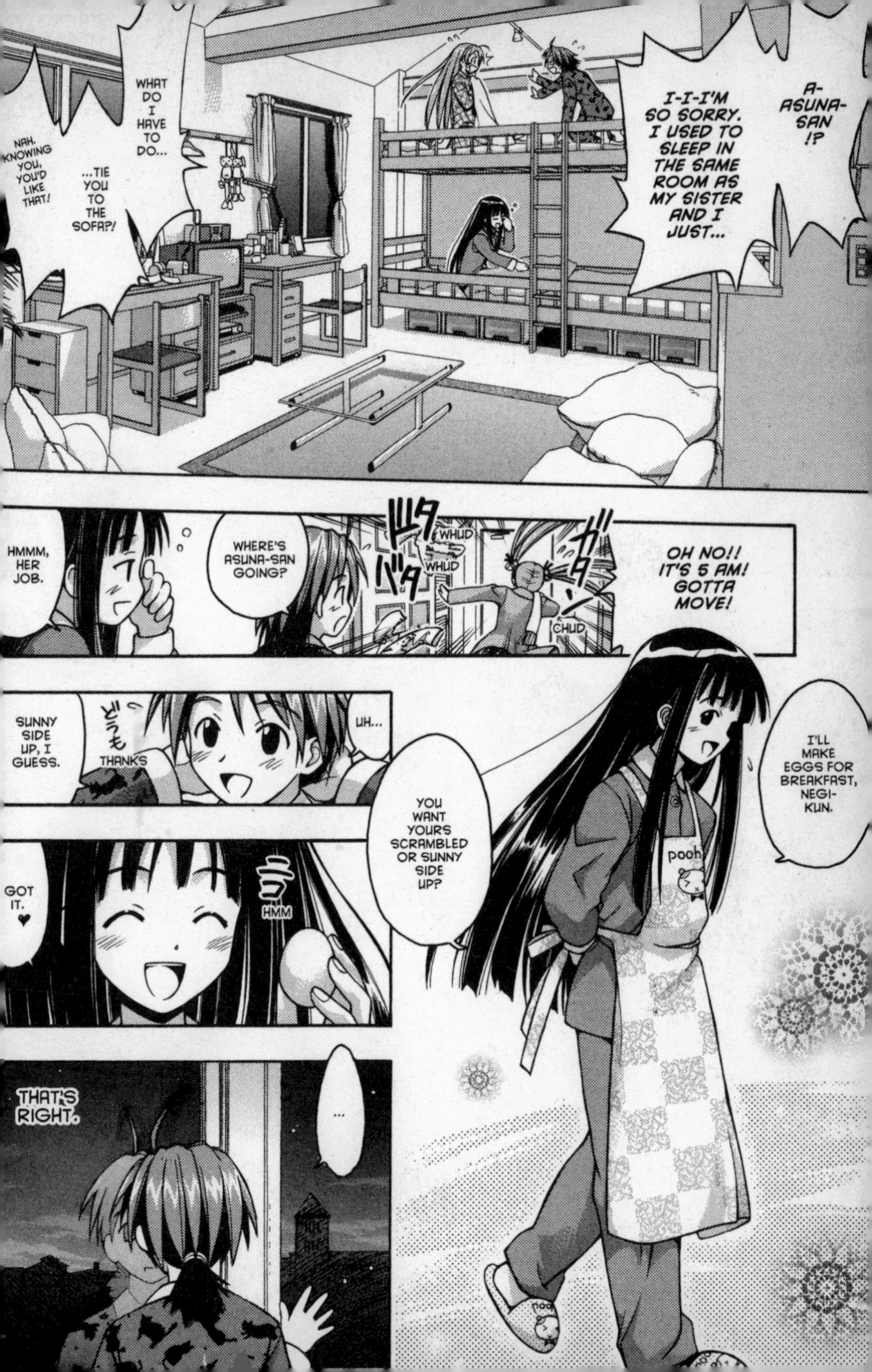
A-ASUNA-SAN!?
I-I-I'M SO SORRY. I USED TO SLEEP IN THE SAME ROOM AS MY SISTER AND I JUST...
WHAT DO I HAVE TO DO...
...TIE YOU TO THE SOFA?!
NAH. KNOWING YOU, YOU'D LIKE THAT!
OH NO!! IT'S 5 AM! GOTTA MOVE!
ガタン
CHUD
ドタバタ
WHUD
WHUD
WHERE'S ASUNA-SAN GOING?
HMMM, HER JOB.
I'LL MAKE EGGS FOR BREAKFAST, NEGI-KUN.
YOU WANT YOURS SCRAMBLED OR SUNNY SIDE UP?
pooh
UH...
どうも
THANKS
SUNNY SIDE UP, I GUESS.
HMM
GOT IT. ❤
...
THAT'S RIGHT.

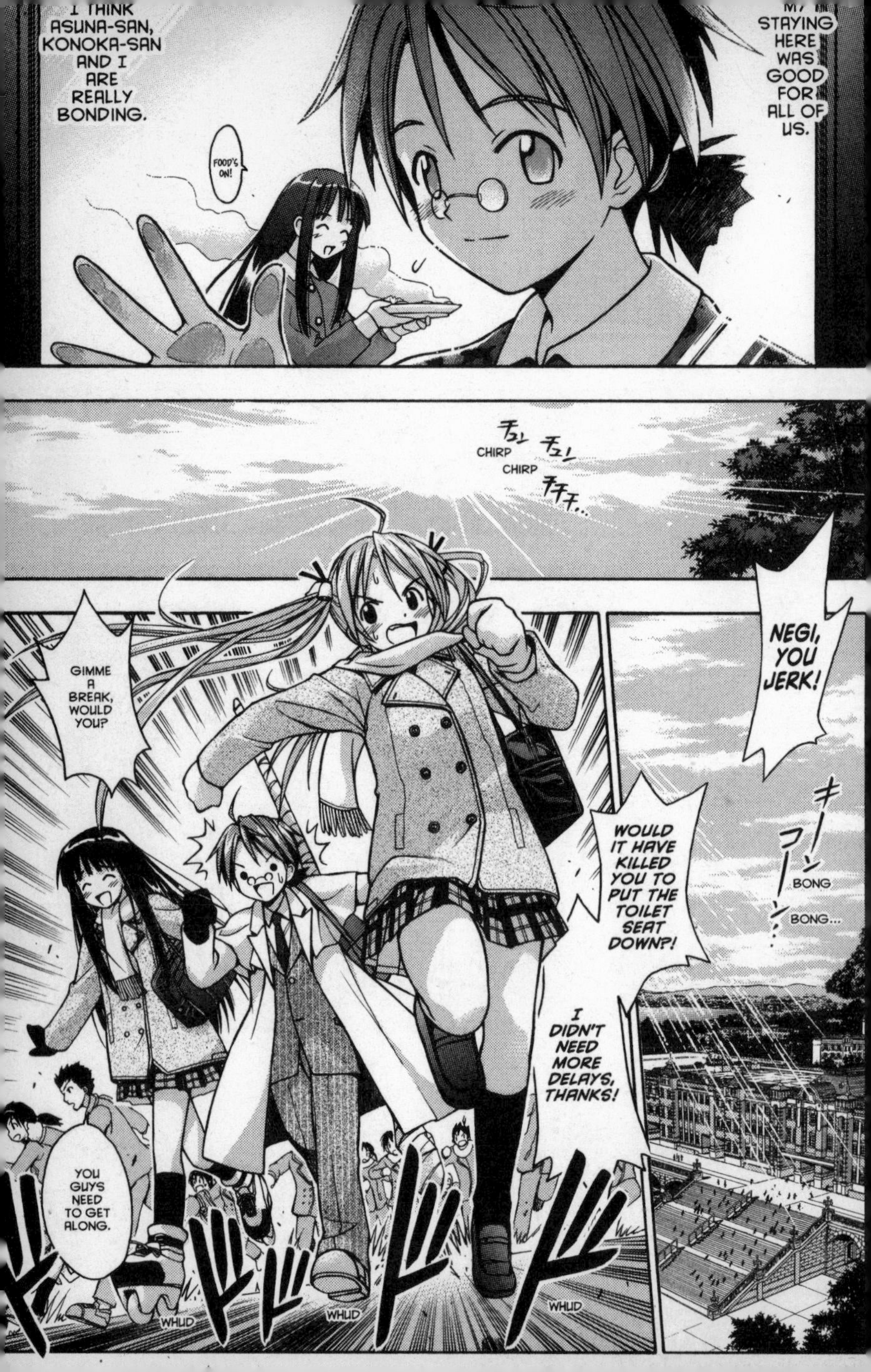
MY STAYING HERE WAS GOOD FOR ALL OF US.
I THINK ASUNA-SAN, KONOKA-SAN AND I ARE REALLY BONDING.
FOOD'S ON!
チュン チュン
CHIRP CHIRP
チチチ...
NEGI, YOU JERK!
キーンコーン
BONG BONG...
WOULD IT HAVE KILLED YOU TO PUT THE TOILET SEAT DOWN?!
I DIDN'T NEED MORE DELAYS, THANKS!
GIMME A BREAK, WOULD YOU?
YOU GUYS NEED TO GET ALONG.
ドドドド
WHUD WHUD WHUD

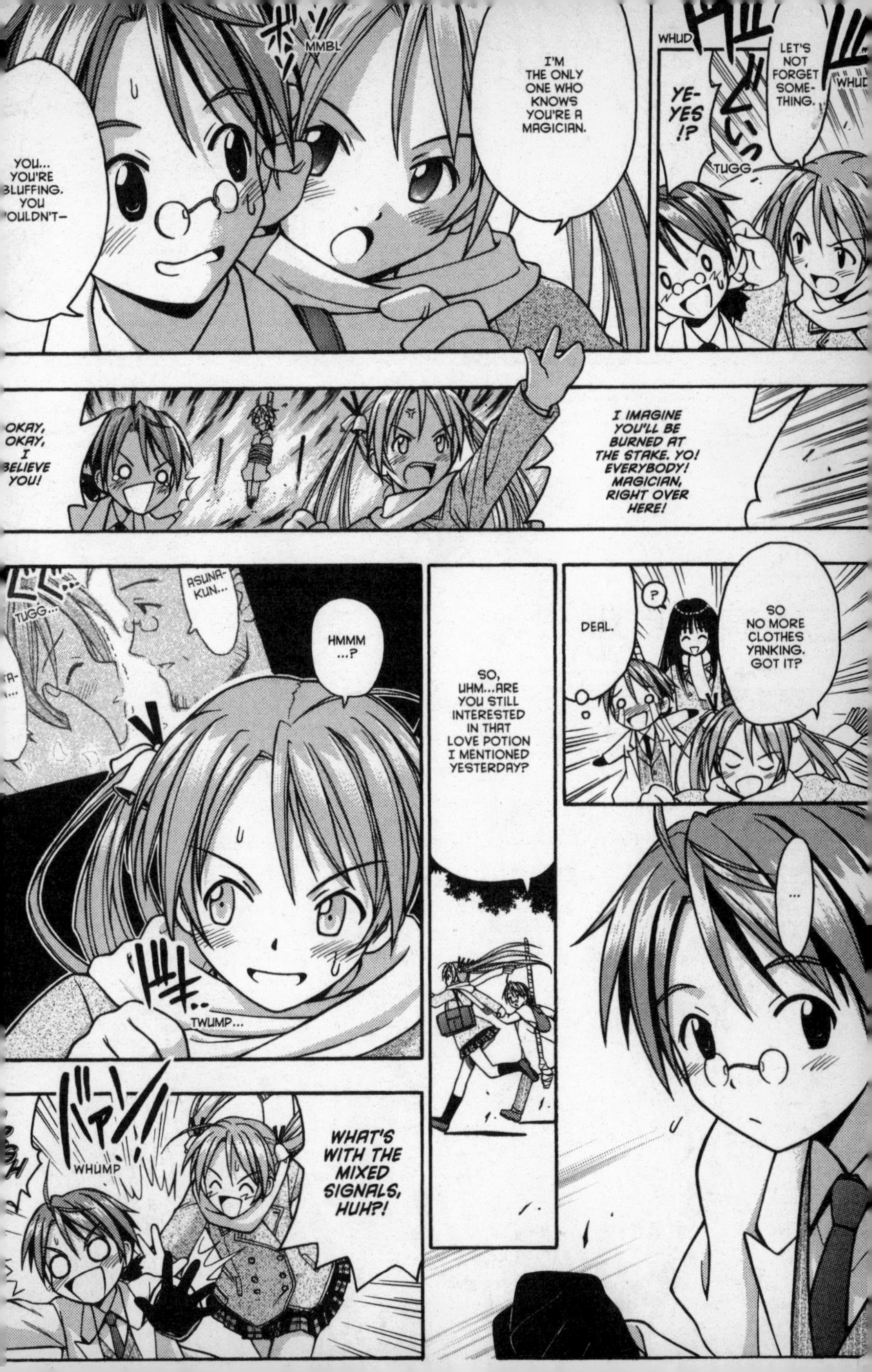

WHUD
LET'S NOT FORGET SOMETHING.
WHUD
YE-YES!?
TUGG
I'M THE ONLY ONE WHO KNOWS YOU'RE A MAGICIAN.
MMBL
YOU... YOU'RE BLUFFING. YOU WOULDN'T–
I IMAGINE YOU'LL BE BURNED AT THE STAKE. YO! EVERYBODY! MAGICIAN, RIGHT OVER HERE!
OKAY, OKAY, I BELIEVE YOU!
SO NO MORE CLOTHES YANKING. GOT IT?
?
DEAL.
...
SO, UHM...ARE YOU STILL INTERESTED IN THAT LOVE POTION I MENTIONED YESTERDAY?
ASUNA-KUN...
TUGG...
HMMM...?
TWUMP...
WHAT'S WITH THE MIXED SIGNALS, HUH?!
WHUMP

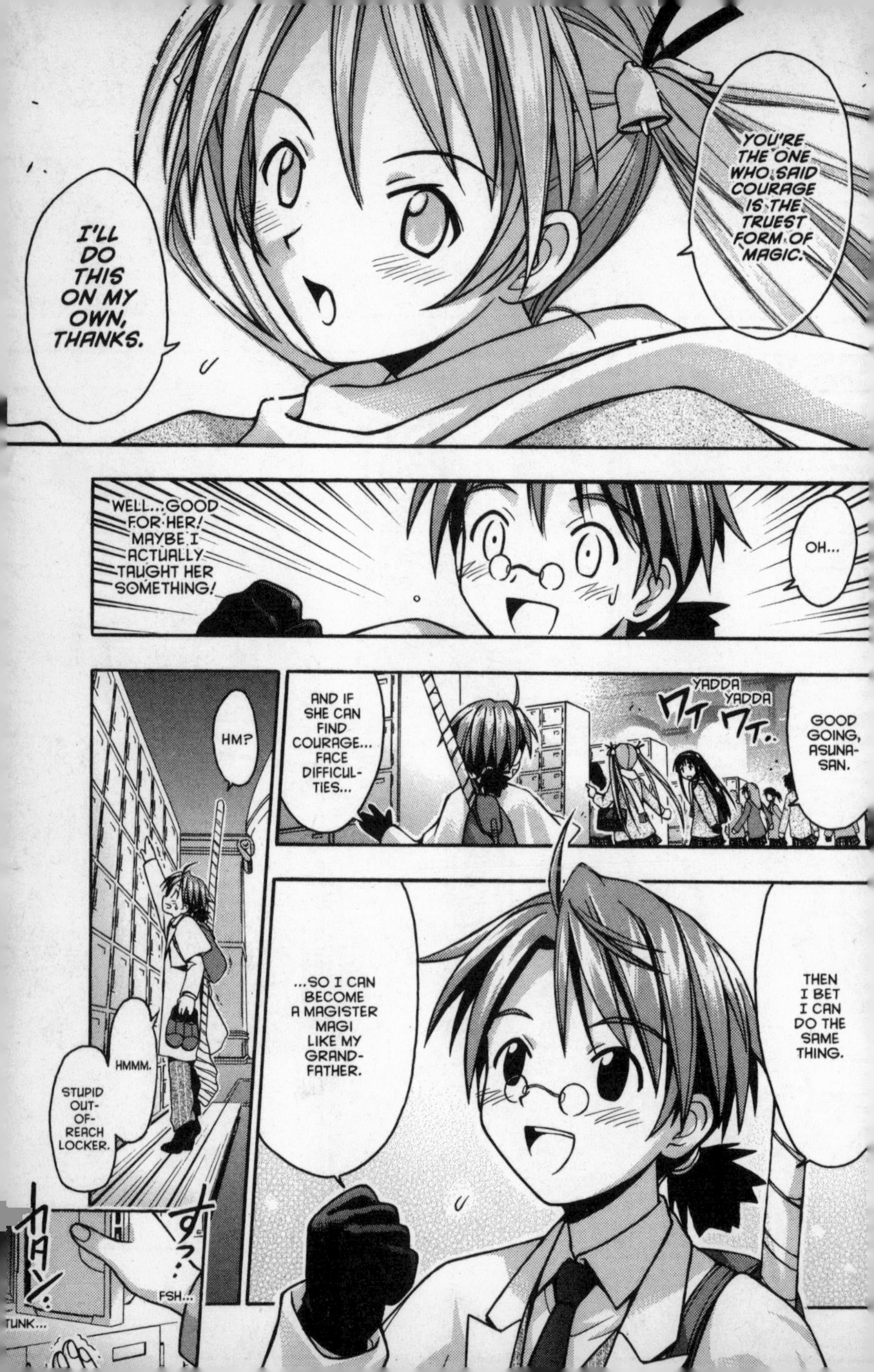
YOU'RE THE ONE WHO SAID COURAGE IS THE TRUEST FORM OF MAGIC.
I'LL DO THIS ON MY OWN, THANKS.
OH...
WELL... GOOD FOR HER! MAYBE I ACTUALLY TAUGHT HER SOMETHING!
GOOD GOING, ASUNA-SAN.
YADDA YADDA
AND IF SHE CAN FIND COURAGE... FACE DIFFICUL-TIES...
THEN I BET I CAN DO THE SAME THING.
...SO I CAN BECOME A MAGISTER MAGI LIKE MY GRAND-FATHER.
HM?
HMMM.
STUPID OUT-OF-REACH LOCKER.
FSH...
TUNK...

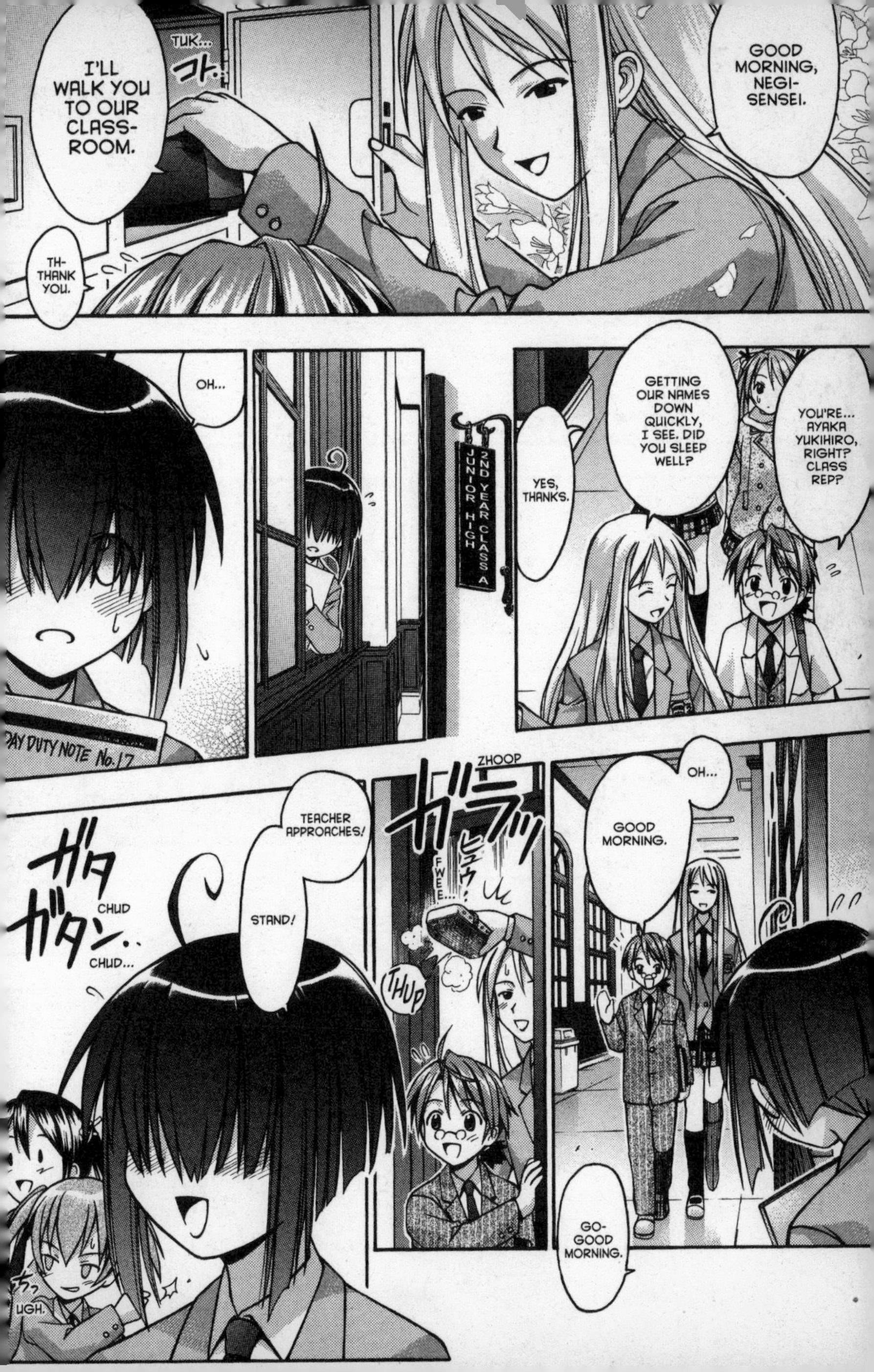
GOOD MORNING, NEGI-SENSEI.
TUK... コト
I'LL WALK YOU TO OUR CLASS-ROOM.
TH-THANK YOU.
YOU'RE... AYAKA YUKIHIRO, RIGHT? CLASS REP?
GETTING OUR NAMES DOWN QUICKLY, I SEE. DID YOU SLEEP WELL?
YES, THANKS.
2ND YEAR CLASS A JUNIOR HIGH
OH...
AY DUTY NOTE No.17
OH...
GOOD MORNING.
GO-GOOD MORNING.
ガラッ ZHOOP
ヒュウ FWEE...
THUP
TEACHER APPROACHES!
STAND!
ガタ CHUD
ガタン.. CHUD...
UGH.

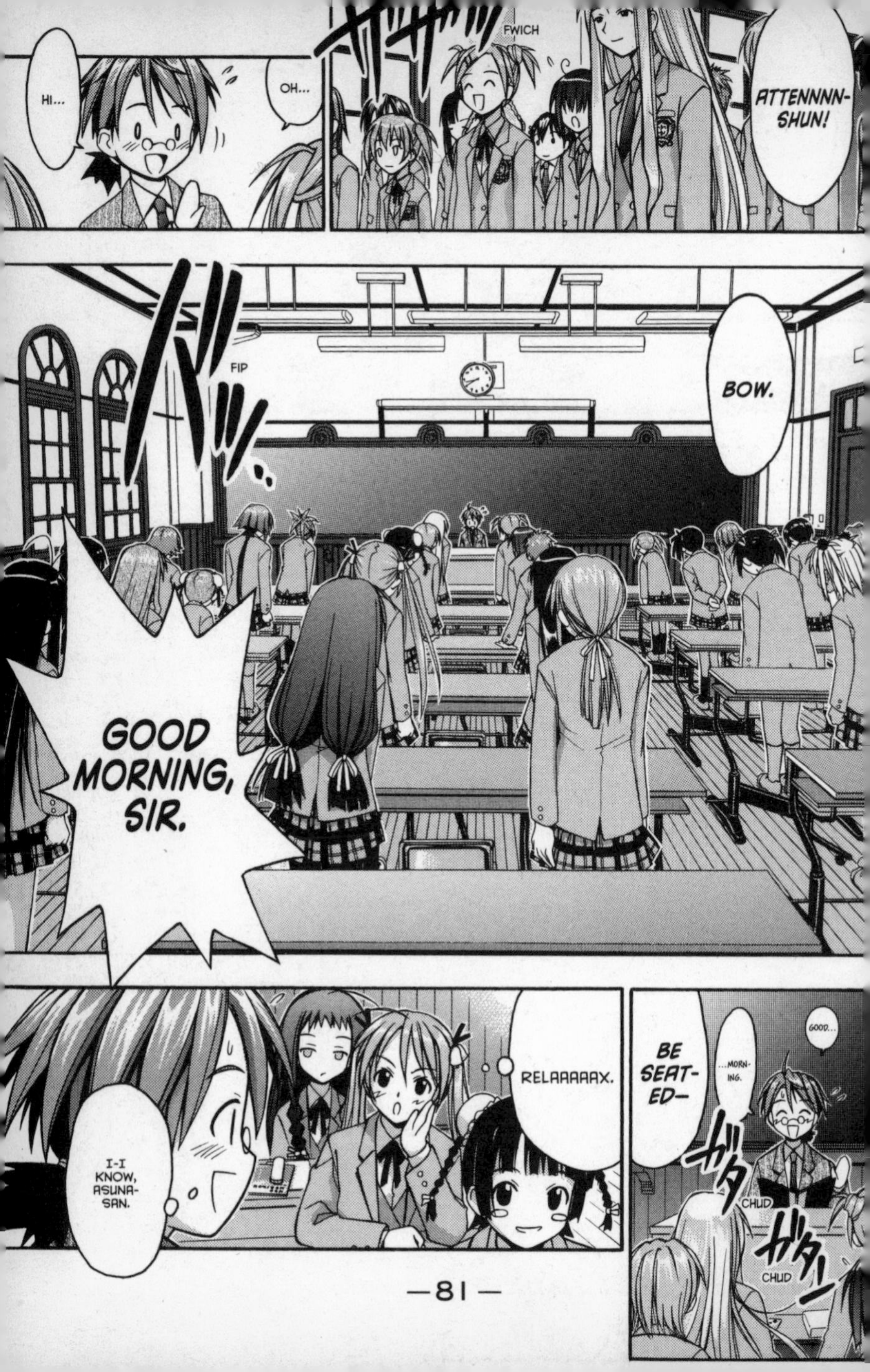
ATTENNNN-SHUN!
FWICH
OH...
HI...
BOW.
FIP
GOOD MORNING, SIR.
GOOD...
BE SEAT-ED—
...MORN-ING.
CHUD
CHUD
RELAAAAAX.
I-I KNOW, ASUNA-SAN.

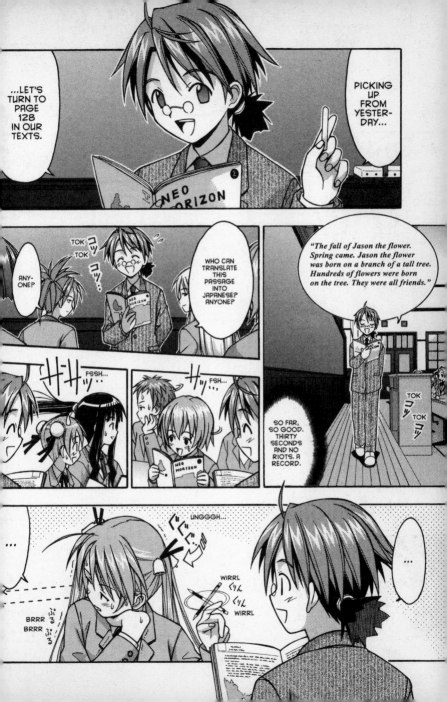

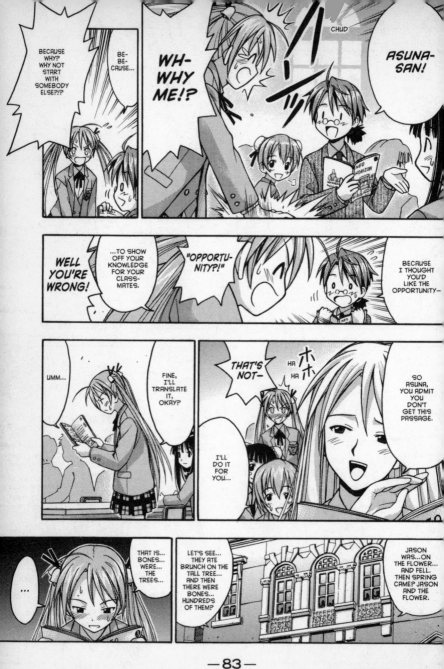

BECAUSE WHY? WHY NOT START WITH SOMEBODY ELSE!?

BE-BE-CAUSE...

WH-WHY ME!?

CHUD

ASUNA-SAN!

NEO HORIZON

WELL YOU'RE WRONG!

...TO SHOW OFF YOUR KNOWLEDGE FOR YOUR CLASS-MATES.

"OPPORTU-NITY?!"

BECAUSE I THOUGHT YOU'D LIKE THE OPPORTUNITY~

UMM...

FINE, I'LL TRANSLATE IT, OKAY?

THAT'S NOT~

HA HA ホホ

SO ASUNA, YOU ADMIT YOU DON'T GET THIS PASSAGE.

I'LL DO IT FOR YOU...

...

THAT IS... BONES... WERE... THE TREES...

LET'S SEE... THEY ATE BRUNCH ON THE TALL TREE... AND THEN THERE WERE BONES... HUNDREDS OF THEM?

JASON WAS...ON THE FLOWER... AND FELL. THEN SPRING CAME? JASON AND THE FLOWER.

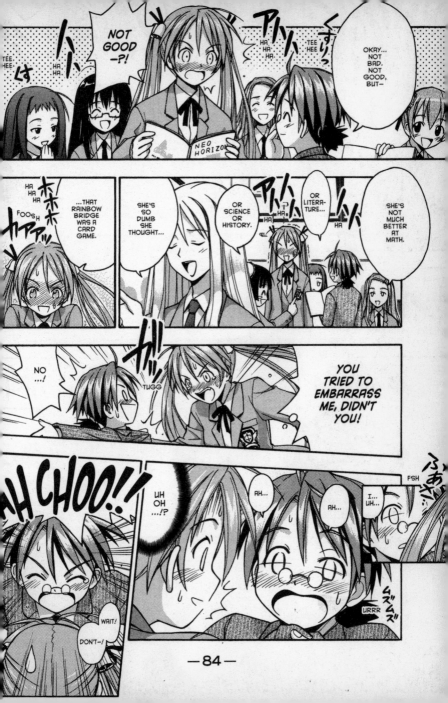

NOT GOOD–?!

TEE HEE

HA, HA,

HA, HA, HA

TEE HEE

OKAY... NOT BAD, NOT GOOD, BUT–

NEO HORIZON

HA HA HA

FOOSH

...THAT RAINBOW BRIDGE WAS A CARD GAME.

SHE'S SO DUMB SHE THOUGHT...

OR SCIENCE OR HISTORY.

OR LITERA-TURE...

HA, HA, HA

HA

SHE'S NOT MUCH BETTER AT MATH.

NO ...!

TUGG

YOU TRIED TO EMBARRASS ME, DIDN'T YOU!

AH CHOO!!

UH OH ...!?

AH...

AH...

I... UH...

FSH

URRR

WAIT!

DON'T–!

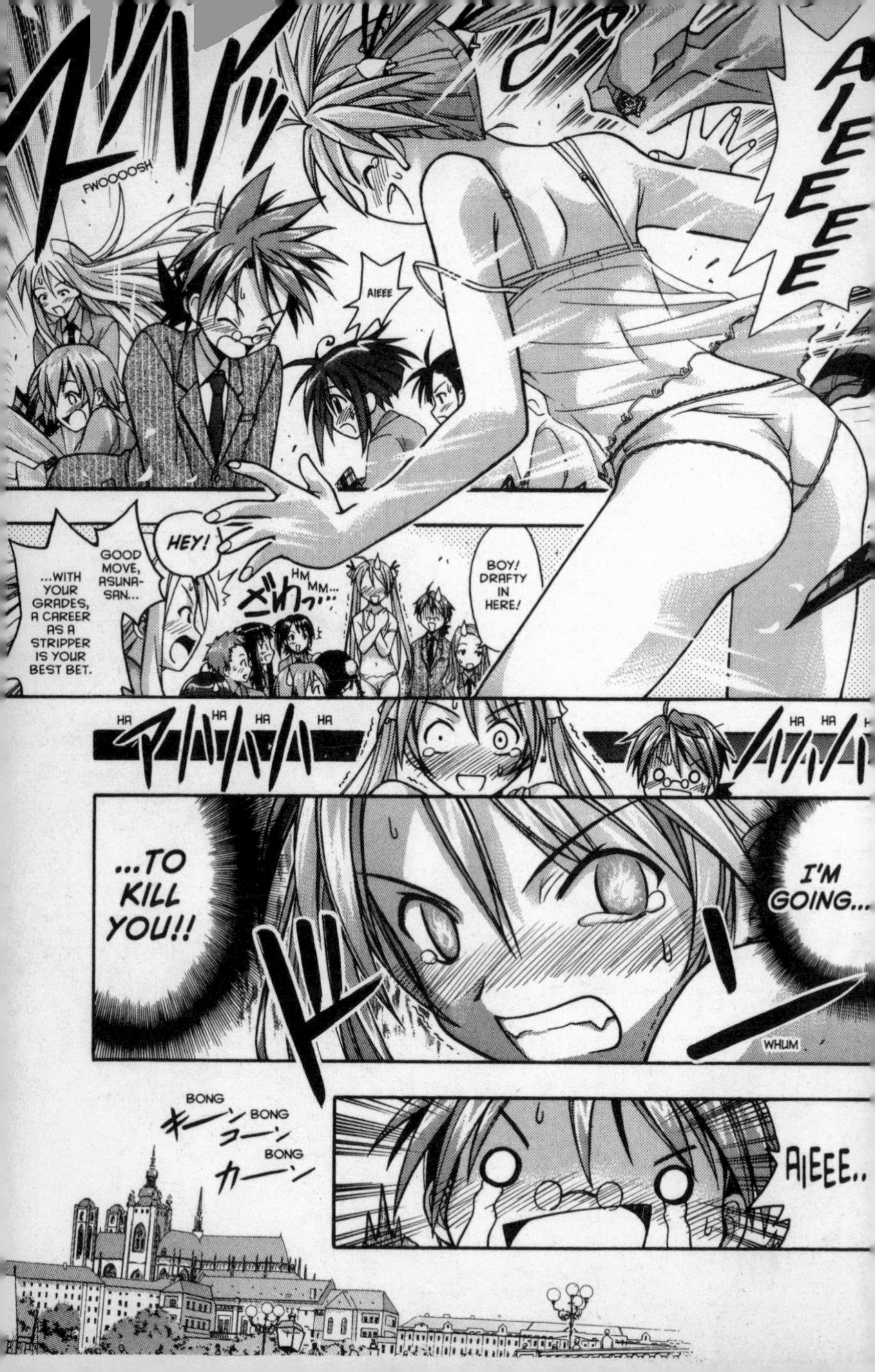
AIEEEEE
AIEEE
FWOOOOSH
BOY! DRAFTY IN HERE!
HMMM...
HEY!
GOOD MOVE, ASUNA-SAN...
...WITH YOUR GRADES, A CAREER AS A STRIPPER IS YOUR BEST BET.
HA HA HA
HA HA HA HA
I'M GOING...
...TO KILL YOU!!
WHUM
AIEEE..
BONG
BONG
BONG

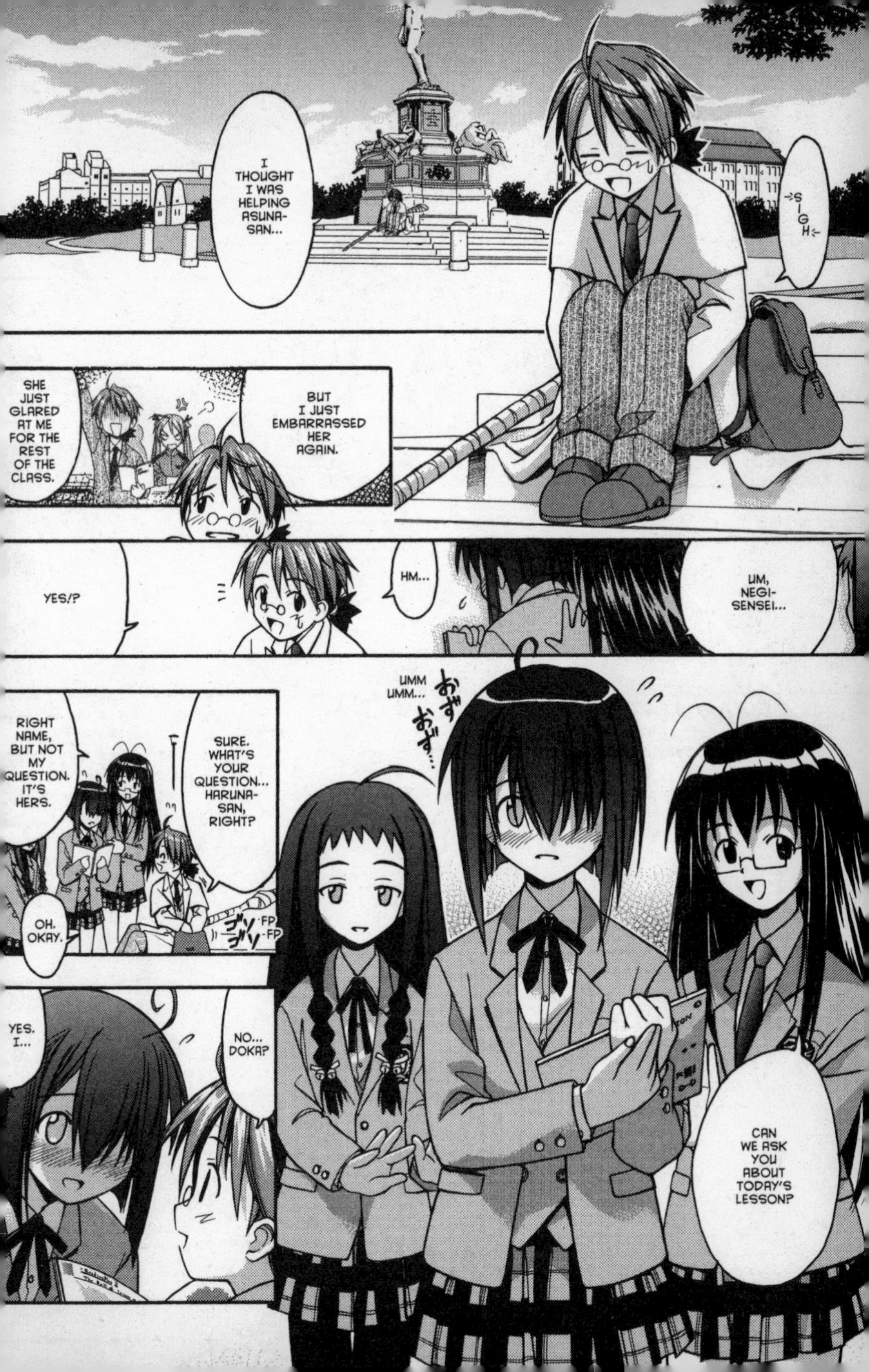
SIGH
I THOUGHT I WAS HELPING ASUNA-SAN...
BUT I JUST EMBARRASSED HER AGAIN.
SHE JUST GLARED AT ME FOR THE REST OF THE CLASS.
UM, NEGI-SENSEI...
HM...
YES!?
UMM UMM...
おず おず...
CAN WE ASK YOU ABOUT TODAY'S LESSON?
SURE. WHAT'S YOUR QUESTION... HARUNA-SAN, RIGHT?
RIGHT NAME, BUT NOT MY QUESTION. IT'S HERS.
FP FP
OH. OKAY.
NO... DOKA?
YES. I...

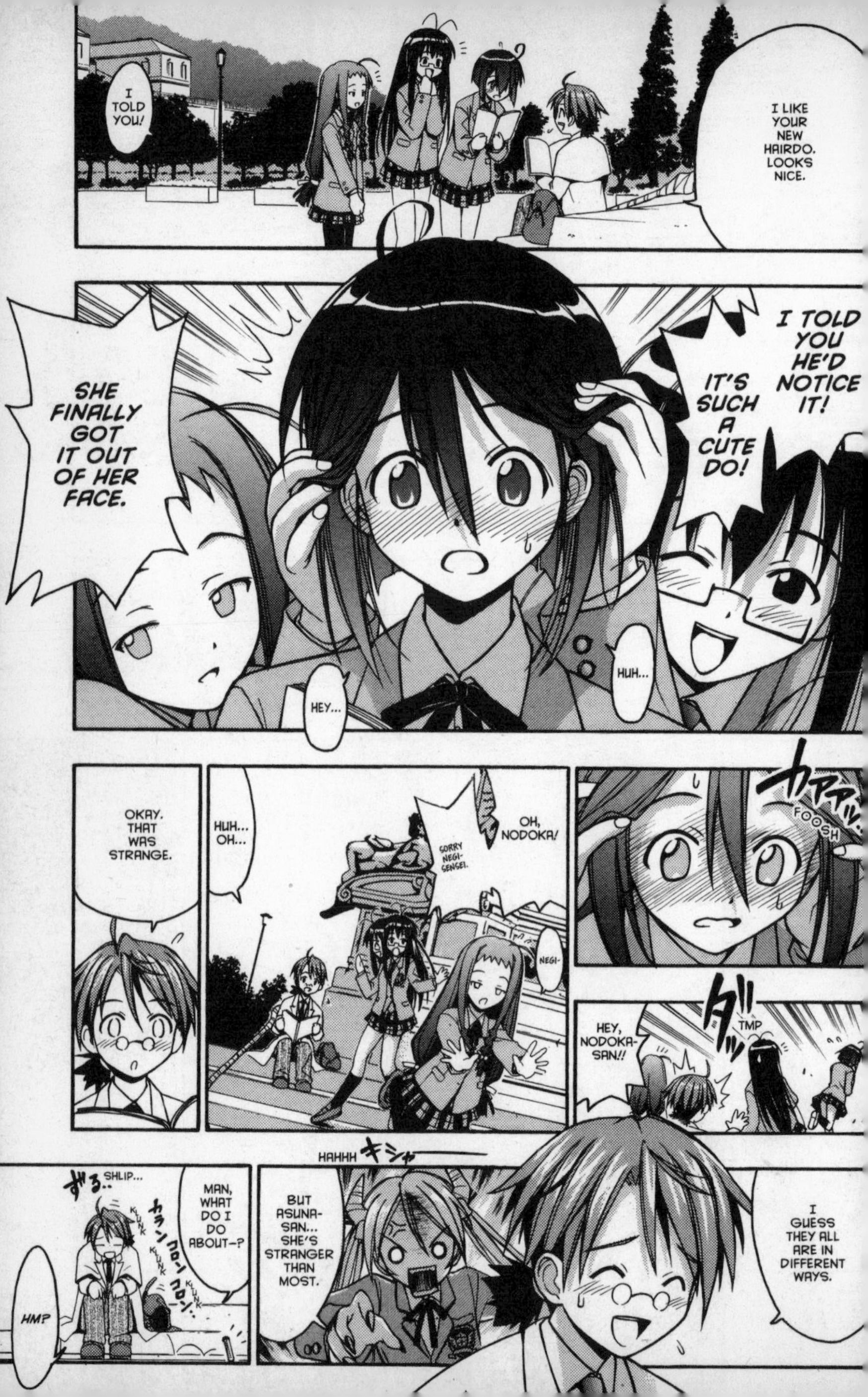
I LIKE YOUR NEW HAIRDO. LOOKS NICE.
I TOLD YOU!
I TOLD YOU HE'D NOTICE IT!
IT'S SUCH A CUTE DO!
SHE FINALLY GOT IT OUT OF HER FACE.
HUH...
HEY...
FOOSH
TMP
HEY, NODOKA-SAN!!
OH, NODOKA!
SORRY NEGI-SENSEI.
HUH... OH...
NEGI-
OKAY. THAT WAS STRANGE.
HAHHH キシャー
I GUESS THEY ALL ARE IN DIFFERENT WAYS.
BUT ASUNA-SAN... SHE'S STRANGER THAN MOST.
MAN, WHAT DO I DO ABOUT—?
ずる.. SHLIP...
KLUNK KLUNK KLUNK
HM?

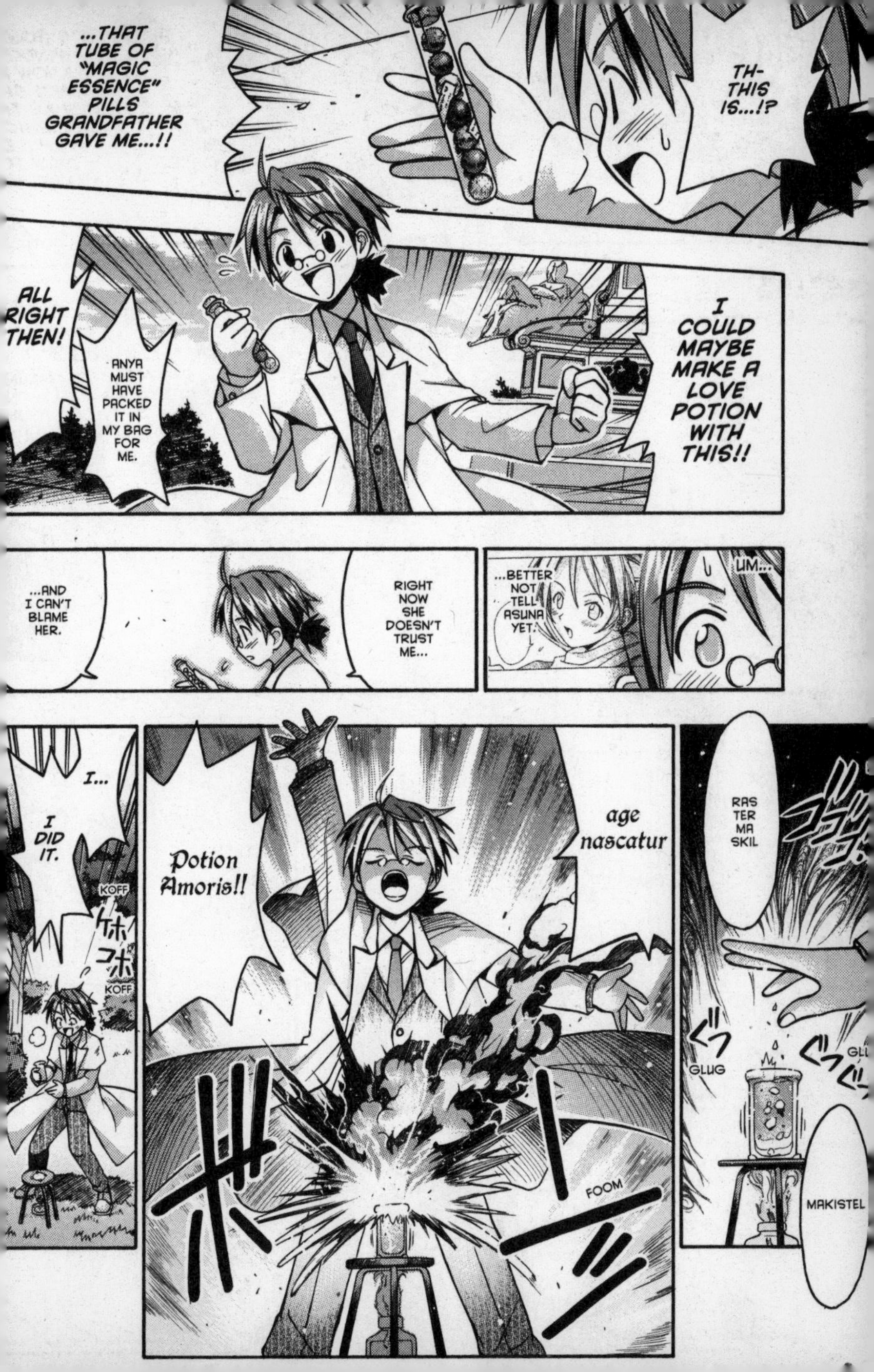

TH- THIS IS...!?
...THAT TUBE OF "MAGIC ESSENCE" PILLS GRANDFATHER GAVE ME...!!
I COULD MAYBE MAKE A LOVE POTION WITH THIS!!
ANYA MUST HAVE PACKED IT IN MY BAG FOR ME.
ALL RIGHT THEN!
UM...
...BETTER NOT TELL ASUNA YET.
RIGHT NOW SHE DOESN'T TRUST ME...
...AND I CAN'T BLAME HER.
RAS TER MA SKIL
GLUG
MAKISTEL
age nascatur
Potion Amoris!!
FOOM
I...
I DID IT.
KOFF
KOFF

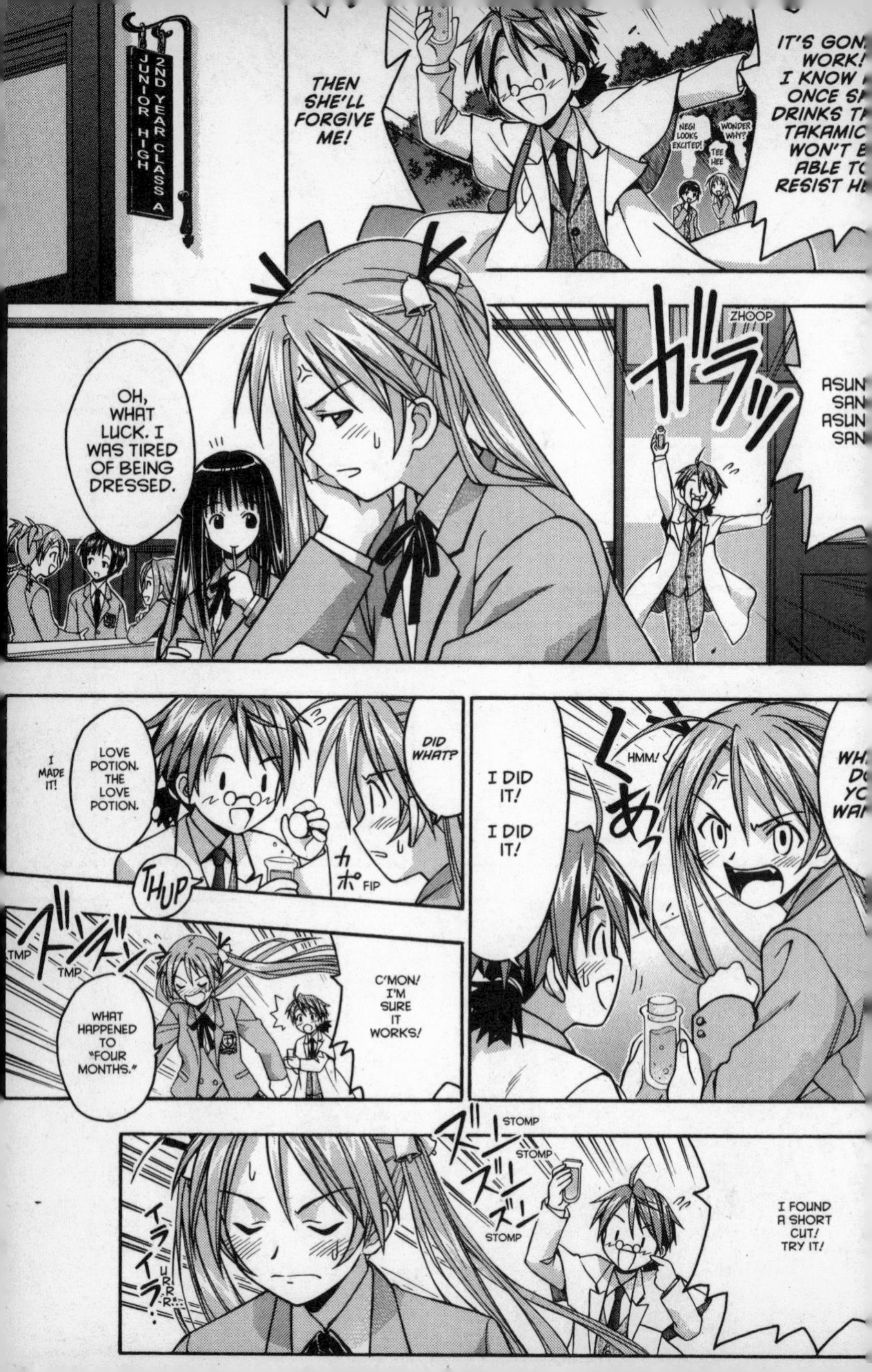
IT'S GON WORK! I KNOW ONCE S DRINKS T TAKAMIC WON'T B ABLE TO RESIST H
NEGI LOOKS EXCITED!
WONDER WHY?
TEE HEE
THEN SHE'LL FORGIVE ME!
2ND YEAR CLASS A
JUNIOR HIGH
ガラッ
ZHOOP
ASUN SAN ASUN SAN
OH, WHAT LUCK. I WAS TIRED OF BEING DRESSED.
WH D YO WA
くあっ
HMM!
I DID IT!
I DID IT!
DID WHAT?
LOVE POTION. THE LOVE POTION.
I MADE IT!
カポ
FIP
THUP
ズンズン
TMP
TMP
C'MON! I'M SURE IT WORKS!
WHAT HAPPENED TO "FOUR MONTHS."
ズーズーズー
STOMP
STOMP
STOMP
I FOUND A SHORT CUT! TRY IT!
イライラ
URRR...

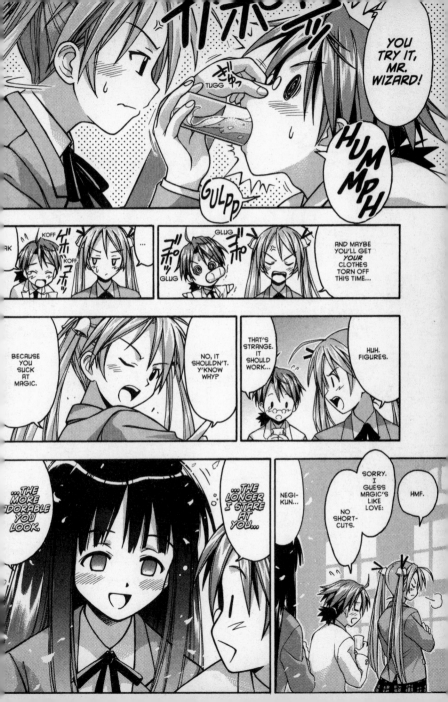

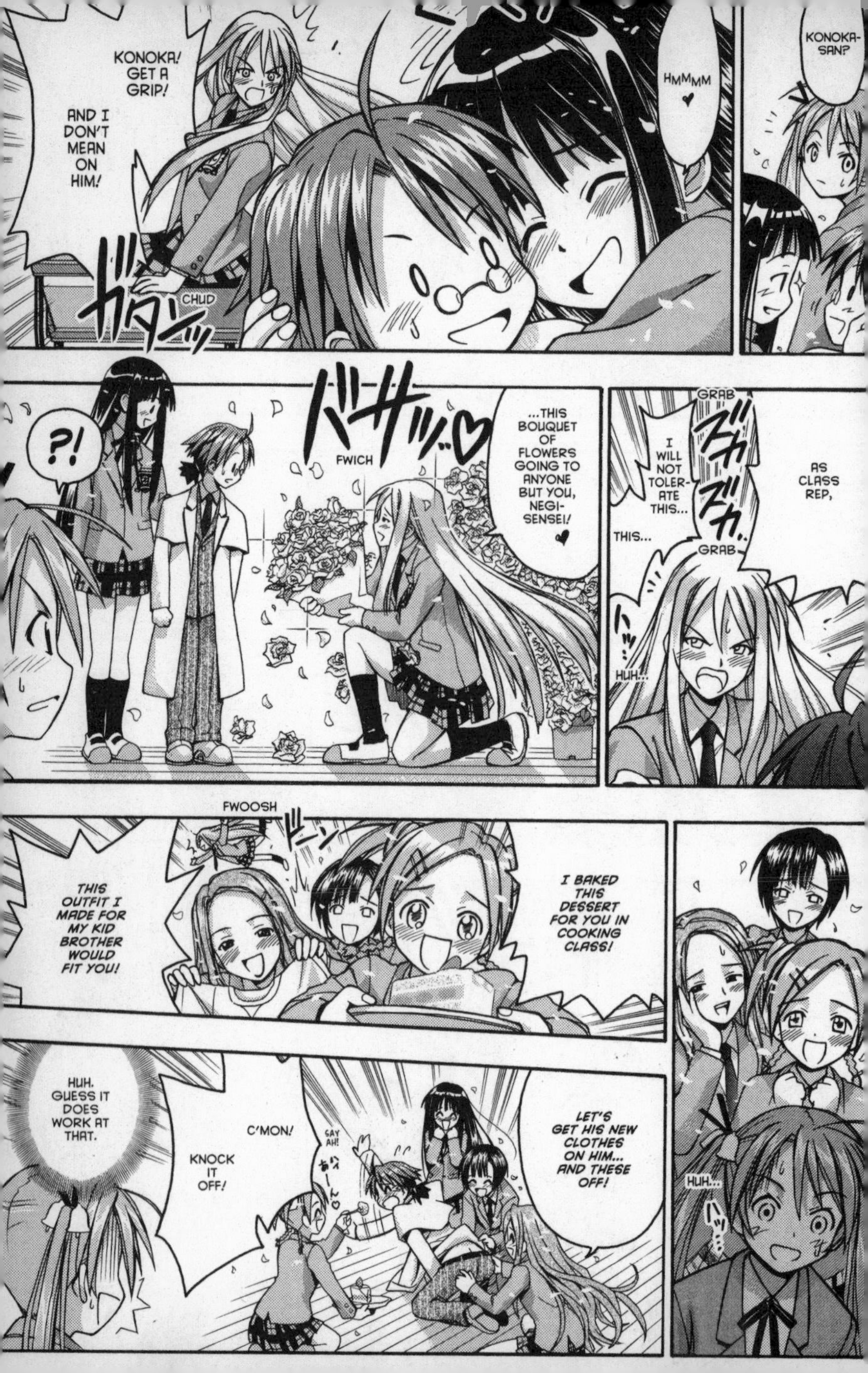
KONOKA-SAN?
HMMMM ♥
KONOKA! GET A GRIP!
AND I DON'T MEAN ON HIM!
CHUD
ガタンッ
AS CLASS REP,
THIS...
I WILL NOT TOLERATE THIS...
GRAB
ズカズカ
GRAB
ハッ
HUH...
...THIS BOUQUET OF FLOWERS GOING TO ANYONE BUT YOU, NEGI-SENSEI! ♥
バサッ♡
FWICH
?!
HUH...
ハッ
I BAKED THIS DESSERT FOR YOU IN COOKING CLASS!
THIS OUTFIT I MADE FOR MY KID BROTHER WOULD FIT YOU!
ドーン
FWOOSH
LET'S GET HIS NEW CLOTHES ON HIM... AND THESE OFF!
SAY AH!
あ～ん♡
C'MON!
KNOCK IT OFF!
HUH. GUESS IT DOES WORK AT THAT.

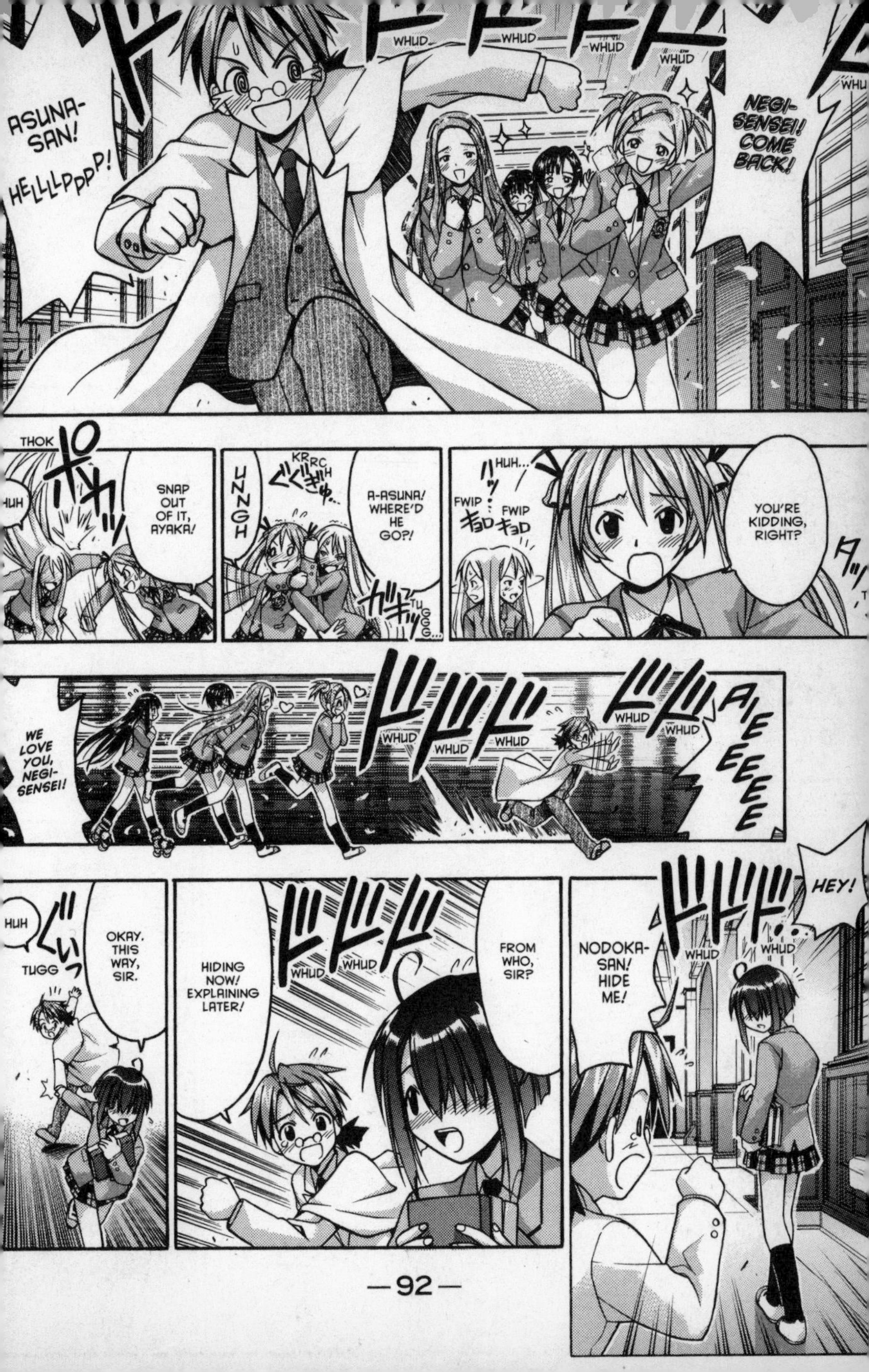
NEGI-SENSEI! COME BACK!
WHU
WHUD
WHUD
WHUD
WHUD
ASUNA-SAN! HELLLLPPPP!
YOU'RE KIDDING, RIGHT?
HUH...
FWIP FWIP
A-ASUNA! WHERE'D HE GO?!
KRRCH
UNNGH
TUGGG...
SNAP OUT OF IT, AYAKA!
THOK
HUH
AIEEEEEE
WHUD WHUD
WHUD WHUD WHUD
WE LOVE YOU, NEGI-SENSEI!
HEY!
WHUD WHUD
NODOKA-SAN! HIDE ME!
FROM WHO, SIR?
WHUD WHUD
HIDING NOW! EXPLAINING LATER!
OKAY. THIS WAY, SIR.
HUH
TUGG

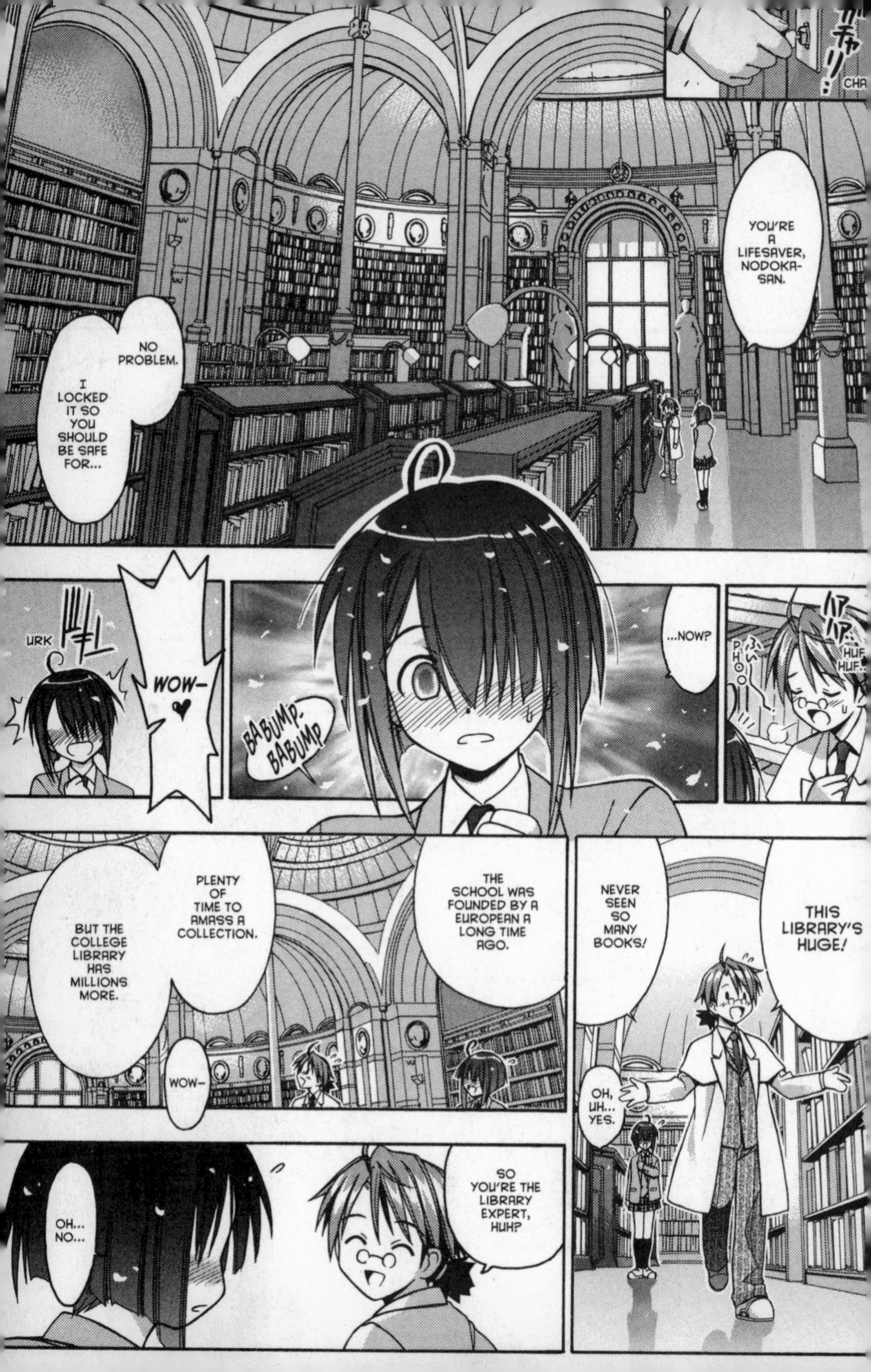

ガチャリ
CHA
YOU'RE A LIFESAVER, NODOKA-SAN.
NO PROBLEM.
I LOCKED IT SO YOU SHOULD BE SAFE FOR...
HUF HUF...
PHOO
...NOW?
BABUMP. BABUMP
WOW-♥
URK
THIS LIBRARY'S HUGE!
NEVER SEEN SO MANY BOOKS!
OH, UH... YES.
THE SCHOOL WAS FOUNDED BY A EUROPEAN A LONG TIME AGO.
PLENTY OF TIME TO AMASS A COLLECTION.
BUT THE COLLEGE LIBRARY HAS MILLIONS MORE.
WOW-
SO YOU'RE THE LIBRARY EXPERT, HUH?
OH... NO...

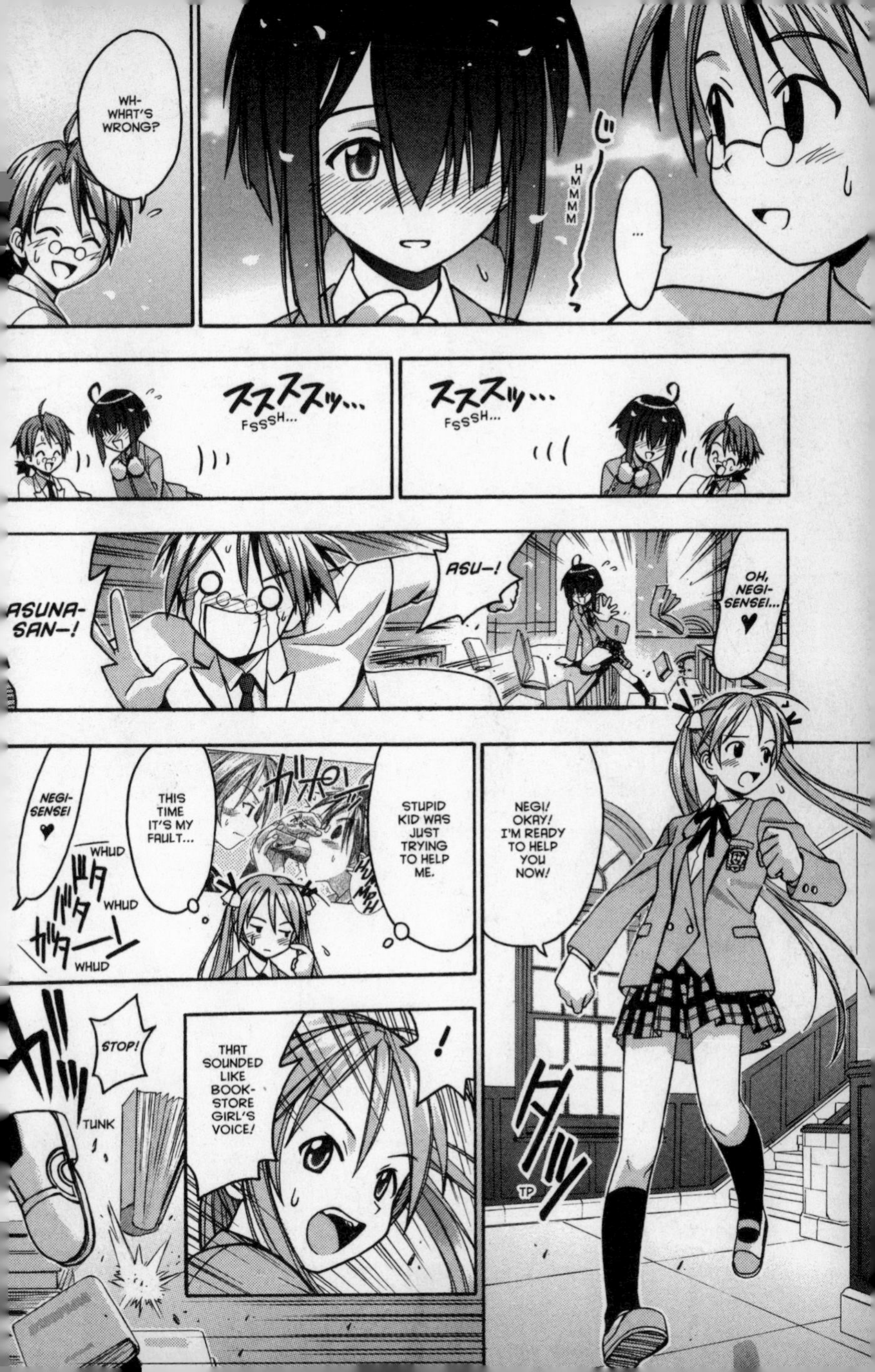

HMMMM
...
WH- WHAT'S WRONG?
スススッ…
FSSSH...
スススッ…
FSSSH...
OH, NEGI-SENSEI... ♥
ASU-!
ASUNA-SAN-!
NEGI! OKAY! I'M READY TO HELP YOU NOW!
TP
STUPID KID WAS JUST TRYING TO HELP ME.
THIS TIME IT'S MY FAULT...
NEGI-SENSEI ♥
WHUD
WHUD
WHUD
!
THAT SOUNDED LIKE BOOK-STORE GIRL'S VOICE!
STOP!
TUNK

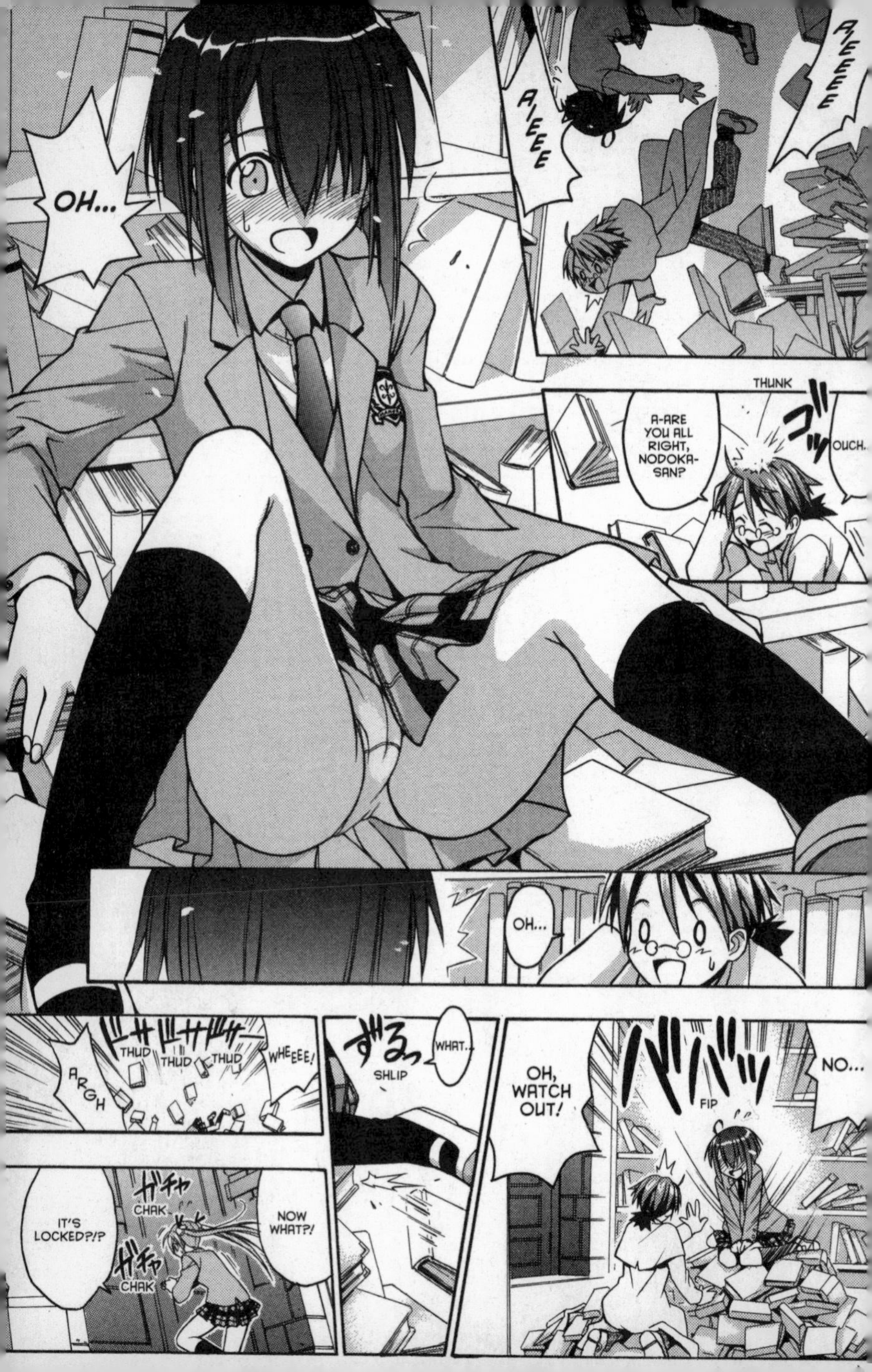
AIEEEEE
AIEEE
THUNK
ゴッ
OUCH.
A-ARE YOU ALL RIGHT, NODOKA-SAN?
OH...
OH...
NO...
バババッ
OH, WATCH OUT!
FIP
WHAT...
ずるっ
SHLIP
WHEEEE!
THUD THUD THUD
ARGH
NOW WHAT?!
ガチャ
CHAK
ガチャ
CHAK
IT'S LOCKED?!?

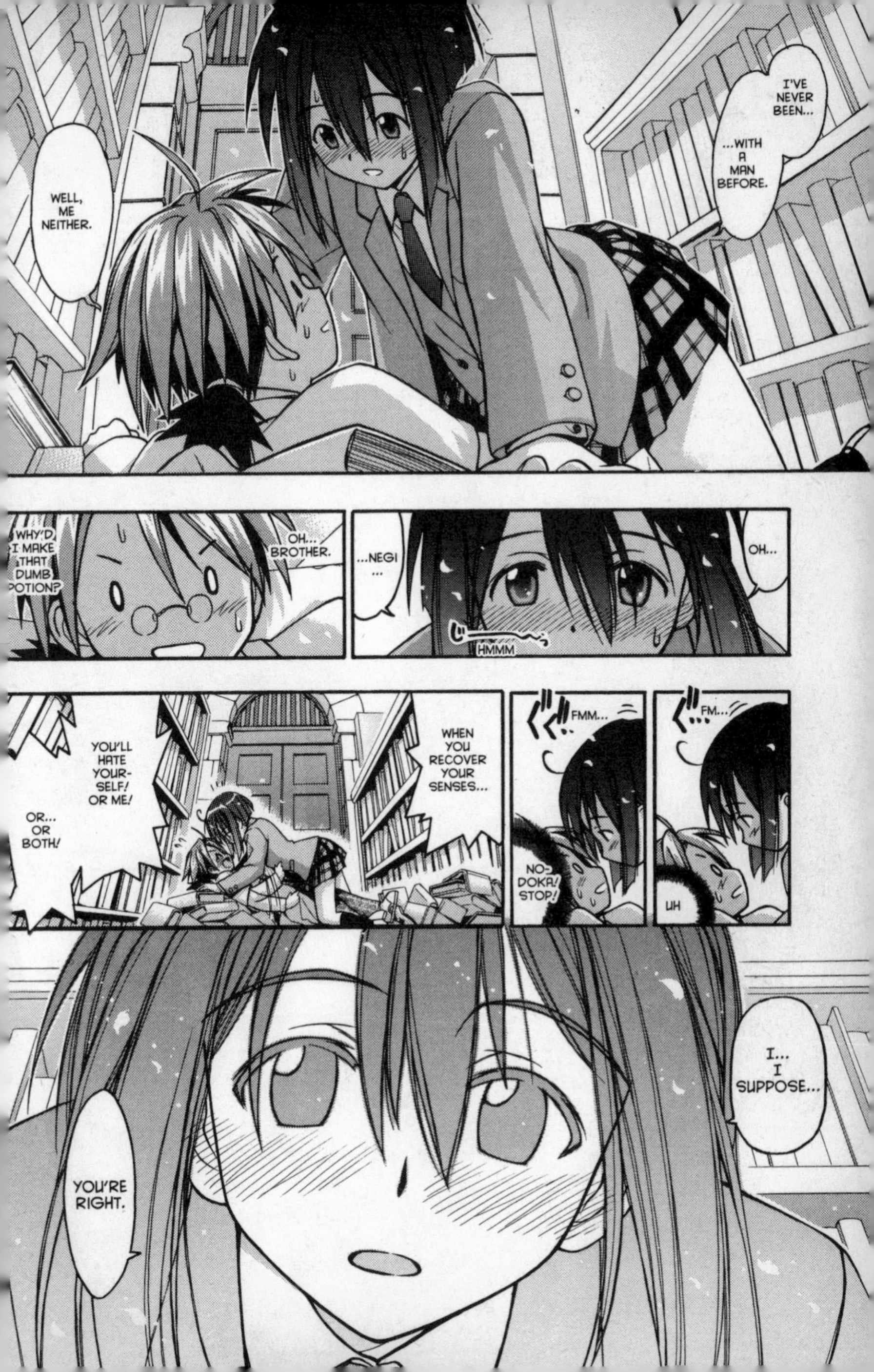
I'VE NEVER BEEN...
...WITH A MAN BEFORE.
WELL, ME NEITHER.
OH...
...NEGI ...
HMMM
OH... BROTHER.
WHY'D I MAKE THAT DUMB POTION?
FM...
UH
FMM...
NO-DOKA! STOP!
WHEN YOU RECOVER YOUR SENSES...
YOU'LL HATE YOUR-SELF! OR ME!
OR... OR BOTH!
I... I SUPPOSE...
YOU'RE RIGHT.

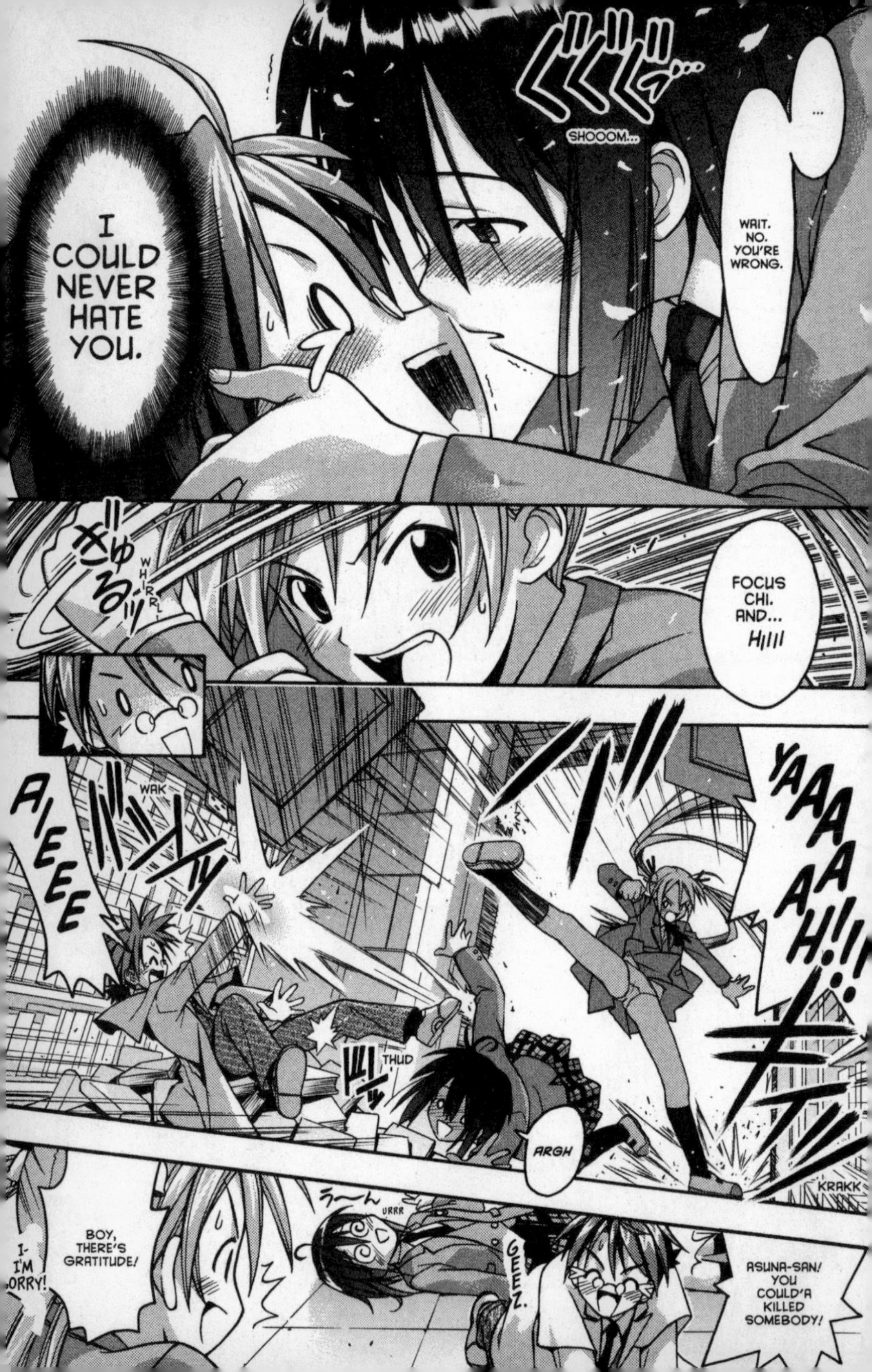
...
WAIT. NO. YOU'RE WRONG.
SHOOOM...
I COULD NEVER HATE YOU.
FOCUS CHI. AND... HIIII
WHIRRL
YAAAAAH!!!
KRAKK
ARGH
THUD
WAK
AIEEEE
ASUNA-SAN! YOU COULD'A KILLED SOMEBODY!
GEEZ.
URRR
BOY, THERE'S GRATITUDE!
I- I'M ORRY!

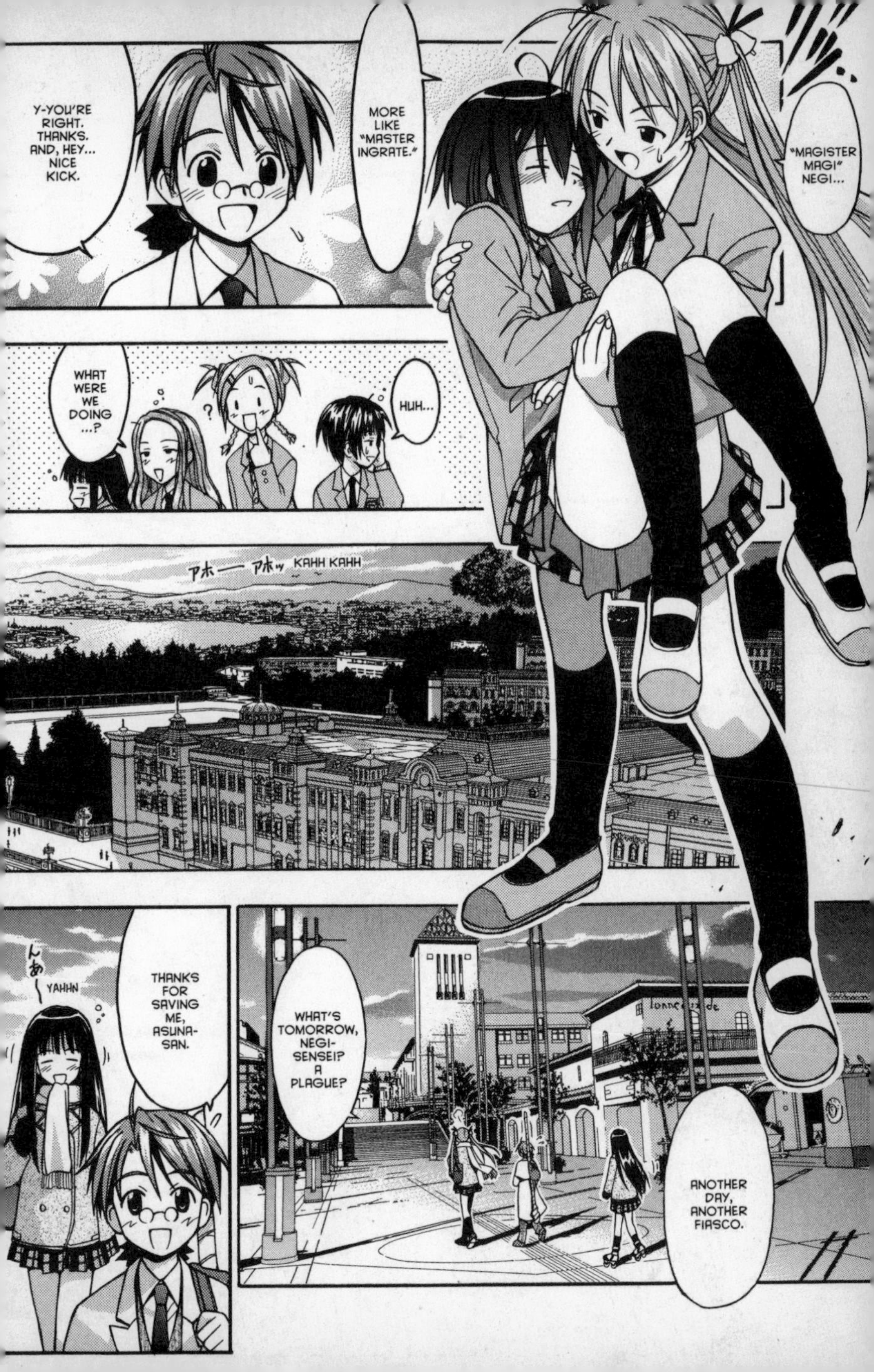
"MAGISTER MAGI" NEGI...
MORE LIKE "MASTER INGRATE."
Y-YOU'RE RIGHT. THANKS. AND, HEY... NICE KICK.
HUH...
WHAT WERE WE DOING ...?
アホー アホッ KAHH KAHH
WHAT'S TOMORROW, NEGI-SENSEI? A PLAGUE?
ANOTHER DAY, ANOTHER FIASCO.
THANKS FOR SAVING ME, ASUNA-SAN.
んあ～ YAHHN

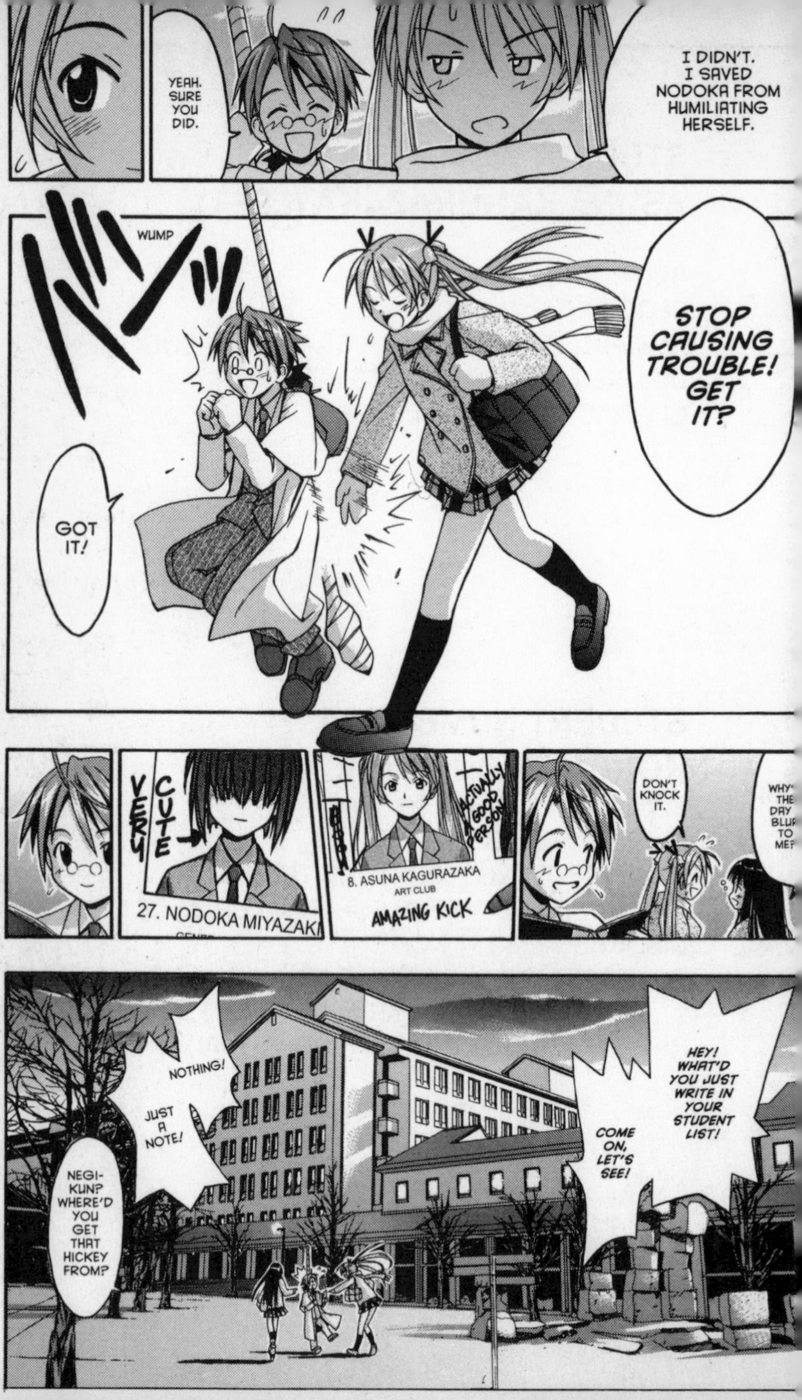
I DIDN'T. I SAVED NODOKA FROM HUMILIATING HERSELF.
YEAH. SURE YOU DID.
STOP CAUSING TROUBLE! GET IT?
WUMP
GOT IT!
DON'T KNOCK IT.
ACTUALLY A GOOD PERSON
8. ASUNA KAGURAZAKA
ART CLUB
AMAZING KICK
VERY CUTE
27. NODOKA MIYAZAKI
HEY! WHAT'D YOU JUST WRITE IN YOUR STUDENT LIST!
COME ON, LET'S SEE!
NOTHING!
JUST A NOTE!
NEGI-KUN? WHERE'D YOU GET THAT HICKEY FROM?

STUDENT NUMBER 8
ASUNA KAGURAZAKA (LEFT)

BIRTHDATE: APRIL 21, 1988
BLOODTYPE: B
FAVORITE THINGS: TAKAHATA-SENSEI, COOL MEN
DISLIKES: KIDS, STUDYING
CLUB ACTIVITIES: ART CLUB

STUDENT NUMBER 13
KONOKA KONOE (RIGHT)
BIRTHDATE: MARCH 18, 1989
BLOODTYPE: AB
FAVORITE THINGS: FORTUNE-TELLING,
                THE SUPERNATURAL, COOKING
DISLIKES: ALMOST NONE
CLUB ACTIVITIES: FORTUNE-TELLING CLUB,
                LIBRARY EXPLORATION CLUB
REMARKS: SCHOOL DEAN'S GRANDDAUGHTER

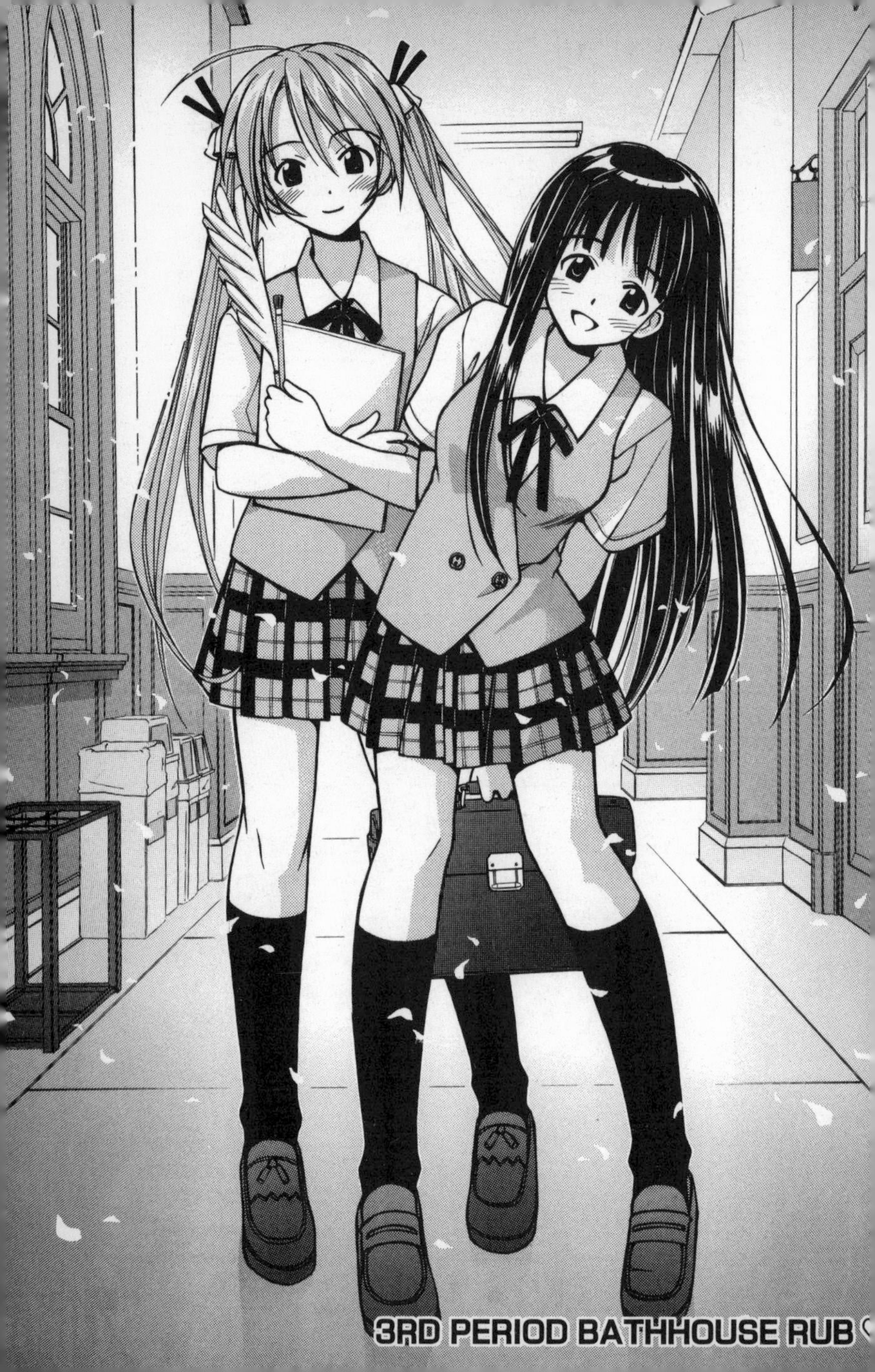

3RD PERIOD BATHHOUSE RUB ♥

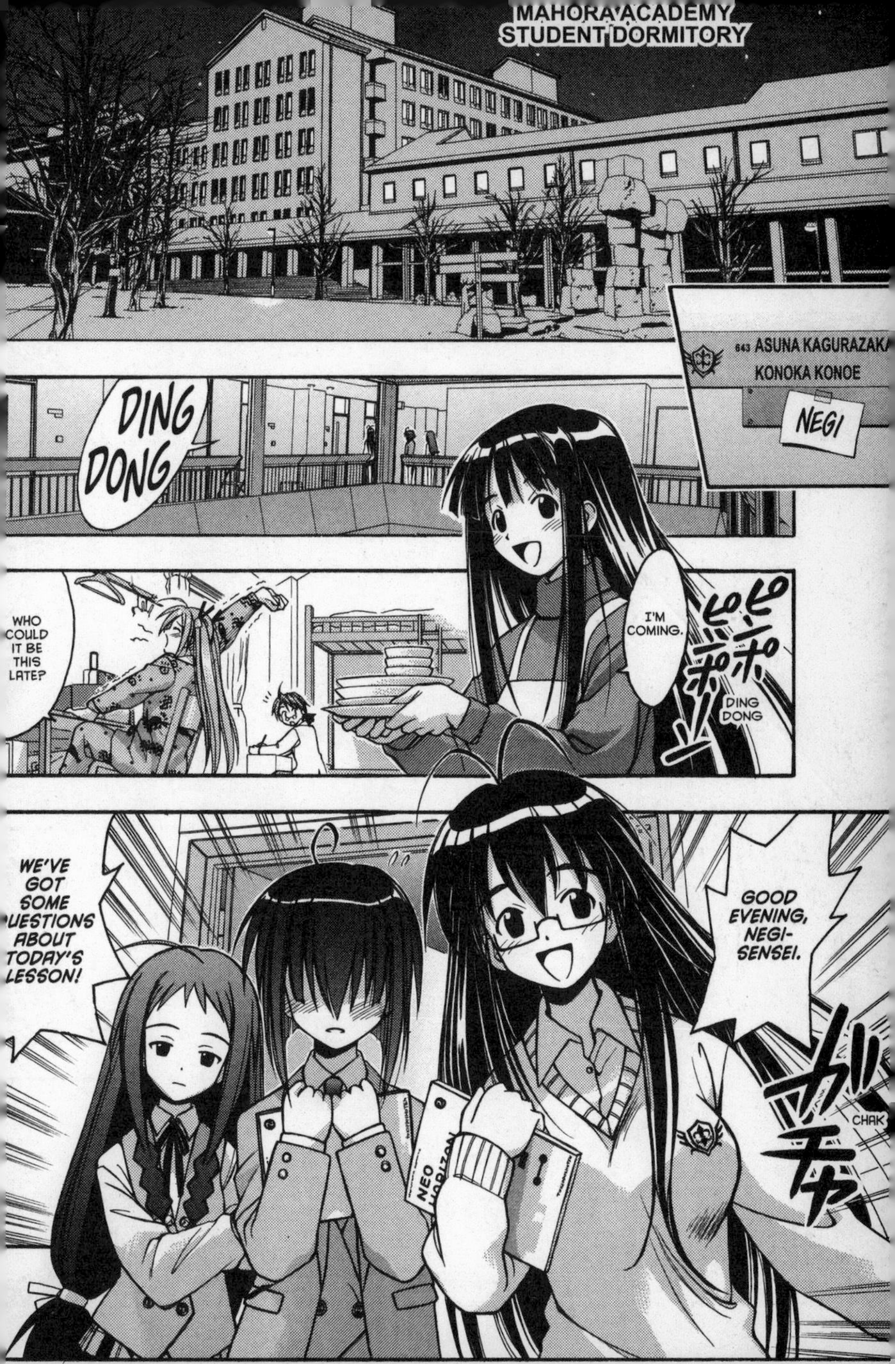
MAHORA ACADEMY STUDENT DORMITORY
643 ASUNA KAGURAZAKA
KONOKA KONOE
NEGI
DING DONG
I'M COMING.
DING DONG
WHO COULD IT BE THIS LATE?
GOOD EVENING, NEGI-SENSEI.
WE'VE GOT SOME QUESTIONS ABOUT TODAY'S LESSON!
CHAK
NEO HORIZON

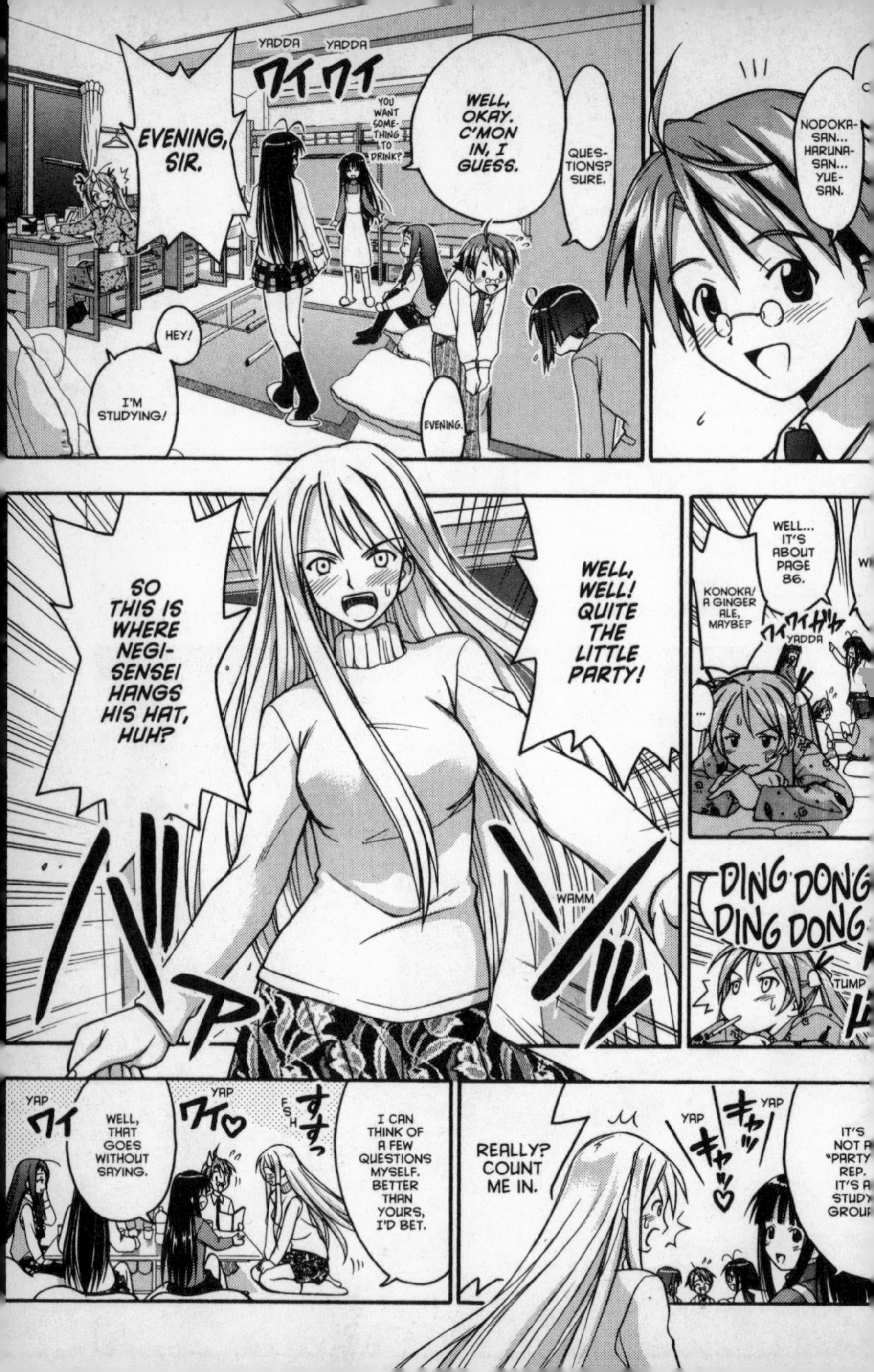
NODOKA-SAN... HARUNA-SAN... YUE-SAN.
QUES-TIONS? SURE.
WELL, OKAY. C'MON IN, I GUESS.
YOU WANT SOME-THING TO DRINK?
YADDA YADDA
ワイワイ
EVENING, SIR.
HEY!
I'M STUDYING!
EVENING.
WELL... IT'S ABOUT PAGE 86.
KONOKA! A GINGER ALE, MAYBE?
YADDA
ワイワイガヤ
...
DING DONG DING DONG
TUMP
WELL, WELL! QUITE THE LITTLE PARTY!
SO THIS IS WHERE NEGI-SENSEI HANGS HIS HAT, HUH?
WAMM
IT'S NOT A "PARTY" REP. IT'S A STUDY GROUP
YAP YAP
キャッキャッ
REALLY? COUNT ME IN.
I CAN THINK OF A FEW QUESTIONS MYSELF. BETTER THAN YOURS, I'D BET.
FSH
すすっ
YAP
ワイ♡
WELL, THAT GOES WITHOUT SAYING.
YAP
ワイ

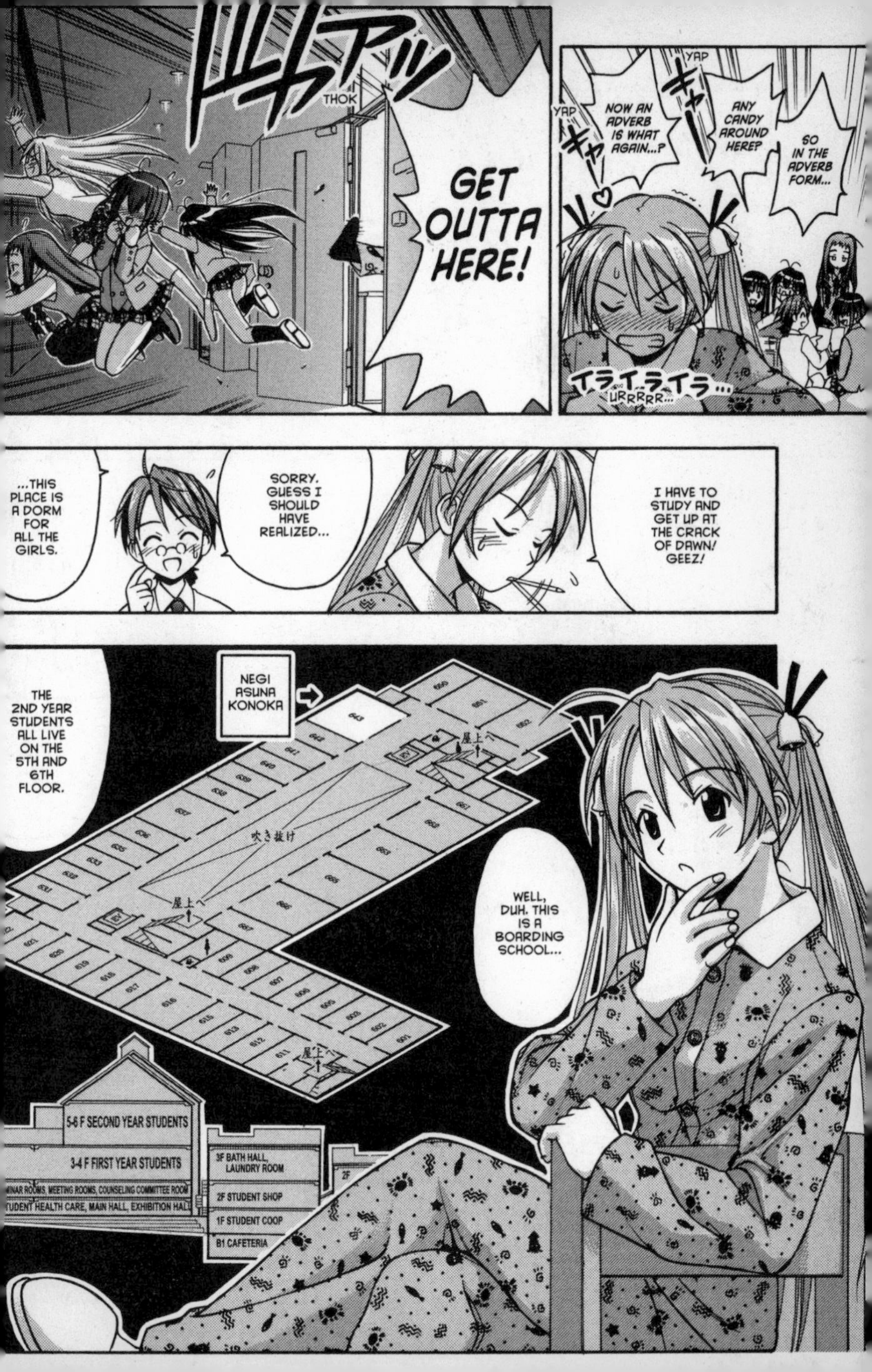

SO IN THE ADVERB FORM...
ANY CANDY AROUND HERE?
キャー
YAP
NOW AN ADVERB IS WHAT AGAIN...?
キャー
YAP
イライライラ...
URRRRR...
ドムアッ
THOK
GET OUTTA HERE!
I HAVE TO STUDY AND GET UP AT THE CRACK OF DAWN! GEEZ!
SORRY. GUESS I SHOULD HAVE REALIZED...
...THIS PLACE IS A DORM FOR ALL THE GIRLS.
WELL, DUH. THIS IS A BOARDING SCHOOL...
NEGI
ASUNA
KONOKA
吹き抜け
屋上へ
THE 2ND YEAR STUDENTS ALL LIVE ON THE 5TH AND 6TH FLOOR.
5-6 F SECOND YEAR STUDENTS
3-4 F FIRST YEAR STUDENTS
MINAR ROOMS, MEETING ROOMS, COUNSELING COMMITTEE ROOM
TUDENT HEALTH CARE, MAIN HALL, EXHIBITION HALL
3F BATH HALL, LAUNDRY ROOM
2F
2F STUDENT SHOP
1F STUDENT COOP
B1 CAFETERIA

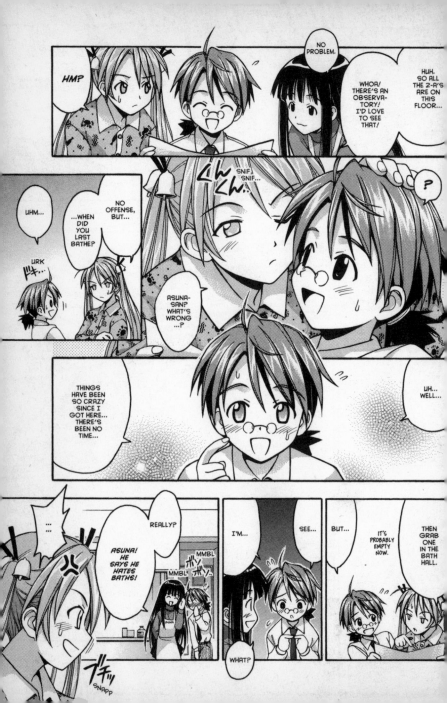

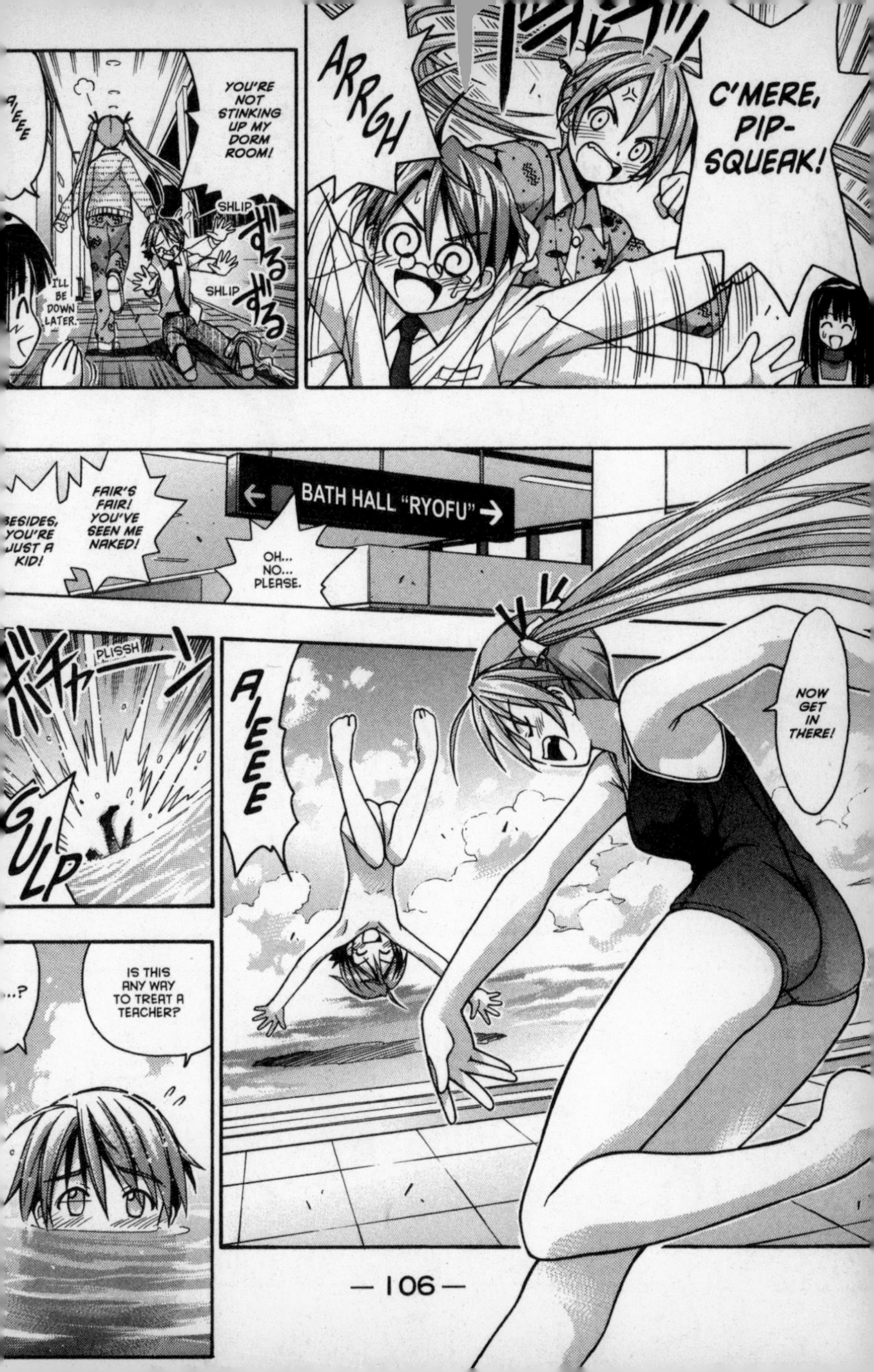
ARRGH
C'MERE, PIP-SQUEAK!
YOU'RE NOT STINKING UP MY DORM ROOM!
SHLIP
ずる
SHLIP
ずる
I'LL BE DOWN LATER.
OH... NO... PLEASE.
← BATH HALL "RYOFU" →
FAIR'S FAIR! YOU'VE SEEN ME NAKED!
BESIDES, YOU'RE JUST A KID!
NOW GET IN THERE!
AIEEE
PLISSH
GULP
IS THIS ANY WAY TO TREAT A TEACHER?
...?

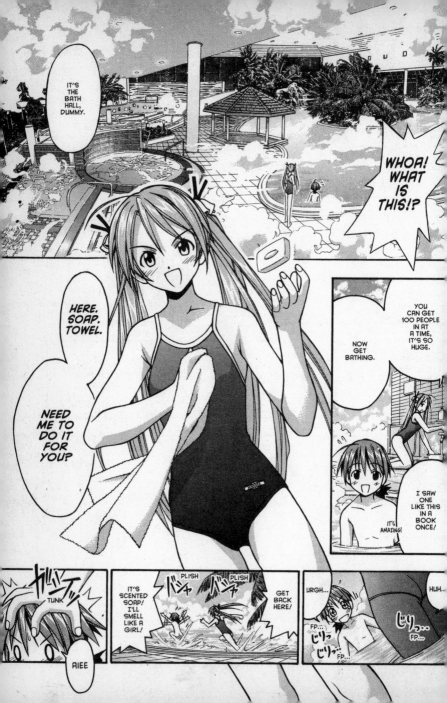

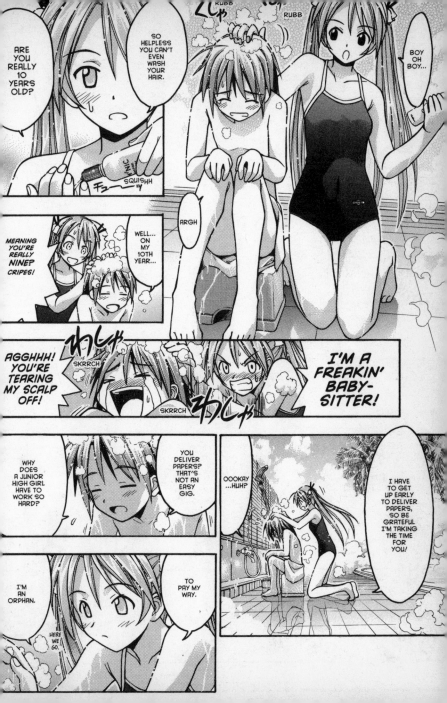

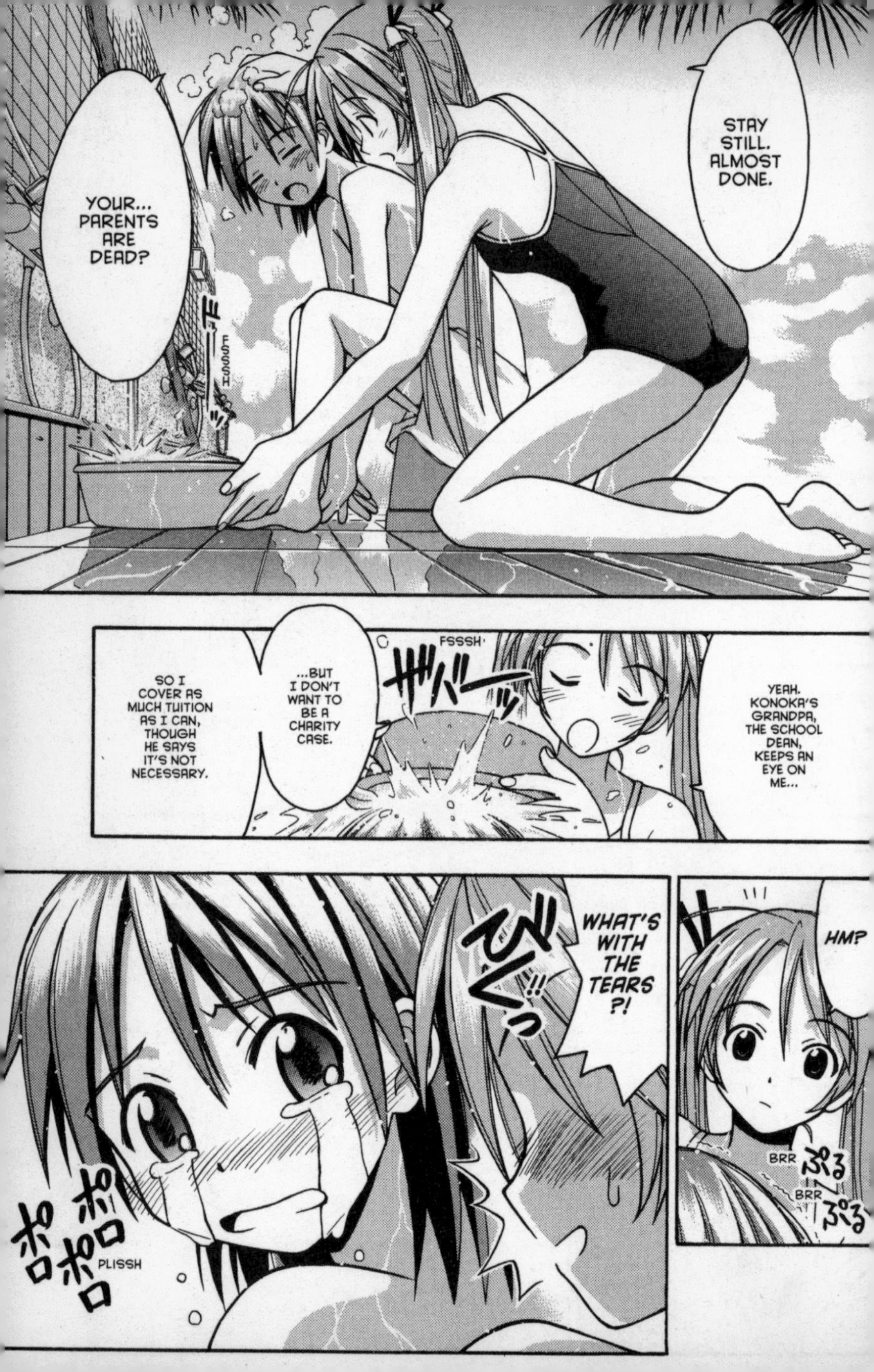

STAY STILL. ALMOST DONE.
YOUR... PARENTS ARE DEAD?
FSSSH
YEAH. KONOKA'S GRANDPA, THE SCHOOL DEAN, KEEPS AN EYE ON ME...
FSSSH
...BUT I DON'T WANT TO BE A CHARITY CASE.
SO I COVER AS MUCH TUITION AS I CAN, THOUGH HE SAYS IT'S NOT NECESSARY.
HM?
BRR ぷる
BRR ぷる
WHAT'S WITH THE TEARS?!
びくっ!!
ポロポロ
ポロポロ
PLISSH

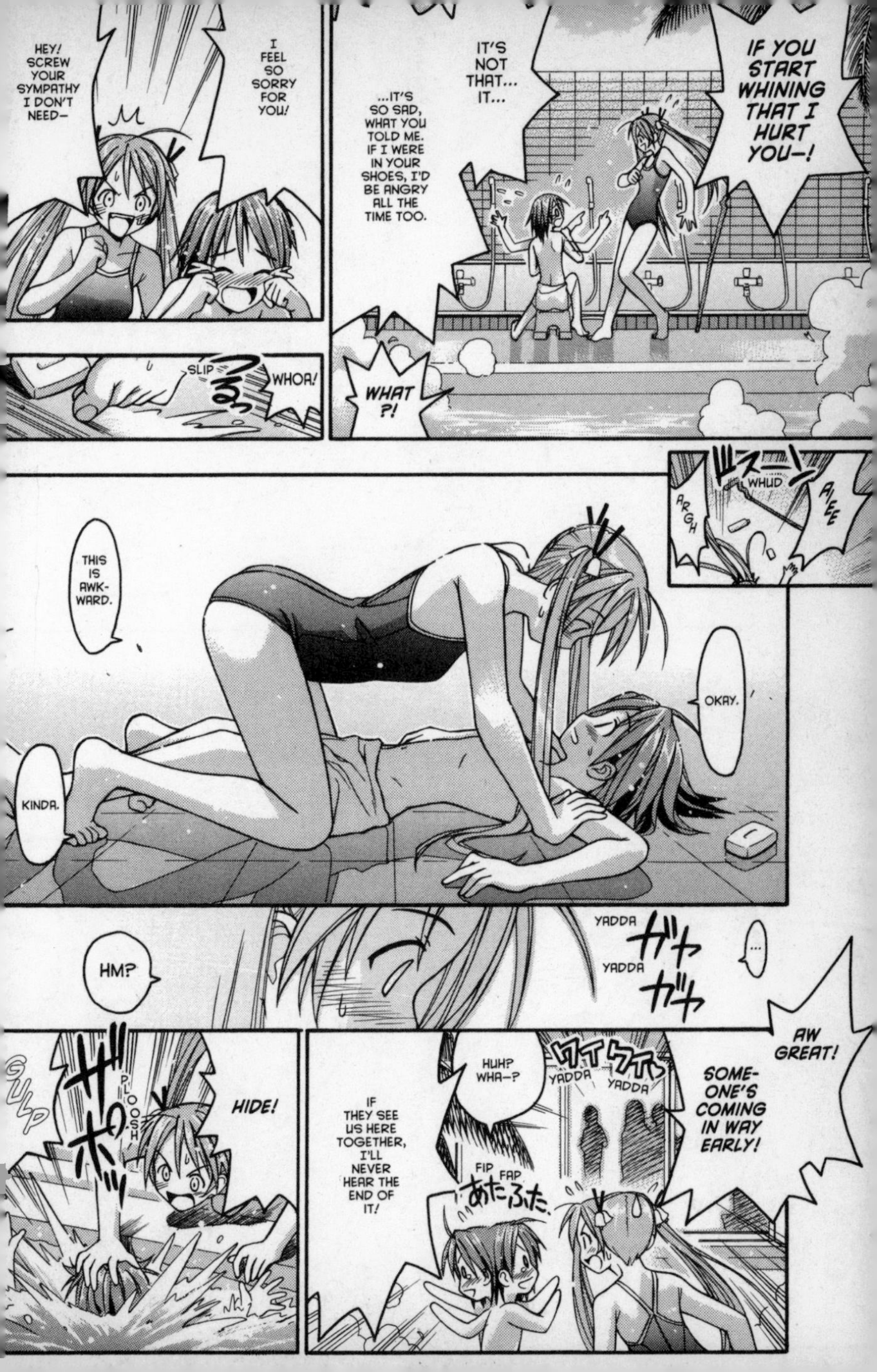
IF YOU START WHINING THAT I HURT YOU—!
IT'S NOT THAT... IT...
...IT'S SO SAD, WHAT YOU TOLD ME. IF I WERE IN YOUR SHOES, I'D BE ANGRY ALL THE TIME TOO.
I FEEL SO SORRY FOR YOU!
HEY! SCREW YOUR SYMPATHY I DON'T NEED—
WHAT ?!
WHOA!
SLIP
WHUD
AIEE
ARGH
OKAY.
THIS IS AWK-WARD.
KINDA.
YADDA
YADDA
...
HM?
AW GREAT!
SOME-ONE'S COMING IN WAY EARLY!
YADDA
YADDA
HUH? WHA—?
IF THEY SEE US HERE TOGETHER, I'LL NEVER HEAR THE END OF IT!
FIP
FAP
HIDE!
PLOOSH
GULP

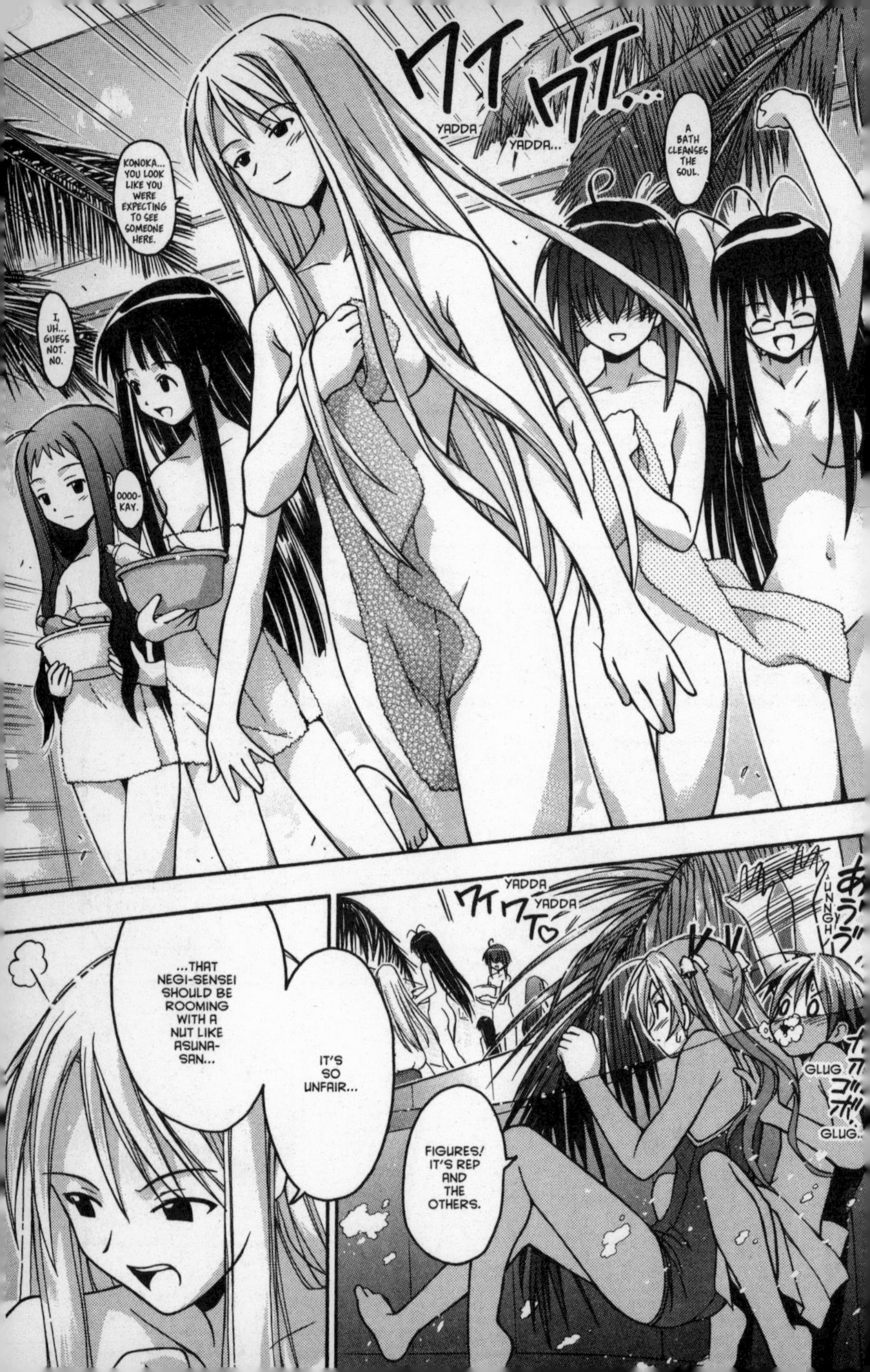
YADDA YADDA...
A BATH CLEANSES THE SOUL.
KONOKA... YOU LOOK LIKE YOU WERE EXPECTING TO SEE SOMEONE HERE.
I, UH... GUESS NOT. NO.
OOOO-KAY.
UNNGH!
YADDA YADDA
GLUG, GLUG...
FIGURES! IT'S REP AND THE OTHERS.
...THAT NEGI-SENSEI SHOULD BE ROOMING WITH A NUT LIKE ASUNA-SAN...
IT'S SO UNFAIR...

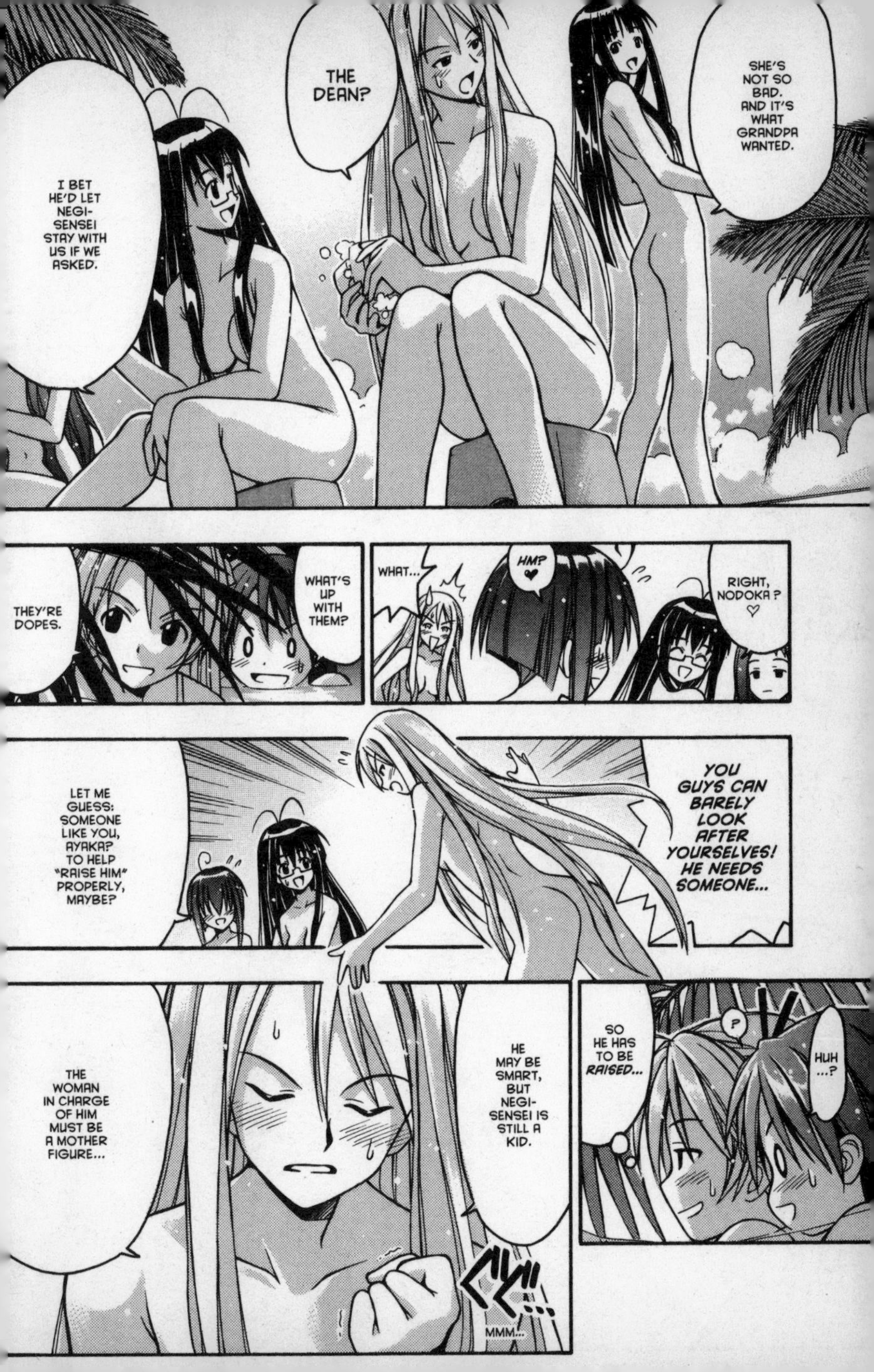

SHE'S NOT SO BAD. AND IT'S WHAT GRANDPA WANTED.
THE DEAN?
I BET HE'D LET NEGI-SENSEI STAY WITH US IF WE ASKED.
RIGHT, NODOKA? ♡
HM? ♥
WHAT...
WHAT'S UP WITH THEM?
THEY'RE DOPES.
YOU GUYS CAN BARELY LOOK AFTER YOURSELVES! HE NEEDS SOMEONE...
LET ME GUESS: SOMEONE LIKE YOU, AYAKA? TO HELP "RAISE HIM" PROPERLY, MAYBE?
HUH ...?
?
SO HE HAS TO BE *RAISED*...
HE MAY BE SMART, BUT NEGI-SENSEI IS STILL A KID.
THE WOMAN IN CHARGE OF HIM MUST BE A MOTHER FIGURE...
MMM...

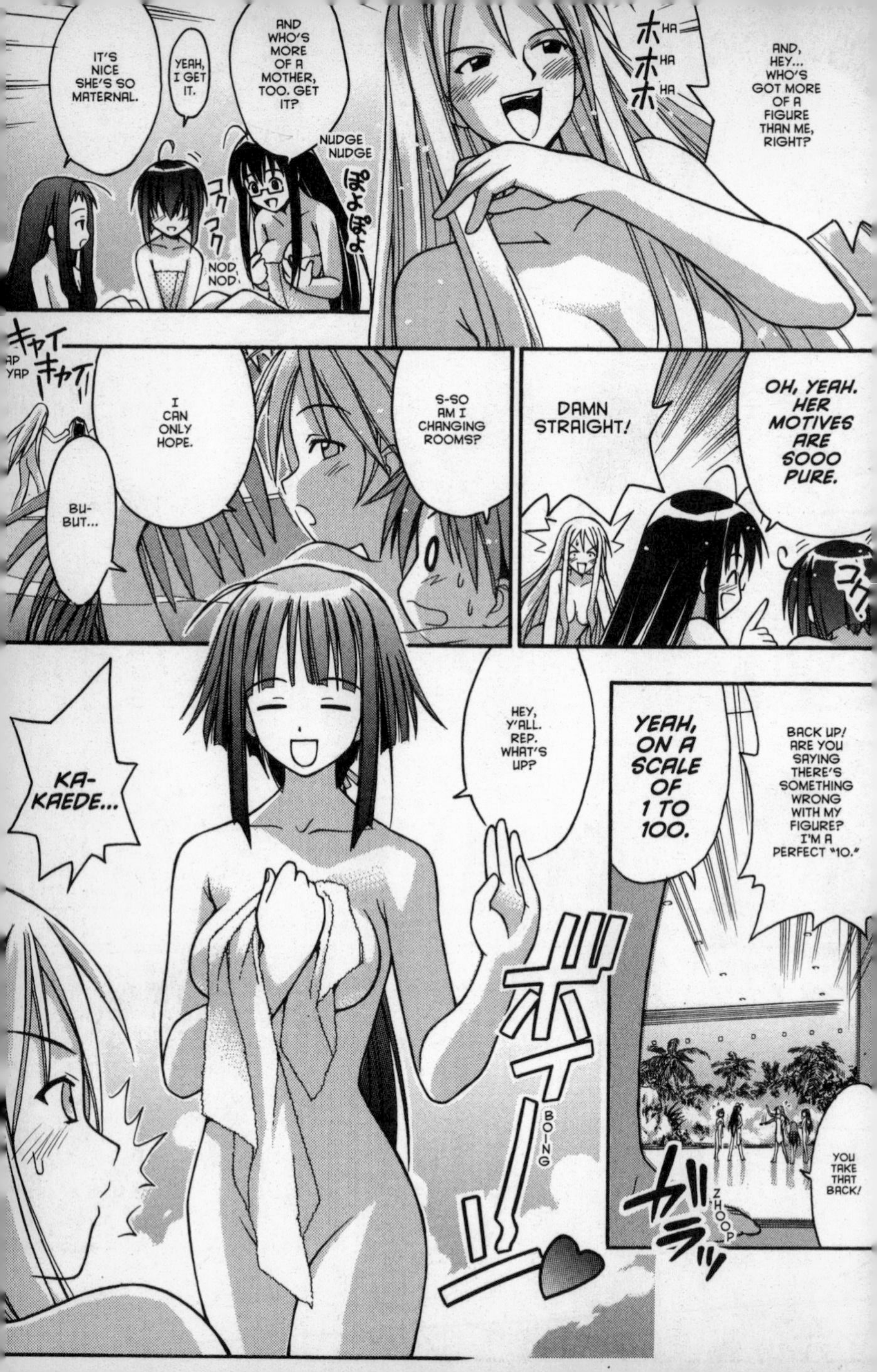
ホホホ
HA HA HA
AND, HEY... WHO'S GOT MORE OF A FIGURE THAN ME, RIGHT?
AND WHO'S MORE OF A MOTHER, TOO. GET IT?
NUDGE NUDGE
ぽよぽよ
YEAH, I GET IT.
IT'S NICE SHE'S SO MATERNAL.
コクコク
NOD NOD
OH, YEAH. HER MOTIVES ARE SOOO PURE.
DAMN STRAIGHT!
S-SO AM I CHANGING ROOMS?
I CAN ONLY HOPE.
キャイキャイ
AP YAP
BU-BUT...
BACK UP! ARE YOU SAYING THERE'S SOMETHING WRONG WITH MY FIGURE? I'M A PERFECT "10."
YEAH, ON A SCALE OF 1 TO 100.
YOU TAKE THAT BACK!
ガラッ
ZHOOP
HEY, Y'ALL. REP. WHAT'S UP?
ボイーン
BOING
KA-KAEDE...

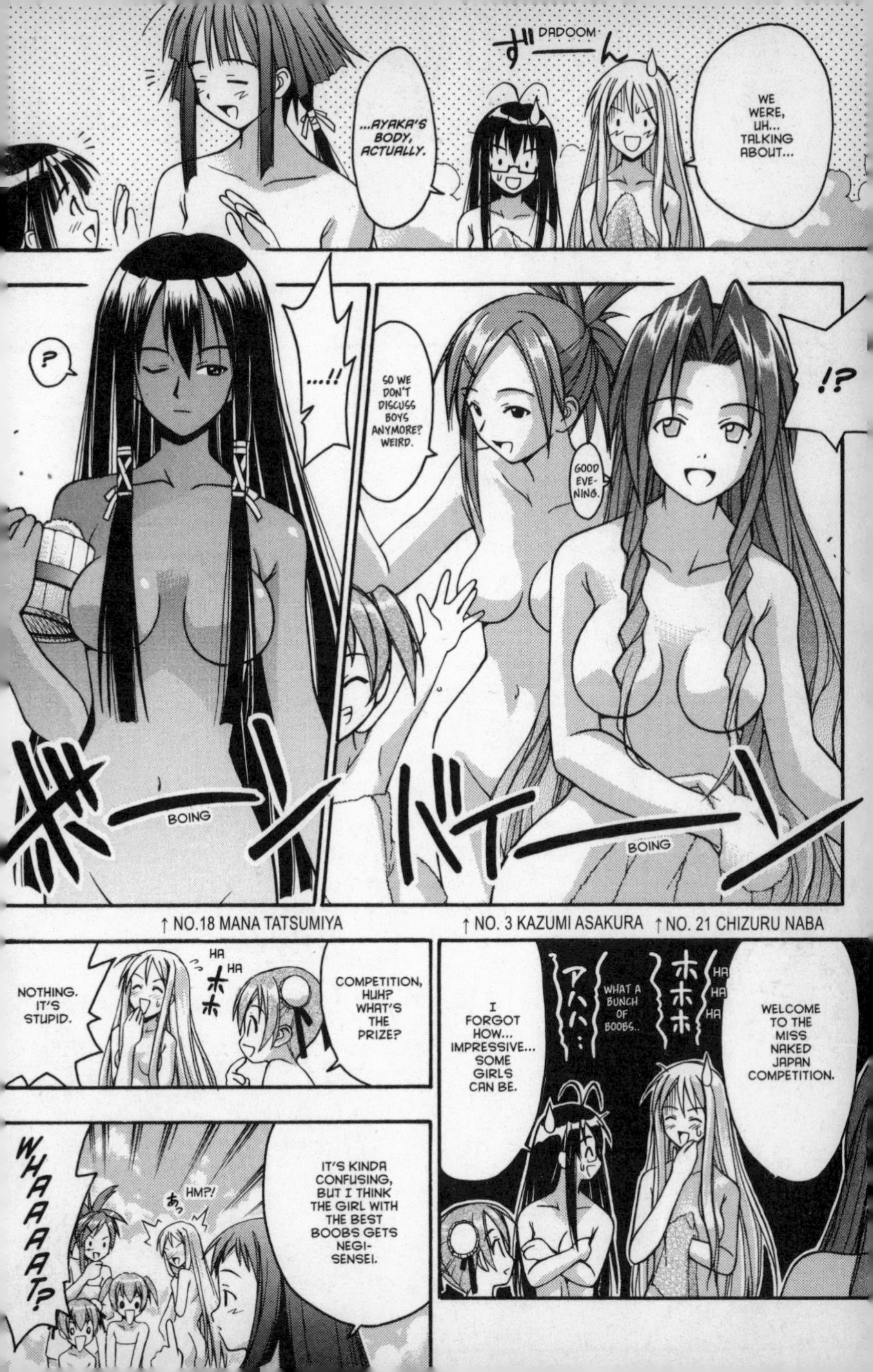
ずーん
DADOOM
WE WERE, UH... TALKING ABOUT...
...AYAKA'S BODY, ACTUALLY.
!?
GOOD EVE-NING.
SO WE DON'T DISCUSS BOYS ANYMORE? WEIRD.
BOING
...!!
?
BOING
↑NO.18 MANA TATSUMIYA
↑NO. 3 KAZUMI ASAKURA
↑NO. 21 CHIZURU NABA
WELCOME TO THE MISS NAKED JAPAN COMPETITION.
HA HA HA
ホホホ
WHAT A BUNCH OF BOOBS..
アハハ…
I FORGOT HOW... IMPRESSIVE... SOME GIRLS CAN BE.
COMPETITION, HUH? WHAT'S THE PRIZE?
HA HA
ホホ
NOTHING. IT'S STUPID.
IT'S KINDA CONFUSING, BUT I THINK THE GIRL WITH THE BEST BOOBS GETS NEGI-SENSEI.
HM?!
あっ
WHAAAAAT?

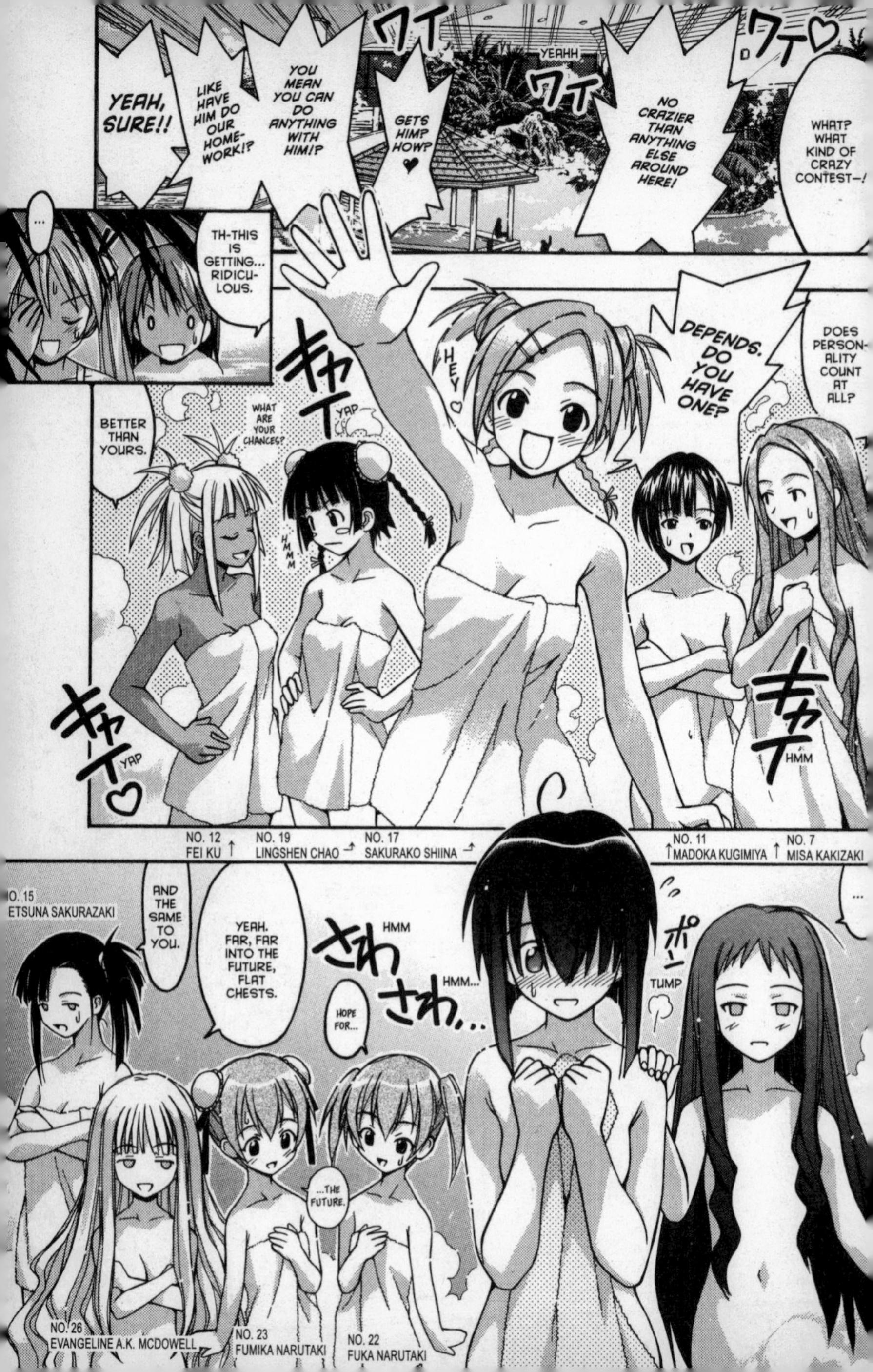
WHAT? WHAT KIND OF CRAZY CONTEST—!
NO CRAZIER THAN ANYTHING ELSE AROUND HERE!
YEAHH
GETS HIM? HOW? ♥
YOU MEAN YOU CAN DO ANYTHING WITH HIM!?
LIKE HAVE HIM DO OUR HOMEWORK!?
YEAH, SURE!!
TH-THIS IS GETTING... RIDICULOUS.
...
DOES PERSONALITY COUNT AT ALL?
DEPENDS. DO YOU HAVE ONE?
HEY ♡
YAP
WHAT ARE YOUR CHANCES?
HMMM
BETTER THAN YOURS.
YAP
HMM
NO. 7 MISA KAKIZAKI
NO. 11 MADOKA KUGIMIYA
NO. 17 SAKURAKO SHIINA
NO. 19 LINGSHEN CHAO
NO. 12 FEI KU
...
TUMP
HMM
HMM...
YEAH. FAR, FAR INTO THE FUTURE, FLAT CHESTS.
AND THE SAME TO YOU.
HOPE FOR...
...THE FUTURE.
NO. 15 ETSUNA SAKURAZAKI
NO. 26 EVANGELINE A.K. MCDOWELL
NO. 23 FUMIKA NARUTAKI
NO. 22 FUKA NARUTAKI

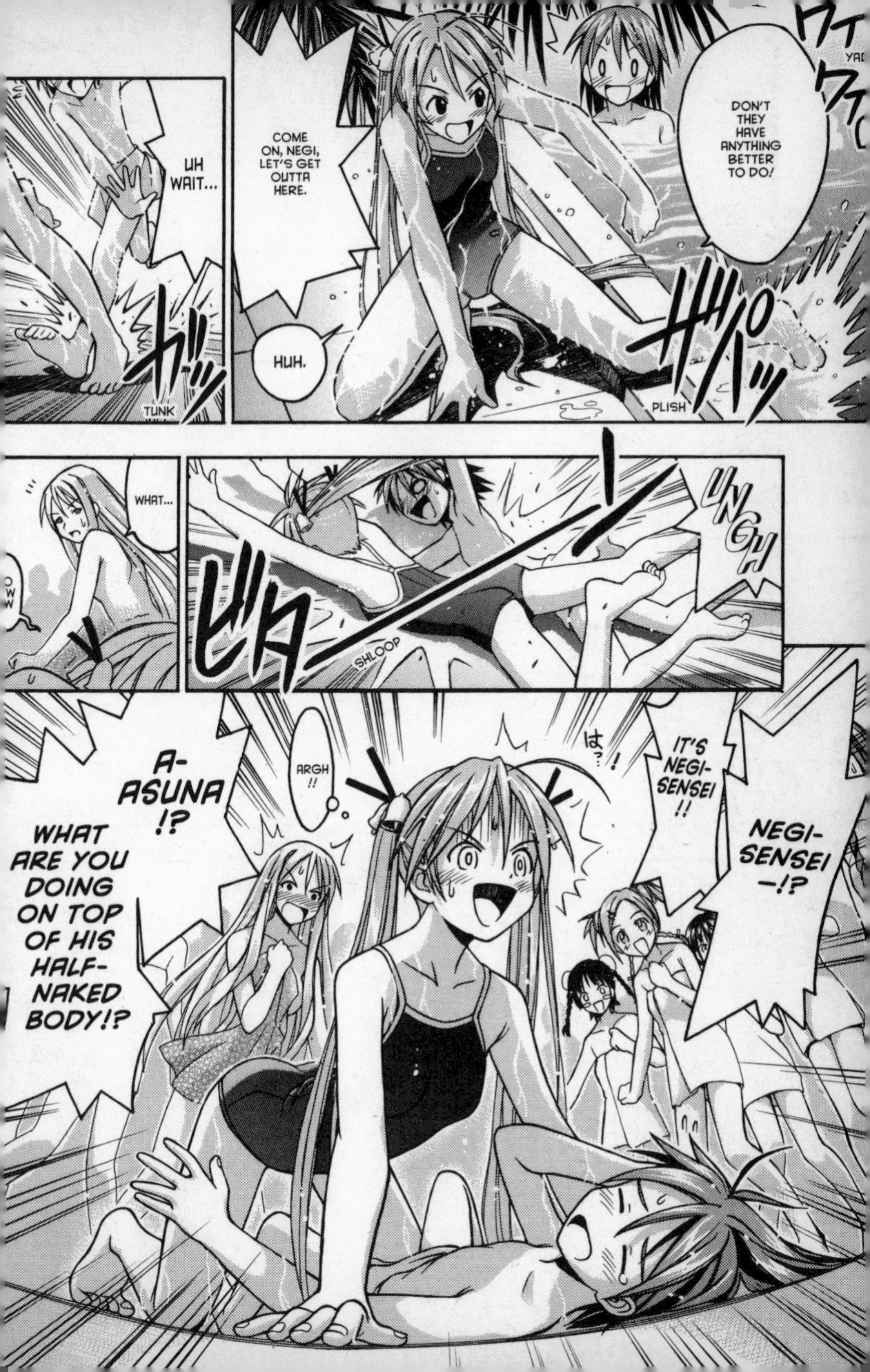
DON'T THEY HAVE ANYTHING BETTER TO DO!
PLISH
COME ON, NEGI, LET'S GET OUTTA HERE.
HUH.
UH WAIT...
TUNK
UNGH
SHLOOP
WHAT...
NEGI-SENSEI—!?
IT'S NEGI-SENSEI!!
はっ!
ARGH!!
A-ASUNA!?
WHAT ARE YOU DOING ON TOP OF HIS HALF-NAKED BODY!?

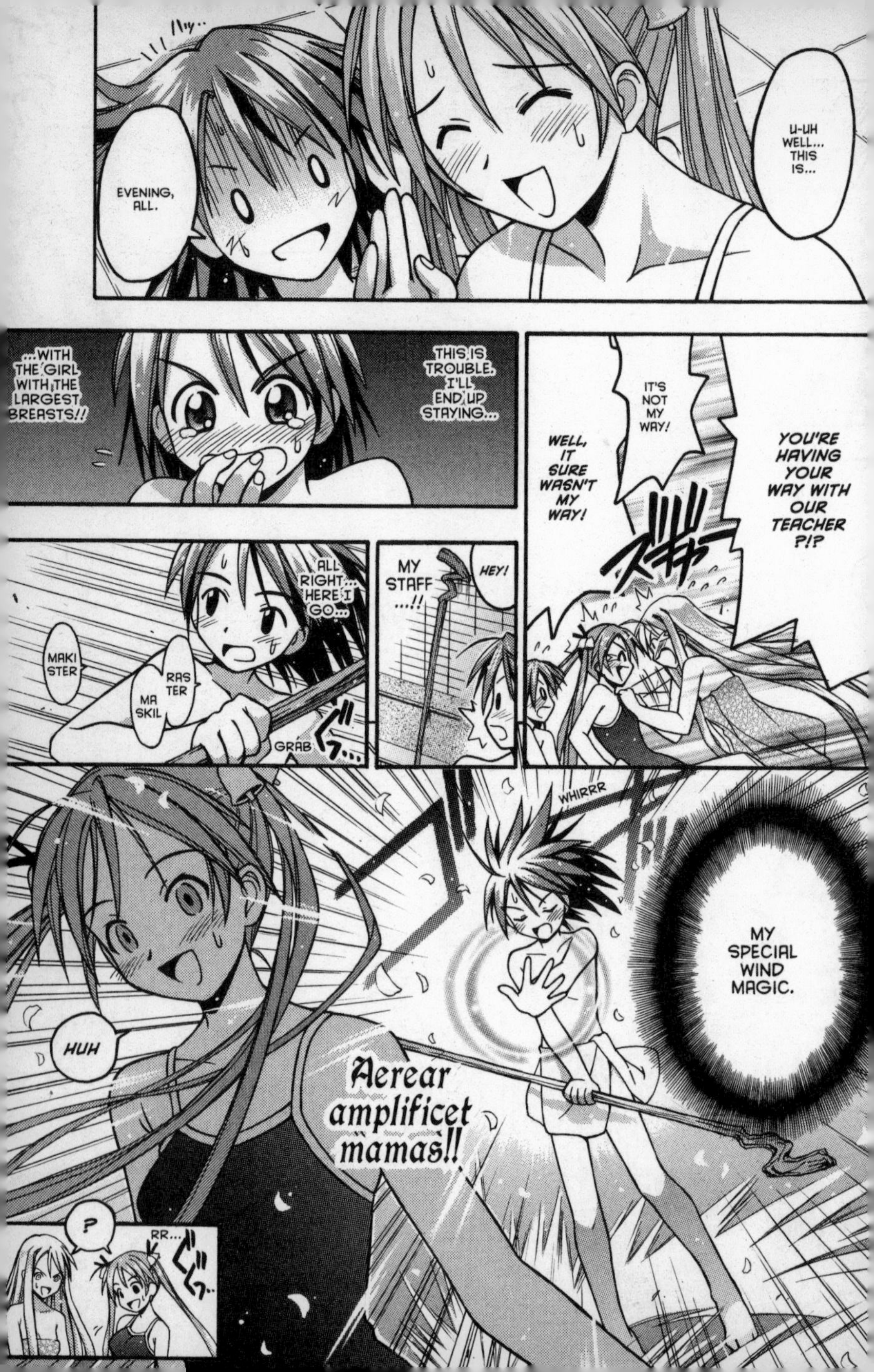

ハッ…
U-UH WELL... THIS IS...
EVENING, ALL.
YOU'RE HAVING YOUR WAY WITH OUR TEACHER?!?
IT'S NOT MY WAY!
WELL, IT SURE WASN'T MY WAY!
THIS IS TROUBLE. I'LL END UP STAYING...
...WITH THE GIRL WITH THE LARGEST BREASTS!!
HEY!
MY STAFF ...!!
ALL RIGHT... HERE I GO...
RASTER MASKIL MAKISTER
GRAB
WHIRRR
MY SPECIAL WIND MAGIC.
Aerear amplificet mamas!!
HUH
?
RR...

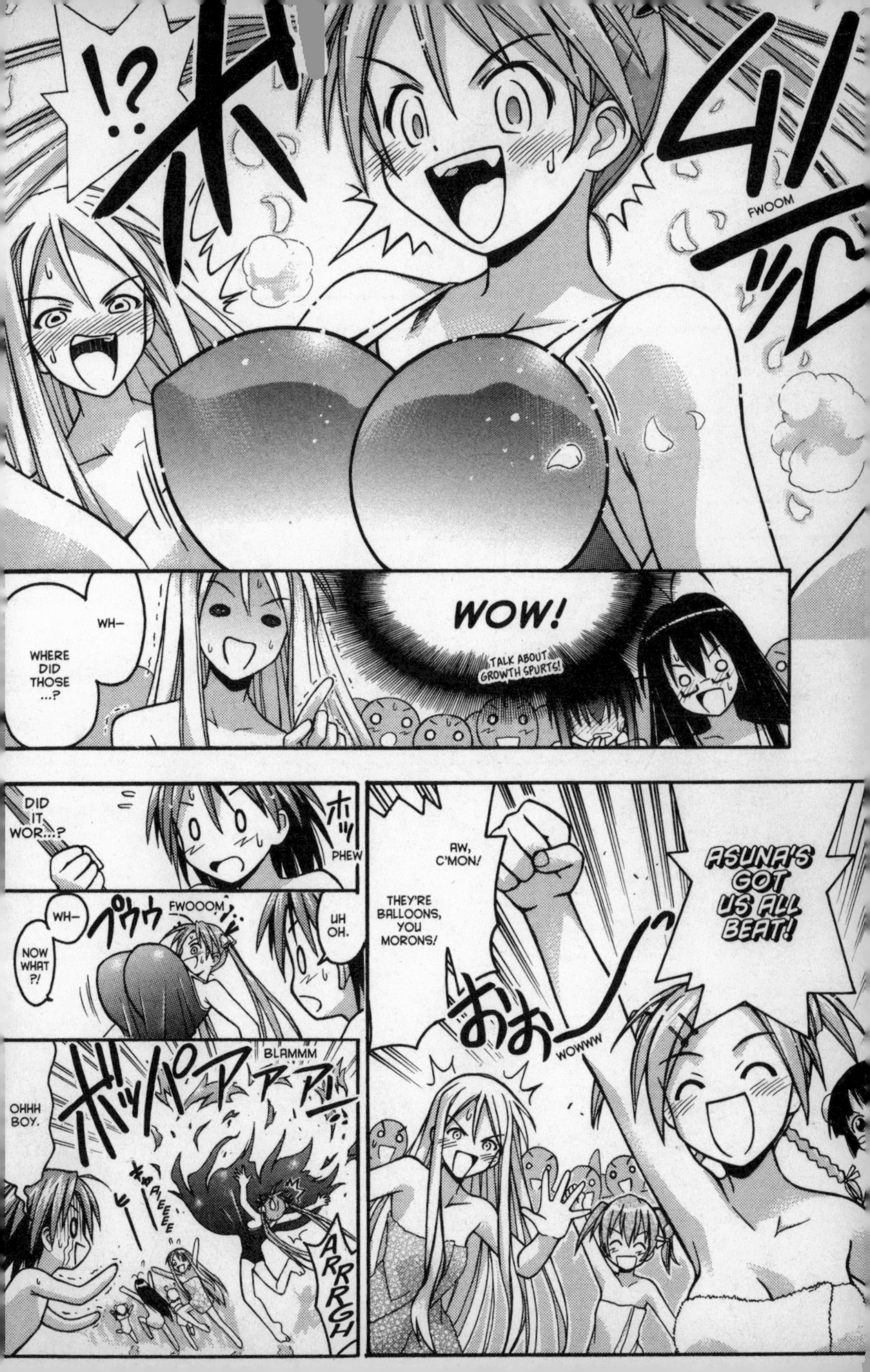

!?
FWOOM
WOW!
TALK ABOUT GROWTH SPURTS!
WH—
WHERE DID THOSE ...?
ASUNA'S GOT US ALL BEAT!
AW, C'MON!
THEY'RE BALLOONS, YOU MORONS!
おおー
WOWWW
PHEW
DID IT WOR...?
UH OH.
プウウ
FWOOOM
WH—
NOW WHAT?!
BLAMMM
ARRRGH
AIEEE
OHHH BOY.

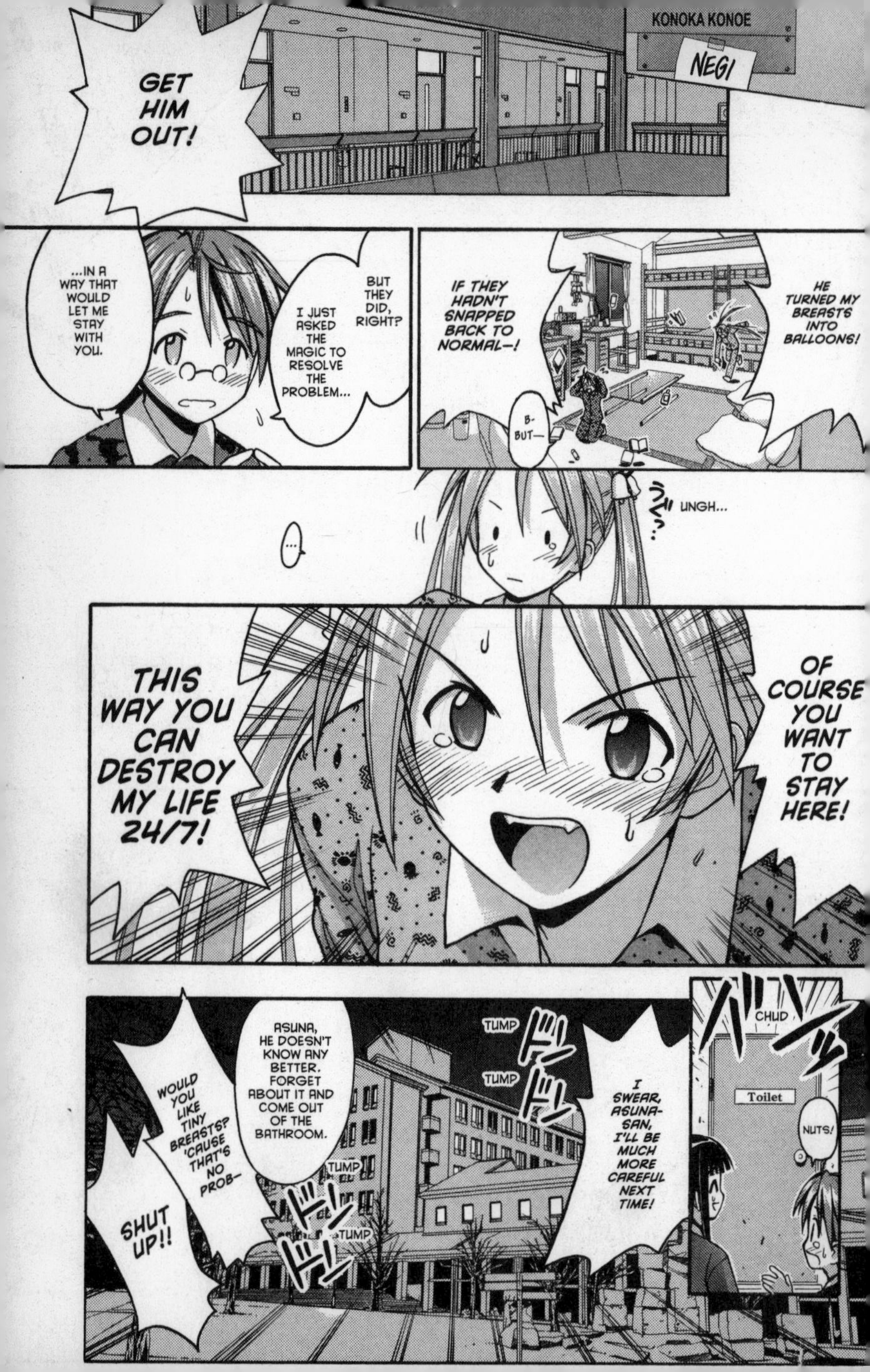
KONOKA KONOE
NEGI
GET HIM OUT!
HE TURNED MY BREASTS INTO BALLOONS!
IF THEY HADN'T SNAPPED BACK TO NORMAL—!
B-BUT—
BUT THEY DID, RIGHT?
I JUST ASKED THE MAGIC TO RESOLVE THE PROBLEM...
...IN A WAY THAT WOULD LET ME STAY WITH YOU.
UNGH...
...
OF COURSE YOU WANT TO STAY HERE!
THIS WAY YOU CAN DESTROY MY LIFE 24/7!
CHUD
Toilet
NUTS!
I SWEAR, ASUNA-SAN, I'LL BE MUCH MORE CAREFUL NEXT TIME!
TUMP
TUMP
ASUNA, HE DOESN'T KNOW ANY BETTER. FORGET ABOUT IT AND COME OUT OF THE BATHROOM.
WOULD YOU LIKE TINY BREASTS? 'CAUSE THAT'S NO PROB—
TUMP
TUMP
SHUT UP!!

★★★ 2-A STUDENT PROFILE ★★★

STUDENT NUMBER 4
YUE AYASE (LEFT)
BIRTHDATE: NOVEMBER 16, 1988
BLOODTYPE: AB
FAVORITE THINGS: READING
DISLIKES: STUDYING FOR SCHOOL
CLUB ACTIVITIES: CHILDREN'S LITERATURE STUDY GROUP,
PHILOSOPHY STUDY GROUP,
LIBRARY CLUB

STUDENT NUMBER 14
HARUNA SAOTOME (RIGHT)
BIRTHDATE: AUGUST 18, 1988
BLOODTYPE: B
FAVORITE THINGS: TEA CEREMONY;
LOTS OF TROUBLE
DISLIKES: REPTILES, DEADLINES
CLUB ACTIVITIES: MANGA CLUB,
LIBRARY EXPLORATION
GROUP
REMARKS: PSEUDONYM "PAL"

STUDENT NUMBER 27
NODOKA MIYAZAKI (MIDDLE)
BIRTHDATE: MAY 10, 1988
BLOODTYPE: O
FAVORITE THINGS: TO BE SURROUNDED BY BOOKS,
ORGANIZING BOOKS
DISLIKES: GUYS
CLUB ACTIVITIES: GENERAL LIBRARY COMMITTEE MEMBER,
LIBRARY REPRESENTATIVE,
LIBRARY CLUB

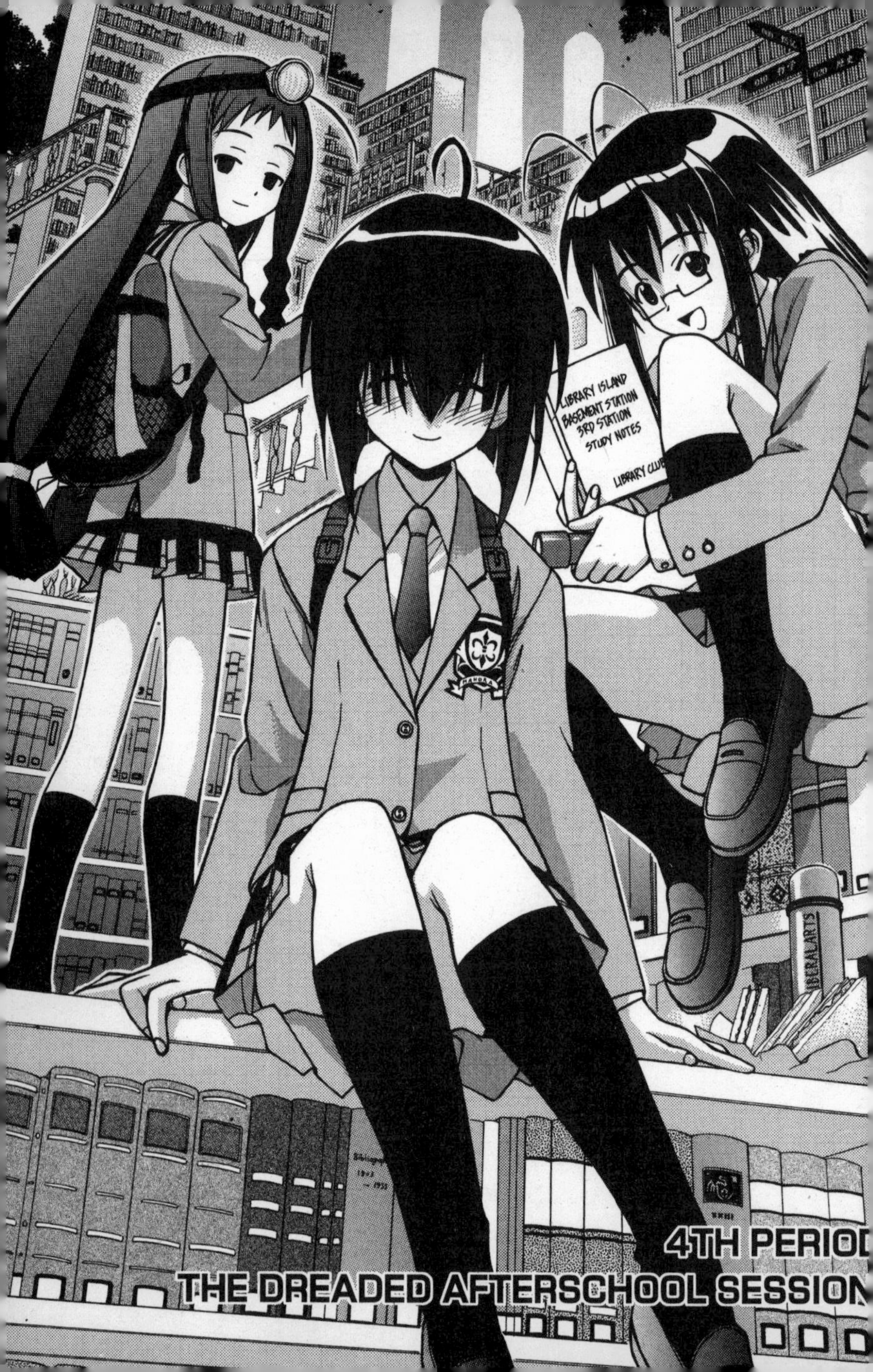
LIBRARY ISLAND
BASEMENT STATION
3RD STATION
STUDY NOTES
LIBRARY CLUB
LIBERAL ARTS
4TH PERIOD
THE DREADED AFTERSCHOOL SESSION

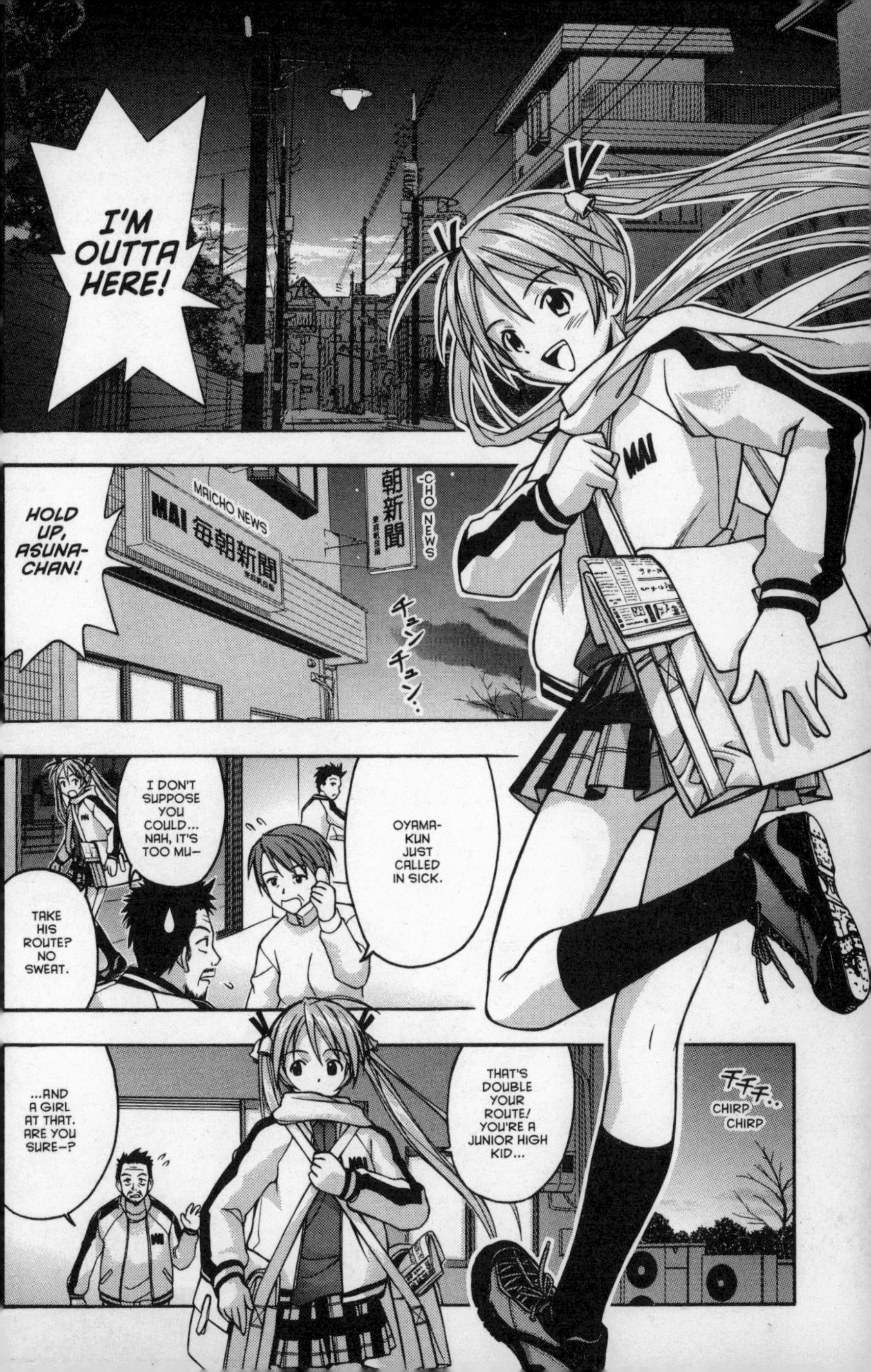
I'M OUTTA HERE!
MAICHO NEWS
MAI 毎朝新聞
朝新聞
-CHO NEWS
チュンチュン…
HOLD UP, ASUNA-CHAN!
OYAMA-KUN JUST CALLED IN SICK.
I DON'T SUPPOSE YOU COULD... NAH, IT'S TOO MU—
TAKE HIS ROUTE? NO SWEAT.
チチチ…
CHIRP CHIRP
THAT'S DOUBLE YOUR ROUTE! YOU'RE A JUNIOR HIGH KID...
...AND A GIRL AT THAT. ARE YOU SURE—?

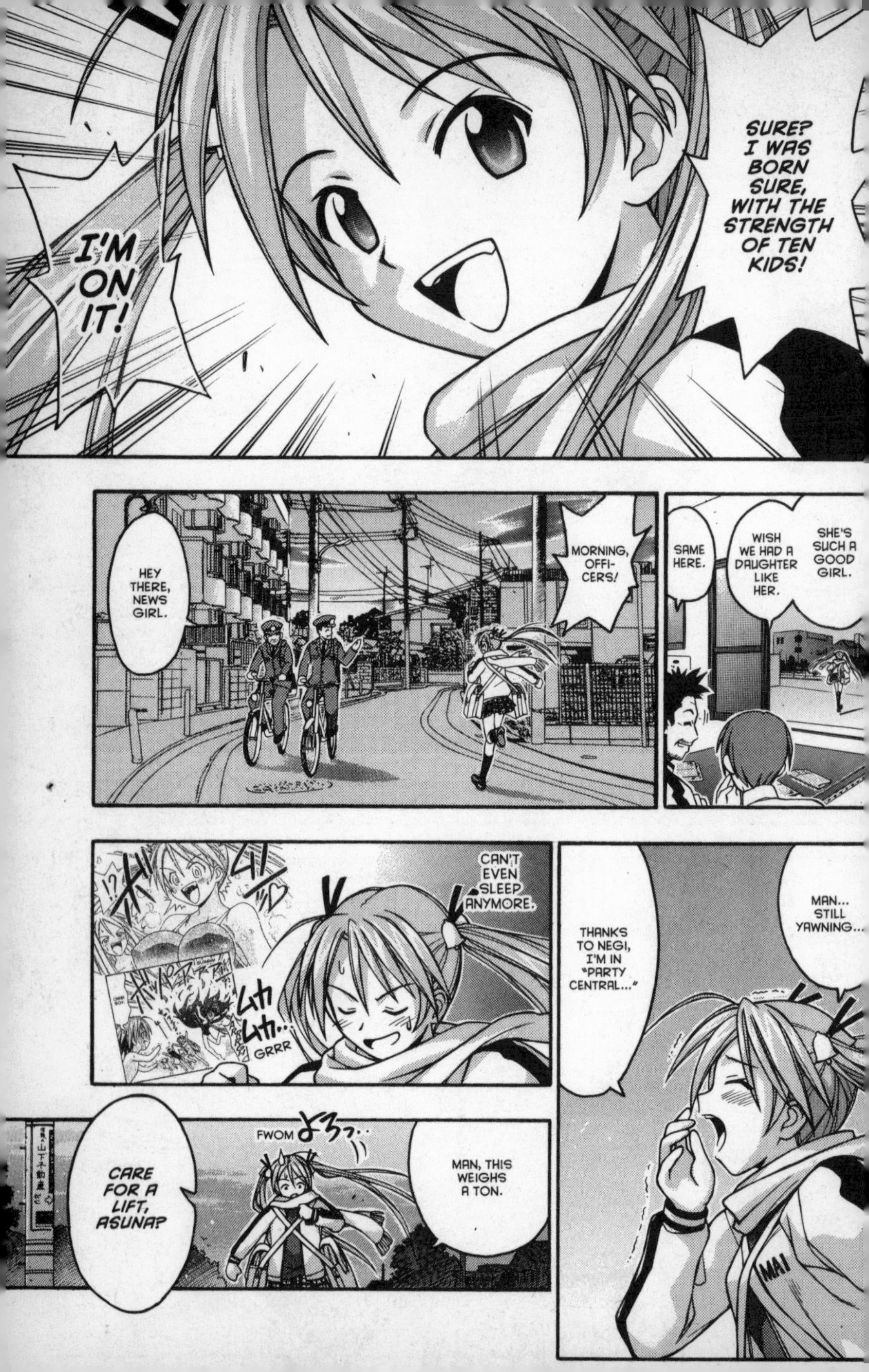
SURE? I WAS BORN SURE, WITH THE STRENGTH OF TEN KIDS!
I'M ON IT!
SHE'S SUCH A GOOD GIRL.
WISH WE HAD A DAUGHTER LIKE HER.
SAME HERE.
MORNING, OFFICERS!
HEY THERE, NEWS GIRL.
MAN... STILL YAWNING...
THANKS TO NEGI, I'M IN "PARTY CENTRAL..."
MAI
CAN'T EVEN SLEEP ANYMORE.
GRRR
MAN, THIS WEIGHS A TON.
FWOM
CARE FOR A LIFT, ASUNA?

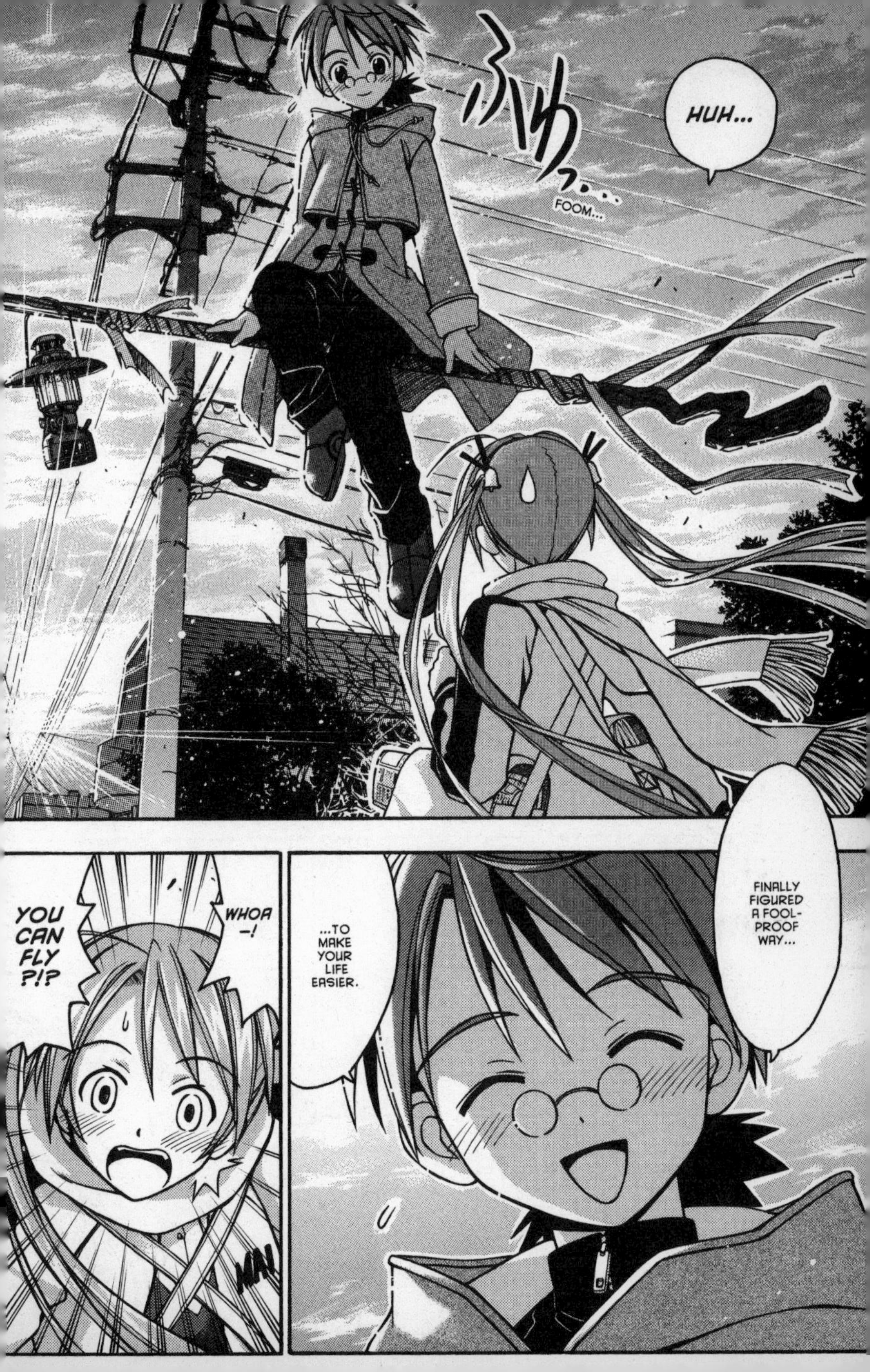
HUH...
ふわっ...
FOOM...
FINALLY FIGURED A FOOL-PROOF WAY...
...TO MAKE YOUR LIFE EASIER.
WHOA—!
YOU CAN FLY?!?

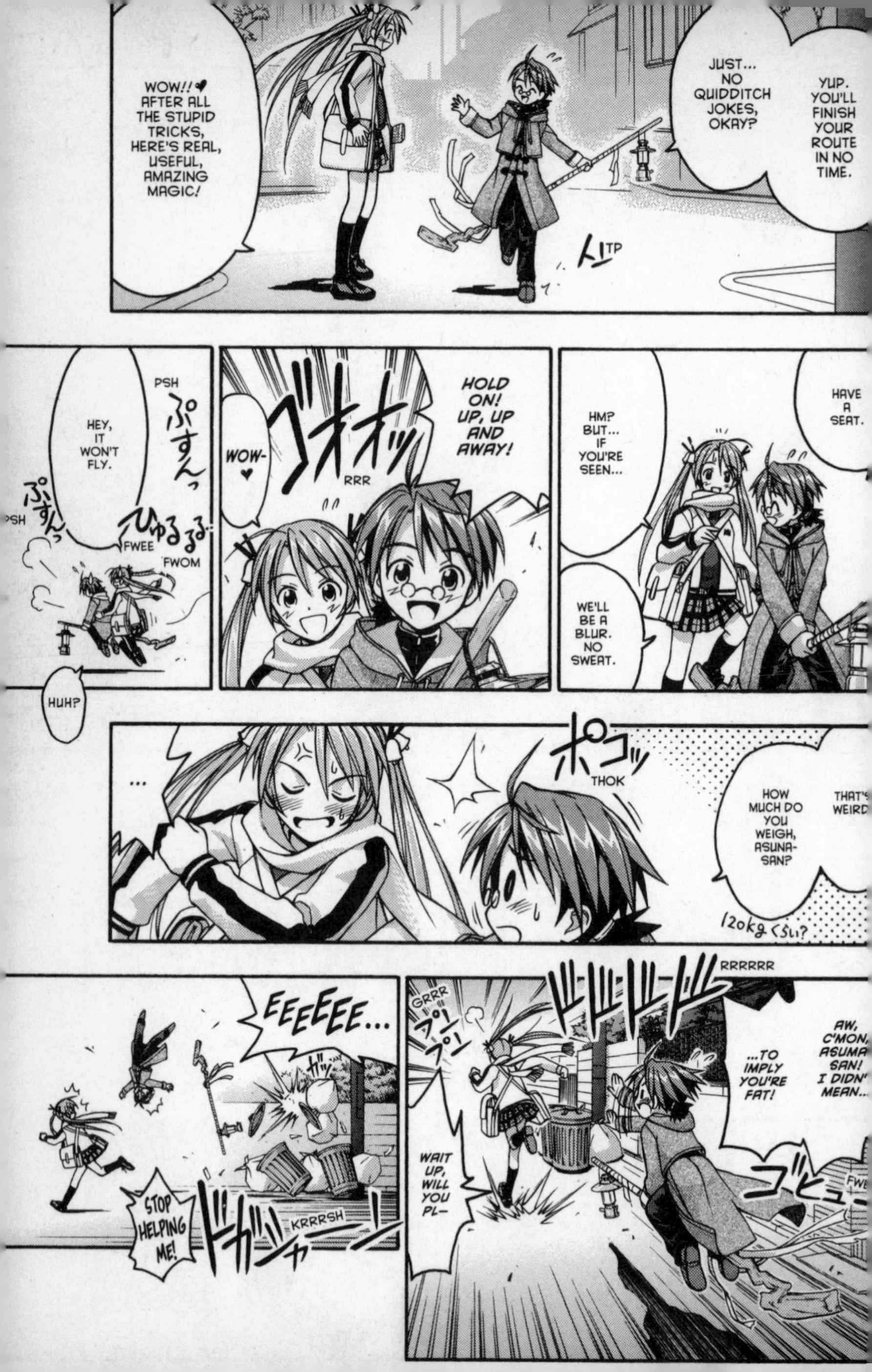
YUP. YOU'LL FINISH YOUR ROUTE IN NO TIME.
JUST... NO QUIDDITCH JOKES, OKAY?
TP
WOW!!♥ AFTER ALL THE STUPID TRICKS, HERE'S REAL, USEFUL, AMAZING MAGIC!
HAVE A SEAT.
HM? BUT... IF YOU'RE SEEN...
WE'LL BE A BLUR. NO SWEAT.
HOLD ON! UP, UP AND AWAY!
ゴオオッ
RRR
WOW-♥
ぷすんっ
PSH
HEY, IT WON'T FLY.
ぷすんっ
PSH
ひゅるるる
FWEE
FWOM
HUH?
THAT'S WEIRD
HOW MUCH DO YOU WEIGH, ASUNA-SAN?
120kgくらい?
ポコッ
THOK
...
AW, C'MON, ASUNA SAN! I DIDN' MEAN...
...TO IMPLY YOU'RE FAT!
ドドドドド
RRRRRR
ゴヒュー
FWE
プンプン
GRRR
WAIT UP, WILL YOU PL—
EEEEEE...
ガッ
ドガシャーン
KRRRSH
STOP HELPING ME!

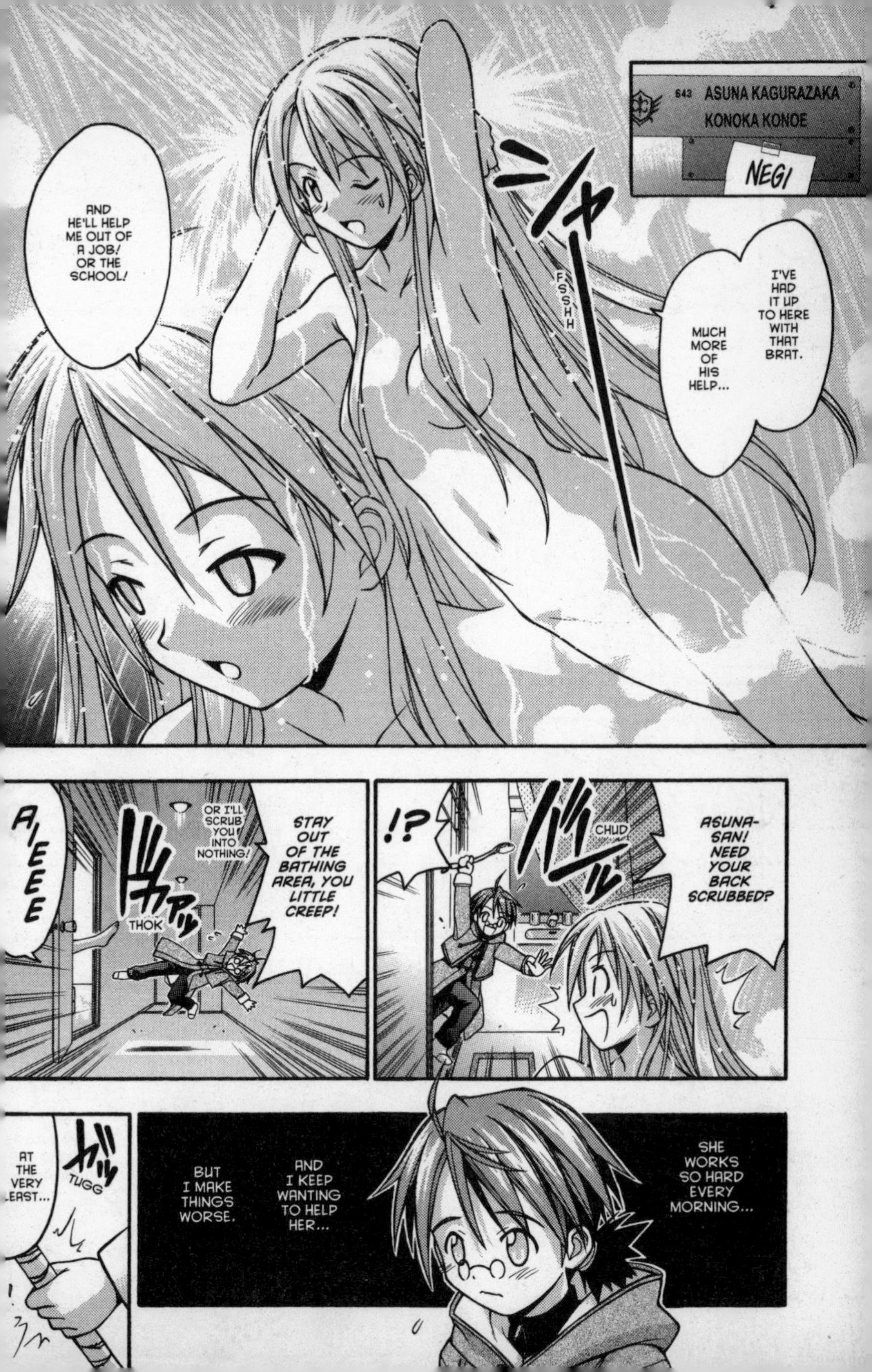
643 ASUNA KAGURAZAKA
KONOKA KONOE
NEGI
I'VE HAD IT UP TO HERE WITH THAT BRAT.
MUCH MORE OF HIS HELP...
FSSHH
AND HE'LL HELP ME OUT OF A JOB! OR THE SCHOOL!
ASUNA-SAN! NEED YOUR BACK SCRUBBED?
CHUD
!?
STAY OUT OF THE BATHING AREA, YOU LITTLE CREEP!
OR I'LL SCRUB YOU INTO NOTHING!
THOK
AIEEEE
SHE WORKS SO HARD EVERY MORNING...
AND I KEEP WANTING TO HELP HER...
BUT I MAKE THINGS WORSE.
TUGG
AT THE VERY LEAST...

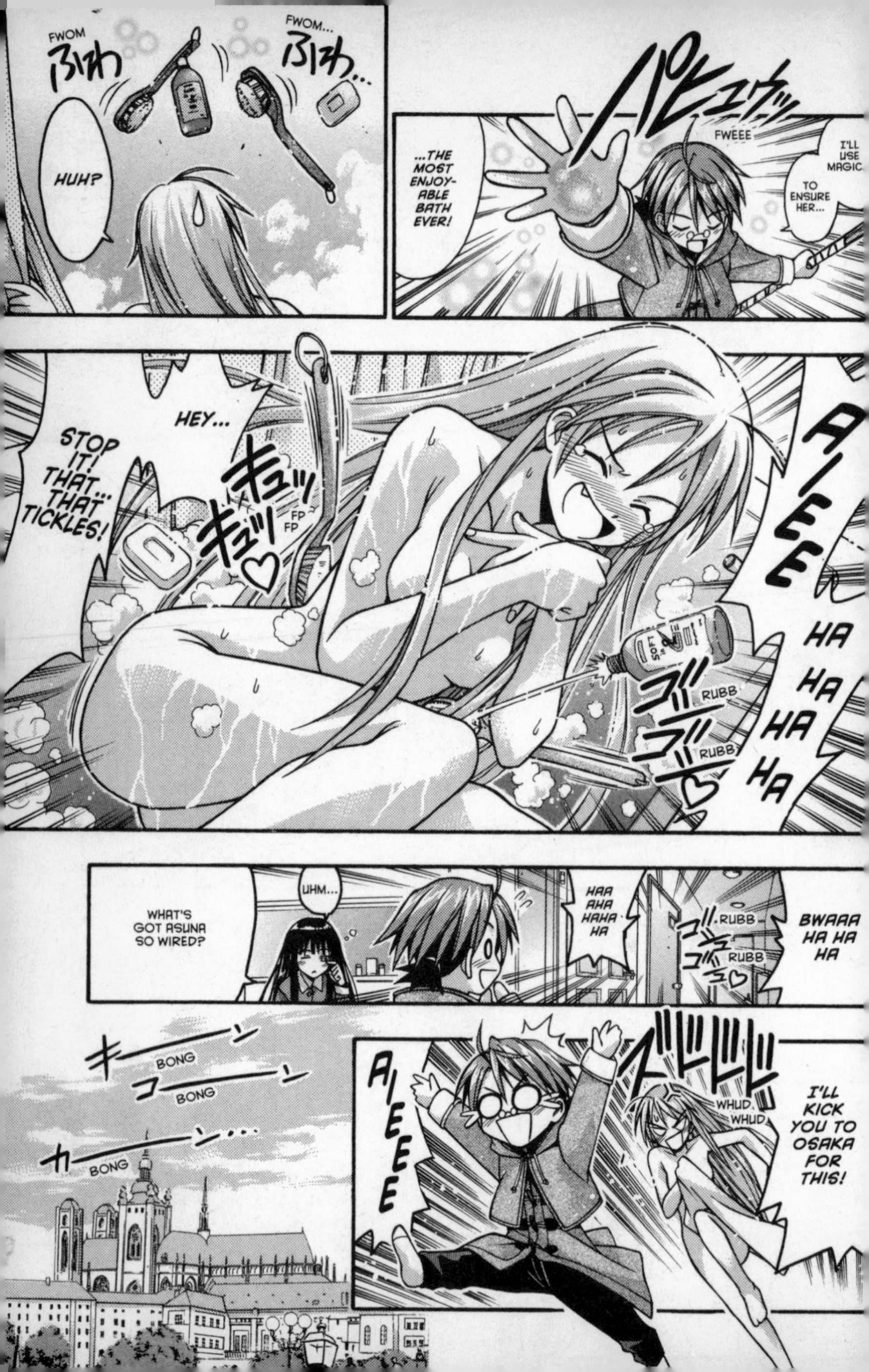
FWEEE
I'LL USE MAGIC
TO ENSURE HER...
...THE MOST ENJOYABLE BATH EVER!
FWOM
ふわ
FWOM...
ふわ...
HUH?
AIEEE
HA HA HA HA HA
RUBB
RUBB
HEY...
STOP IT! THAT... THAT TICKLES!
FP FP
BWAAA HA HA HA
RUBB
RUBB
HAA AHA HAHA HA
UHM...
WHAT'S GOT ASUNA SO WIRED?
I'LL KICK YOU TO OSAKA FOR THIS!
WHUD
WHUD
AIEEE
BONG
BONG
BONG

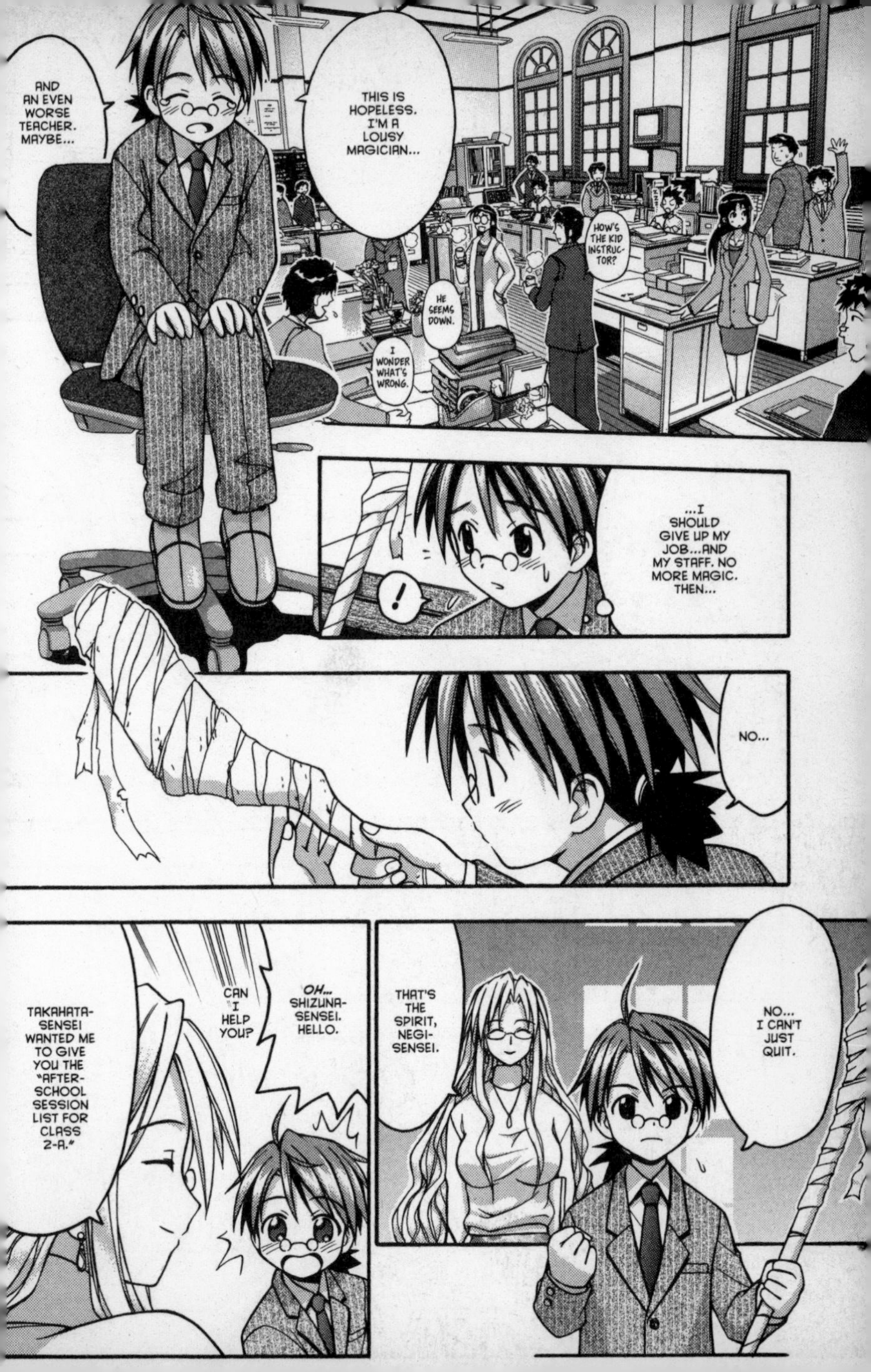
HOW'S THE KID INSTRUCTOR?
HE SEEMS DOWN.
I WONDER WHAT'S WRONG.
THIS IS HOPELESS. I'M A LOUSY MAGICIAN...
AND AN EVEN WORSE TEACHER. MAYBE...
...I SHOULD GIVE UP MY JOB...AND MY STAFF. NO MORE MAGIC. THEN...
!
NO...
NO... I CAN'T JUST QUIT.
THAT'S THE SPIRIT, NEGI-SENSEI.
OH... SHIZUNA-SENSEI. HELLO.
CAN I HELP YOU?
TAKAHATA-SENSEI WANTED ME TO GIVE YOU THE "AFTER-SCHOOL SESSION LIST FOR CLASS 2-A."

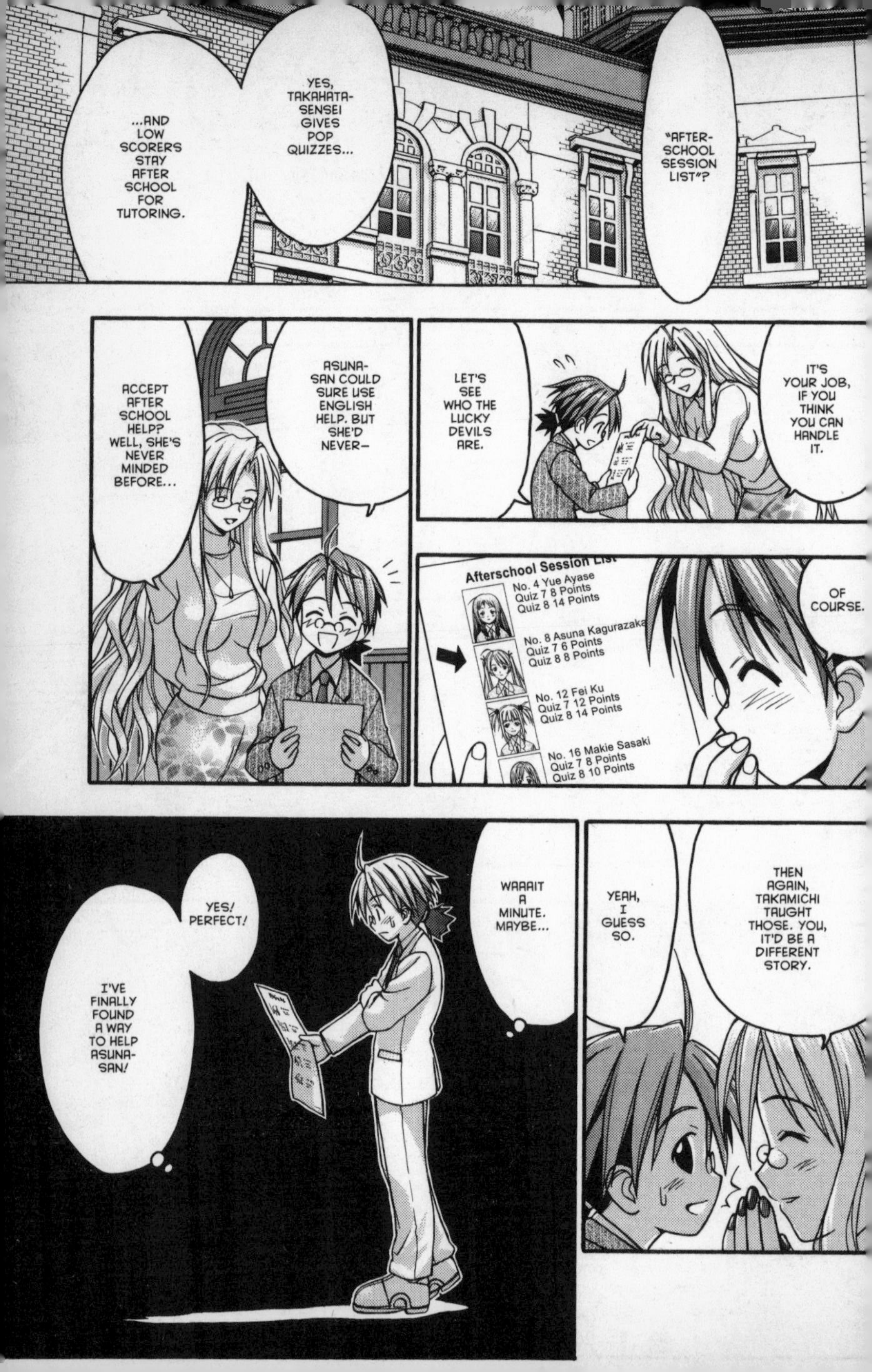
"AFTER-SCHOOL SESSION LIST"?
YES, TAKAHATA-SENSEI GIVES POP QUIZZES...
...AND LOW SCORERS STAY AFTER SCHOOL FOR TUTORING.
IT'S YOUR JOB, IF YOU THINK YOU CAN HANDLE IT.
LET'S SEE WHO THE LUCKY DEVILS ARE.
OF COURSE.
Afterschool Session List
No. 4 Yue Ayase
Quiz 7 8 Points
Quiz 8 14 Points
No. 8 Asuna Kagurazaka
Quiz 7 6 Points
Quiz 8 8 Points
No. 12 Fei Ku
Quiz 7 12 Points
Quiz 8 14 Points
No. 16 Makie Sasaki
Quiz 7 8 Points
Quiz 8 10 Points
ASUNA-SAN COULD SURE USE ENGLISH HELP. BUT SHE'D NEVER—
ACCEPT AFTER SCHOOL HELP? WELL, SHE'S NEVER MINDED BEFORE...
THEN AGAIN, TAKAMICHI TAUGHT THOSE. YOU, IT'D BE A DIFFERENT STORY.
YEAH, I GUESS SO.
WAAAIT A MINUTE. MAYBE...
YES! PERFECT!
I'VE FINALLY FOUND A WAY TO HELP ASUNA-SAN!

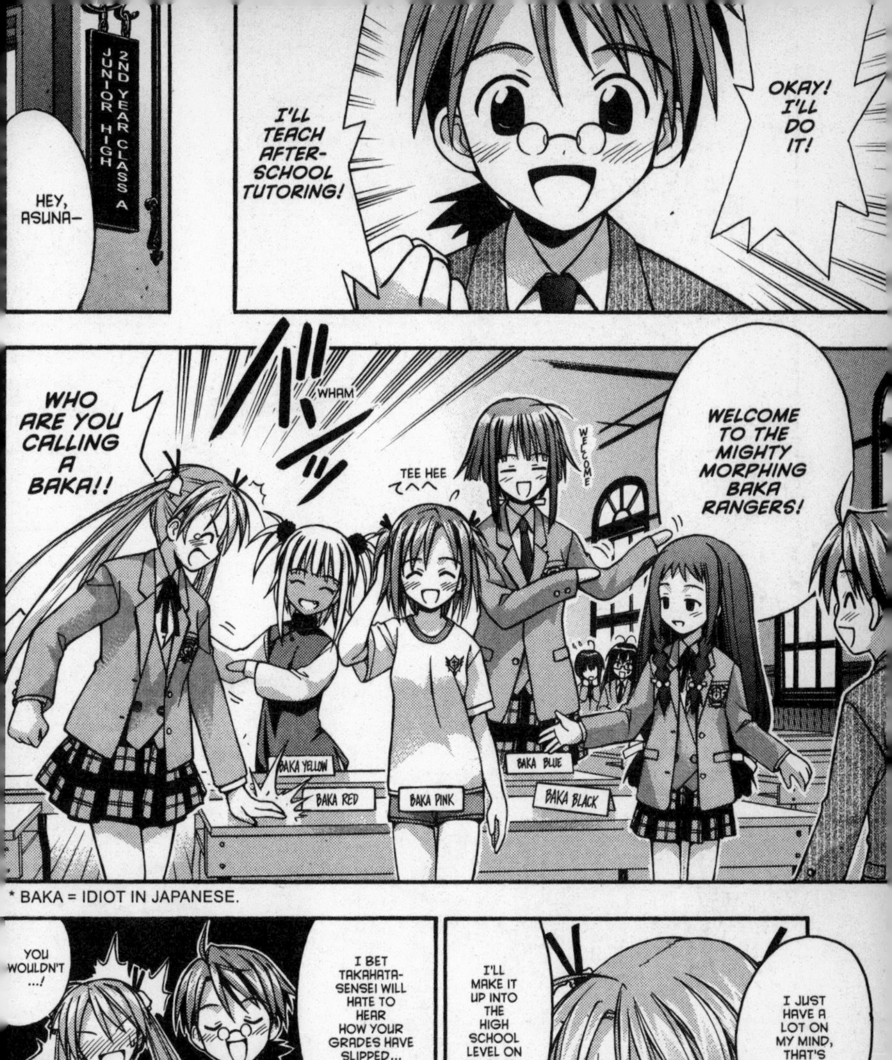
OKAY! I'LL DO IT!
I'LL TEACH AFTER-SCHOOL TUTORING!
2ND YEAR CLASS A JUNIOR HIGH
HEY, ASUNA—
WELCOME TO THE MIGHTY MORPHING BAKA RANGERS!
WELCOME
TEE HEE てへへ
WHAM
WHO ARE YOU CALLING A BAKA!!
BAKA BLUE
BAKA BLACK
BAKA PINK
BAKA YELLOW
BAKA RED

* BAKA = IDIOT IN JAPANESE.

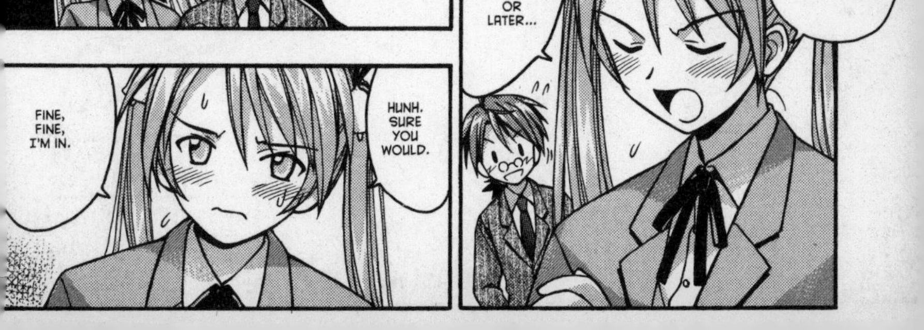
I JUST HAVE A LOT ON MY MIND, THAT'S ALL.
I'LL MAKE IT UP INTO THE HIGH SCHOOL LEVEL ON MY OWN... SOONER OR LATER...
I BET TAKAHATA-SENSEI WILL HATE TO HEAR HOW YOUR GRADES HAVE SLIPPED...
YOU WOULDN'T ...!
HUNH. SURE YOU WOULD.
FINE, FINE, I'M IN.

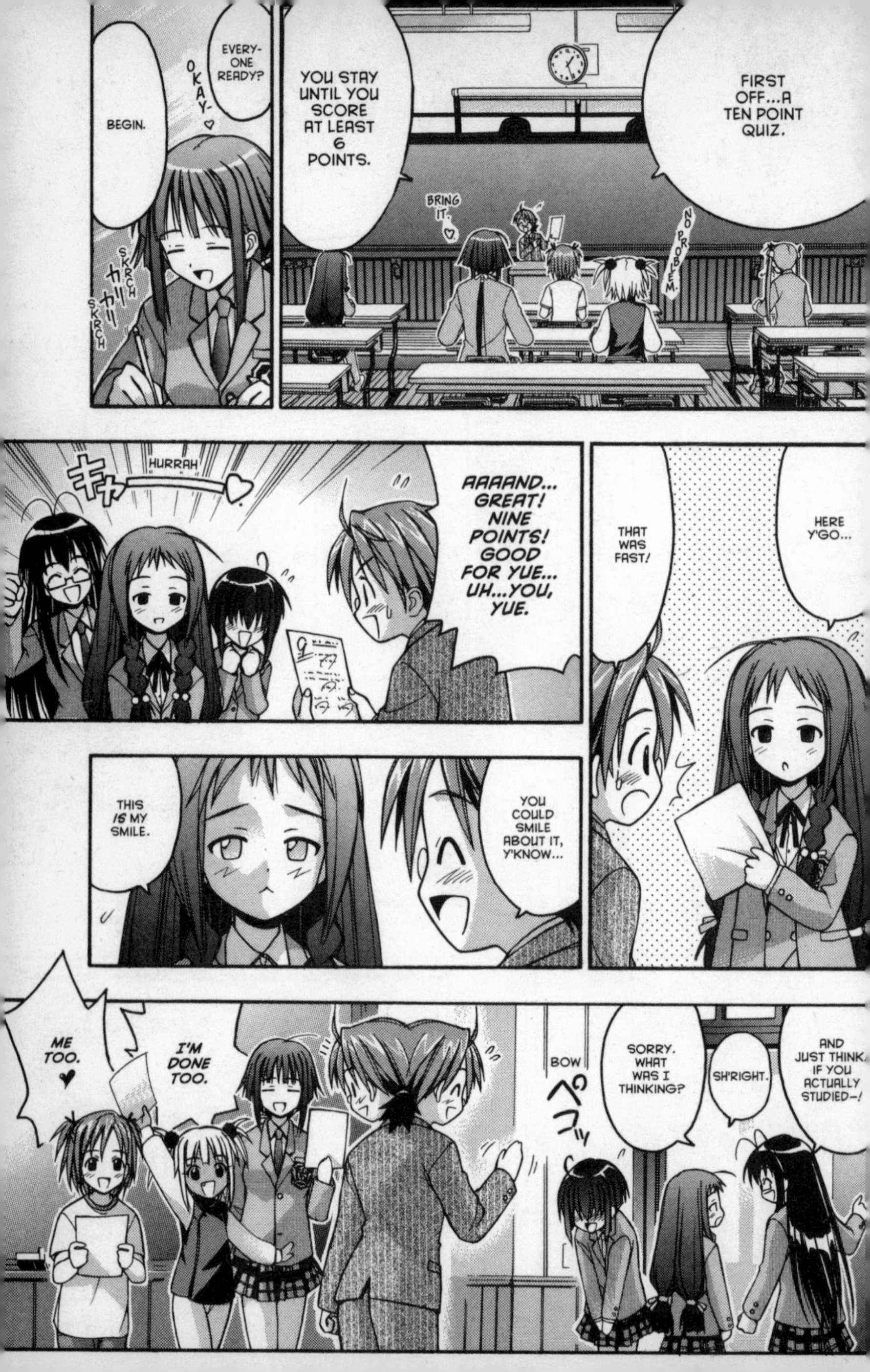
FIRST OFF...A TEN POINT QUIZ.
YOU STAY UNTIL YOU SCORE AT LEAST 6 POINTS.
NO PROBLEM.
BRING IT. ♡
EVERY-ONE READY?
OKAY-♡
BEGIN.
SKRCH
SKRCH
HERE Y'GO...
THAT WAS FAST!
AAAAND... GREAT! NINE POINTS! GOOD FOR YUE... UH...YOU, YUE.
HURRAH
YOU COULD SMILE ABOUT IT, Y'KNOW...
THIS *IS* MY SMILE.
AND JUST THINK IF YOU ACTUALLY STUDIED—!
SH'RIGHT.
SORRY. WHAT WAS I THINKING?
BOW
I'M DONE TOO.
ME TOO. ♥

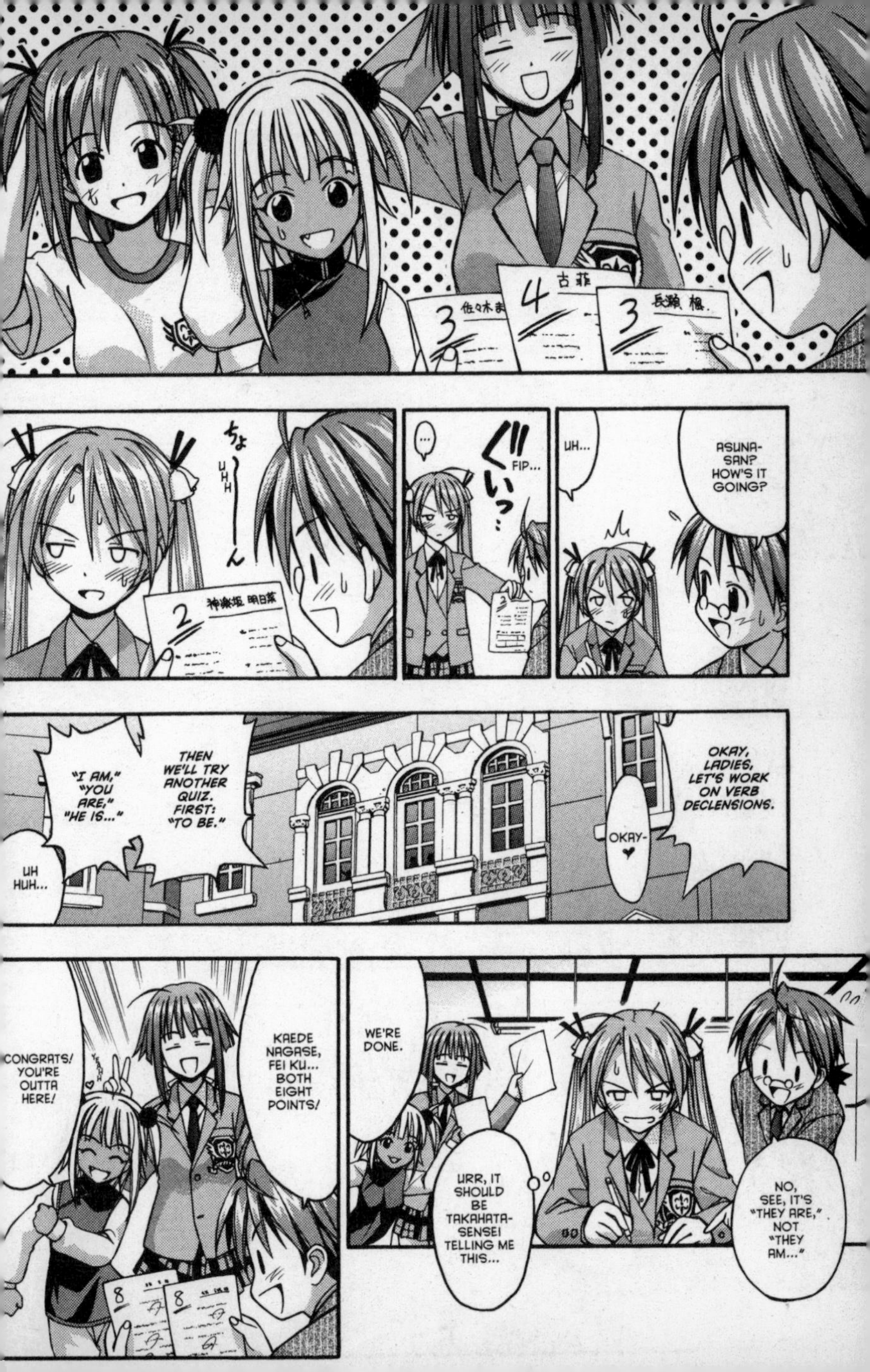
佐々木ま
古菲
長瀬 楓
ASUNA-SAN? HOW'S IT GOING?
UH...
...
ぐいっ
FIP...
UHH
神楽坂 明日菜
OKAY, LADIES, LET'S WORK ON VERB DECLENSIONS.
OKAY-♥
THEN WE'LL TRY ANOTHER QUIZ. FIRST: "TO BE."
"I AM," "YOU ARE," "HE IS..."
UH HUH...
WE'RE DONE.
NO, SEE, IT'S "THEY ARE," NOT "THEY AM..."
URR, IT SHOULD BE TAKAHATA-SENSEI TELLING ME THIS...
KAEDE NAGASE, FEI KU... BOTH EIGHT POINTS!
CONGRATS! YOU'RE OUTTA HERE!

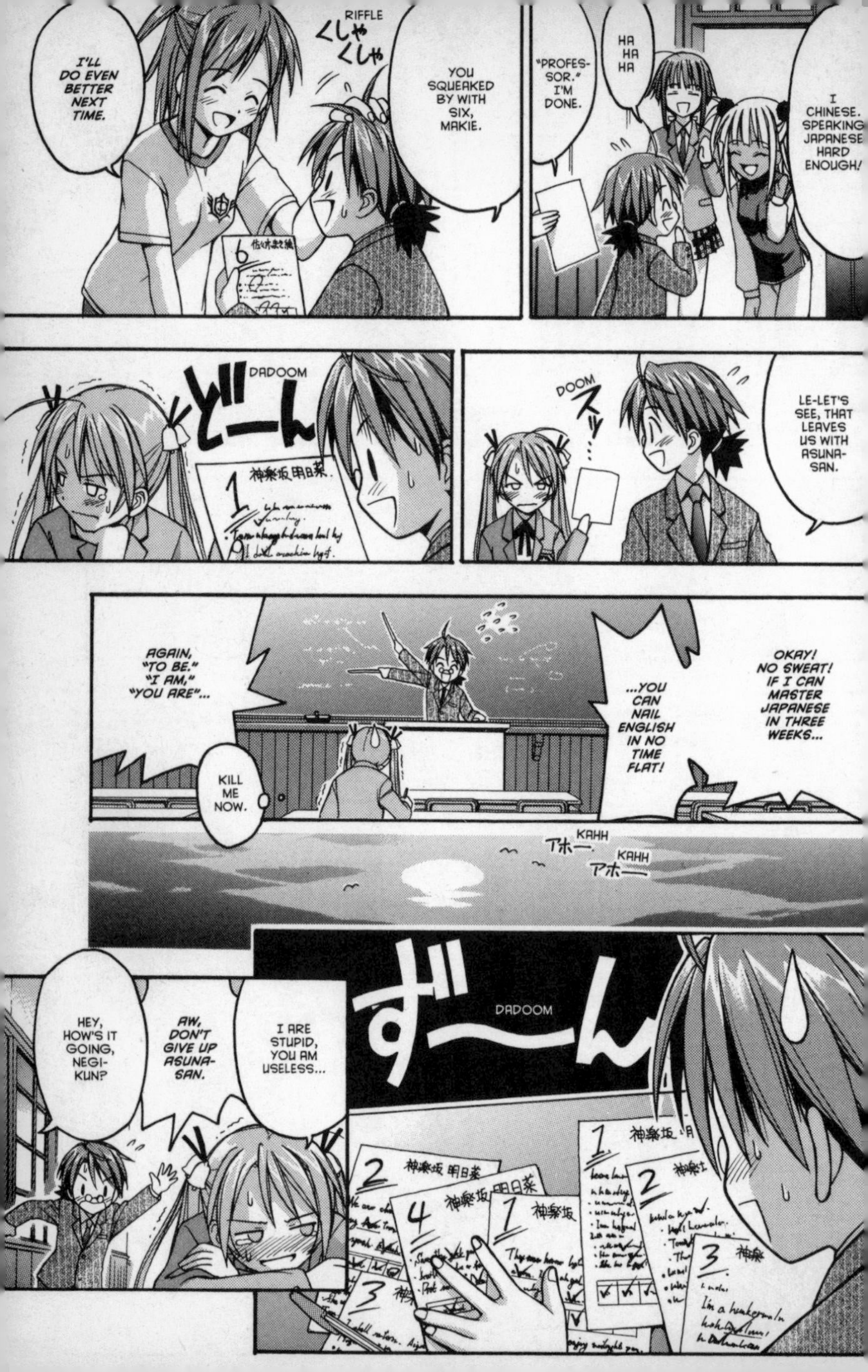
I CHINESE. SPEAKING JAPANESE HARD ENOUGH!
HA HA HA
“PROFES-SOR.” I'M DONE.
YOU SQUEAKED BY WITH SIX, MAKIE.
RIFFLE
くしゃくしゃ
I'LL DO EVEN BETTER NEXT TIME.
LE-LET'S SEE, THAT LEAVES US WITH ASUNA-SAN.
DOOM
スッ…
DADOOM
どーん
神楽坂明日菜
OKAY! NO SWEAT! IF I CAN MASTER JAPANESE IN THREE WEEKS...
...YOU CAN NAIL ENGLISH IN NO TIME FLAT!
AGAIN, “TO BE.” “I AM,” “YOU ARE”...
KILL ME NOW.
KAHH
アホー
KAHH
アホー
DADOOM
ずーん
I ARE STUPID, YOU AM USELESS...
AW, DON'T GIVE UP ASUNA-SAN.
HEY, HOW'S IT GOING, NEGI-KUN?

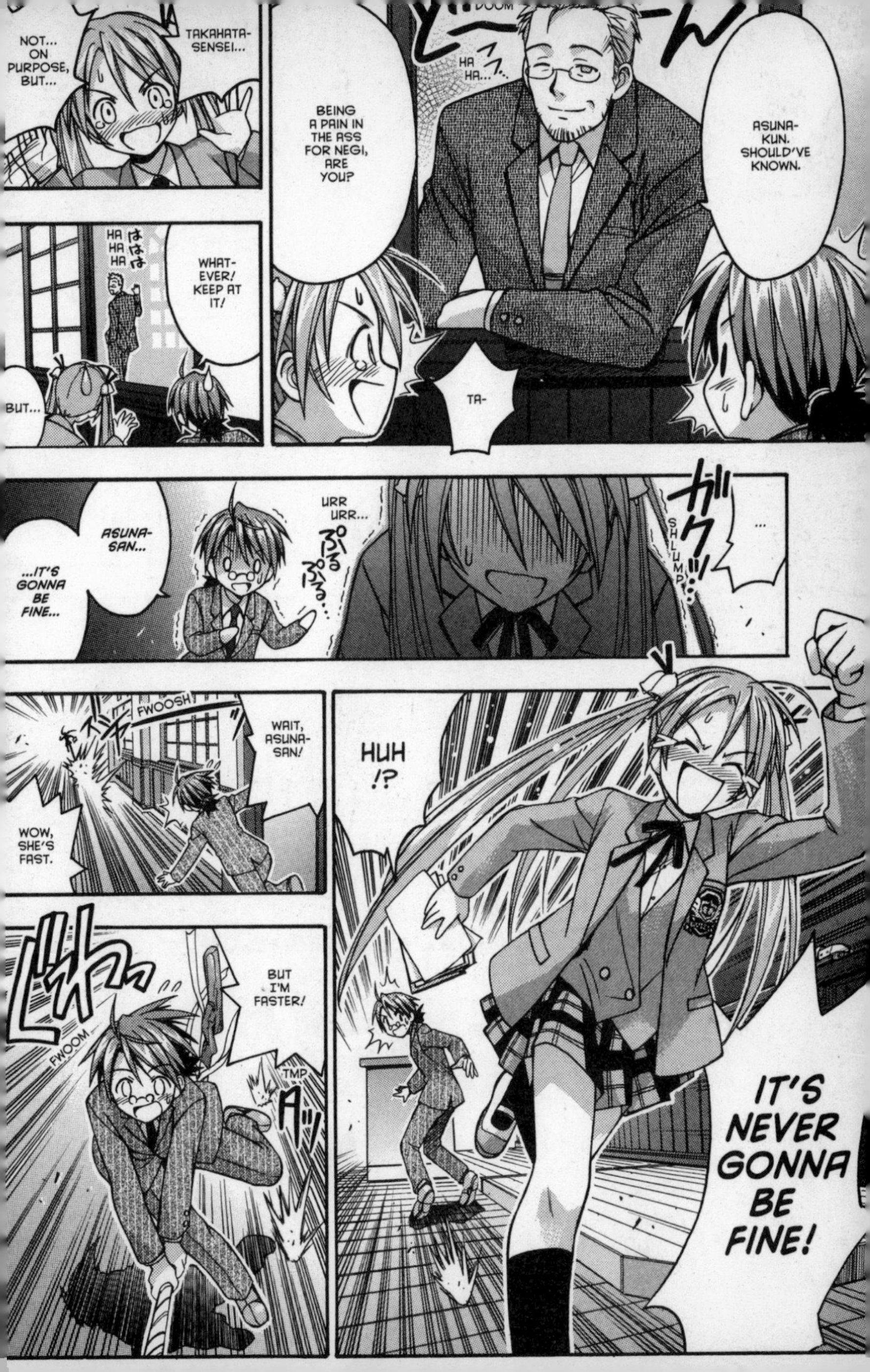
DOOM
ASUNA-KUN. SHOULD'VE KNOWN.
HA HA...
BEING A PAIN IN THE ASS FOR NEGI, ARE YOU?
TA-
TAKAHATA-SENSEI...
NOT... ON PURPOSE, BUT...
HA HA HA ははは
WHAT-EVER! KEEP AT IT!
BUT...
SHLUMP
...
URR URR... ぷるぷる...
ASUNA-SAN...
...IT'S GONNA BE FINE...
IT'S NEVER GONNA BE FINE!
HUH !?
FWOOSH
WAIT, ASUNA-SAN!
WOW, SHE'S FAST.
BUT I'M FASTER!
FWOOM
TMP

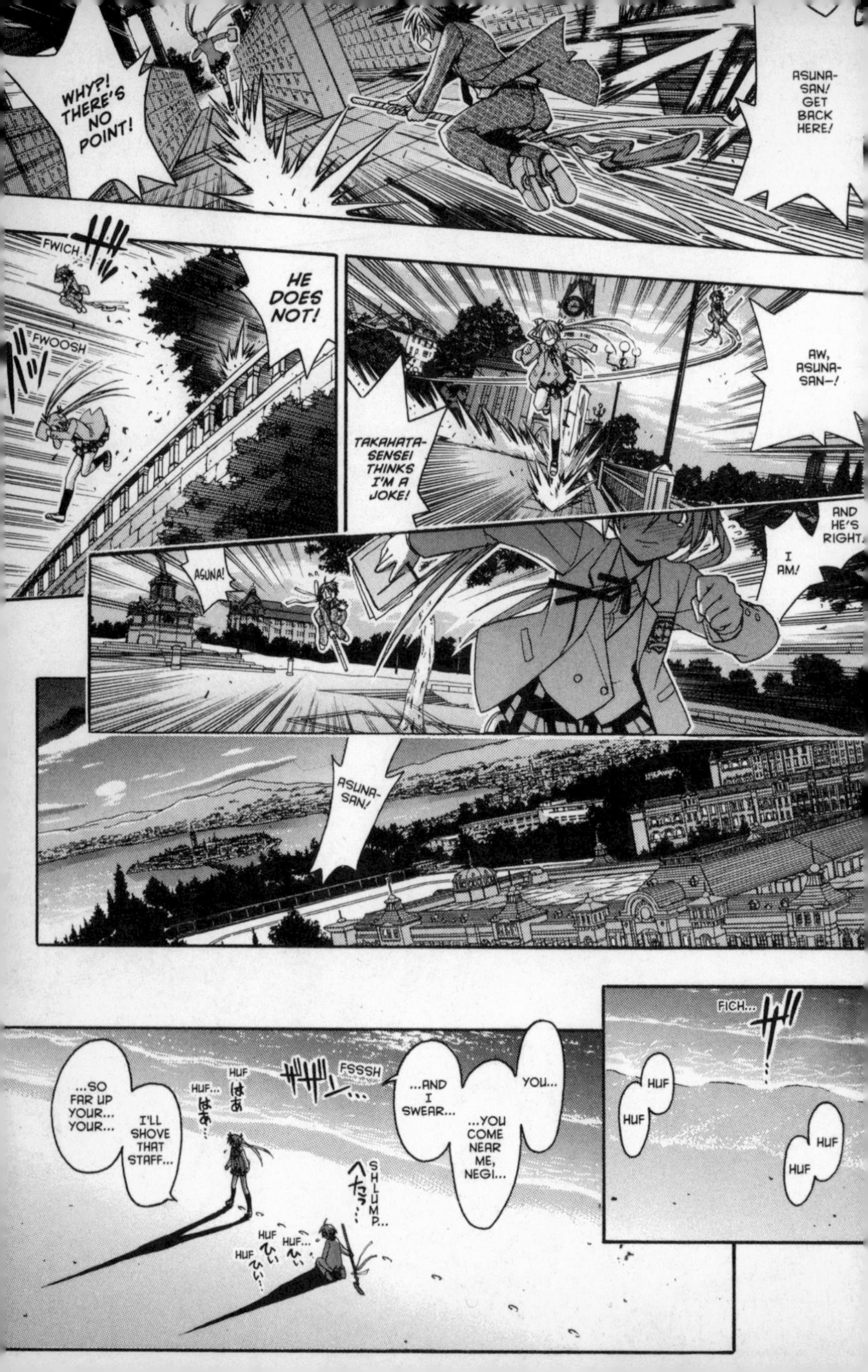
ASUNA-SAN! GET BACK HERE!
WHY?! THERE'S NO POINT!
AW, ASUNA-SAN—!
TAKAHATA-SENSEI THINKS I'M A JOKE!
FWICH
HE DOES NOT!
FWOOSH
AND HE'S RIGHT.
I AM!
ASUNA!
ASUNA-SAN!
FICH...
HUF
HUF
HUF
HUF
YOU...
...YOU COME NEAR ME, NEGI...
...AND I SWEAR...
FSSSH
I'LL SHOVE THAT STAFF...
...SO FAR UP YOUR... YOUR...
HUF はあ
HUF... はあ...
SHLUMP...
HUF... ひい
HUF ひい...

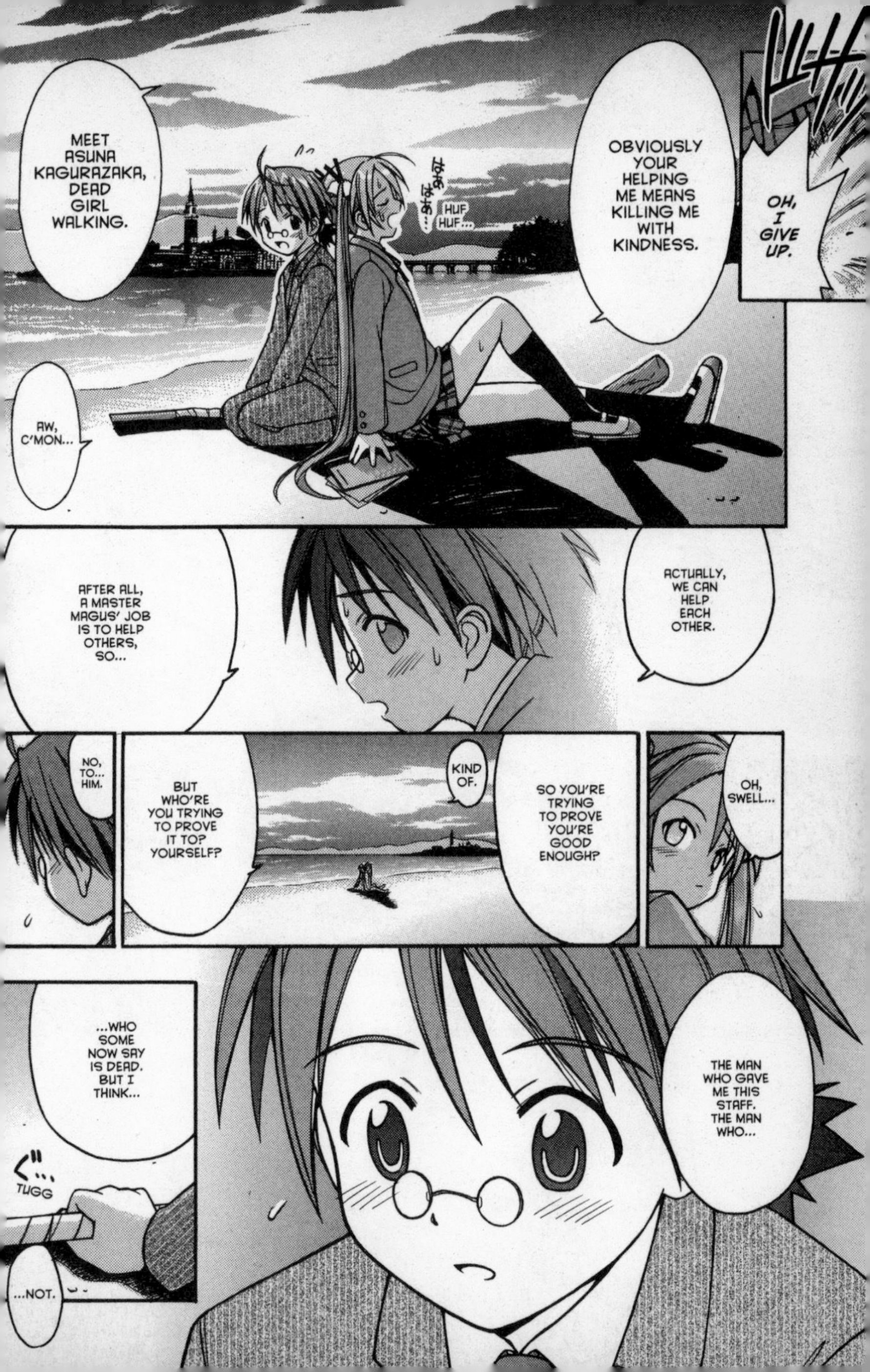
OH, I GIVE UP.
OBVIOUSLY YOUR HELPING ME MEANS KILLING ME WITH KINDNESS.
はあ はあ…
HUF HUF...
MEET ASUNA KAGURAZAKA, DEAD GIRL WALKING.
AW, C'MON...
ACTUALLY, WE CAN HELP EACH OTHER.
AFTER ALL, A MASTER MAGUS' JOB IS TO HELP OTHERS, SO...
OH, SWELL...
SO YOU'RE TRYING TO PROVE YOU'RE GOOD ENOUGH?
KIND OF.
BUT WHO'RE YOU TRYING TO PROVE IT TO? YOURSELF?
NO, TO... HIM.
THE MAN WHO GAVE ME THIS STAFF. THE MAN WHO...
...WHO SOME NOW SAY IS DEAD. BUT I THINK...
ぐ…,
TUGG
...NOT.

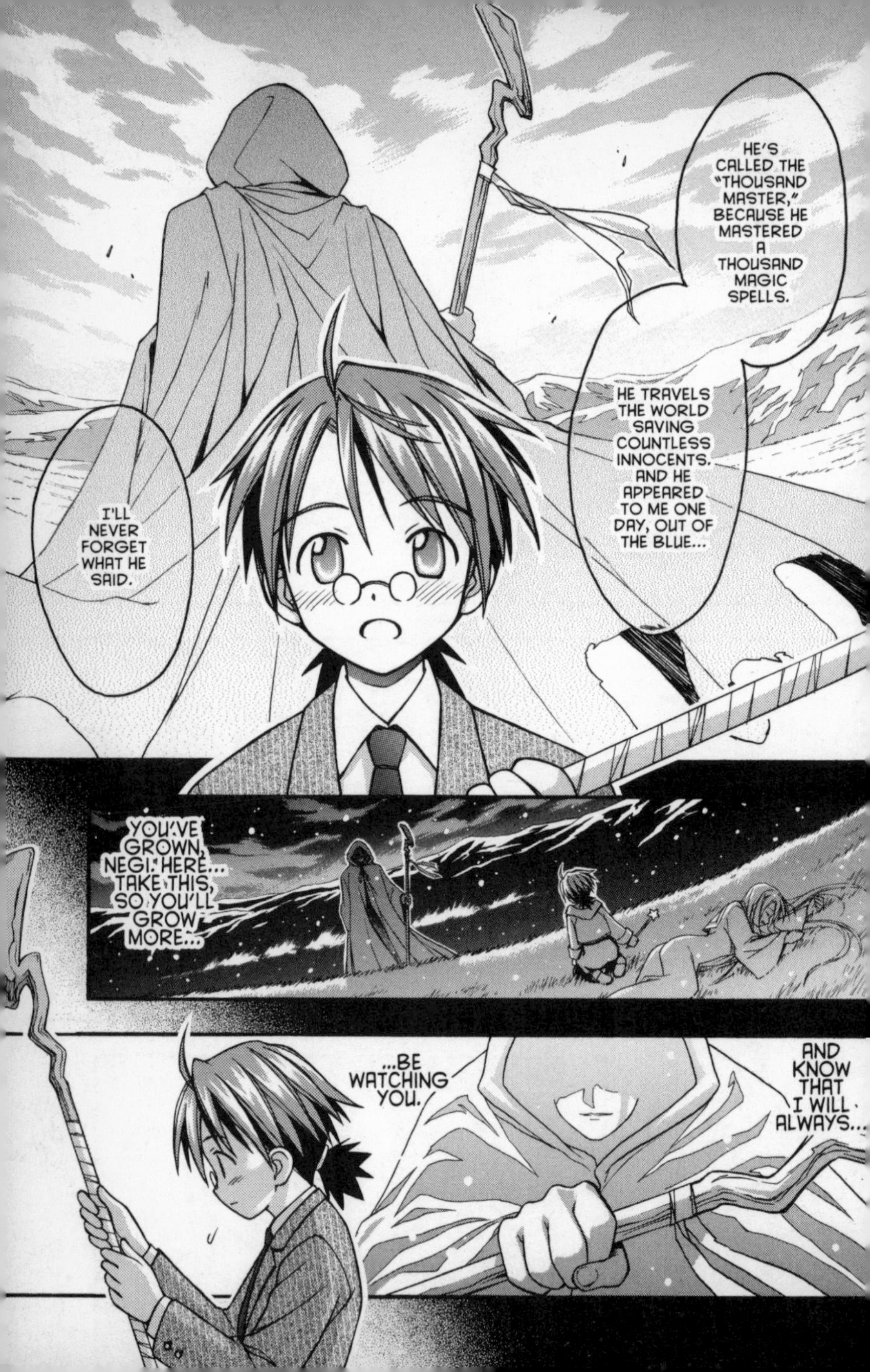
HE'S CALLED THE "THOUSAND MASTER," BECAUSE HE MASTERED A THOUSAND MAGIC SPELLS.
HE TRAVELS THE WORLD SAVING COUNTLESS INNOCENTS. AND HE APPEARED TO ME ONE DAY, OUT OF THE BLUE...
I'LL NEVER FORGET WHAT HE SAID.
YOU'VE GROWN, NEGI. HERE... TAKE THIS, SO YOU'LL GROW MORE...
AND KNOW THAT I WILL ALWAYS...
...BE WATCHING YOU.

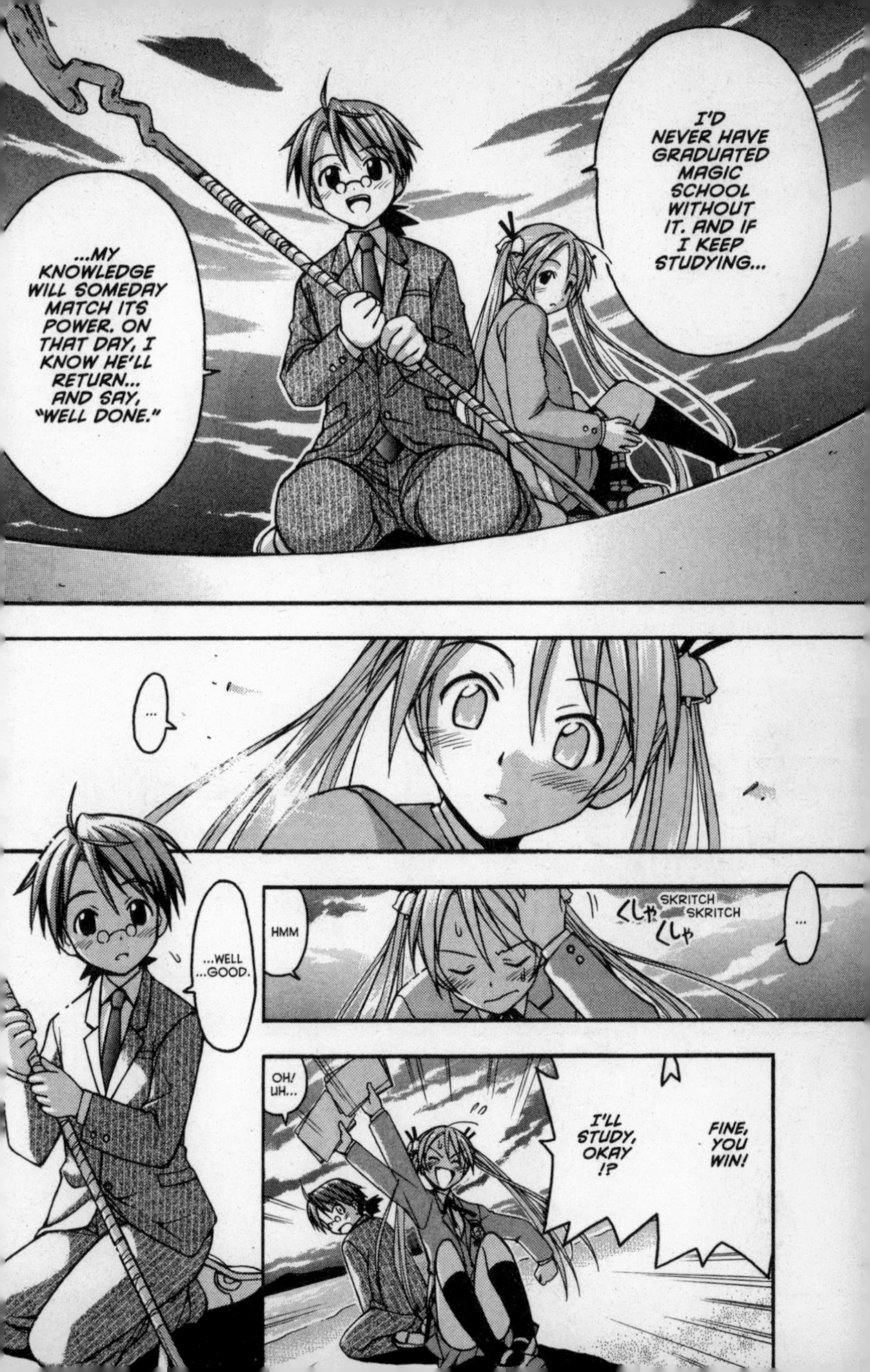
I'D NEVER HAVE GRADUATED MAGIC SCHOOL WITHOUT IT. AND IF I KEEP STUDYING...
...MY KNOWLEDGE WILL SOMEDAY MATCH ITS POWER. ON THAT DAY, I KNOW HE'LL RETURN... AND SAY, "WELL DONE."
...
...
くしゃ SKRITCH
くしゃ SKRITCH
HMM
FINE, YOU WIN!
I'LL STUDY, OKAY !?
OH! UH...
...WELL ...GOOD.

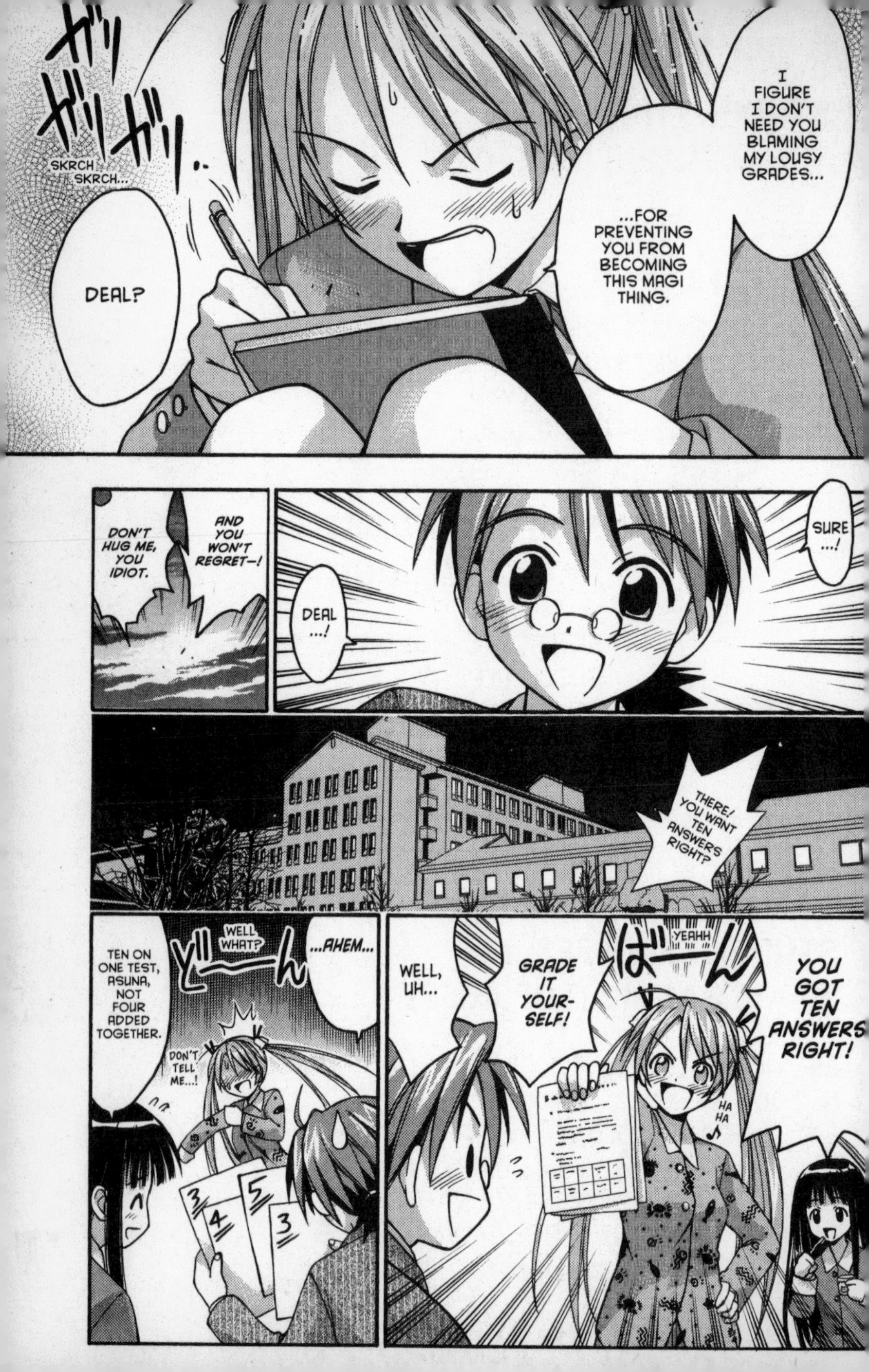
I FIGURE I DON'T NEED YOU BLAMING MY LOUSY GRADES...
...FOR PREVENTING YOU FROM BECOMING THIS MAGI THING.
SKRCH SKRCH...
DEAL?
SURE...!
DEAL...!
AND YOU WON'T REGRET—!
DON'T HUG ME, YOU IDIOT.
THERE! YOU WANT TEN ANSWERS RIGHT?
YOU GOT TEN ANSWERS RIGHT!
YEAHH
HA HA
GRADE IT YOURSELF!
WELL, UH...
...AHEM...
WELL WHAT?
TEN ON ONE TEST, ASUNA, NOT FOUR ADDED TOGETHER.
DON'T TELL ME...!

2-A STUDENT PROFILE

STUDENT NUMBER 2
YUNA AKASHI (BOTTOM)

BIRTHDATE: JUNE 1, 1988
BLOODTYPE: A
FAVORITE THINGS: FATHER
DISLIKES: BAD CLOTHES,
           SHIRTS HANGING OUT,
           SLOPPY LIFESTYLE
CLUB ACTIVITIES: BASKETBALL

STUDENT NUMBER 5
AKO IZUMI (RIGHT)

BIRTHDATE: NOVEMBER 21, 1988
BLOODTYPE: A
FAVORITE THINGS: CUTE BANDAIDS,
                 DOING LAUNDRY
DISLIKES: BLOOD, FIGHTS
CLUB ACTIVITIES: NURSE'S OFFICE,
                 BOYS' SOCCER
                 TEAM MANAGER

STUDENT NUMBER 16
MAKIE SASAKI (TOP LEFT)

BIRTHDATE: MARCH 7, 1989
BLOODTYPE: O
FAVORITE THINGS: DEVOTED TO RHYTHMIC GYMNASTICS,
                 NEGI, CUTE THINGS
DISLIKES: SLIMY THINGS LIKE NATTO
CLUB ACTIVITIES: RHYTHMIC GYMNASTICS

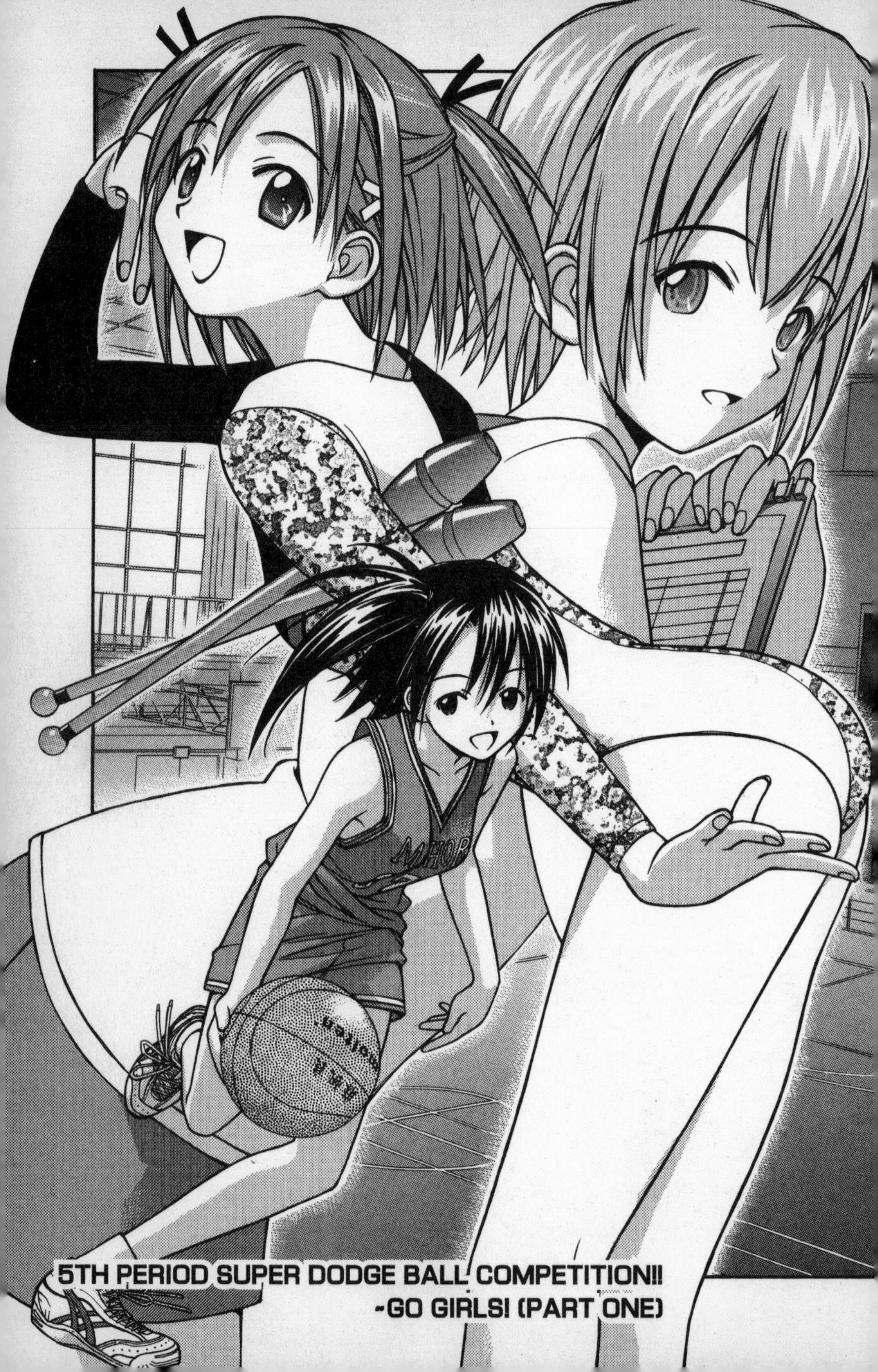
5TH PERIOD SUPER DODGE BALL COMPETITION!!
-GO GIRLS! (PART ONE)

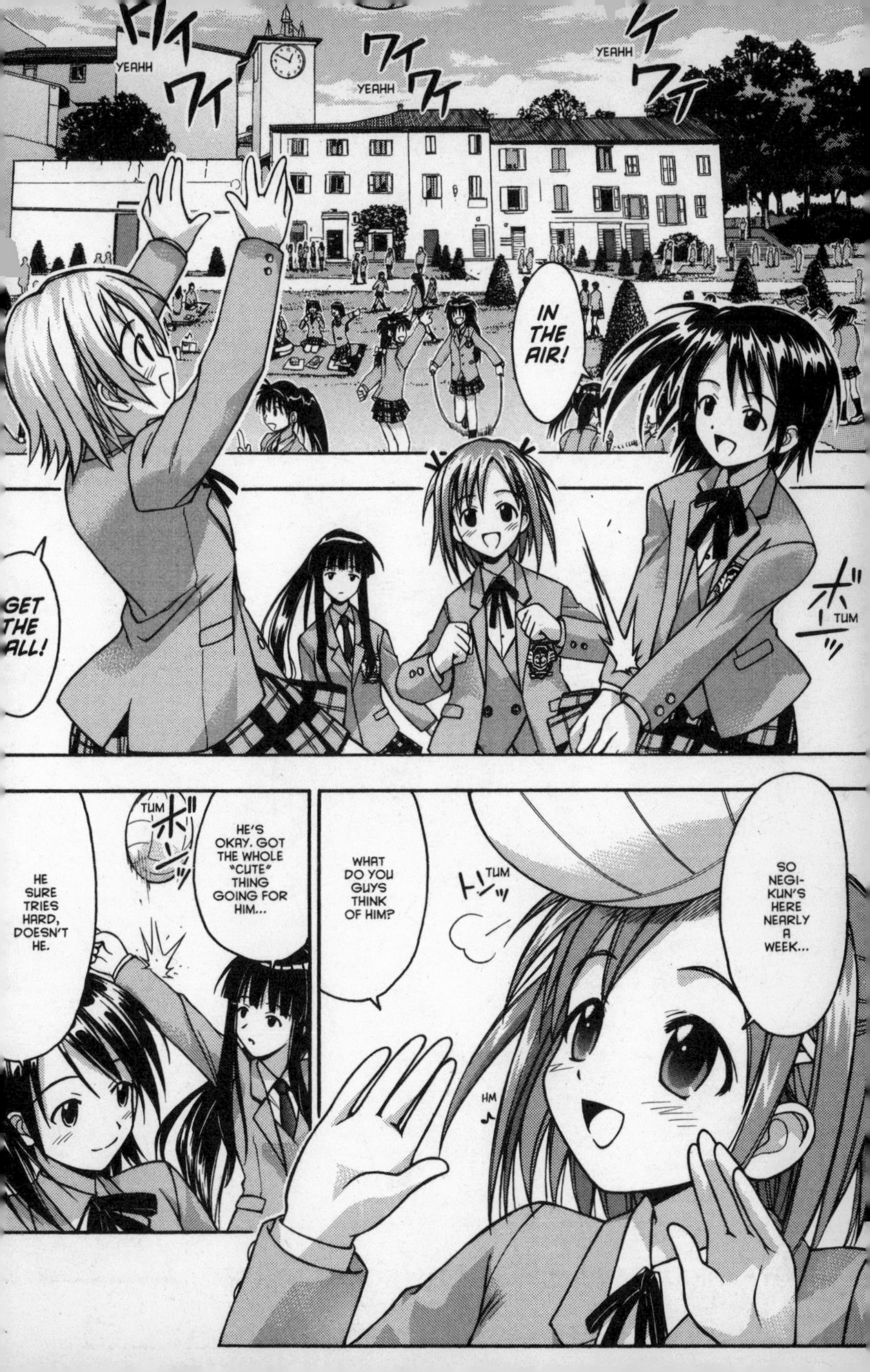
YEAHH
YEAHH
YEAHH
IN THE AIR!
GET THE ALL!
TUM
SO NEGI-KUN'S HERE NEARLY A WEEK...
TUM
WHAT DO YOU GUYS THINK OF HIM?
HM
HE'S OKAY. GOT THE WHOLE "CUTE" THING GOING FOR HIM...
TUM
HE SURE TRIES HARD, DOESN'T HE.

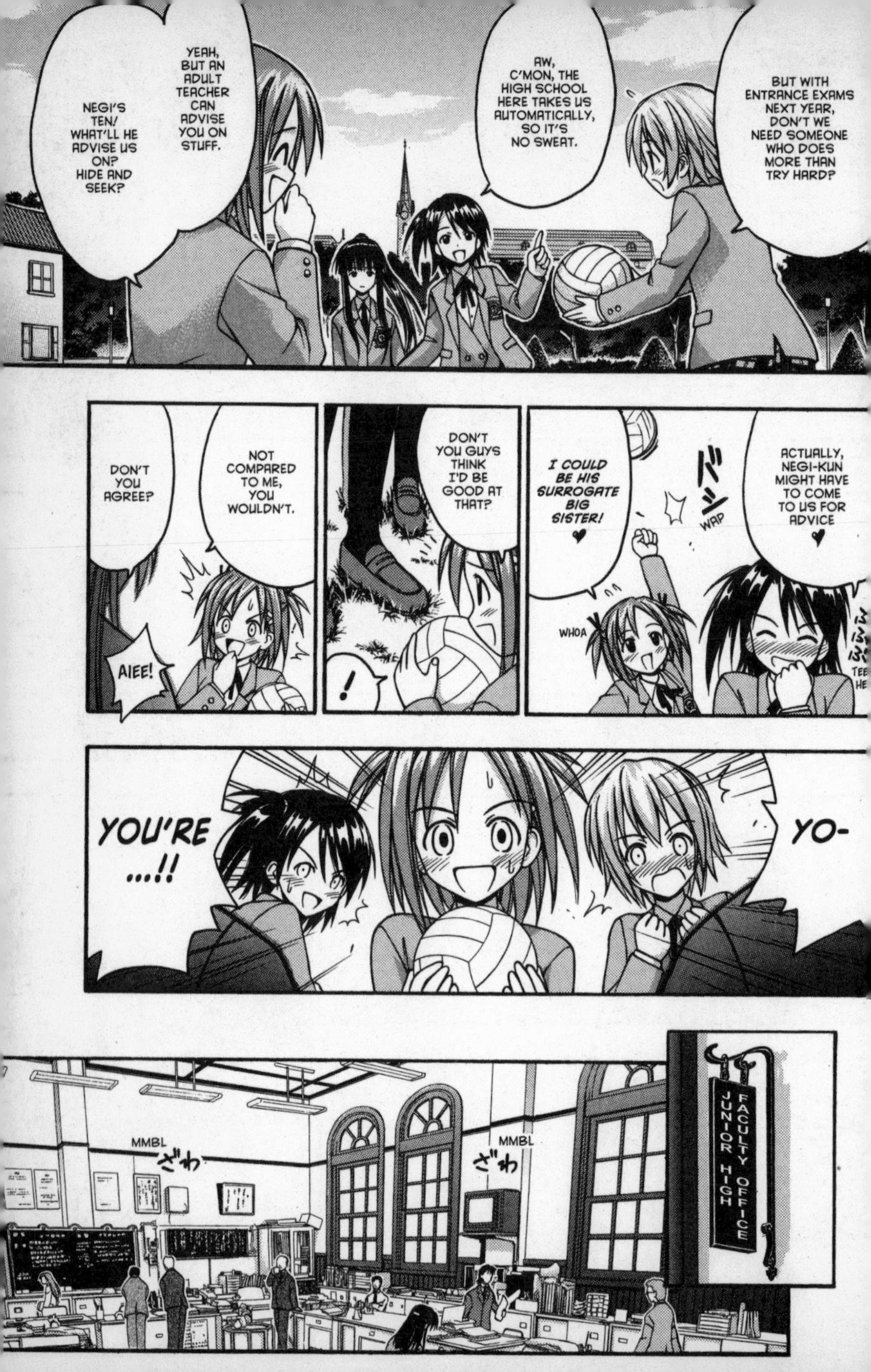
BUT WITH ENTRANCE EXAMS NEXT YEAR, DON'T WE NEED SOMEONE WHO DOES MORE THAN TRY HARD?
AW, C'MON, THE HIGH SCHOOL HERE TAKES US AUTOMATICALLY, SO IT'S NO SWEAT.
YEAH, BUT AN ADULT TEACHER CAN ADVISE YOU ON STUFF.
NEGI'S TEN! WHAT'LL HE ADVISE US ON? HIDE AND SEEK?
ACTUALLY, NEGI-KUN MIGHT HAVE TO COME TO US FOR ADVICE ♥
ふふ TEE HE
ドシ WAP
I COULD BE HIS SURROGATE BIG SISTER! ♥
WHOA
DON'T YOU GUYS THINK I'D BE GOOD AT THAT?
!
NOT COMPARED TO ME, YOU WOULDN'T.
DON'T YOU AGREE?
AIEE!
YO-
YOU'RE ...!!
JUNIOR HIGH FACULTY OFFICE
ざわ MMBL
ざわ MMBL

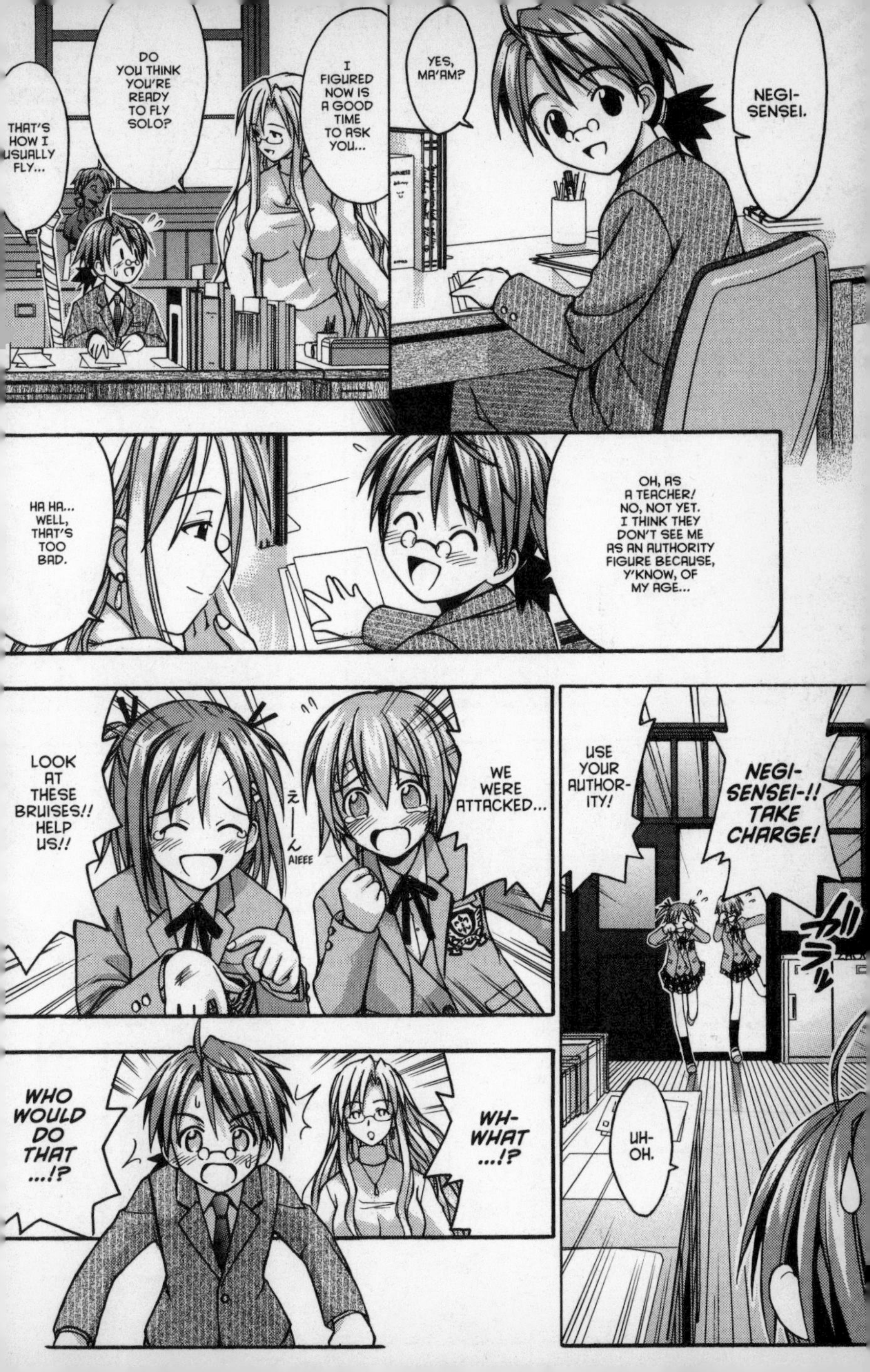
NEGI-SENSEI.
YES, MA'AM?
I FIGURED NOW IS A GOOD TIME TO ASK YOU...
DO YOU THINK YOU'RE READY TO FLY SOLO?
THAT'S HOW I USUALLY FLY...
OH, AS A TEACHER! NO, NOT YET. I THINK THEY DON'T SEE ME AS AN AUTHORITY FIGURE BECAUSE, Y'KNOW, OF MY AGE...
HA HA... WELL, THAT'S TOO BAD.
ガラッ
NEGI-SENSEI-!! TAKE CHARGE!
USE YOUR AUTHORITY!
UH-OH.
WE WERE ATTACKED...
えーん
AIEEE
LOOK AT THESE BRUISES!! HELP US!!
WH-WHAT ...!?
WHO WOULD DO THAT ...!?

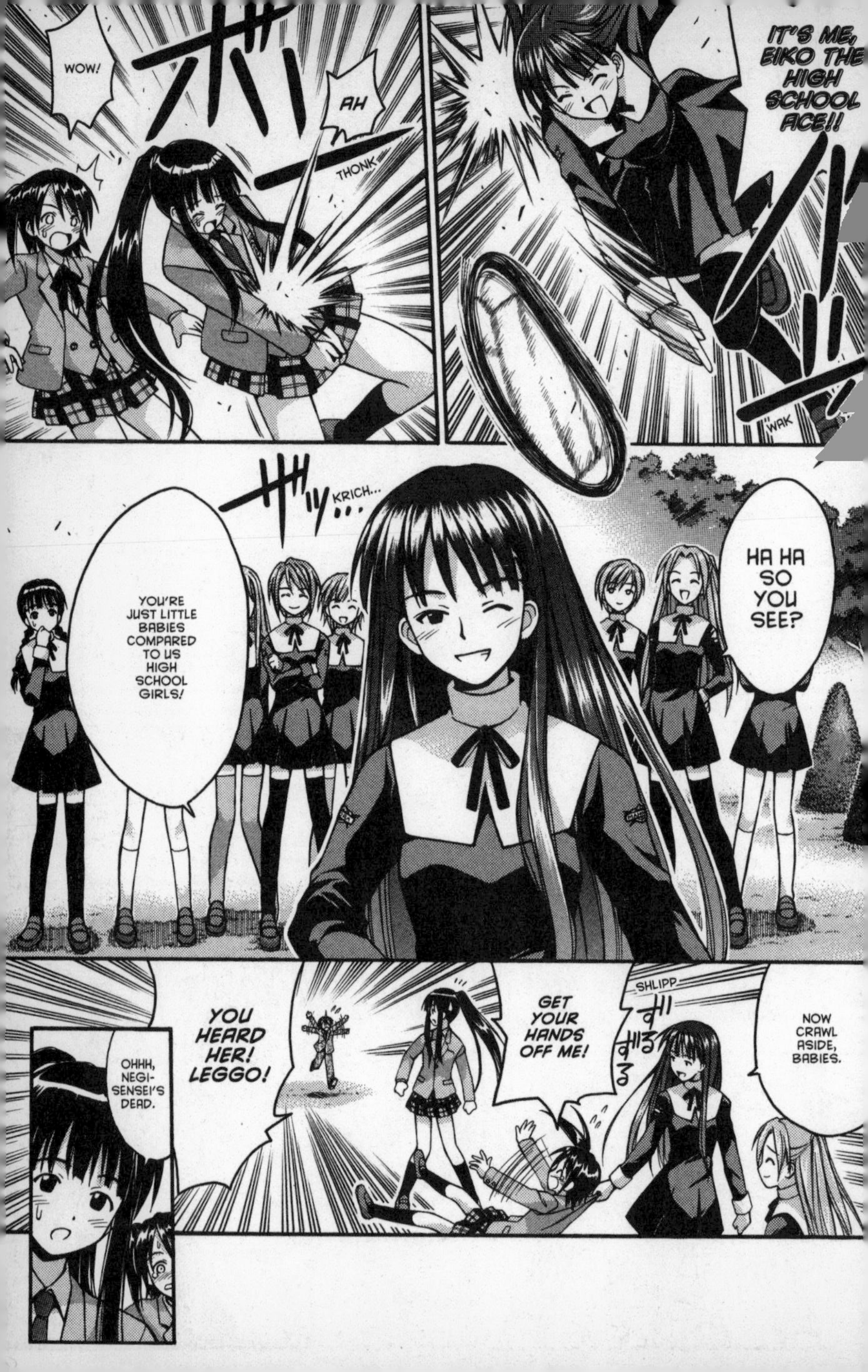
IT'S ME, EIKO THE HIGH SCHOOL ACE!!
WAK
AH
THONK
WOW!
HA HA SO YOU SEE?
KRICH...
YOU'RE JUST LITTLE BABIES COMPARED TO US HIGH SCHOOL GIRLS!
NOW CRAWL ASIDE, BABIES.
SHLIPP
GET YOUR HANDS OFF ME!
YOU HEARD HER! LEGGO!
OHHH, NEGI-SENSEI'S DEAD.

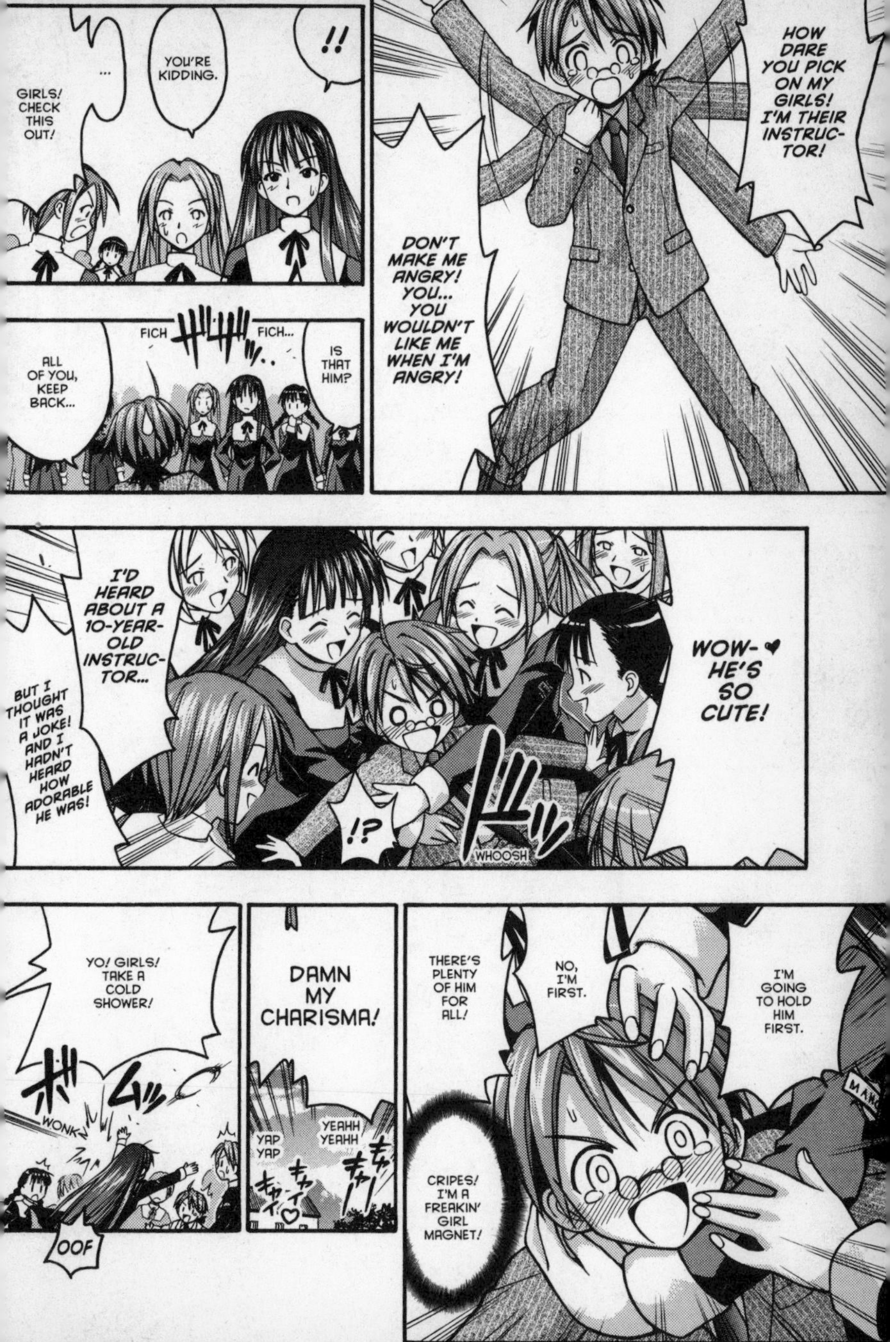
HOW DARE YOU PICK ON MY GIRLS! I'M THEIR INSTRUCTOR!
DON'T MAKE ME ANGRY! YOU... YOU WOULDN'T LIKE ME WHEN I'M ANGRY!
!!
YOU'RE KIDDING.
...
GIRLS! CHECK THIS OUT!
IS THAT HIM?
FICH... FICH
ALL OF YOU, KEEP BACK...
WOW-♥ HE'S SO CUTE!
I'D HEARD ABOUT A 10-YEAR-OLD INSTRUCTOR...
BUT I THOUGHT IT WAS A JOKE! AND I HADN'T HEARD HOW ADORABLE HE WAS!
!?
WHOOSH
I'M GOING TO HOLD HIM FIRST.
NO, I'M FIRST.
THERE'S PLENTY OF HIM FOR ALL!
CRIPES! I'M A FREAKIN' GIRL MAGNET!
DAMN MY CHARISMA!
YEAHH YEAHH
YAP YAP
YO! GIRLS! TAKE A COLD SHOWER!
WONK
OOF

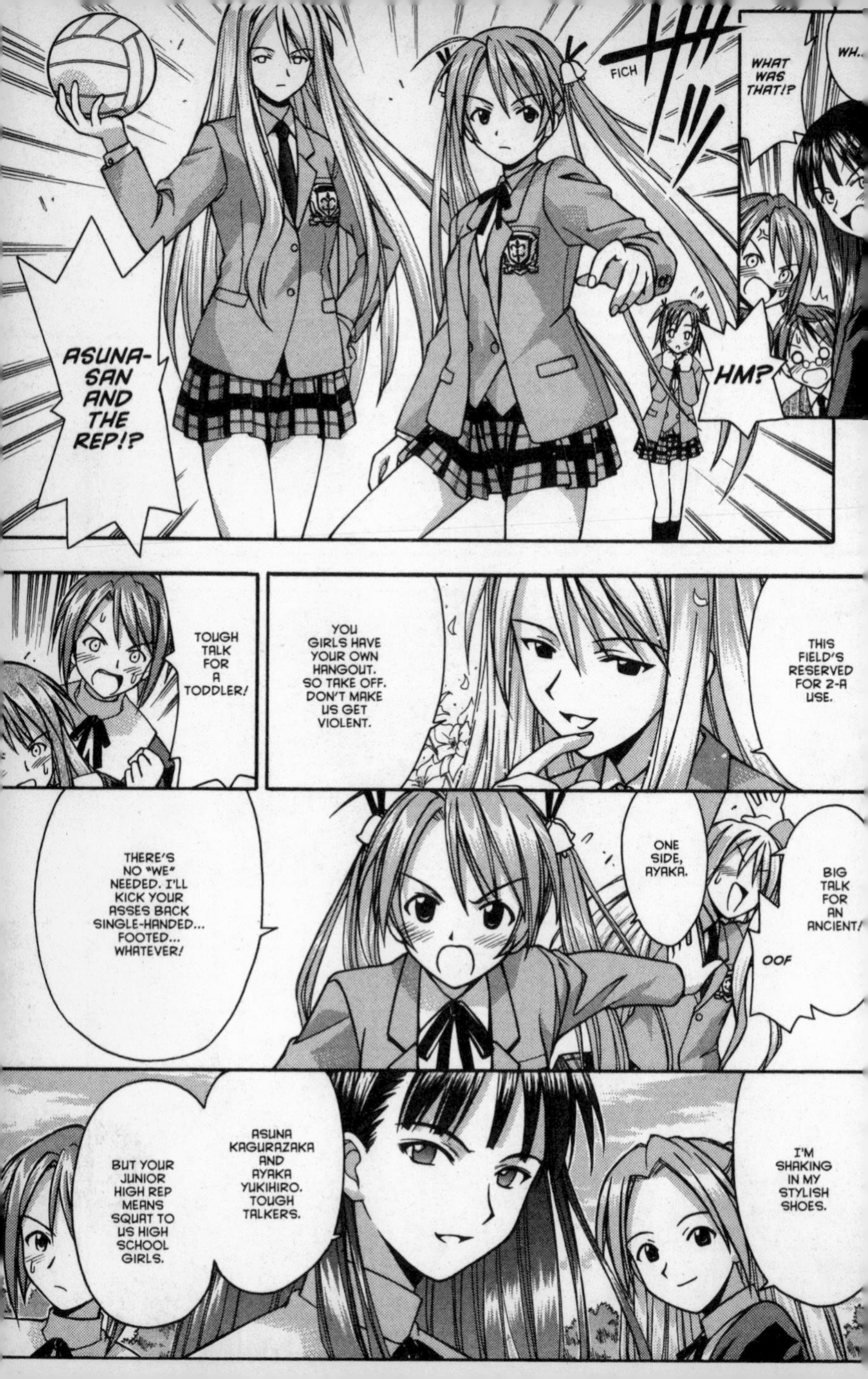
WH..
WHAT WAS THAT!?
FICH
HM?
ASUNA-SAN AND THE REP!?
THIS FIELD'S RESERVED FOR 2-A USE.
YOU GIRLS HAVE YOUR OWN HANGOUT. SO TAKE OFF. DON'T MAKE US GET VIOLENT.
TOUGH TALK FOR A TODDLER!
BIG TALK FOR AN ANCIENT!
OOF
ONE SIDE, AYAKA.
THERE'S NO "WE" NEEDED. I'LL KICK YOUR ASSES BACK SINGLE-HANDED... FOOTED... WHATEVER!
I'M SHAKING IN MY STYLISH SHOES.
ASUNA KAGURAZAKA AND AYAKA YUKIHIRO. TOUGH TALKERS.
BUT YOUR JUNIOR HIGH REP MEANS SQUAT TO US HIGH SCHOOL GIRLS.

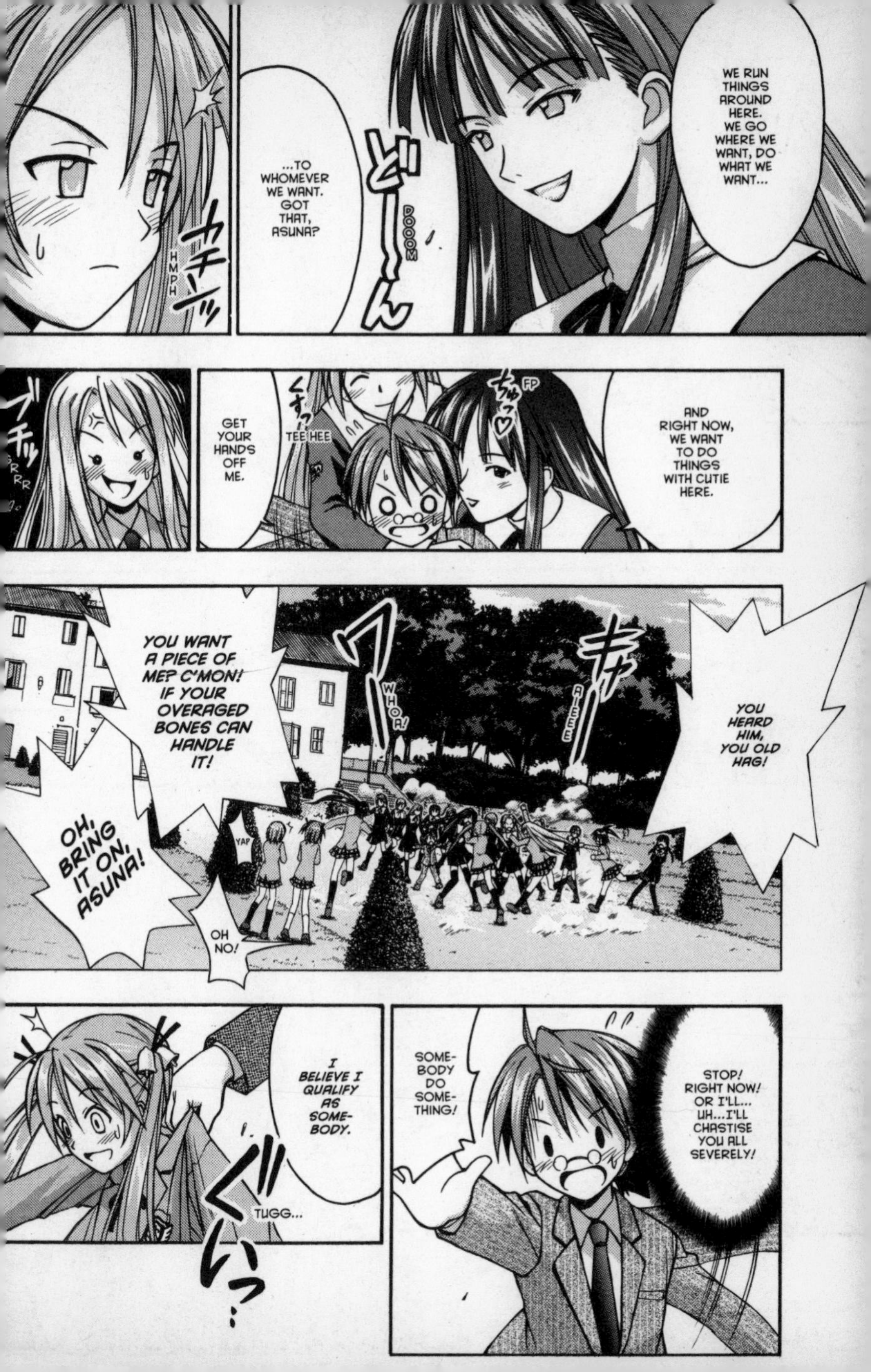
WE RUN THINGS AROUND HERE. WE GO WHERE WE WANT, DO WHAT WE WANT...
DOOOM
...TO WHOMEVER WE WANT. GOT THAT, ASUNA?
HMPH
FP
AND RIGHT NOW, WE WANT TO DO THINGS WITH CUTIE HERE.
TEE HEE
GET YOUR HANDS OFF ME.
GRRR
YOU HEARD HIM, YOU OLD HAG!
AIEEE
WHOA!
YOU WANT A PIECE OF ME? C'MON! IF YOUR OVERAGED BONES CAN HANDLE IT!
OH, BRING IT ON, ASUNA!
YAP
OH NO!
STOP! RIGHT NOW! OR I'LL... UH...I'LL CHASTISE YOU ALL SEVERELY!
SOME-BODY DO SOME-THING!
I BELIEVE I QUALIFY AS SOME-BODY.
TUGG...

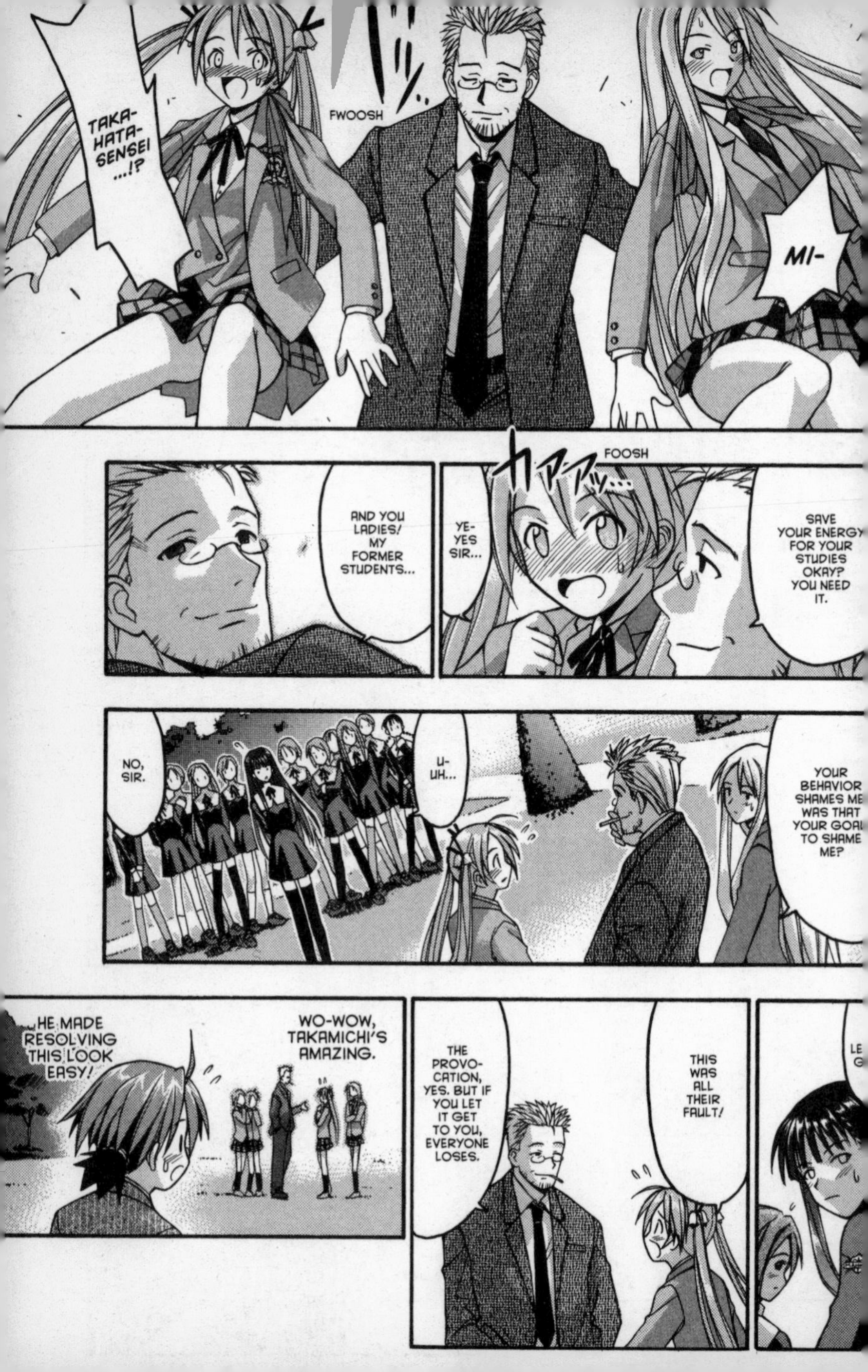
MI-
FWOOSH
TAKA-HATA-SENSEI ...!?
FOOSH
カァァッ...
SAVE YOUR ENERGY FOR YOUR STUDIES OKAY? YOU NEED IT.
YE- YES SIR...
AND YOU LADIES! MY FORMER STUDENTS...
YOUR BEHAVIOR SHAMES ME WAS THAT YOUR GOAL TO SHAME ME?
U- UH...
NO, SIR.
LE G
THIS WAS ALL THEIR FAULT!
THE PROVOCATION, YES. BUT IF YOU LET IT GET TO YOU, EVERYONE LOSES.
WO-WOW, TAKAMICHI'S AMAZING.
HE MADE RESOLVING THIS LOOK EASY!

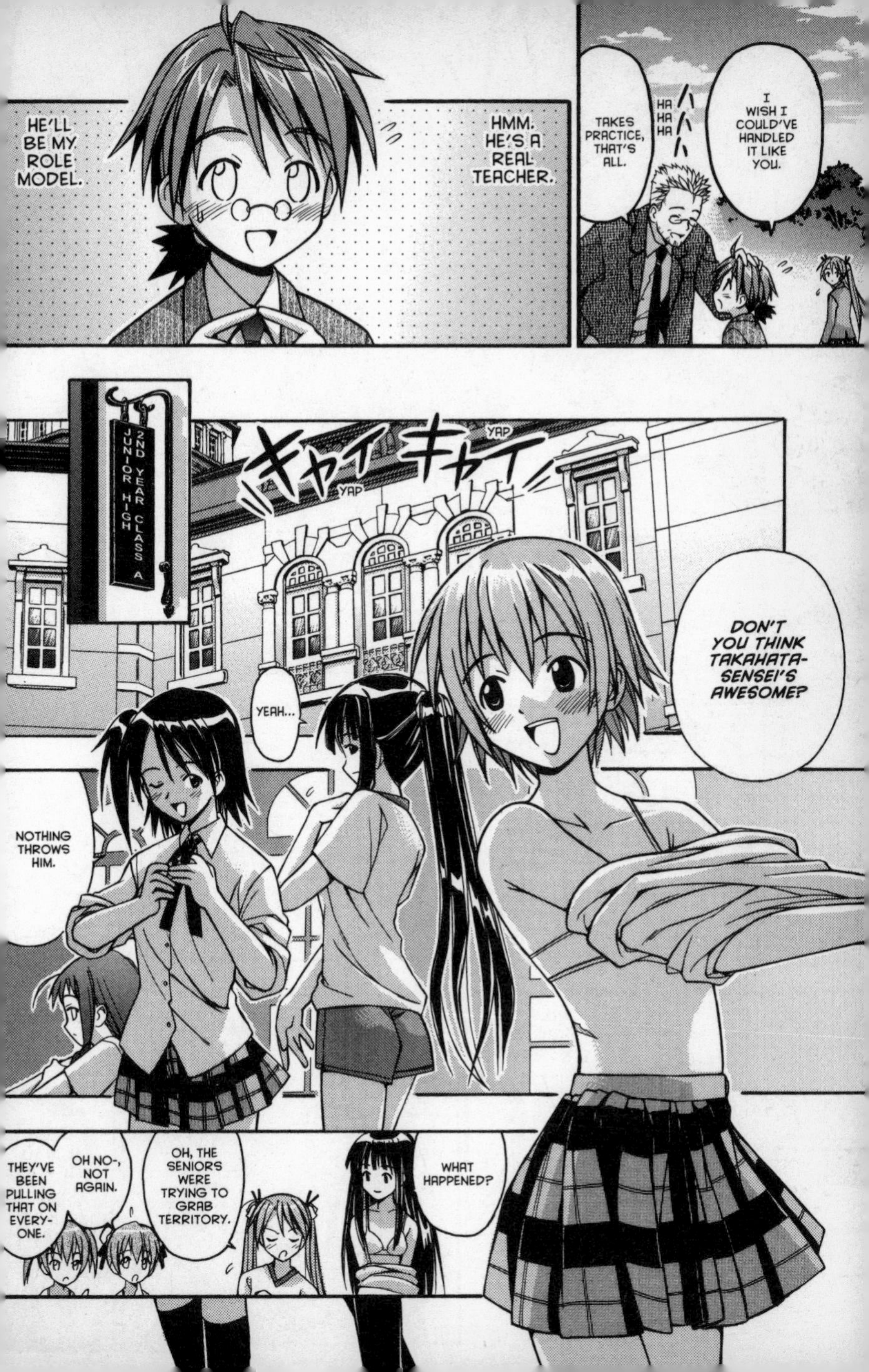
I WISH I COULD'VE HANDLED IT LIKE YOU.
HA HA HA
TAKES PRACTICE, THAT'S ALL.
HMM. HE'S A REAL TEACHER.
HE'LL BE MY ROLE MODEL.
2ND YEAR CLASS A
JUNIOR HIGH
YAP
YAP
DON'T YOU THINK TAKAHATA-SENSEI'S AWESOME?
YEAH...
NOTHING THROWS HIM.
WHAT HAPPENED?
OH, THE SENIORS WERE TRYING TO GRAB TERRITORY.
OH NO-, NOT AGAIN.
THEY'VE BEEN PULLING THAT ON EVERYONE.

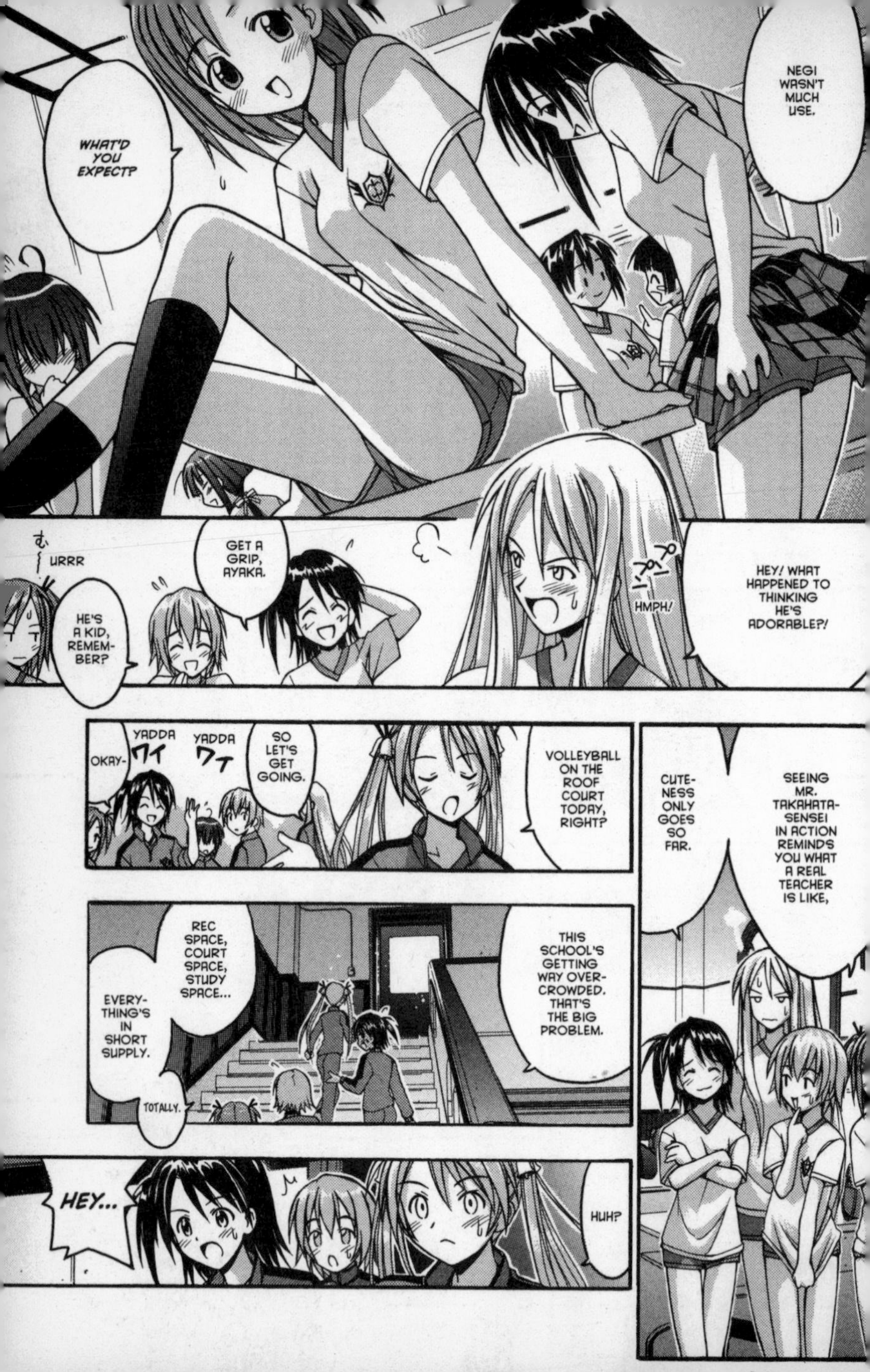
NEGI WASN'T MUCH USE.
WHAT'D YOU EXPECT?
HEY! WHAT HAPPENED TO THINKING HE'S ADORABLE?!
HMPH!
GET A GRIP, AYAKA.
HE'S A KID, REMEMBER?
URRR
SEEING MR. TAKAHATA-SENSEI IN ACTION REMINDS YOU WHAT A REAL TEACHER IS LIKE,
CUTENESS ONLY GOES SO FAR.
VOLLEYBALL ON THE ROOF COURT TODAY, RIGHT?
SO LET'S GET GOING.
YADDA ワィ
YADDA ワイ
OKAY-
THIS SCHOOL'S GETTING WAY OVERCROWDED. THAT'S THE BIG PROBLEM.
REC SPACE, COURT SPACE, STUDY SPACE...
EVERYTHING'S IN SHORT SUPPLY.
TOTALLY.
HUH?
HEY...

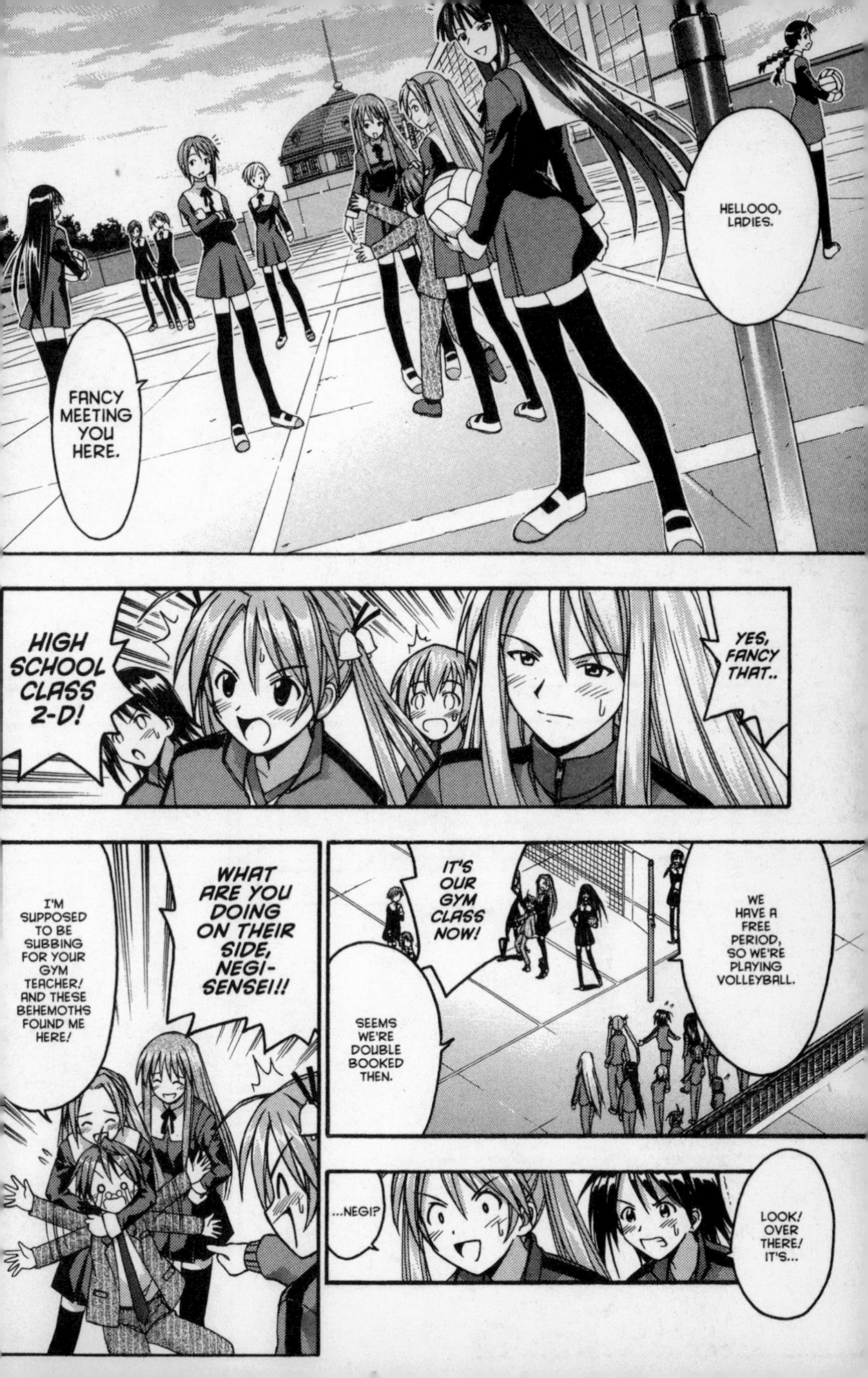
HELLOOO, LADIES.
FANCY MEETING YOU HERE.
YES, FANCY THAT..
HIGH SCHOOL CLASS 2-D!
WE HAVE A FREE PERIOD, SO WE'RE PLAYING VOLLEYBALL.
IT'S OUR GYM CLASS NOW!
SEEMS WE'RE DOUBLE BOOKED THEN.
LOOK! OVER THERE! IT'S...
...NEGI!?
WHAT ARE YOU DOING ON THEIR SIDE, NEGI-SENSEI!!
I'M SUPPOSED TO BE SUBBING FOR YOUR GYM TEACHER! AND THESE BEHEMOTHS FOUND ME HERE!

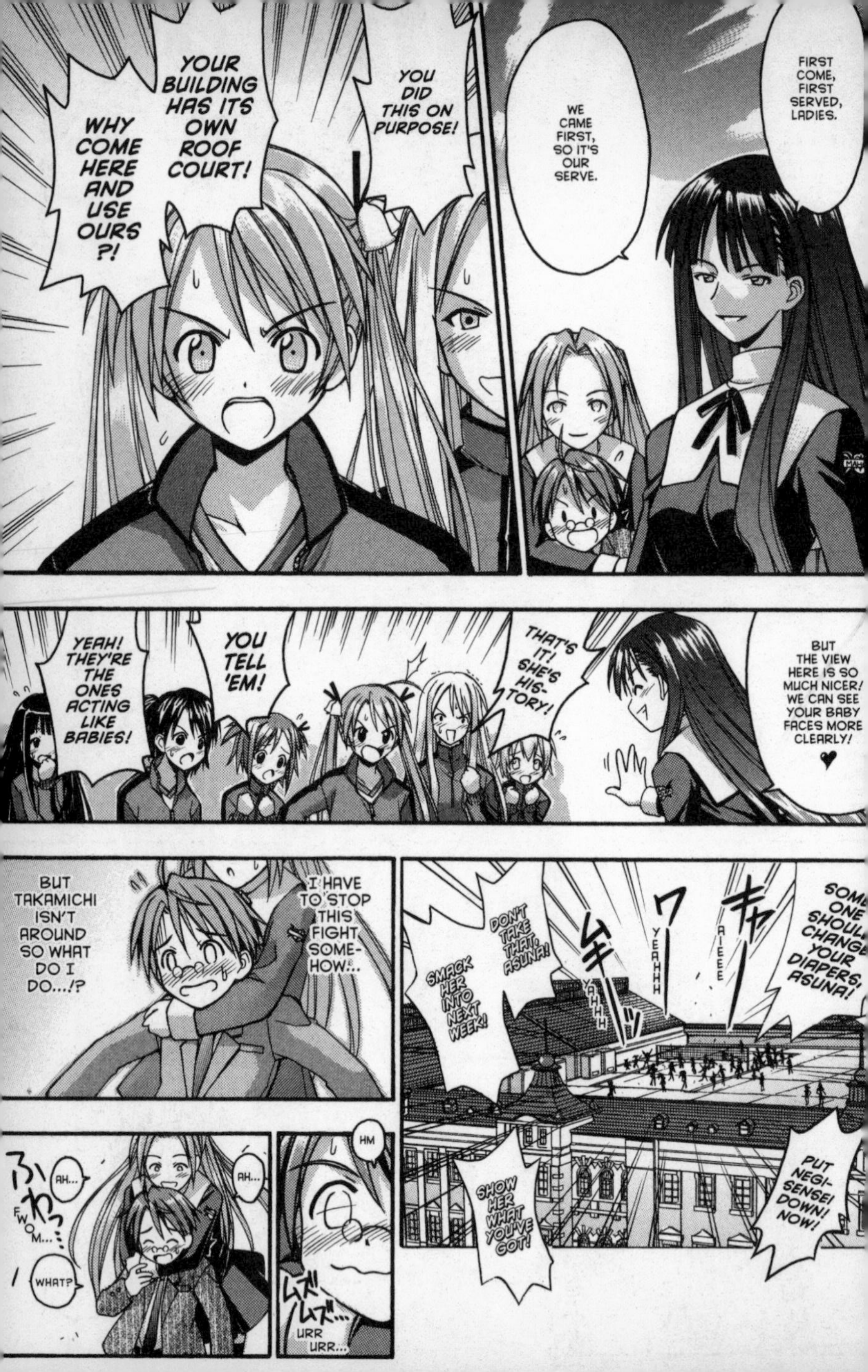
FIRST COME, FIRST SERVED, LADIES.
WE CAME FIRST, SO IT'S OUR SERVE.
YOU DID THIS ON PURPOSE!
YOUR BUILDING HAS ITS OWN ROOF COURT!
WHY COME HERE AND USE OURS?!
BUT THE VIEW HERE IS SO MUCH NICER! WE CAN SEE YOUR BABY FACES MORE CLEARLY! ♥
THAT'S IT! SHE'S HISTORY!
YOU TELL 'EM!
YEAH! THEY'RE THE ONES ACTING LIKE BABIES!
SOMEONE SHOULD CHANGE YOUR DIAPERS, ASUNA!
キャー
AIEEE
ワー
YEAHHH
ムキーッ
YAHHH
DON'T TAKE THAT, ASUNA!
SMACK HER INTO NEXT WEEK!
PUT NEGI-SENSEI DOWN! NOW!
SHOW HER WHAT YOU'VE GOT!
I HAVE TO STOP THIS FIGHT SOMEHOW...
BUT TAKAMICHI ISN'T AROUND SO WHAT DO I DO...!?
HM
ムズムズ...
URR URR...
AH...
AH...
ふわっ
FWOM...
WHAT?

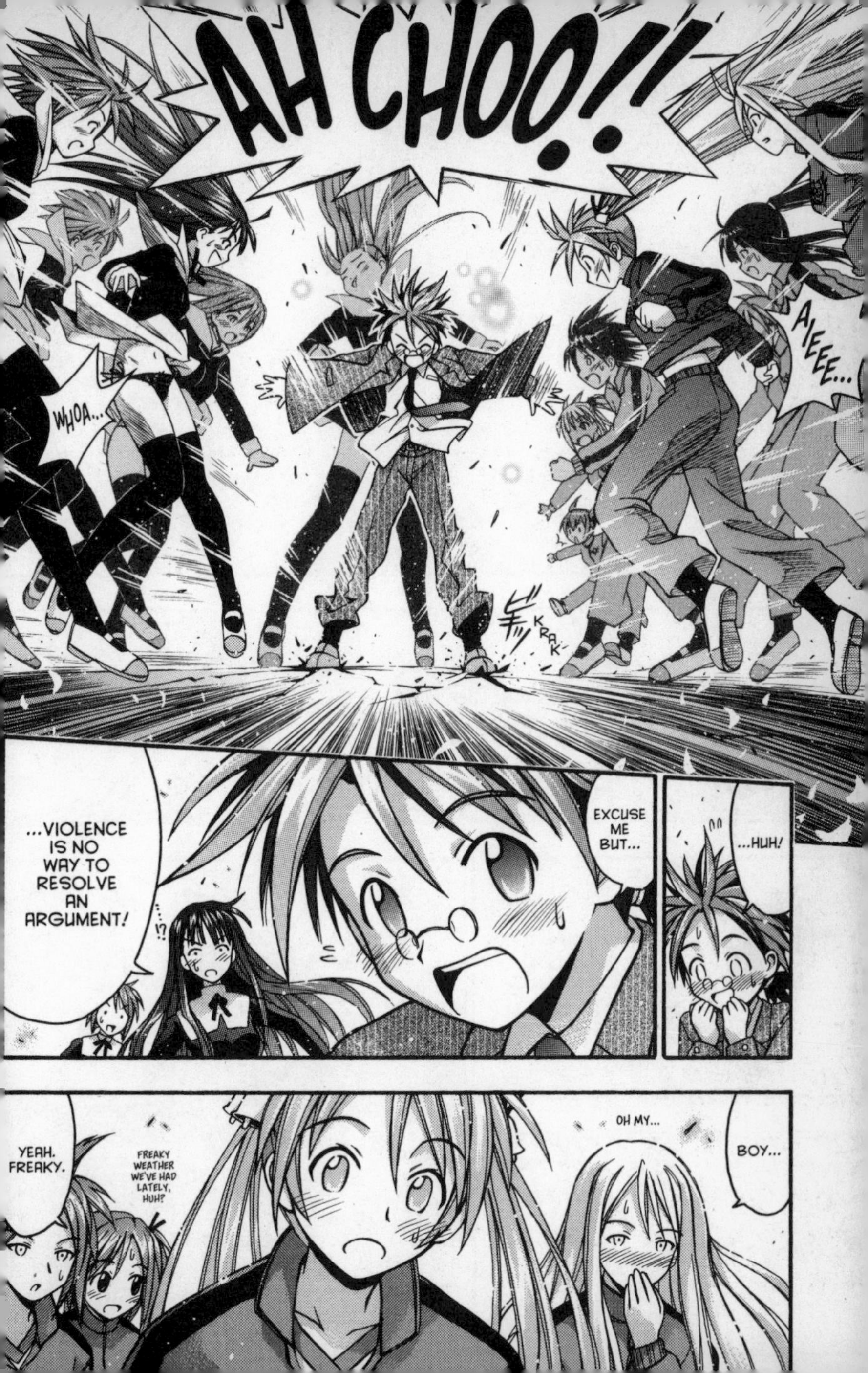
AH CHOO!!
AIEEE...
KRAK
WHOA...
...HUH!
EXCUSE ME BUT...
...!?
...VIOLENCE IS NO WAY TO RESOLVE AN ARGUMENT!
BOY...
OH MY...
FREAKY WEATHER WE'VE HAD LATELY, HUH?
YEAH. FREAKY.

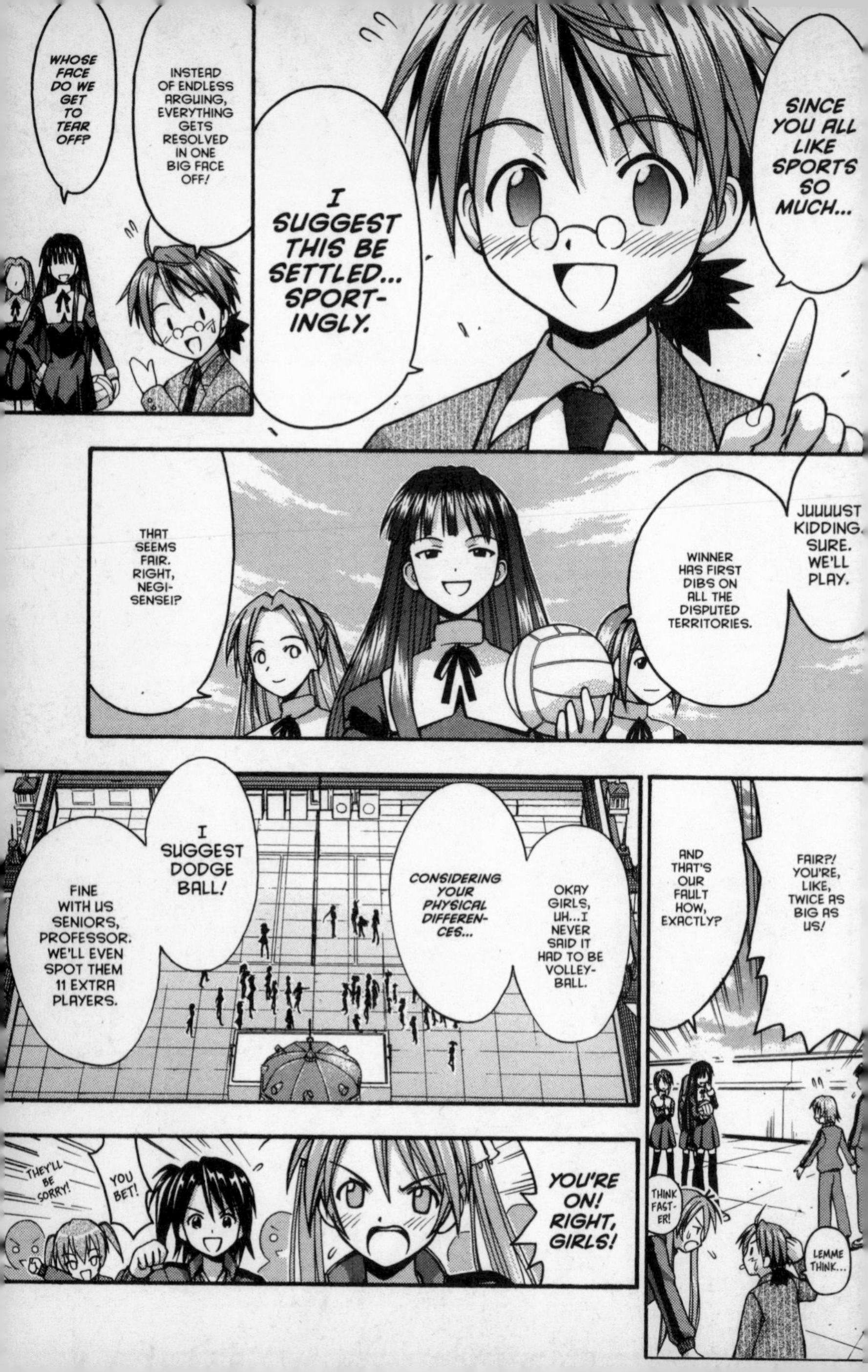
SINCE YOU ALL LIKE SPORTS SO MUCH...
I SUGGEST THIS BE SETTLED... SPORT-INGLY.
INSTEAD OF ENDLESS ARGUING, EVERYTHING GETS RESOLVED IN ONE BIG FACE OFF!
WHOSE FACE DO WE GET TO TEAR OFF?
JUUUUST KIDDING. SURE. WE'LL PLAY.
WINNER HAS FIRST DIBS ON ALL THE DISPUTED TERRITORIES.
THAT SEEMS FAIR. RIGHT, NEGI-SENSEI?
FAIR?! YOU'RE, LIKE, TWICE AS BIG AS US!
AND THAT'S OUR FAULT HOW, EXACTLY?
THINK FAST-ER!
LEMME THINK...
OKAY GIRLS, UH...I NEVER SAID IT HAD TO BE VOLLEY-BALL.
CONSIDERING YOUR PHYSICAL DIFFEREN-CES...
I SUGGEST DODGE BALL!
FINE WITH US SENIORS, PROFESSOR. WE'LL EVEN SPOT THEM 11 EXTRA PLAYERS.
YOU'RE ON! RIGHT, GIRLS!
YOU BET!
THEY'LL BE SORRY!

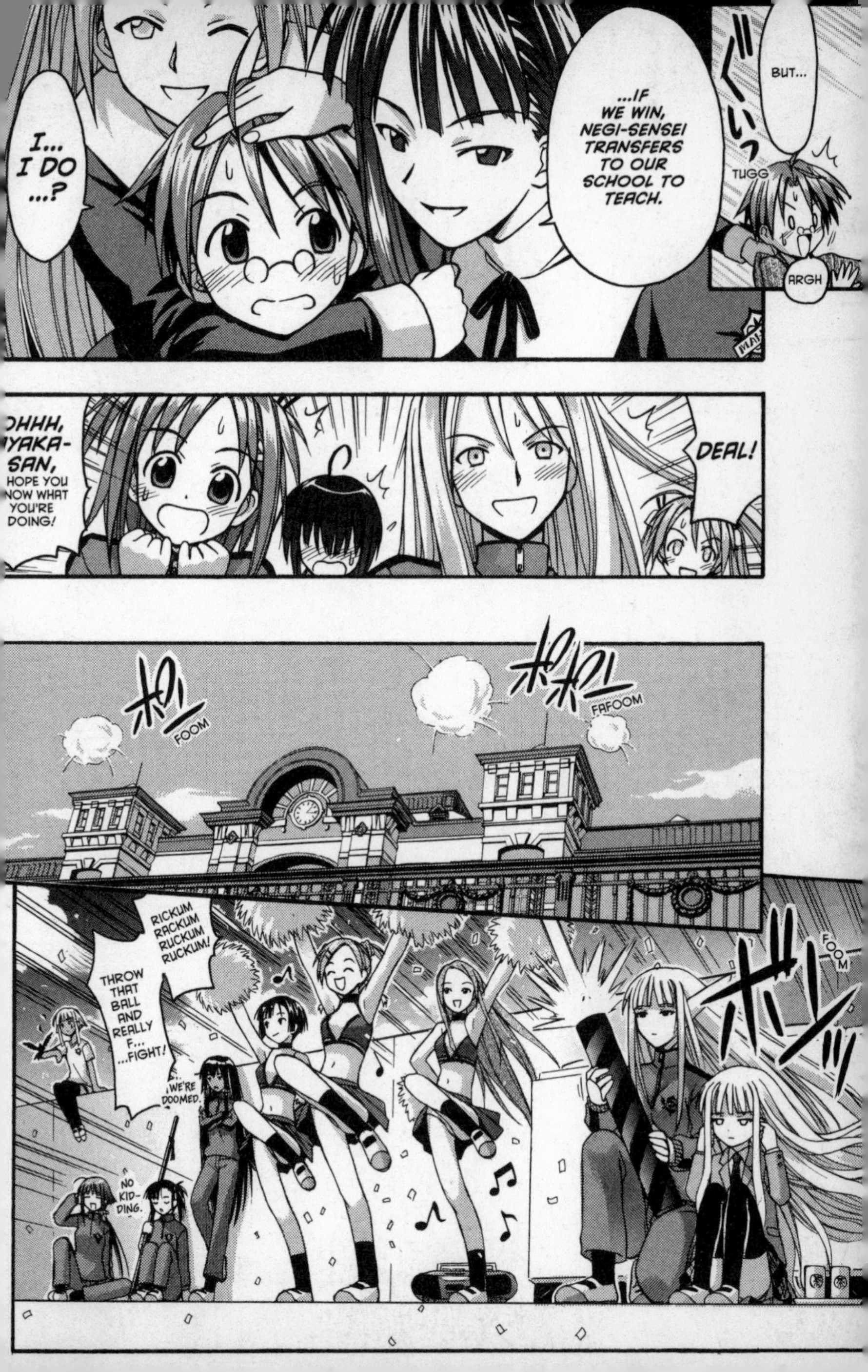
BUT...
TUGG
ARGH
...IF WE WIN, NEGI-SENSEI TRANSFERS TO OUR SCHOOL TO TEACH.
I... I DO ...?
DEAL!
OHHH, YAKA-SAN, HOPE YOU NOW WHAT YOU'RE DOING!
FAFOOM
FOOM
FOOM
RICKUM RACKUM RUCKUM RUCKUM!
THROW THAT BALL AND REALLY F... ...FIGHT!
WE'RE DOOMED.
NO KID-DING.

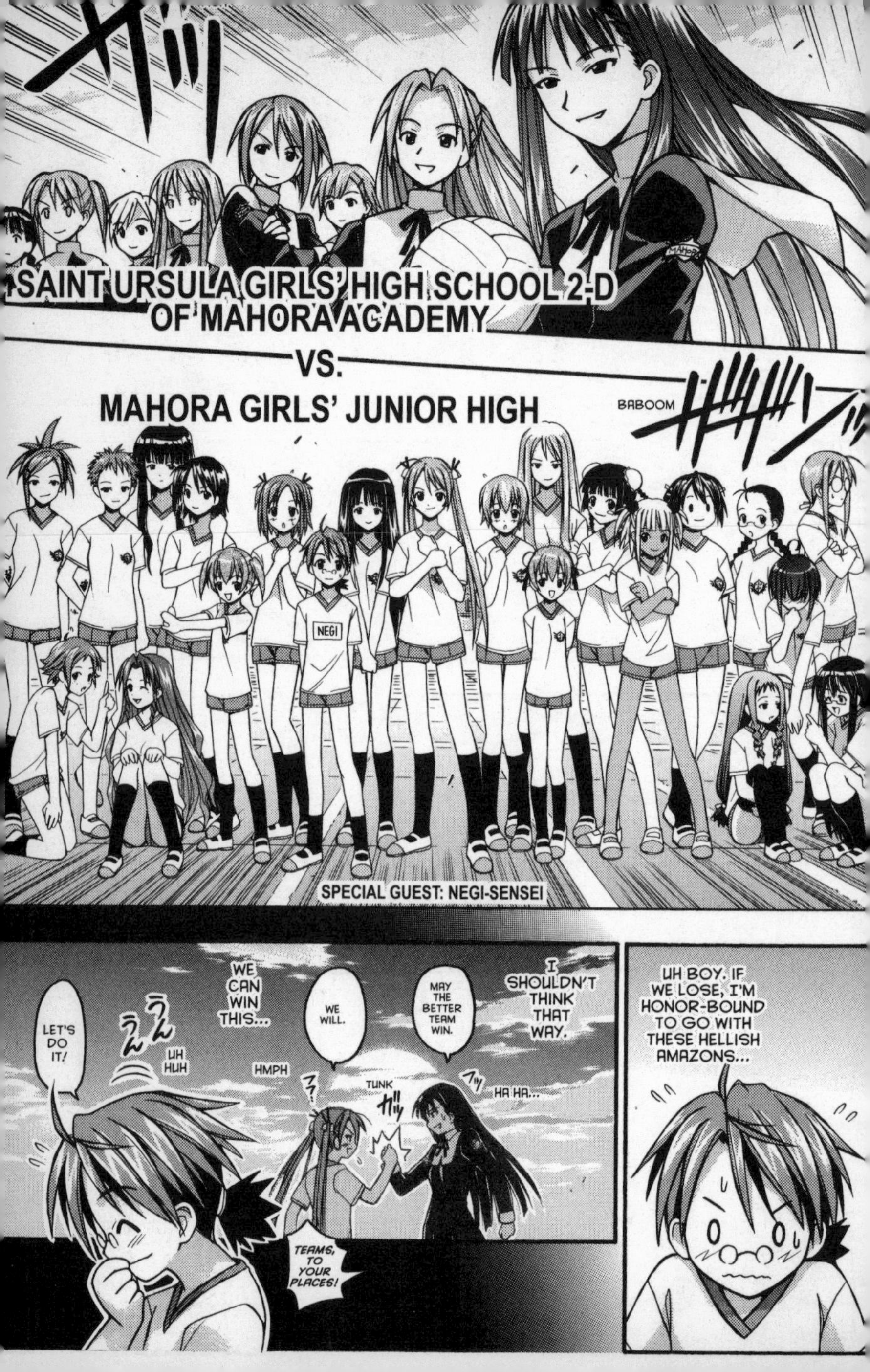
SAINT URSULA GIRLS' HIGH SCHOOL 2-D
OF MAHORA ACADEMY
VS.
MAHORA GIRLS' JUNIOR HIGH
BABOOM
NEGI
SPECIAL GUEST: NEGI-SENSEI
UH BOY. IF WE LOSE, I'M HONOR-BOUND TO GO WITH THESE HELLISH AMAZONS...
I SHOULDN'T THINK THAT WAY.
MAY THE BETTER TEAM WIN.
HA HA...
WE WILL.
TUNK
HMPH
WE CAN WIN THIS...
UH HUH
LET'S DO IT!
TEAMS, TO YOUR PLACES!

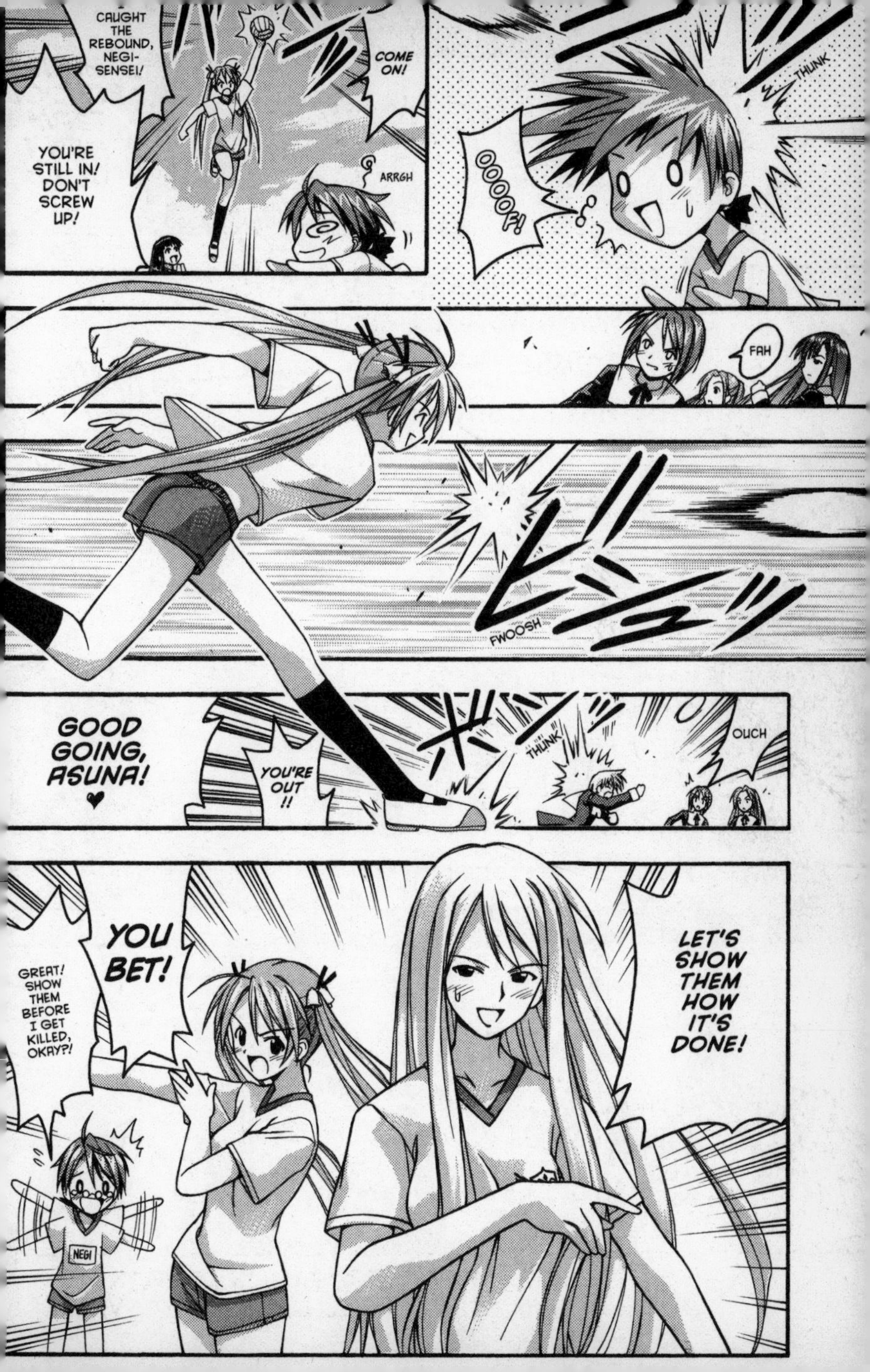
THUNK
OOOOF!
COME ON!
CAUGHT THE REBOUND, NEGI-SENSEI!
ARRGH
YOU'RE STILL IN! DON'T SCREW UP!
FAH
FWOOSH
OUCH
THUNK
YOU'RE OUT!!
GOOD GOING, ASUNA! ♥
LET'S SHOW THEM HOW IT'S DONE!
YOU BET!
GREAT! SHOW THEM BEFORE I GET KILLED, OKAY?!

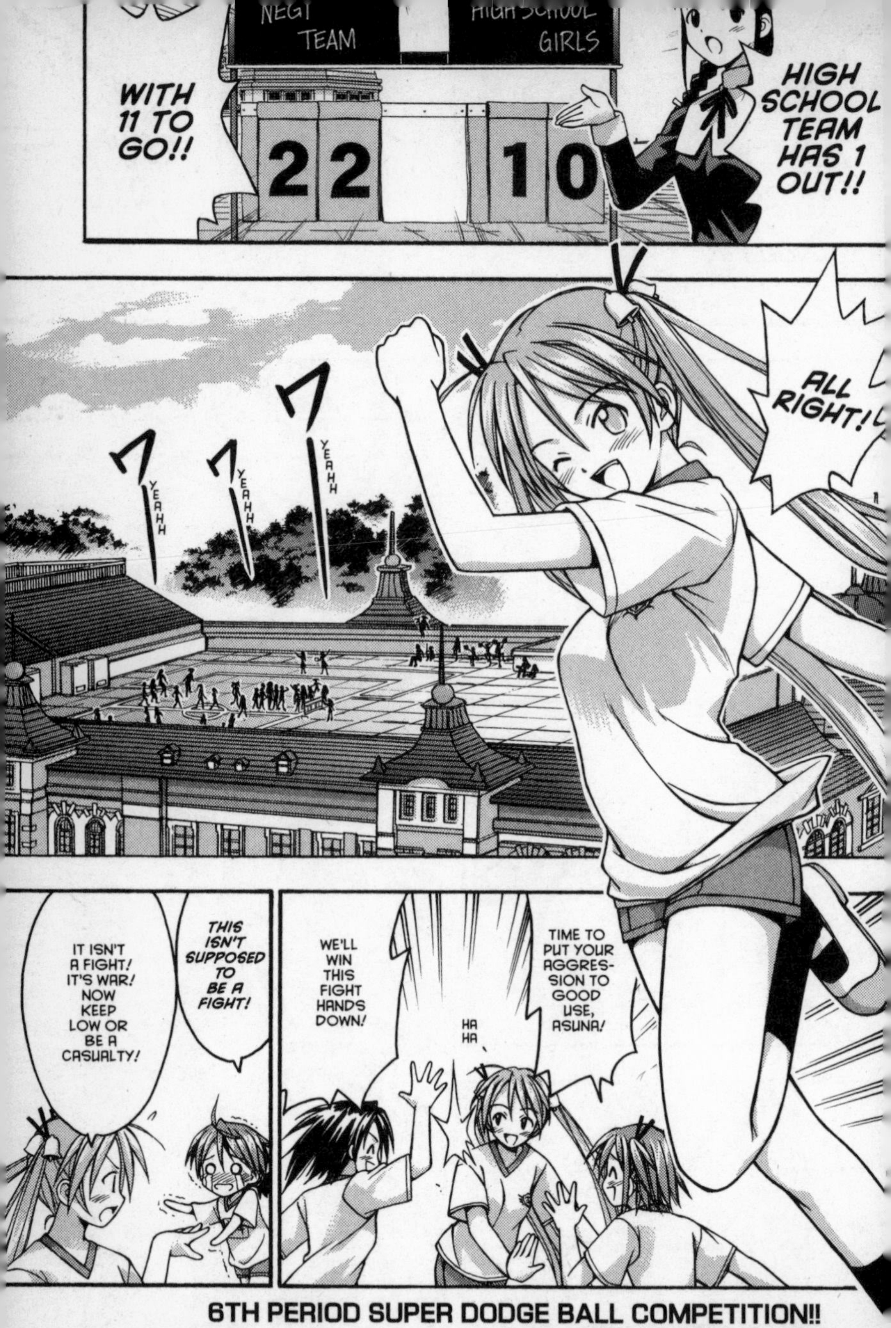
NEGI TEAM
HIGH SCHOOL GIRLS
22
10
HIGH SCHOOL TEAM HAS 1 OUT!!
WITH 11 TO GO!!
ALL RIGHT!!
YEAHH
YEAHH
YEAHH
TIME TO PUT YOUR AGGRESSION TO GOOD USE, ASUNA!
HA HA
WE'LL WIN THIS FIGHT HANDS DOWN!
THIS ISN'T SUPPOSED TO BE A FIGHT!
IT ISN'T A FIGHT! IT'S WAR! NOW KEEP LOW OR BE A CASUALTY!

6TH PERIOD SUPER DODGE BALL COMPETITION!!
-GO GIRLS! (PART TWO)

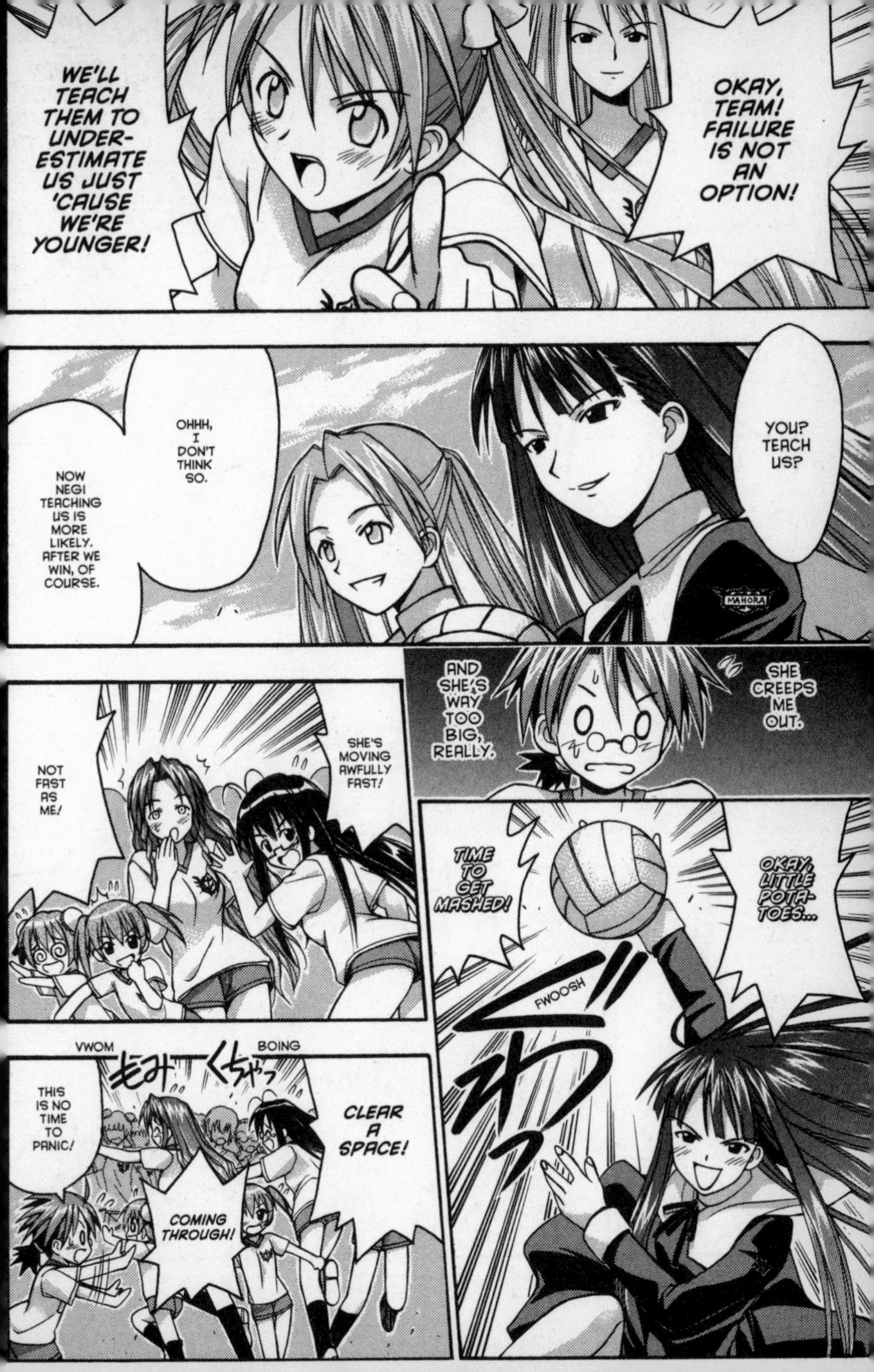
OKAY, TEAM! FAILURE IS NOT AN OPTION!
WE'LL TEACH THEM TO UNDER-ESTIMATE US JUST 'CAUSE WE'RE YOUNGER!
YOU? TEACH US?
OHHH, I DON'T THINK SO.
NOW NEGI TEACHING US IS MORE LIKELY. AFTER WE WIN, OF COURSE.
SHE CREEPS ME OUT.
AND SHE'S WAY TOO BIG, REALLY.
OKAY, LITTLE POTATOES...
TIME TO GET MASHED!
FWOOSH
SHE'S MOVING AWFULLY FAST!
NOT FAST AS ME!
BOING
VWOM
CLEAR A SPACE!
THIS IS NO TIME TO PANIC!
COMING THROUGH!

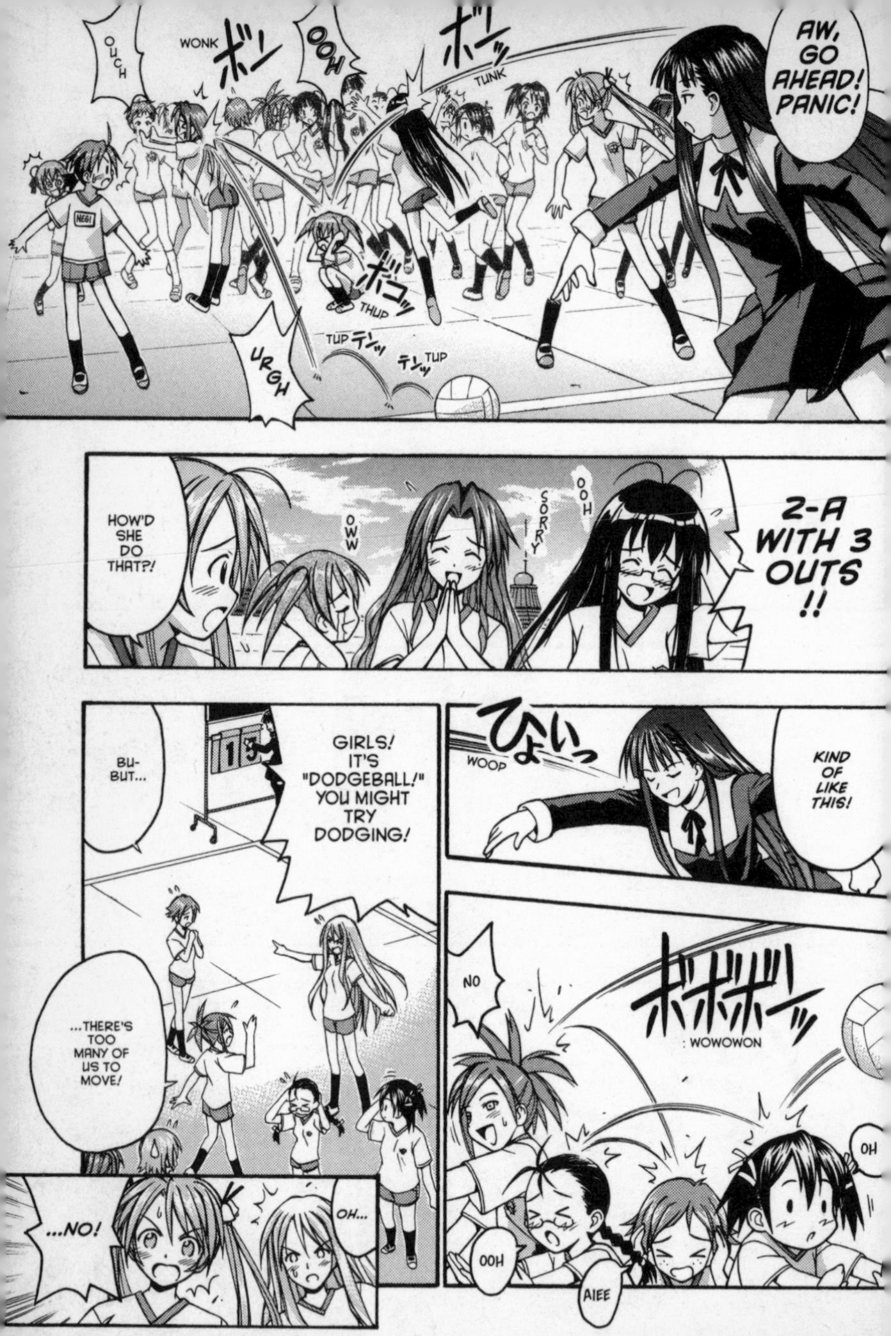
AW, GO AHEAD! PANIC!
ボーッ
TUNK
OOH
ボン
WONK
OUCH
ボゴッ
THUD
テンッ
TUP
テンッ
TUP
URGH
2-A WITH 3 OUTS !!
OOH
SORRY
OWW
HOW'D SHE DO THAT?!
KIND OF LIKE THIS!
ひょいっ
WOOP
OH
ボボボーッ
WOWOWON
NO
OOH
AIEE
GIRLS! IT'S "DODGEBALL!" YOU MIGHT TRY DODGING!
BU- BUT...
...THERE'S TOO MANY OF US TO MOVE!
OH...
...NO!

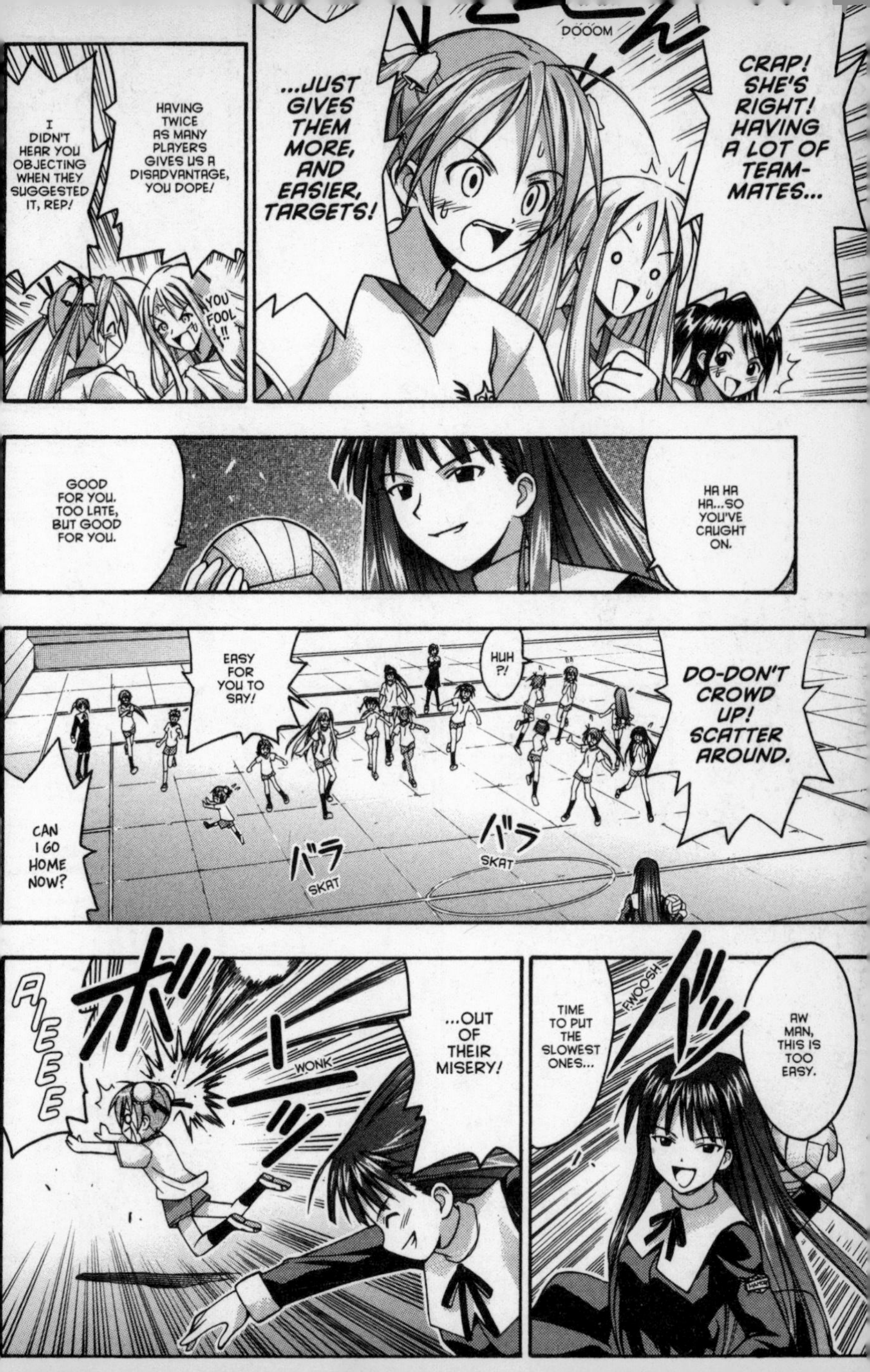
DOOOM
CRAP! SHE'S RIGHT! HAVING A LOT OF TEAM-MATES...
...JUST GIVES THEM MORE, AND EASIER, TARGETS!
HAVING TWICE AS MANY PLAYERS GIVES US A DISADVANTAGE, YOU DOPE!
I DIDN'T HEAR YOU OBJECTING WHEN THEY SUGGESTED IT, REP!
YOU FOOL!!
HA HA HA...SO YOU'VE CAUGHT ON.
GOOD FOR YOU. TOO LATE, BUT GOOD FOR YOU.
DO-DON'T CROWD UP! SCATTER AROUND.
HUH?!
EASY FOR YOU TO SAY!
バラ
SKAT
バラ
SKAT
CAN I GO HOME NOW?
AW MAN, THIS IS TOO EASY.
FWOOSH
TIME TO PUT THE SLOWEST ONES...
...OUT OF THEIR MISERY!
WONK
AIEEEE

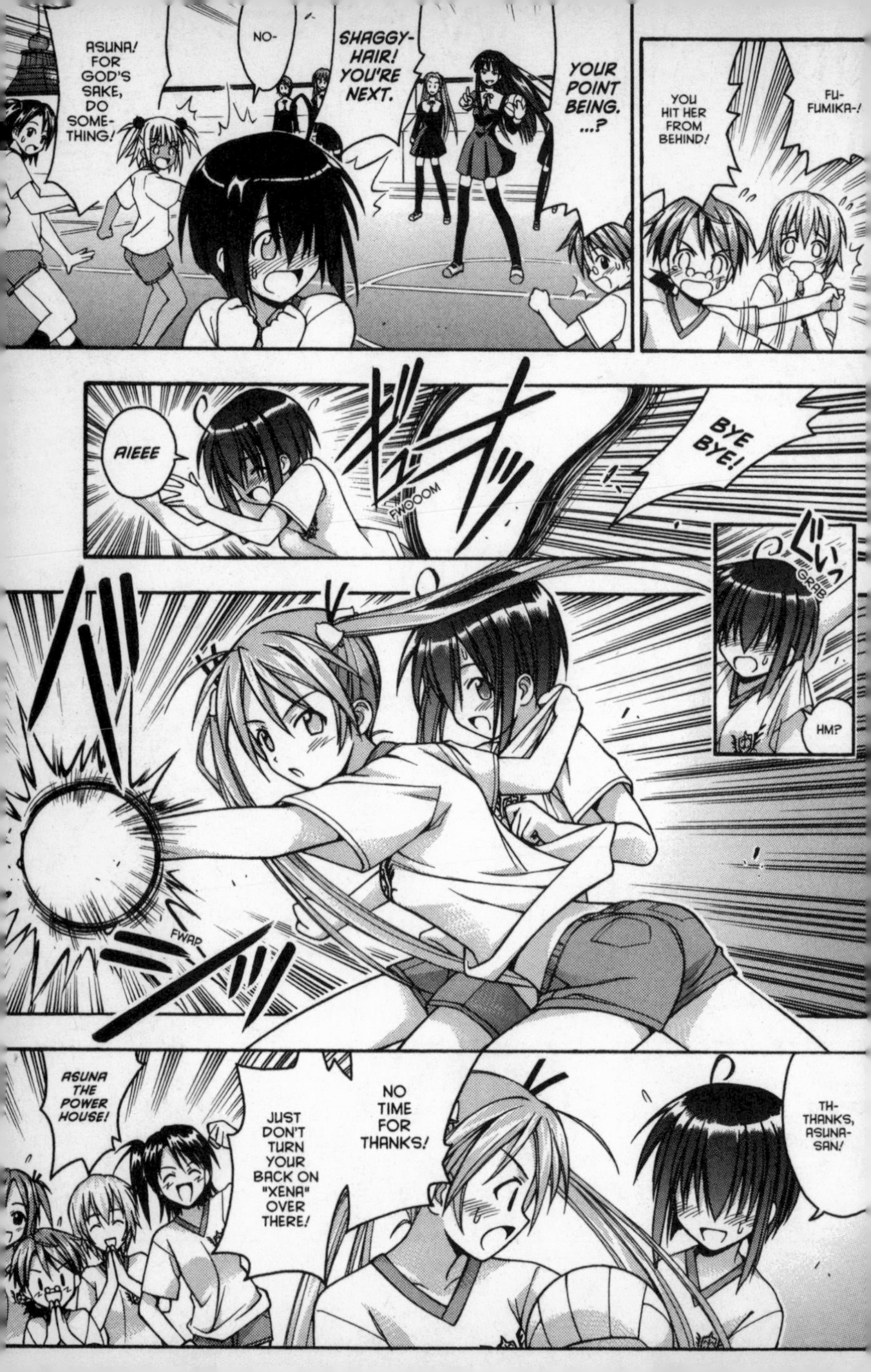
FU-FUMIKA-!
YOU HIT HER FROM BEHIND!
YOUR POINT BEING. ...?
SHAGGY-HAIR! YOU'RE NEXT.
NO-
ASUNA! FOR GOD'S SAKE, DO SOME-THING!
BYE BYE!
FWOOOM
AIEEE
ぐいっ
GRAB
HM?
FWAP
TH-THANKS, ASUNA-SAN!
NO TIME FOR THANKS!
JUST DON'T TURN YOUR BACK ON "XENA" OVER THERE!
ASUNA THE POWER HOUSE!

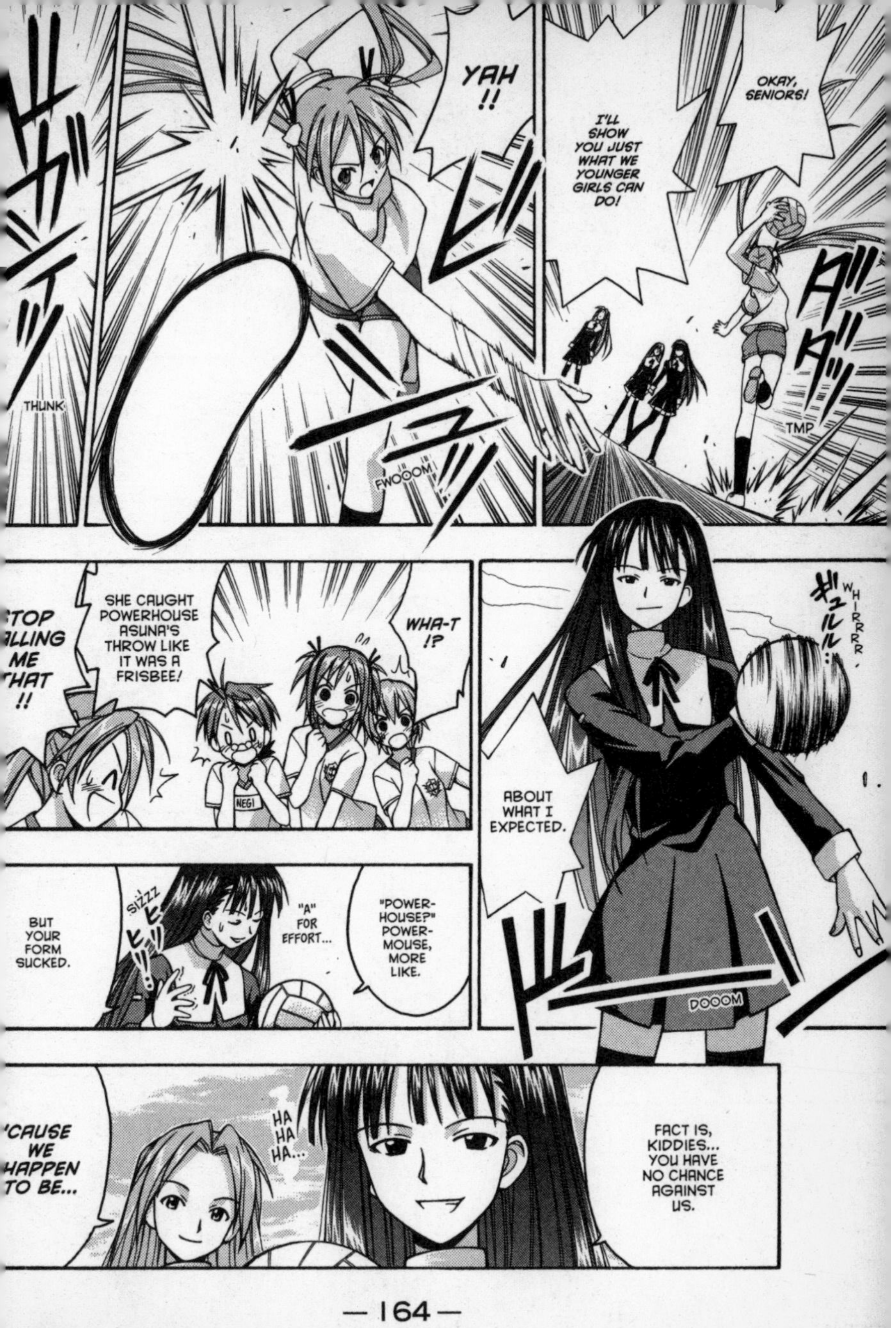
OKAY, SENIORS!
I'LL SHOW YOU JUST WHAT WE YOUNGER GIRLS CAN DO!
TMP
YAH!!
FWOOOM
THUNK
WHIRRRR
ABOUT WHAT I EXPECTED.
DOOOM
WHA-T!?
SHE CAUGHT POWERHOUSE ASUNA'S THROW LIKE IT WAS A FRISBEE!
TOP ALLING ME HAT!!
NEGI
"POWER-HOUSE?" POWER-MOUSE, MORE LIKE.
"A" FOR EFFORT...
SIZZZ
BUT YOUR FORM SUCKED.
FACT IS, KIDDIES... YOU HAVE NO CHANCE AGAINST US.
HA HA HA...
'CAUSE WE HAPPEN TO BE...

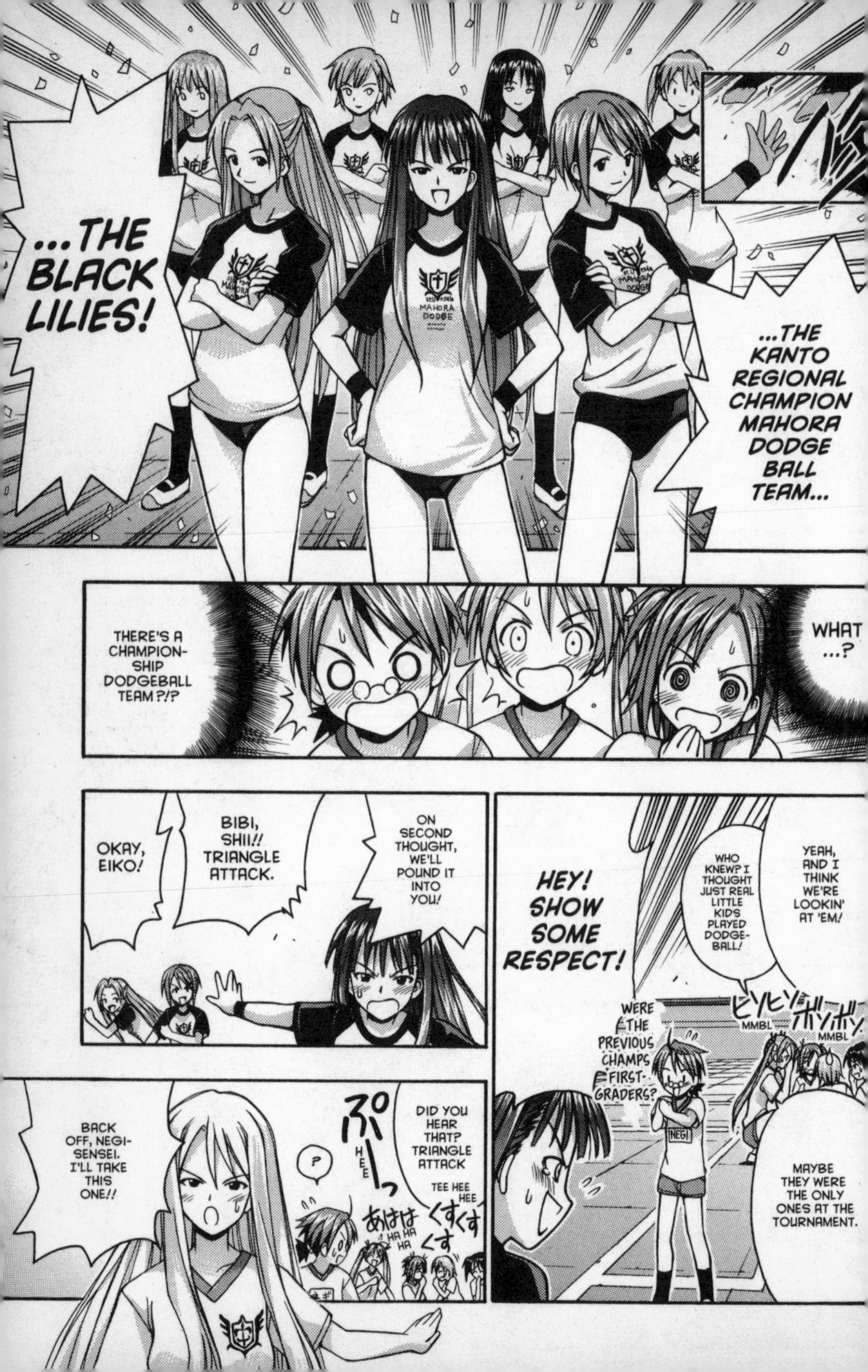
...THE KANTO REGIONAL CHAMPION MAHORA DODGE BALL TEAM...
...THE BLACK LILIES!
WHAT ...?
THERE'S A CHAMPIONSHIP DODGEBALL TEAM?!?
YEAH, AND I THINK WE'RE LOOKIN' AT 'EM!
WHO KNEW? I THOUGHT JUST REAL LITTLE KIDS PLAYED DODGE-BALL!
HEY! SHOW SOME RESPECT!
ボソボソ MMBL
ヒソヒソ MMBL
ON SECOND THOUGHT, WE'LL POUND IT INTO YOU!
BIBI, SHII!! TRIANGLE ATTACK.
OKAY, EIKO!
MAYBE THEY WERE THE ONLY ONES AT THE TOURNAMENT.
WERE THE PREVIOUS CHAMPS FIRST-GRADERS?
NEGI
DID YOU HEAR THAT? TRIANGLE ATTACK
ぷーっ HEE
くすくすくす TEE HEE HEE
あはは HA HA HA
?
BACK OFF, NEGI-SENSEI. I'LL TAKE THIS ONE!!

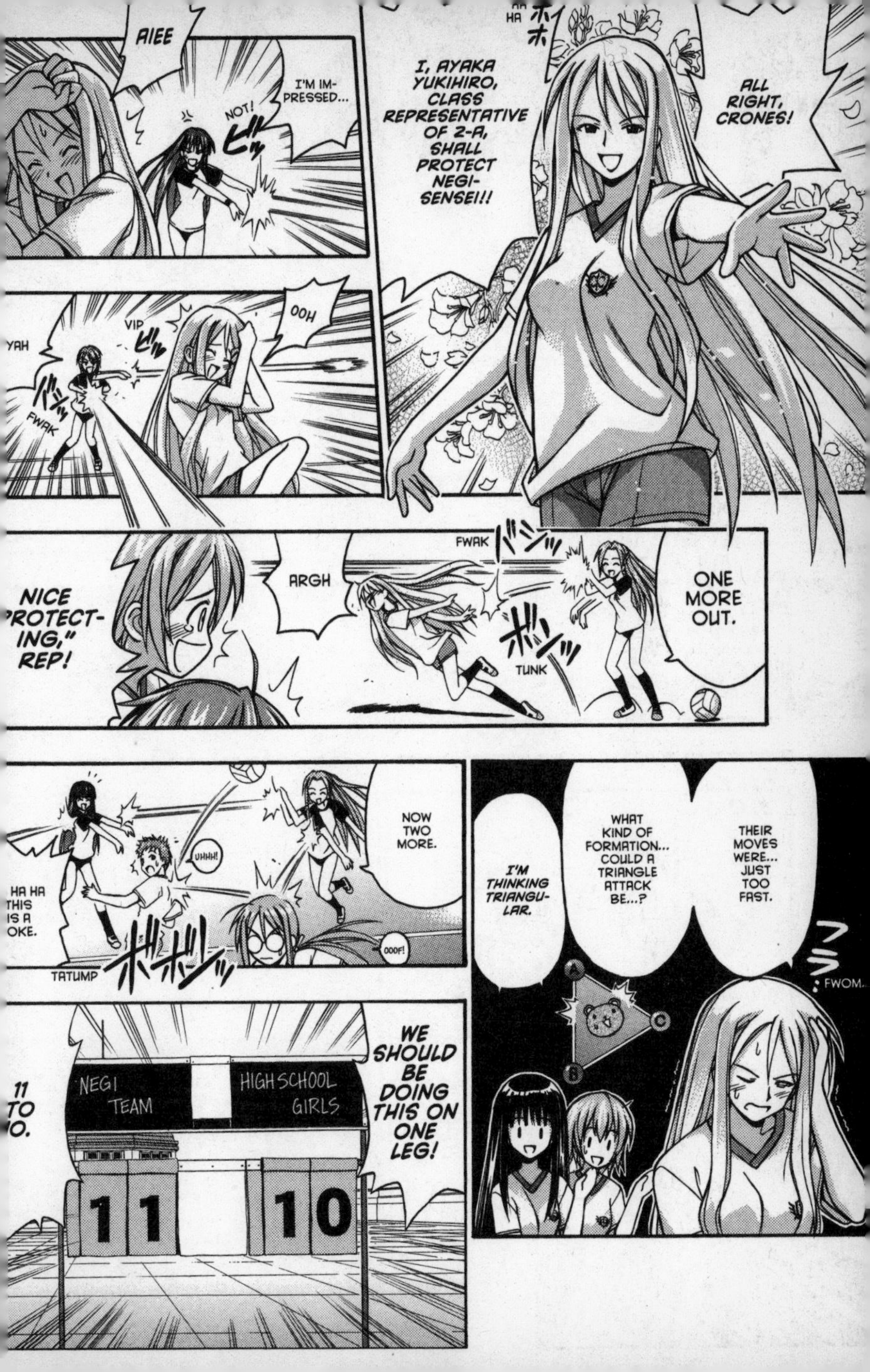
HA HA
ALL RIGHT, CRONES!
I, AYAKA YUKIHIRO, CLASS REPRESENTATIVE OF 2-A, SHALL PROTECT NEGI-SENSEI!!
I'M IM-PRESSED...
NOT!
AIEE
OOH
VIP
YAH
FWAK
ONE MORE OUT.
FWAK
ARGH
TUNK
NICE PROTECTING," REP!
THEIR MOVES WERE... JUST TOO FAST.
WHAT KIND OF FORMATION... COULD A TRIANGLE ATTACK BE...?
I'M THINKING TRIANGULAR.
FWOM...
NOW TWO MORE.
UHHH!
OOOF!
HA HA THIS IS A OKE.
TATUMP
WE SHOULD BE DOING THIS ON ONE LEG!
NEGI TEAM
HIGH SCHOOL GIRLS
11
10
11 TO

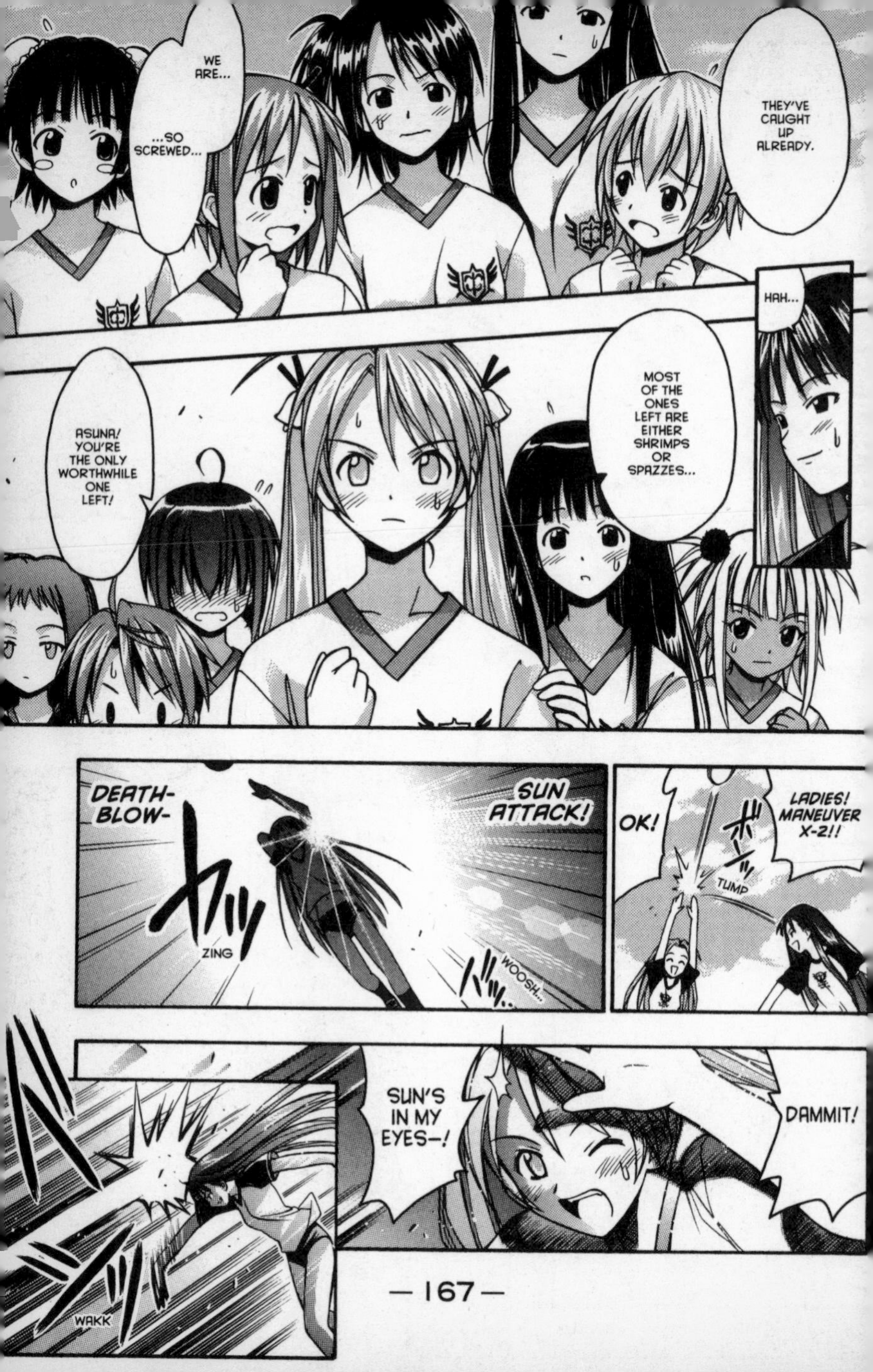
THEY'VE CAUGHT UP ALREADY.
WE ARE...
...SO SCREWED...
HAH...
MOST OF THE ONES LEFT ARE EITHER SHRIMPS OR SPAZZES...
ASUNA! YOU'RE THE ONLY WORTHWHILE ONE LEFT!
LADIES! MANEUVER X-2!!
OK!
TUMP
DEATH-BLOW-
SUN ATTACK!
ZING
WOOSH...
DAMMIT!
SUN'S IN MY EYES—!
WAKK

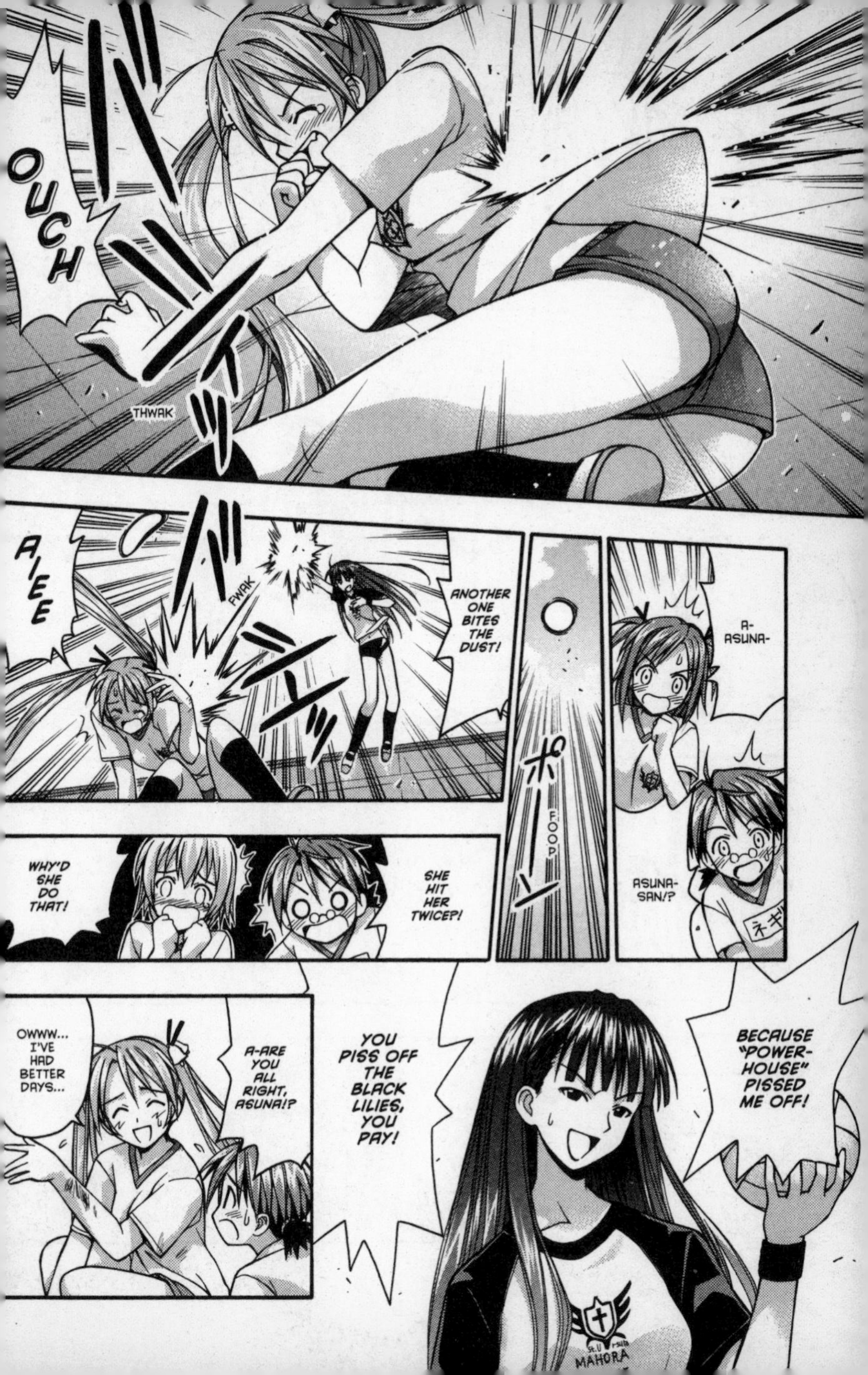
OUCH
THWAK
A-ASUNA-
ASUNA-SAN!?
FOOP
ANOTHER ONE BITES THE DUST!
FWAK
AIEE
SHE HIT HER TWICE!?
WHY'D SHE DO THAT!
BECAUSE "POWER-HOUSE" PISSED ME OFF!
YOU PISS OFF THE BLACK LILIES, YOU PAY!
MAHORA
A-ARE YOU ALL RIGHT, ASUNA!?
OWWW... I'VE HAD BETTER DAYS...

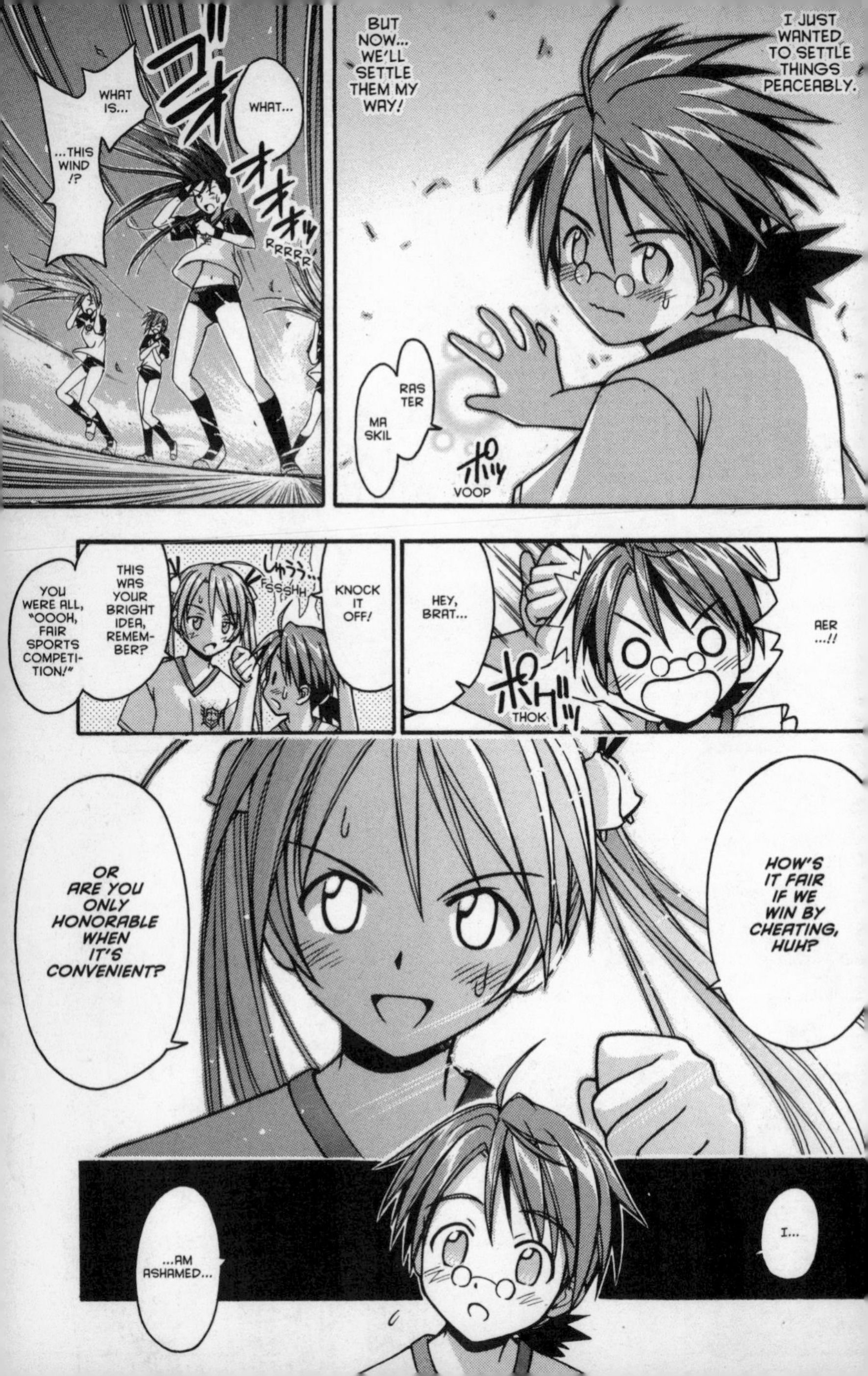
I JUST WANTED TO SETTLE THINGS PEACEABLY.
BUT NOW... WE'LL SETTLE THEM MY WAY!
RASTER MASKIL
VOOP
WHAT...
WHAT IS...
...THIS WIND !?
RRRRRR
AER ...!!
HEY, BRAT...
THOK
KNOCK IT OFF!
FSSSHH
THIS WAS YOUR BRIGHT IDEA, REMEMBER?
YOU WERE ALL, "OOOH, FAIR SPORTS COMPETITION!"
HOW'S IT FAIR IF WE WIN BY CHEATING, HUH?
OR ARE YOU ONLY HONORABLE WHEN IT'S CONVENIENT?
I...
...AM ASHAMED...

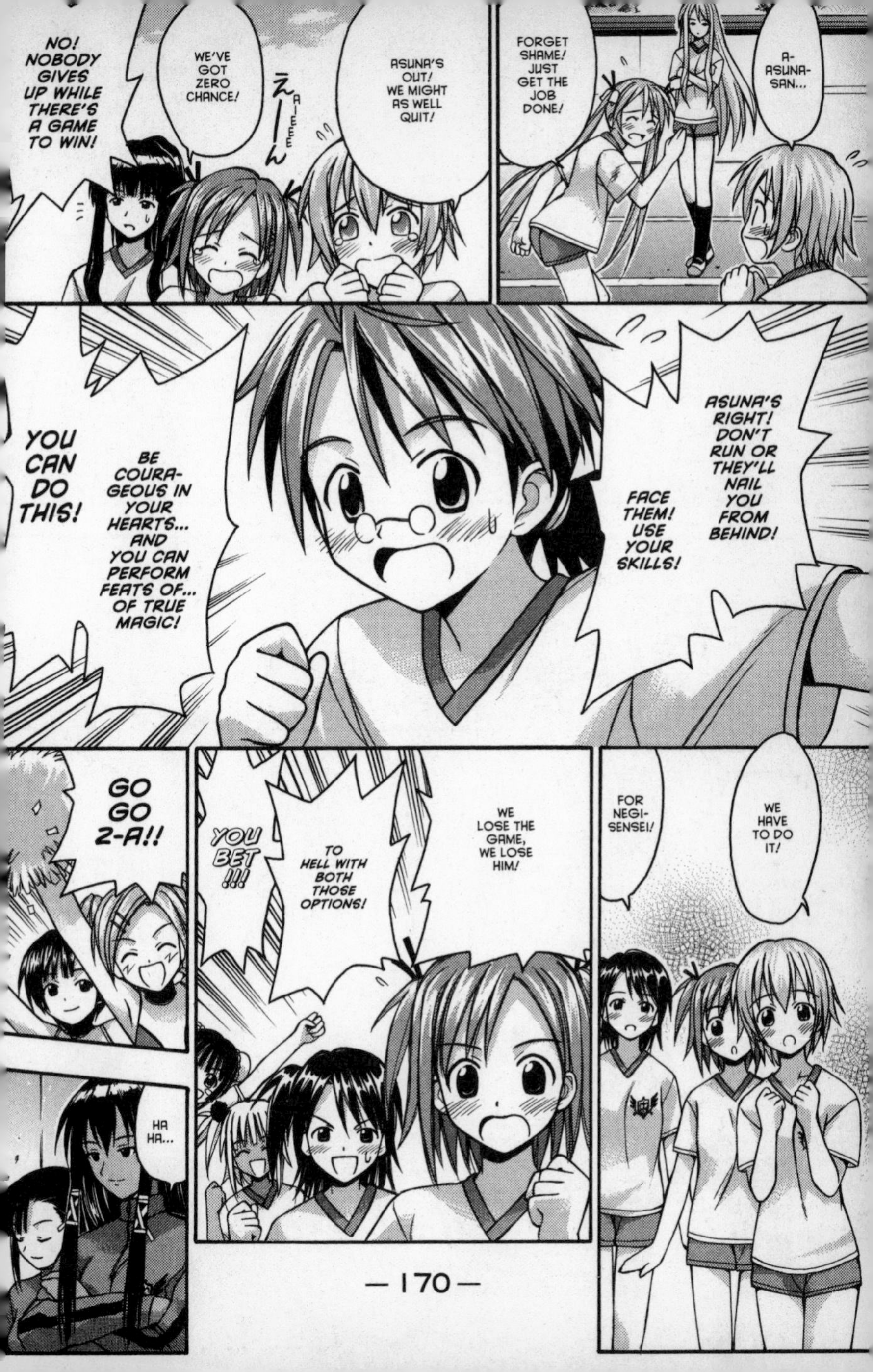
A-ASUNA-SAN...
FORGET SHAME! JUST GET THE JOB DONE!
ASUNA'S OUT! WE MIGHT AS WELL QUIT!
AIEEE
WE'VE GOT ZERO CHANCE!
NO! NOBODY GIVES UP WHILE THERE'S A GAME TO WIN!
ASUNA'S RIGHT! DON'T RUN OR THEY'LL NAIL YOU FROM BEHIND!
FACE THEM! USE YOUR SKILLS!
BE COURAGEOUS IN YOUR HEARTS... AND YOU CAN PERFORM FEATS OF... OF TRUE MAGIC!
YOU CAN DO THIS!
WE HAVE TO DO IT!
FOR NEGI-SENSEI!
WE LOSE THE GAME, WE LOSE HIM!
TO HELL WITH BOTH THOSE OPTIONS!
YOU BET!!!
GO GO 2-A!!
HA HA...

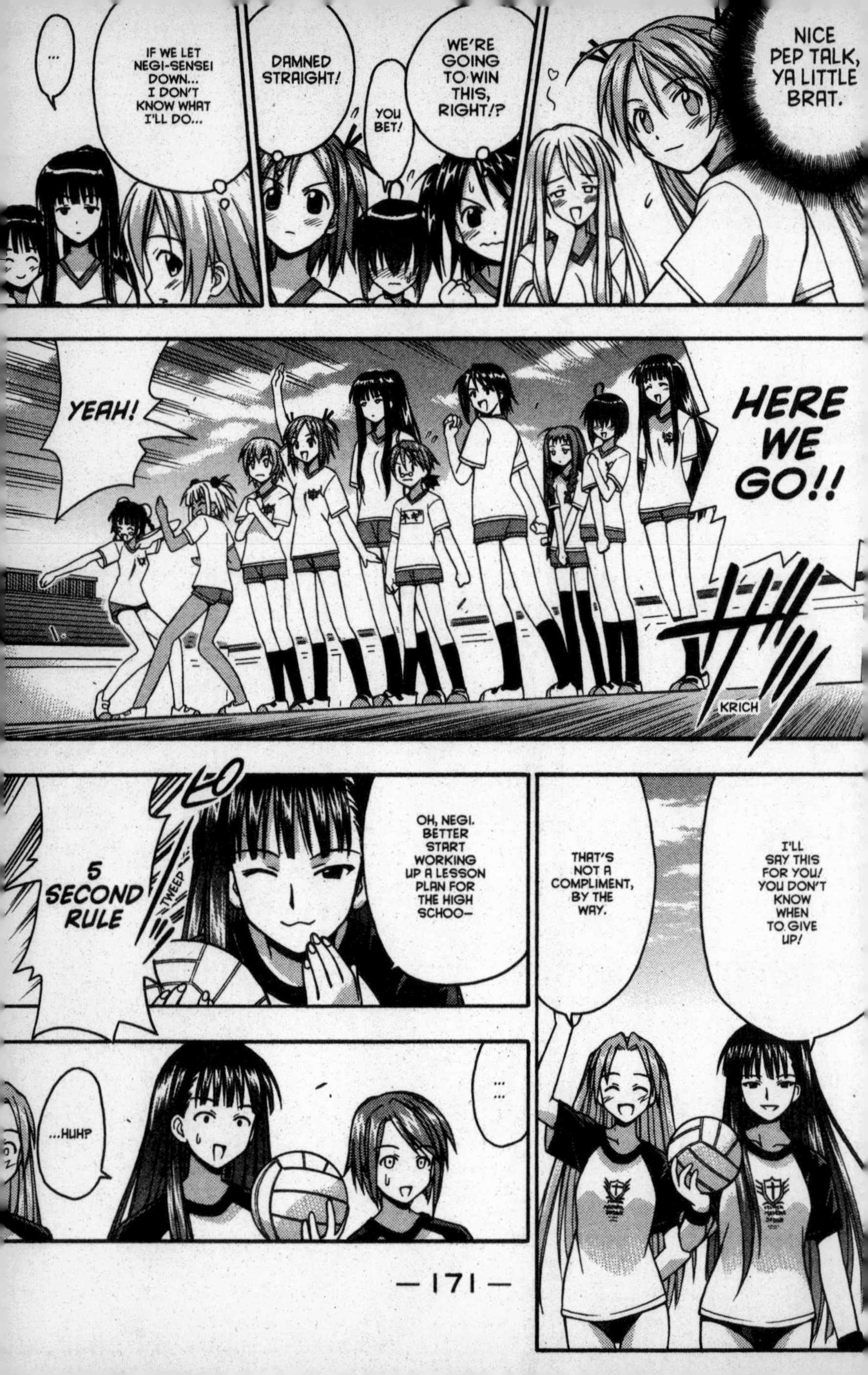
NICE PEP TALK, YA LITTLE BRAT.
WE'RE GOING TO WIN THIS, RIGHT!?
YOU BET!
DAMNED STRAIGHT!
IF WE LET NEGI-SENSEI DOWN... I DON'T KNOW WHAT I'LL DO...
...
HERE WE GO!!
KRICH
YEAH!
I'LL SAY THIS FOR YOU! YOU DON'T KNOW WHEN TO GIVE UP!
THAT'S NOT A COMPLIMENT, BY THE WAY.
OH, NEGI. BETTER START WORKING UP A LESSON PLAN FOR THE HIGH SCHOO—
TWEEP
5 SECOND RULE
... ...
...HUH?

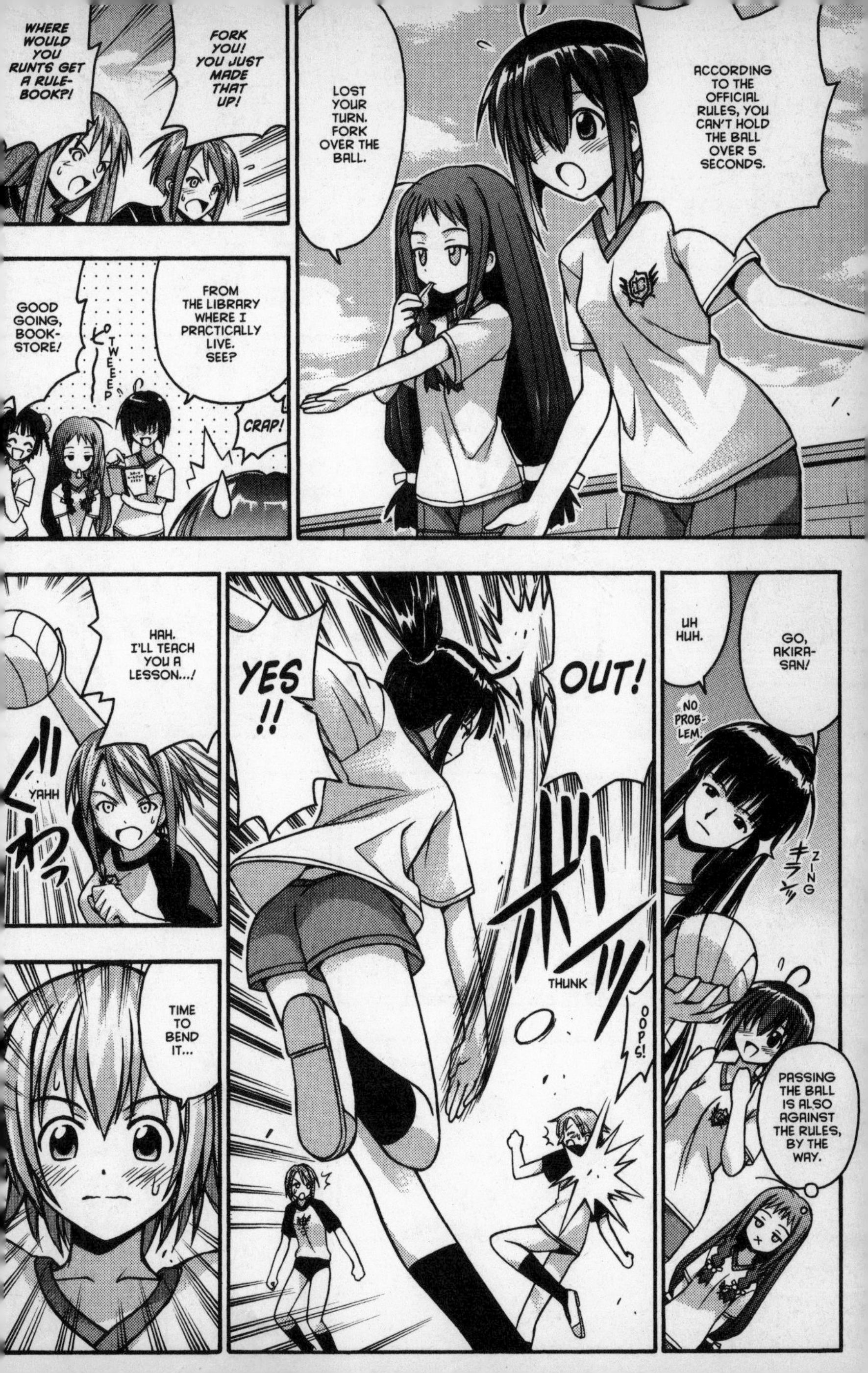
ACCORDING TO THE OFFICIAL RULES, YOU CAN'T HOLD THE BALL OVER 5 SECONDS.
LOST YOUR TURN. FORK OVER THE BALL.
FORK YOU! YOU JUST MADE THAT UP!
WHERE WOULD YOU RUNTS GET A RULE-BOOK?!
FROM THE LIBRARY WHERE I PRACTICALLY LIVE. SEE?
TWEEEP
GOOD GOING, BOOK-STORE!
CRAP!
GO, AKIRA-SAN!
UH HUH.
NO PROB-LEM.
ZING
PASSING THE BALL IS ALSO AGAINST THE RULES, BY THE WAY.
OUT!
YES !!
THUNK
OOPS!
HAH. I'LL TEACH YOU A LESSON...!
YAHH
TIME TO BEND IT...

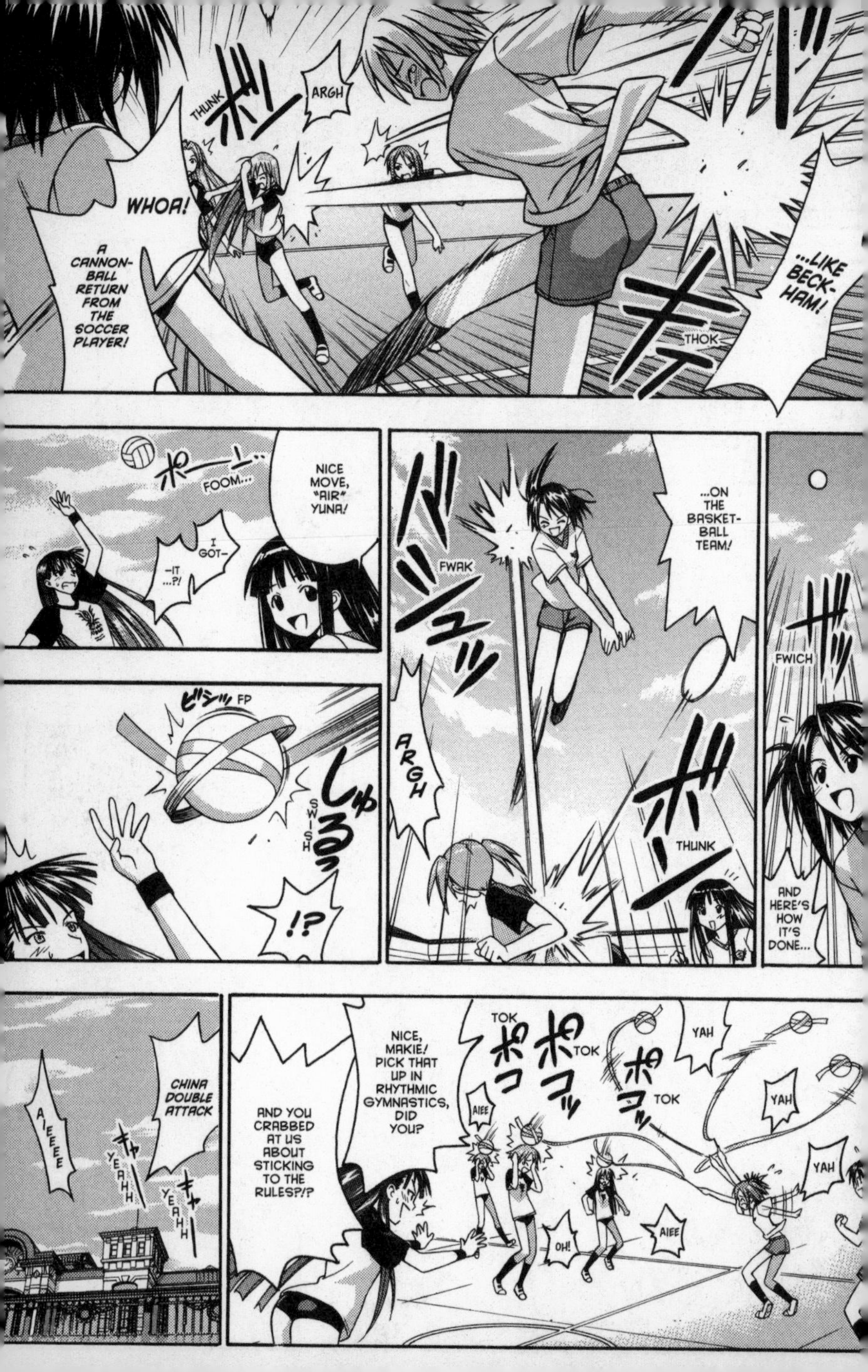
...LIKE BECKHAM!
THOK
ARGH
THUNK
WHOA!
A CANNONBALL RETURN FROM THE SOCCER PLAYER!
FWICH
AND HERE'S HOW IT'S DONE...
...ON THE BASKETBALL TEAM!
FWAK
ARGH
THUNK
NICE MOVE, "AIR" YUNA!
FOOM...
I GOT—
—IT ...?!
FP
SWISH
!?
YAH
YAH
YAH
TOK
TOK
TOK
NICE, MAKIE! PICK THAT UP IN RHYTHMIC GYMNASTICS, DID YOU?
AIEE
AIEE
OH!
AND YOU CRABBED AT US ABOUT STICKING TO THE RULES?!?
CHINA DOUBLE ATTACK
AIEEEE
YEAHH
YEAHH

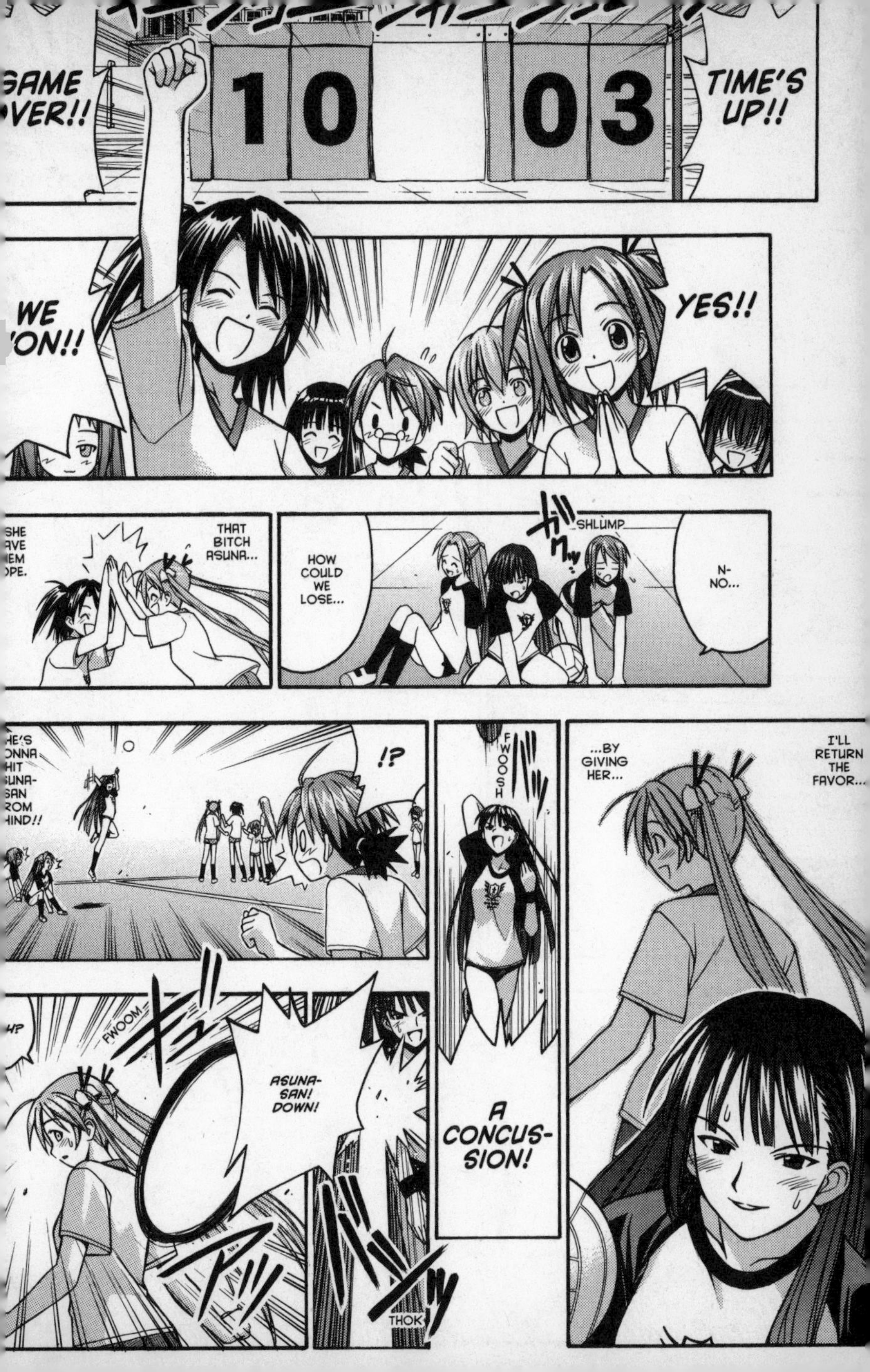
TIME'S UP!!
10 03
GAME
YES!!
N- NO...
SHLUMP
HOW COULD WE LOSE...
THAT BITCH ASUNA...
I'LL RETURN THE FAVOR...
...BY GIVING HER...
FWOOSH
A CONCUS-SION!
!?
ASUNA-SAN! DOWN!
FWOOM
THOK

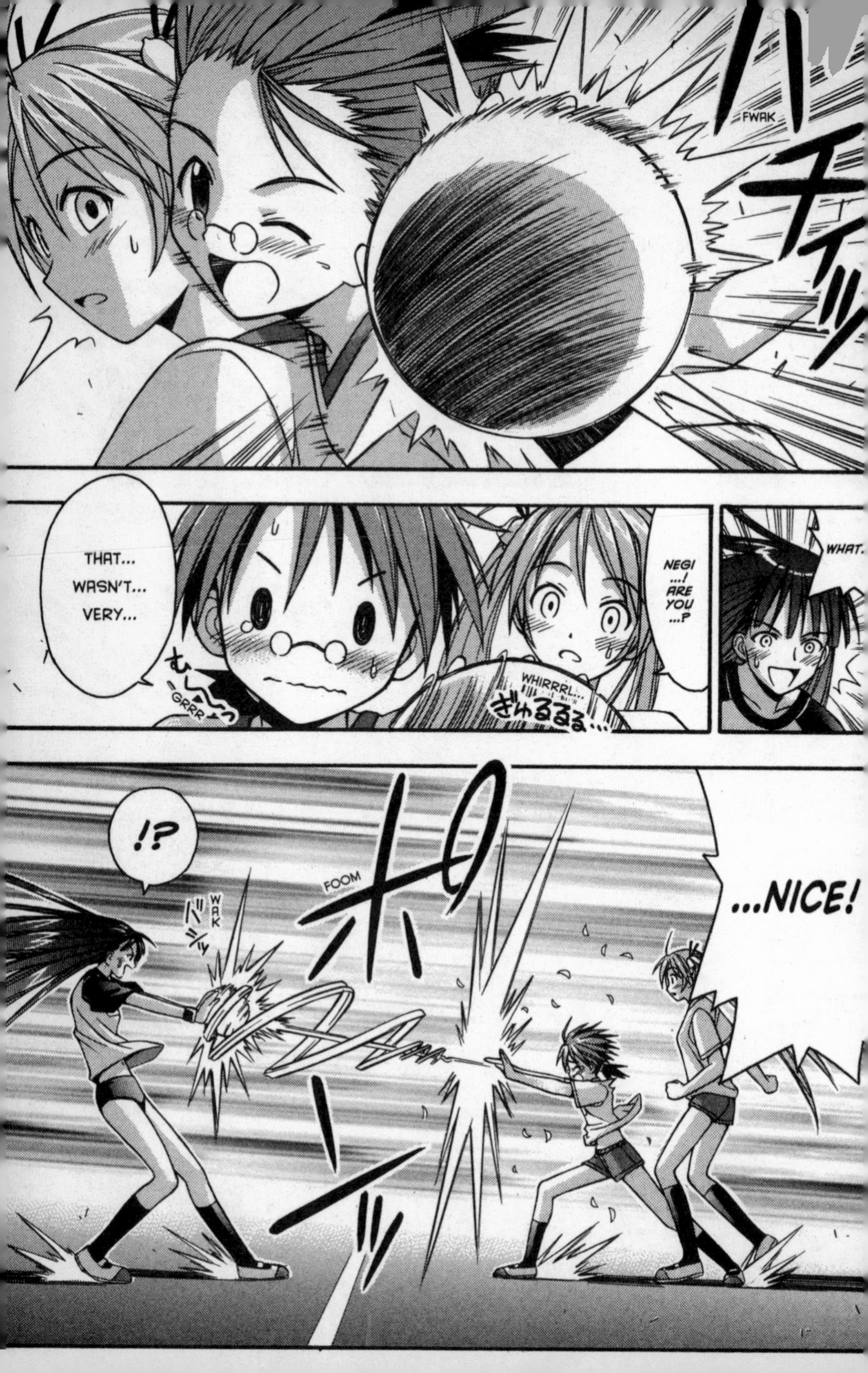
FWAK
WHAT.
NEGI ...! ARE YOU ...?
THAT... WASN'T... VERY...
WHIRRRL...
GRRR
...NICE!
FOOM
WAK
!?

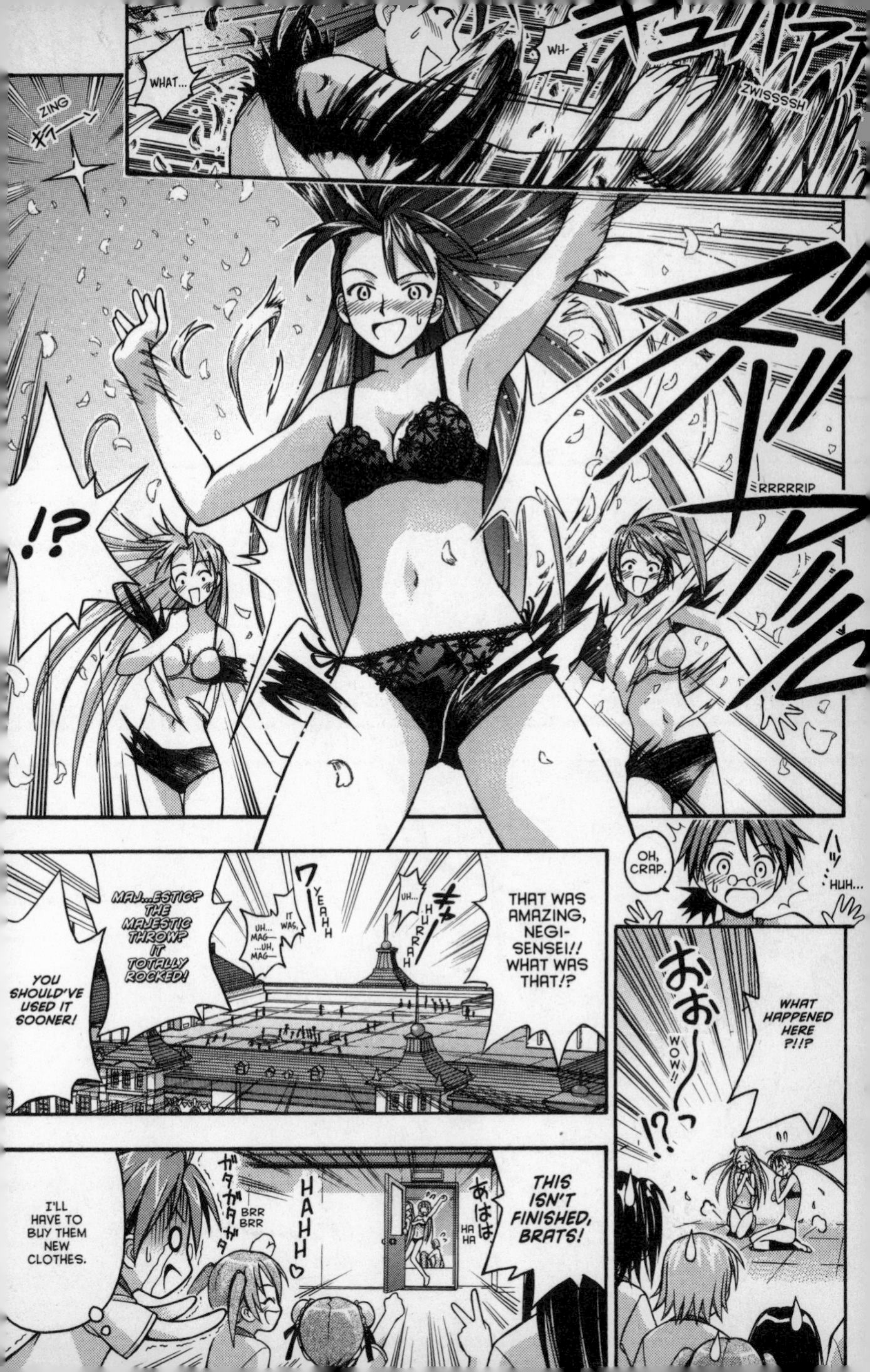

WH-
WHAT...
ZWISSSSH
ZING
RRRRRIP
!?
OH, CRAP.
HUH...
WHAT HAPPENED HERE?!?
WOW!!
!?
THAT WAS AMAZING, NEGI-SENSEI!! WHAT WAS THAT!?
UH...
HURRAH
YEAHH
IT WAS,
UH... MAG— ...UH, MAG—
MAJ...ESTIC? THE MAJESTIC THROW? IT TOTALLY ROCKED!
YOU SHOULD'VE USED IT SOONER!
THIS ISN'T FINISHED, BRATS!
HA HA
HAHH
BRR BRR
I'LL HAVE TO BUY THEM NEW CLOTHES.

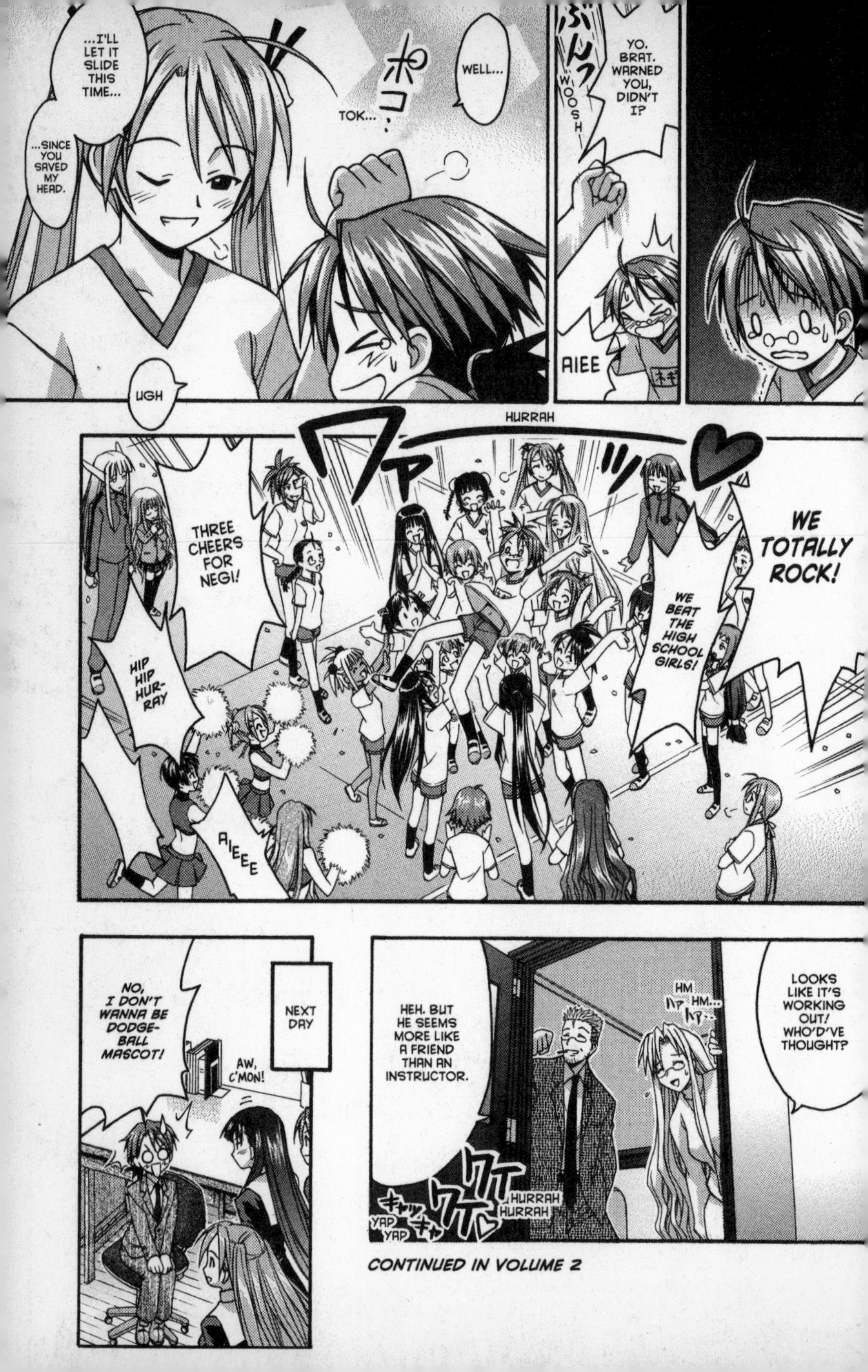
ぶんっ
WOOSH
YO. BRAT. WARNED YOU, DIDN'T I?
AIEE
WELL...
ポコ
TOK...
...I'LL LET IT SLIDE THIS TIME...
...SINCE YOU SAVED MY HEAD.
UGH
ワァッ
HURRAH
WE TOTALLY ROCK!
WE BEAT THE HIGH SCHOOL GIRLS!
THREE CHEERS FOR NEGI!
HIP HIP HUR-RAY
AIEEE
LOOKS LIKE IT'S WORKING OUT! WHO'D'VE THOUGHT?
ハァ ハァ
HM HM...
HEH. BUT HE SEEMS MORE LIKE A FRIEND THAN AN INSTRUCTOR.
ワイワイ
HURRAH HURRAH
キャッキャ
YAP YAP
NEXT DAY
NO, I DON'T WANNA BE DODGE-BALL MASCOT!
AW, C'MON!

CONTINUED IN VOLUME 2

– STAFF –

Ken Akamatsu
Takashi Takemoto
Kenichi Nakamura
Masaki Ohyama
Keiichi Yamashita
Chigusa Amagasaki ·
Takaaki Miyahara
Kei Nishikawa

Thanks To

Ran Ayanaga
Toshiko Akamatsu

Welcome. . .

. . . to the launch of the Del Rey Manga line! It all starts here, with four new series from Japan: *Negima!* by Ken Akamatsu! *Gundam SEED* by Masatsuga Iwase! And *Tsubasa: Reservoir Chronicle* and *xxxHOLiC*, both by CLAMP! Together, these four series represent some of the best and most popular manga series published in Japan.

We're dedicated to providing our readers with the most enjoyable, authentic manga experience possible. Our books are printed from right to left, in the Japanese printing format. We strive to keep the translations as true to the original as possible, while giving the English versions the same sense of adventure and fun. We keep Japanese honorifics intact, translate all sound effects, and give you extras at the back of the books to help you understand the context of the stories and keep track of all the characters. It's the next best thing to being able to read Japanese yourself!

For information on upcoming releases, visit www.delreymanga.com, and while you're there be sure to sign up for our newsletter. If you do, you'll be the first to hear all the scoop on Del Rey Manga, and you'll have the opportunity to talk back directly to the editor (that would be me) and say what works for you in our books, and what doesn't. Manga wouldn't be the red-hot phenomenon it is without your support, and we want your feedback.

See you in volume 2!

Dallas Middaugh

Dallas Middaugh
Director of Manga, Del Rey Books

About the Creator

Negima! is only Ken Akamatsu's third manga, although he started working in the field in 1994 with *AI Ga Tomaranai*. Like all of Akamatsu's work to date, it was published in Kodansha's *Shonen Magazine*. *AI Ga Tomaranai* ran for five years before concluding in 1999. In 1998, however, Akamatsu began the work that would make him one of the most popular manga artists in Japan: *Love Hina*. *Love Hina* ran for four years, and before its conclusion in 2002, it would cause Akamatsu to be granted the prestigious Manga of the Year award from Kodansha, as well as going on to become one of the best-selling manga in the United States.

"PROFESSOR" NEGI, MAGUS
PROVISIONAL 3-A HEIGHT CHART

180
170
160
150
SAKURAZAKI
IZUMI
AYASE
NABA
MURAKAMI
NAKASE
TATSUMIYA
YOTSUYA
SHIINA
THE NARUTAKIS
SASAKI
KONOE
KAGURAZAKA
YUKIHIRO
EVANGELINE
MIYAZAKI
HASEGAWA
ZAZIE
NAGASE
RAKUSO
ASAKURA
ASASHI
KASUGA
TOBISAKA
OTSU
AKUSAWA
KU
KAKIZAKE
SAOTOME
KUGIMIYA

"MAGISTER NEGIMA!" CONCEPT ART COLLECTION

OFFICIAL PROVISIONAL VERSION

COMMENTS BY KEN AKAMATSU

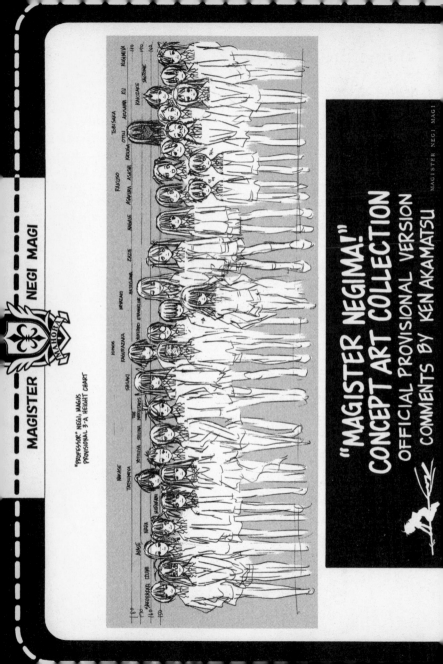

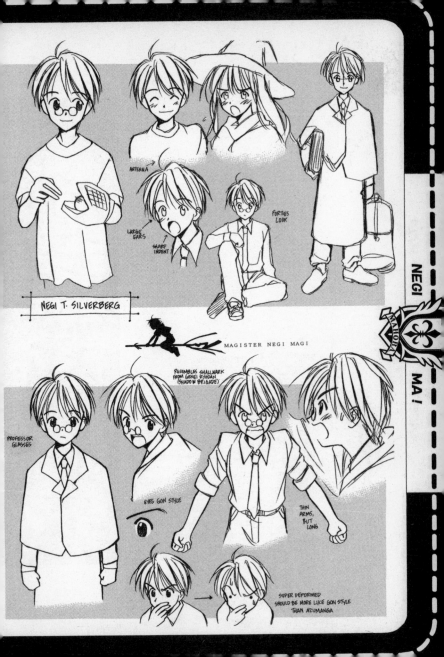

ANTENNA

LARGE
EARS

SHARP
INDENT

FORTIES
LOOK

NEGI T. SILVERBERG

MAGISTER NEGI MAGI

RESEMBLES SHALLNARK
FROM GENEI RYODAN
(SHADOW BRIGADE)

PROFESSOR
GLASSES

EYES GON STYLE

THIN
ARMS,
BUT
LONG

SUPER DEFORMED
SHOULD BE MORE LIKE GON STYLE
THAN AZUMANGA

MAHORA

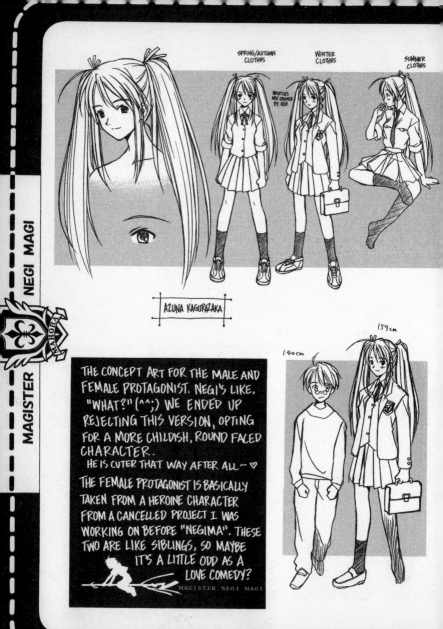

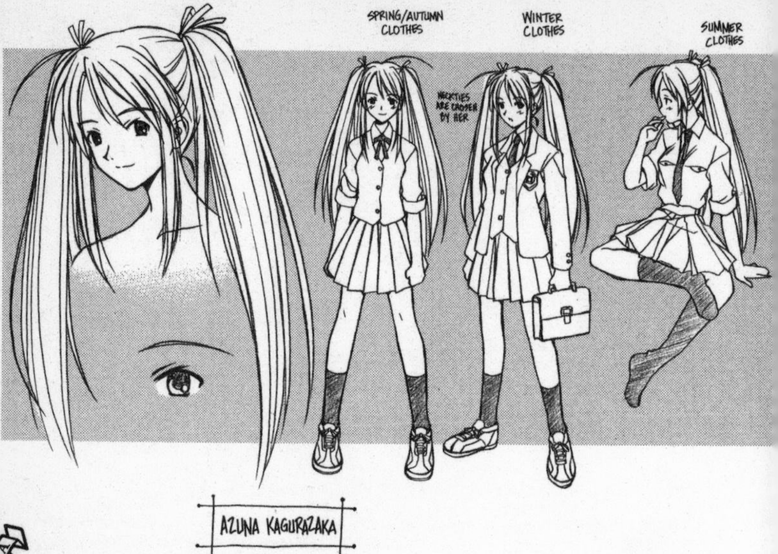
SPRING/AUTUMN CLOTHES
WINTER CLOTHES
SUMMER CLOTHES
NECKTIES ARE CHOSEN BY HER
AZUNA KAGURAZAKA

THE CONCEPT ART FOR THE MALE AND FEMALE PROTAGONIST. NEGI'S LIKE, "WHAT?" (^^;) WE ENDED UP REJECTING THIS VERSION, OPTING FOR A MORE CHILDISH, ROUND FACED CHARACTER.
HE IS CUTER THAT WAY AFTER ALL~ ♡
THE FEMALE PROTAGONIST IS BASICALLY TAKEN FROM A HEROINE CHARACTER FROM A CANCELLED PROJECT I WAS WORKING ON BEFORE "NEGIMA". THESE TWO ARE LIKE SIBLINGS, SO MAYBE IT'S A LITTLE ODD AS A LOVE COMEDY?

MAGISTER NEGI MAGI

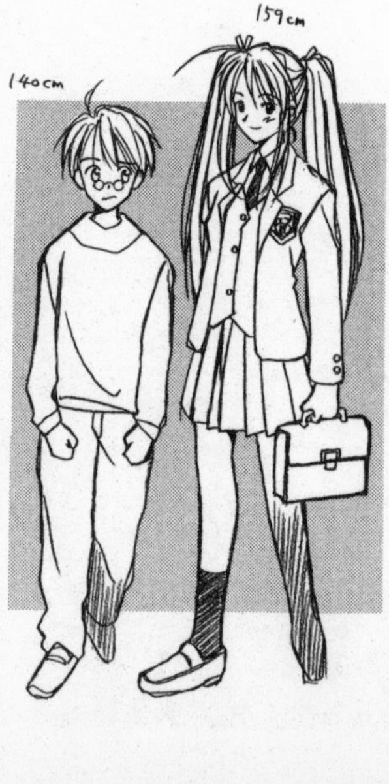
159 cm
140 cm

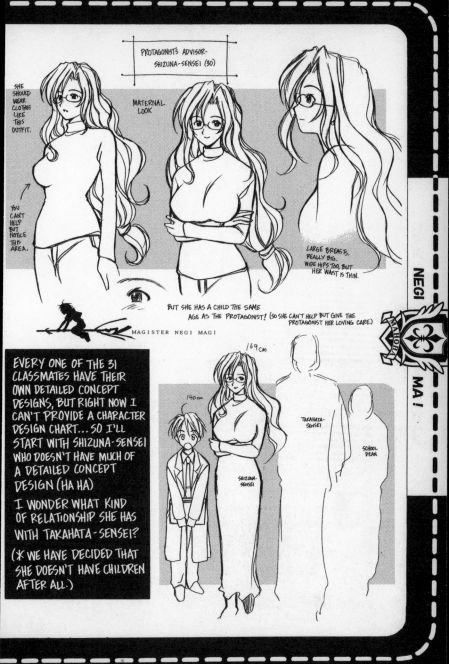

PROTAGONIST'S ADVISOR-
SHIZUNA-SENSEI (30)

SHE SHOULD WEAR CLOTHES LIKE THIS OUTFIT.

MATERNAL LOOK

YOU CAN'T HELP BUT NOTICE THIS AREA.

LARGE BREASTS. REALLY BIG. WIDE HIPS TOO, BUT HER WAIST IS THIN.

BUT SHE HAS A CHILD THE SAME AGE AS THE PROTAGONIST! (SO SHE CAN'T HELP BUT GIVE THE PROTAGONIST HER LOVING CARE.)

MAGISTER NEGI MAGI

EVERY ONE OF THE 31 CLASSMATES HAVE THEIR OWN DETAILED CONCEPT DESIGNS, BUT RIGHT NOW I CAN'T PROVIDE A CHARACTER DESIGN CHART... SO I'LL START WITH SHIZUNA-SENSEI WHO DOESN'T HAVE MUCH OF A DETAILED CONCEPT DESIGN (HA HA)

I WONDER WHAT KIND OF RELATIONSHIP SHE HAS WITH TAKAHATA-SENSEI?

(✳ WE HAVE DECIDED THAT SHE DOESN'T HAVE CHILDREN AFTER ALL.)

169cm

140cm

SHIZUNA-SENSEI

TAKAHATA-SENSEI

SCHOOL DEAN

NEGI MA!

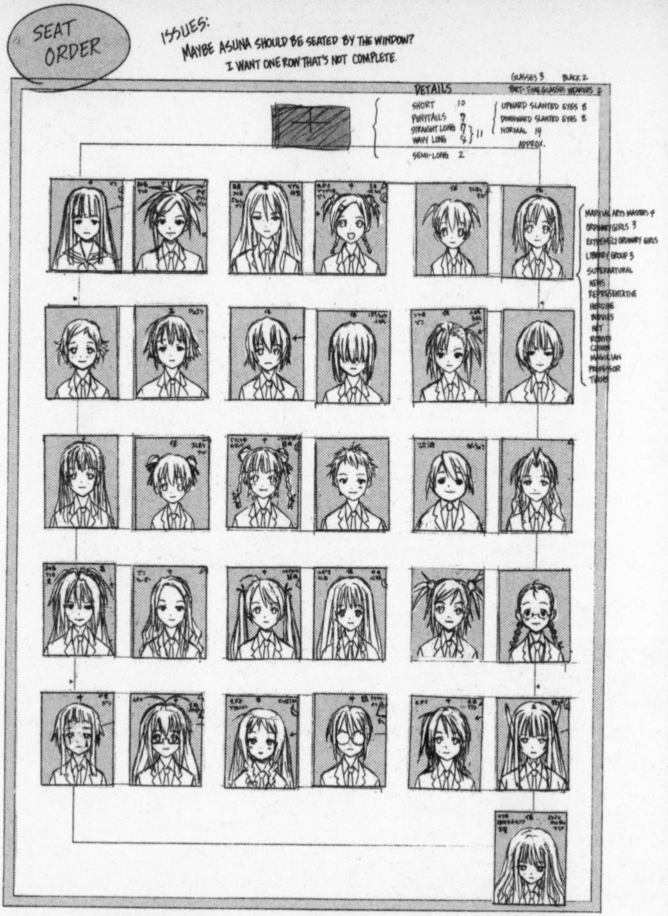
SEAT ORDER
ISSUES:
MAYBE ASUNA SHOULD BE SEATED BY THE WINDOW?
I WANT ONE ROW THAT'S NOT COMPLETE.
GLASSES 3 BLACK 2
DETAILS
SHORT 10
PONYTAILS 7
STRAIGHT LONG 7
WAVY LONG 4
11
SEMI-LONG 2
UPWARD SLANTED EYES 8
DOWNWARD SLANTED EYES 8
NORMAL 14
APPROX.
MARTIAL ARTS MASTERS 4
ORDINARY GIRLS 3
LIBRARY GROUP 3
SUPERNATURAL
NEWS
REPRESENTATIVE
HEROINE
ROBOTS
MAGICIAN
PROFESSOR

NEXT, WE'LL BE SHOWING THE CLASSMATE CONCEPT DESIGNS ~ (^^).

MAYBE YOUR FAVORITE GAL WILL SHOW UP. SEE YOU IN VOLUME 2 THEN!

MAGISTER NEGI MAGI MAGISTER NEG

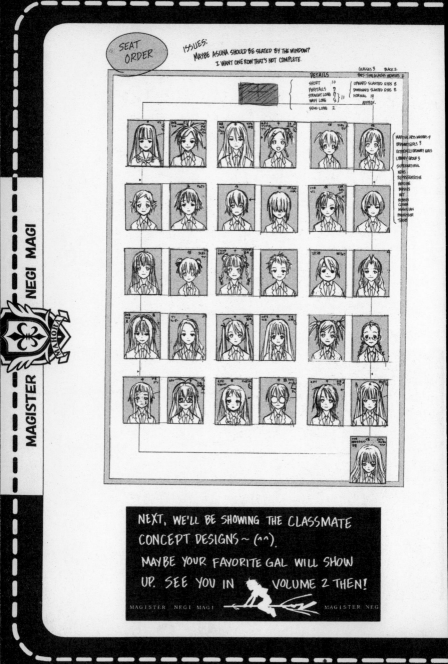

Translation Notes

Japanese is a tricky language for most westerners, and translation is often more art than science. For your edification and reading pleasure, here are notes on some of the places where we could have gone in a different direction in our translation of the work, or where a Japanese cultural reference is used.

If you're reading all of the manga from the launch (and if you're not, go pick up *Gundam SEED*, *xxxHOLiC*, and *Tsubasa* right now!), you'll have seen that we've gone to great effort to keep our translations as authentic as possible. Nowhere did that pose such a challenge, however, as with *Negima!*

Two decisions we made early on in planning the line were to maintain Japanese honorifics as appropriate (for example, if a manga were set in, say, America, there would be little point in keeping them), and to translate all sound effects. We've managed to do both of these things in all of our books, but *Negima!* has been the most—shall we say—troublesome.

To begin with, take a look through the book at all of the sound effects. Akamatsu-sensei sure does like to use them, doesn't he? Where in our other manga we were experiencing 0 to 5 sound effects per page, with several pages lacking effects entirely, *Negima!* has more like 2 to 10 effects and asides per page! As difficult as it was to translate them all (and I'm not certain, but it's possible we managed to miss some along the way), *Negima!* highlights why it is so necessary to do the extra translation work and provide the reader with a more complete, immersive reading experience.

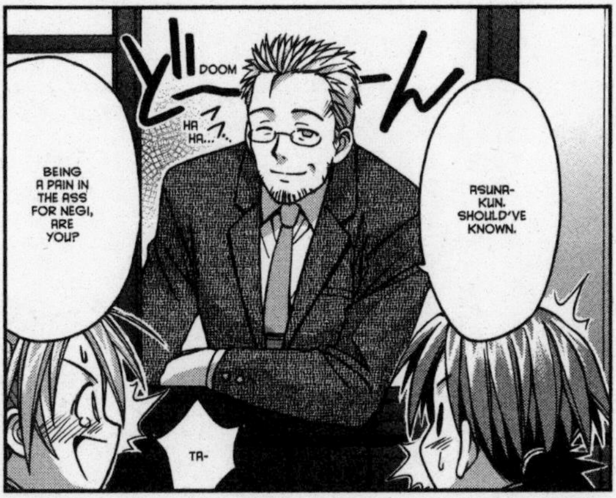
ASUNA-KUN. SHOULD'VE KNOWN.
DOOM
HA HA...
BEING A PAIN IN THE ASS FOR NEGI, ARE YOU?
TA-

While honorifics came up in our other manga, they were definitely a major necessity in *Negima!* because it takes place in a school—a very formal setting in Japan. An understanding of Japanese honorifics drives home the relationships between the characters. Look at when Negi first runs into Takahata—he calls him by his first name with no honorific at all, clearly indicating they are good friends.

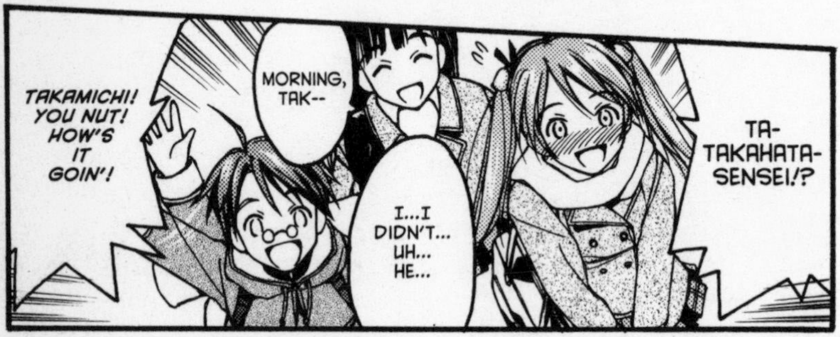
TA- TAKAHATA-SENSEI!?
MORNING, TAK--
I...I DIDN'T... UH... HE...
TAKAMICHI! YOU NUT! HOW'S IT GOIN'!

Likewise, when Takahata interrupts Asuna and Negi after school, he calls them both Asuna-kun and Negi-kun, which to Negi should indicate friendship, while to Asuna it's simply an acknowledgment that she is a student and Takahata is a teacher.

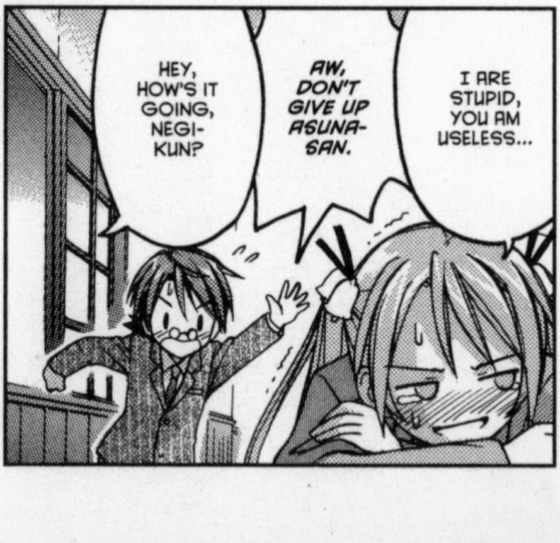
I ARE STUPID, YOU AM USELESS...
AW, DON'T GIVE UP ASUNA-SAN.
HEY, HOW'S IT GOING, NEGI-KUN?

Preview of Volume 2

Here is an excerpt from Volume 2, on sale in English now.

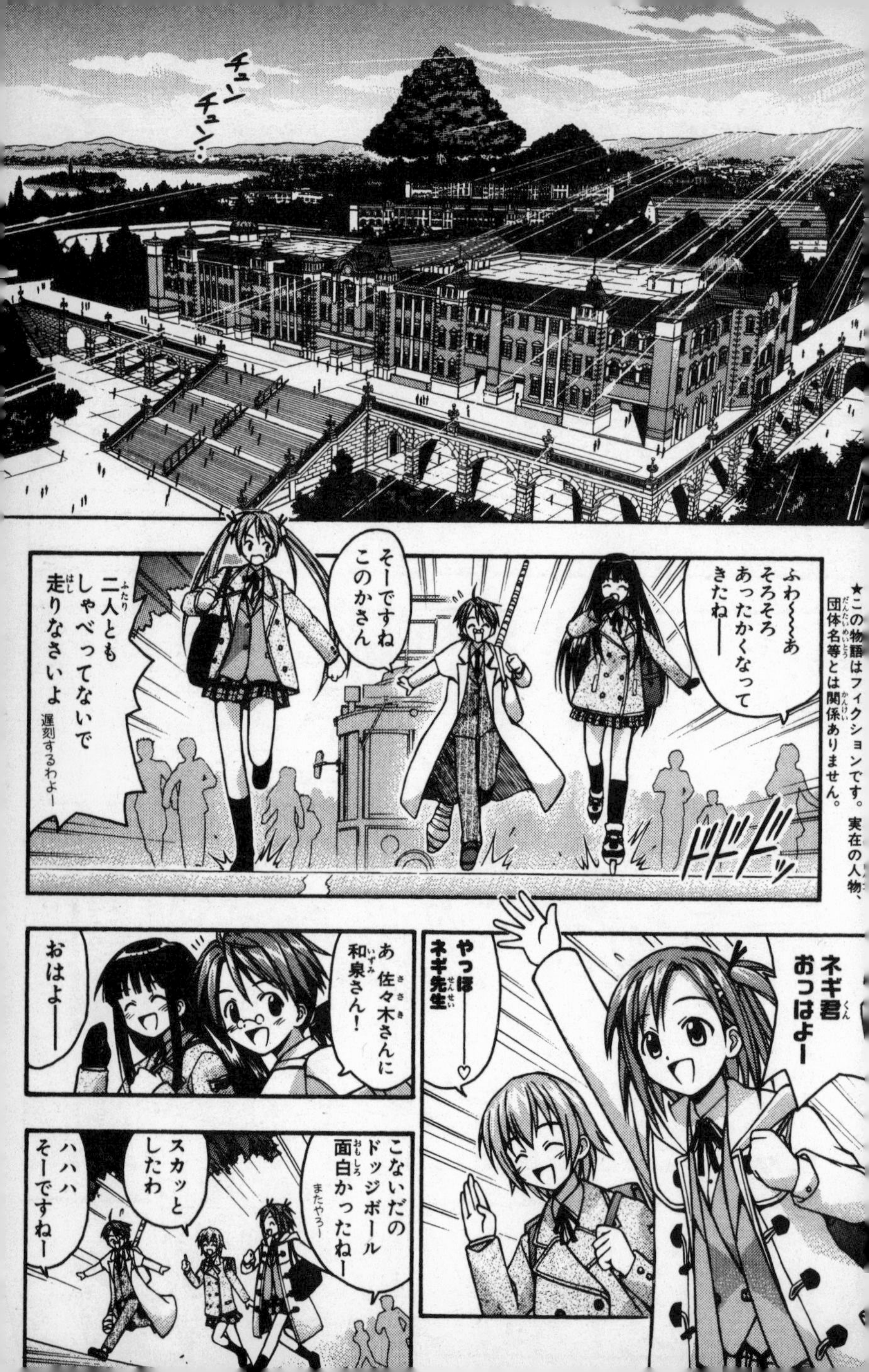
チュンチュン…
ふわ〜〜あ そろそろあったかくなってきたね――
そーですね このかさん
二人ともしゃべってないで走りなさいよ
遅刻するわよー
ドドドッ
ネギ君おっはよー
やっほーネギ先生♡
あ 佐々木さんに和泉さん!
おはよーー
こないだのドッジボール面白かったねー
またやろー
スカッとしたわ
ハハハ そーですねー

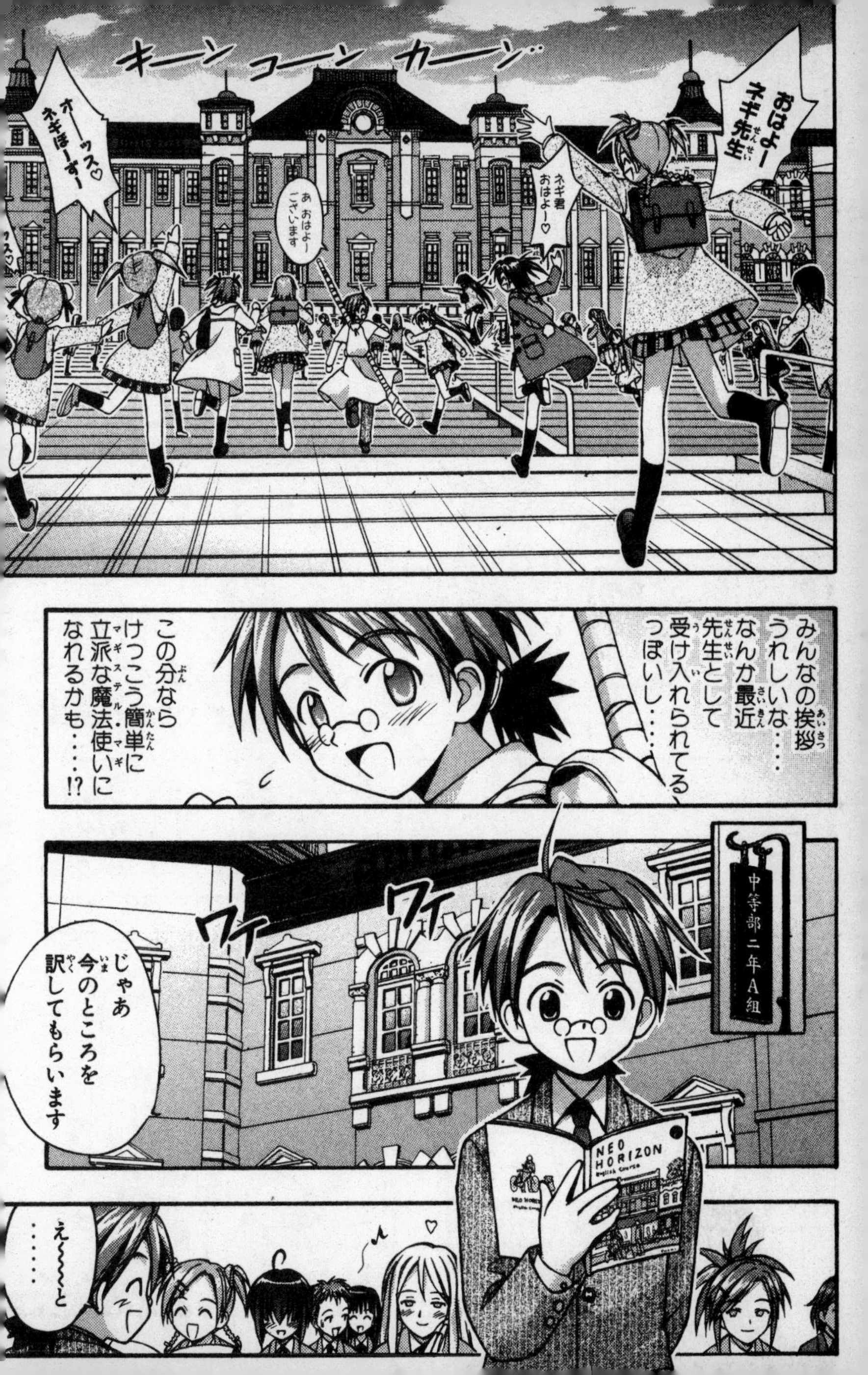
キーン コーン カーン
おはよーネギ先生
ネギ君おはよー♡
あ おはよーございます
オーッスネギぼーずー♡
みんなの挨拶うれしいな……なんか最近先生として受け入れられてるっぽいし……
この分ならけっこう簡単に立派な魔法使いになれるかも……!?
中等部二年A組
ワイワイ
NEO HORIZON English Course
じゃあ今のところを訳してもらいます
え〜〜〜と……

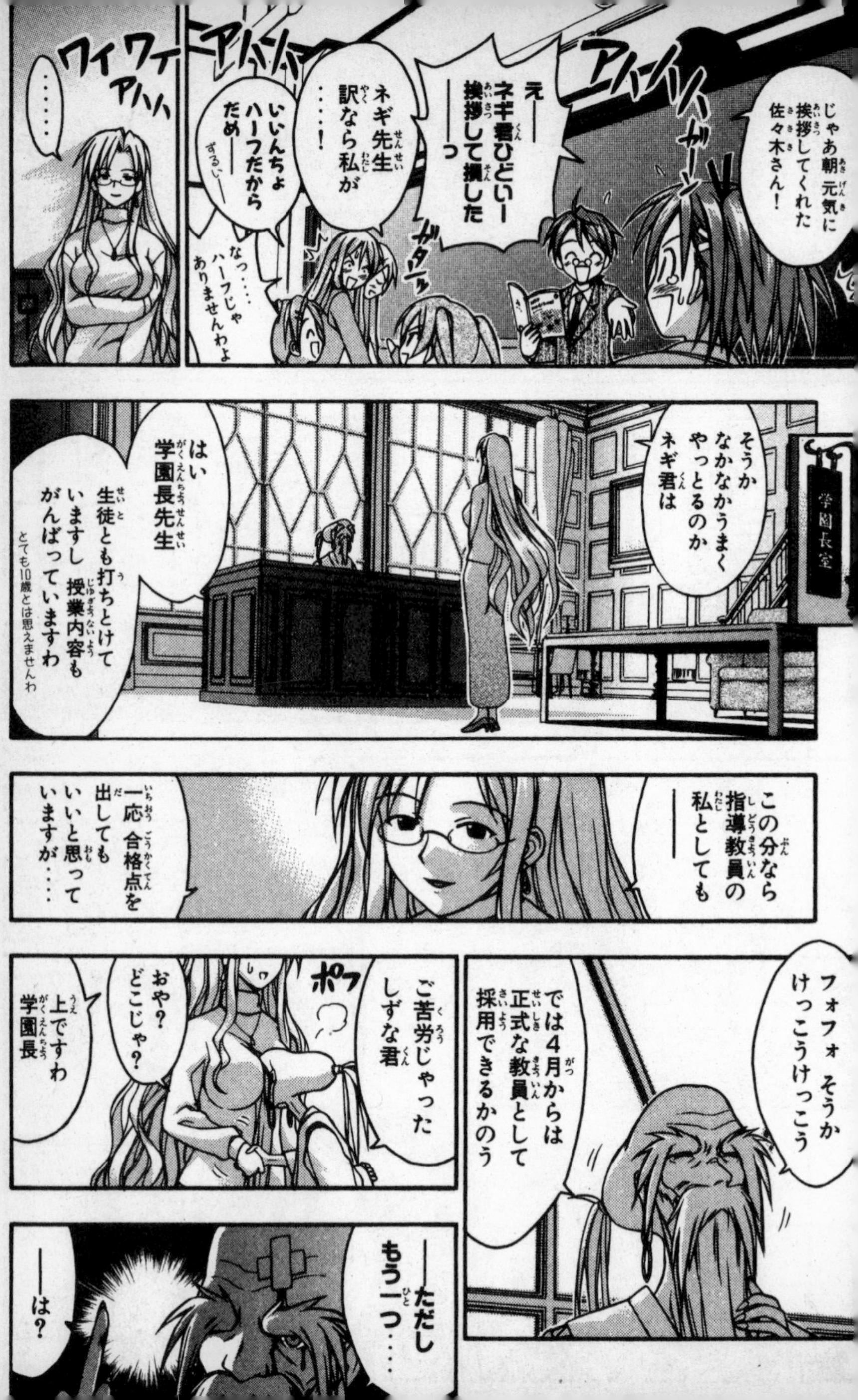

じゃあ朝元気に挨拶してくれた佐々木さん!
アハハハ
えーネギ君ひどいーー挨拶して損したーっ
ガタッ
ネギ先生訳なら私が……!
いいんちょハーフだからだめーー
ずるいーー
なっ……ハーフじゃありませんわよ
ワイワイ
アハハ
……
そうかなかなかうまくやっとるのかネギ君は
学園長室
はい学園長先生
生徒とも打ちとけていますし 授業内容もがんばっていますわ
とても10歳とは思えませんわ
この分なら指導教員の私としても――
一応合格点を出してもいいと思っていますが……
フォフォ そうかけっこうけっこう
では4月からは正式な教員として採用できるかのう
ご苦労じゃったしずな君
ポフ
おや?どこじゃ?
上ですわ学園長
――ただしもう一つ……
――は?

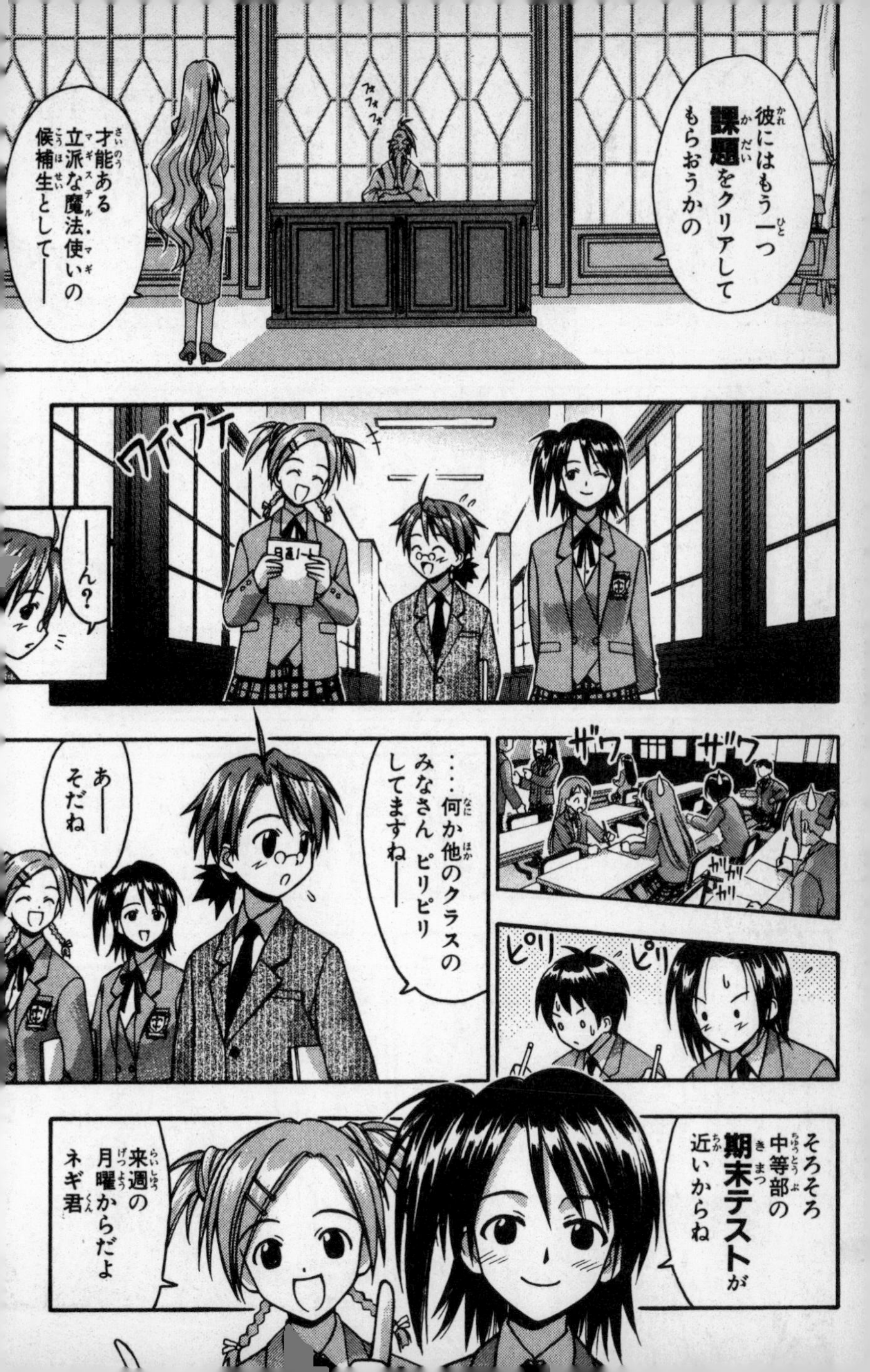
彼にはもう一つ課題をクリアしてもらおうかの
フォフォフォ
才能ある立派な魔法使いの候補生として——
ワイワイ
——ん？
ザワ ザワ
ガリガリ
ピリ ピリ
…何か他のクラスのみなさん ピリピリしてますね——
あ——そだね
そろそろ中等部の期末テストが近いからね
来週の月曜からだよネギ君

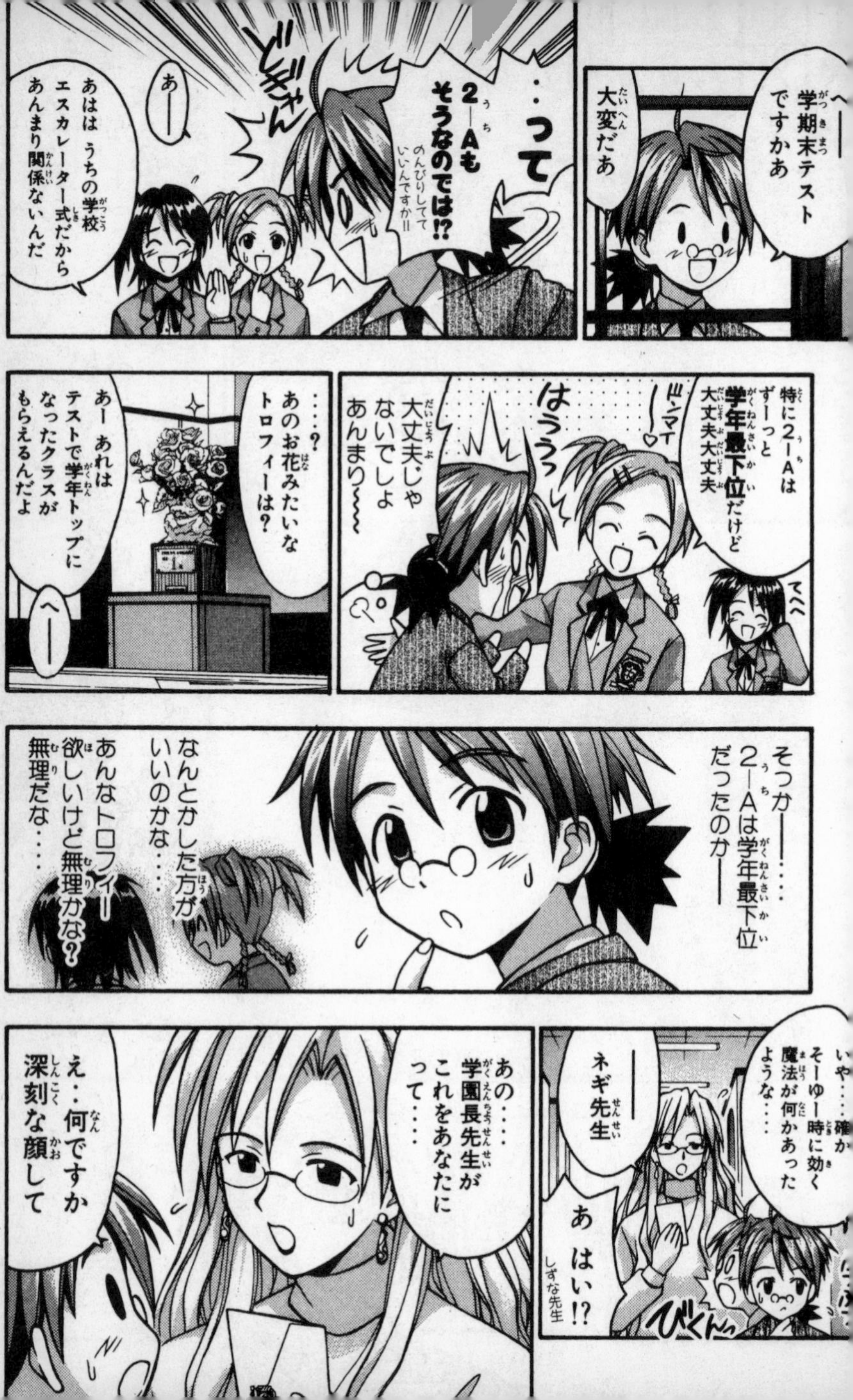
へーー学期末テストですかあ
大変だあ
...って
2ーAもそうなのでは!?
のんびりしてていいんですか!!
どぎゃん
あーー
あはは うちの学校エスカレーター式だからあんまり関係ないんだ
特に2ーAはずーっと学年最下位だけど大丈夫大丈夫
ドンマイ～♡
はううっ
大丈夫じゃないでしょあんまり～～
てへへ
...?あのお花みたいなトロフィーは?
あー あれはテストで学年トップになったクラスがもらえるんだよ
へーー
そっかーー....2ーAは学年最下位だったのかーー
なんとかした方がいいのかな....
あんなトロフィー欲しいけど無理かな?無理だな....
いや....確かそーゆー時に効く魔法が何かあったような....
ーネギ先生
あ はい!?
しずな先生
びくんっ
あの....学園長先生がこれをあなたにって....
え:何ですか深刻な顔して

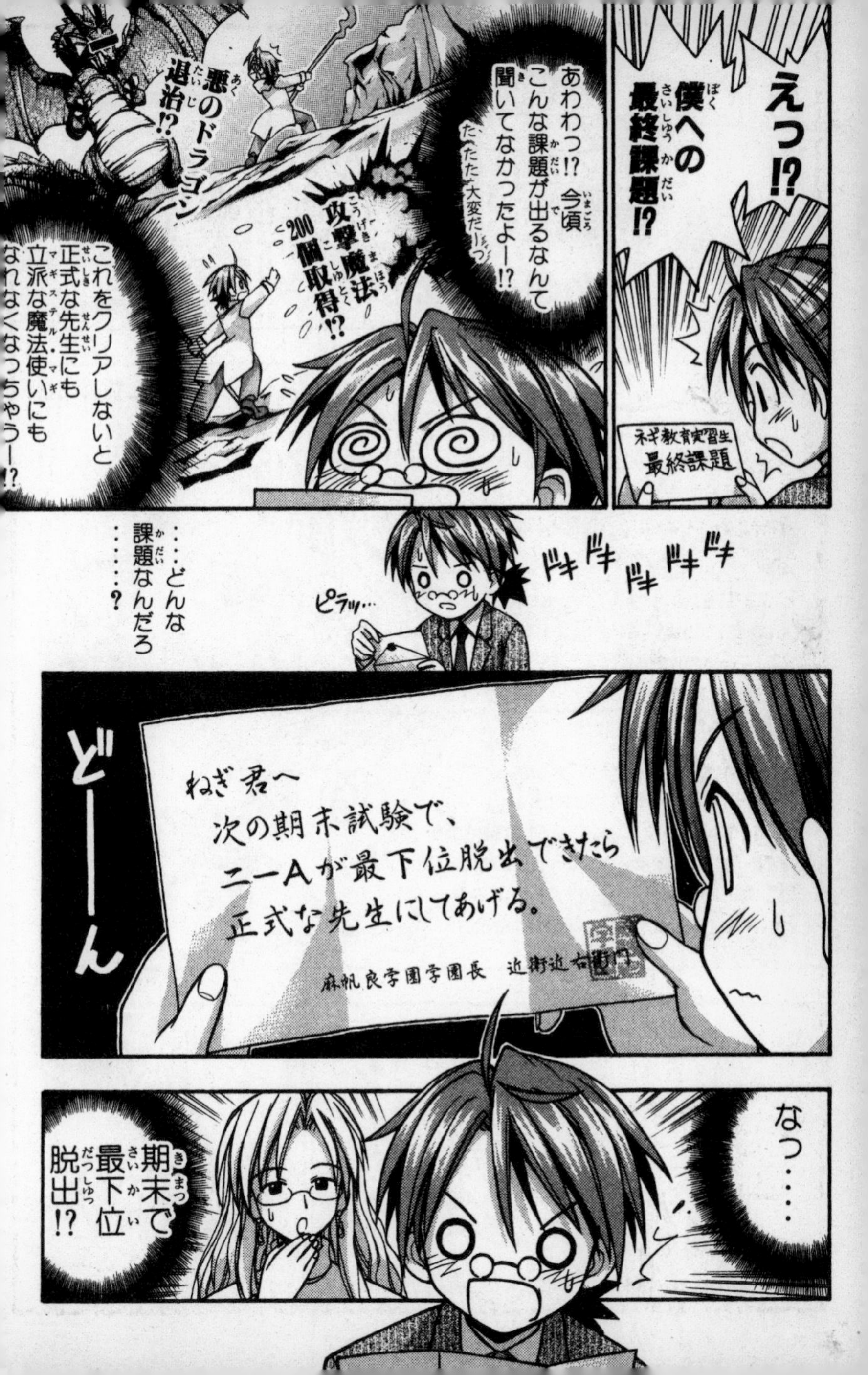

えっ!?
僕への最終課題!?
ネギ教育実習生
最終課題
あわわっ!? 今頃こんな課題が出るなんて聞いてなかったよー!?
たたた大変だーっ
攻撃魔法200個取得!?
悪のドラゴン退治!?
これをクリアしないと正式な先生にも立派な魔法使いにもなれなくなっちゃうー!?
ドキドキドキドキドキ
ピラッ…
……どんな課題なんだろ……?
ねぎ君へ
次の期末試験で、
二ーAが最下位脱出できたら
正式な先生にしてあげる。
麻帆良学園学園長 近衛近右衛門
どーーん
なっ……
期末で最下位脱出!?

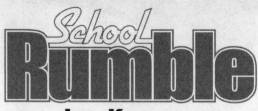

School Rumble

BY JIN KOBAYASHI

SUBTLETY IS FOR WIMPS!

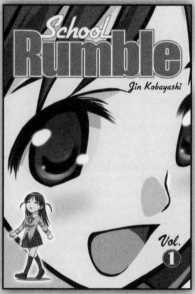

She . . . is a second-year high school student with a single all-consuming question: Will the boy she likes ever really notice her?

He . . . is the school's most notorious juvenile delinquent, and he's suddenly come to a shocking realization: He's got a huge crush, and now he must tell her how he feels.

Life-changing obsessions, colossal foul-ups, grand schemes, deep-seated anxieties, and raging hormones—School Rumble portrays high school as it really is: over-the-top comedy!

Ages: 16 +

Special extras in each volume! Read them all!

GENSHIKEN

The Society for the Study of Modern Visual Culture

BY KIO SHIMOKU

ARE YOU OTAKU?

It's the spring of freshman year, and Kanji Sasahara is in a quandary. Should he fulfill his long-cherished dream of joining an otaku club? Saki Kasukabe also faces a dilemma. Can she ever turn her boyfriend, anime fanboy Kousaka, into a normal guy? Kanji triumphs where Saki fails, when both Kanji and Kousaka sign up for Genshiken: The Society for the Study of Modern Visual Culture.

Undeterred, Saki chases Kousaka through various activities of the club, from cosplay and comic conventions to video gaming and collecting anime figures—all the while discovering more than she ever wanted to know about the humorous world of the Japanese otaku!

1
Kio Shimoku
GENSHIKEN
The Society for the Study of Modern Visual Culture

Ages: 16+

Special extras in each volume! Read them all!

DEL REY

VISIT WWW.DELREYMANGA.COM TO:

- **View release date calendars for upcoming volumes**
- **Sign up for Del Rey's free manga e-newsletter**
- **Find out the latest about new Del Rey Manga series**

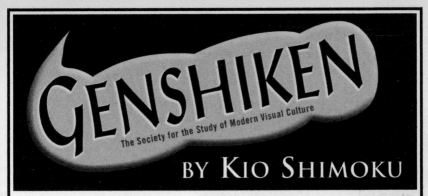

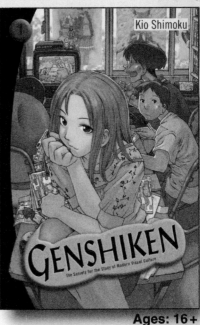

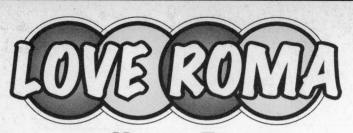

LOVE ROMA

BY MINORU TOYODA

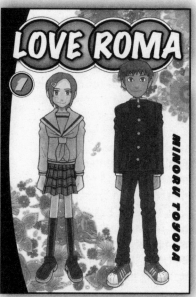

"We have been telling all the people we meet to read this manga!"
—CLAMP, creators of Tsubasa

A fun, romantic comedy, Love Roma is about the simple kind of relationships we all longed for when we were young. It's a story of love at first sight—literally. When Hoshino sees Negishi for the first time, he asks her to be his girlfriend. Shocked, Negishi nevertheless agrees to allow Hoshino to walk her home, while he explains why he is in love with her. Touched, Negishi begins to feel something for this strange young boy from her school.

Ages: 16+

Special extras in each volume! Read them all!

xxxHOLiC™

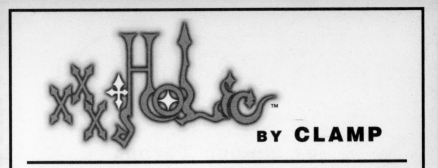

BY CLAMP

Watanuki Kimihiro is haunted by visions. When he finds himself irresistibly drawn into a shop owned by Yûko, a mysterious witch, he is offered the chance to rid himself of the spirits that plague him. He accepts, but soon realizes that he's just been tricked into working for the shop to pay off the cost of Yûko's services! But this isn't any ordinary kind of shop . . . In this shop, Yûko grants wishes to those in need. But they must have the strength of will not only to truly understand their need, but to give up something incredibly precious in return.

CLAMP
CREATORS OF CHOBITS!
1
xxxHOLiC

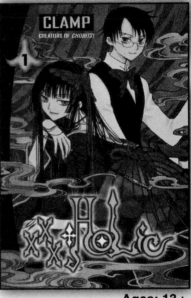

Ages: 13+

Special extras in each volume! Read them all!

DEL REY

VISIT WWW.DELREYMANGA.COM TO:

- View release date calendars for upcoming volumes
- Sign up for Del Rey's free manga e-newsletter
- Find out the latest about new Del Rey Manga series

TOMARE!

[STOP!]

You're going the wrong way!

Manga is a completely different type of reading experience.

To start at the *beginning*, go to the *end*!

That's right! Authentic manga is read the traditional Japanese way—from right to left. Exactly the *opposite* of how American books are read. It's easy to follow: Just go to the other end of the book, and read each page—and each panel—from right side to left side, starting at the top right. Now you're experiencing manga as it was meant to be.